On behalf of Mainfreight I hope you enjoy
this celebration of the company's journey.

*Don Braid*

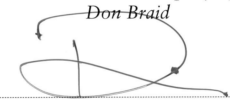

# READY FIRE AIM

## THE MAINFREIGHT STORY

### KEITH DAVIES

**How a Kiwi freight company went global**

RANDOM HOUSE
NEW ZEALAND

A RANDOM HOUSE BOOK published by Random House New Zealand
18 Poland Road, Glenfield, Auckland, New Zealand

For more information about our titles go to www.randomhouse.co.nz

A catalogue record for this book is available from the
National Library of New Zealand

Random House New Zealand is part of the Random House Group
New York   London   Sydney   Auckland   Delhi   Johannesburg


First published 2013

© 2013 Keith Davies

The moral rights of the author have been asserted

ISBN 978 1 77553 290 3
eISBN 978 1 77553 346 7

Design: Carla Sy
Front cover photograph and images on pages 5, 19, 24, 101, 119, 124, 134 (bottom),
162, 188, 213, 224, 229, 243, 246, 250, 260, 270, 288, 294, 299, 306 (top), 308,
315, 318, 323, 331 by Alistair Guthrie. All other images, Mainfreight collection.

Printed in China by Everbest Printing Co Ltd

Mainfreight in Times Square, New York

# Contents

# THINK LIKE A CAPITAL

ST

# FOREWORD

THIS IS THE story of a company built on the belief that with passion anything is possible, that you should 'go anywhere as long as it's forward'. In the process, it revolutionised transport in New Zealand then took its message to the world.

It is the story of Mainfreight, founded by the visionary Bruce Plested, who set out to make the company a family, a team, in which everyone would have a share in the riches. A team in which everyone has the authority to make decisions and mistakes. The instruction manual is painfully short: Feel the fear but do it anyway.

It's a world based on the philosophy 'Ready, Fire, Aim' — and that's no mere slogan, it's a way of life. A world so transparent that the weekly profit and loss figures of each branch, its innermost secrets, right down to how much it banks each day, are posted on the lunchroom walls. And they are profits in which every team member gets an equal share. It's a world where branch managers sit in the lunchroom with drivers and loaders and receptionists, and with managing directors and board members.

It's a world where budgets are deemed 'bullshit'. Why spend time preparing figures that are invariably out of date before the ink is dry? What are we trying to do? Make more than last year. There is just one question to ask about anything we might do: Will it make the company money? If not, why are we doing it?

Bruce Plested's philosophy is simple enough. He wants everyone to think like a capitalist. 'I have never seen capitalism as greedy. The more wealthy you can help make all the people in your establishment, the more money everyone will make with more satisfaction.'

Perhaps the single most empowering moment in the company's history to date was when they asked: Why not think of ourselves as a 100-year company? Once they did that anything was possible — they could plan for the long term without having to worry about the impact on the immediate future.

Mainfreight's simple objective is to attract only those customers who appreciate added value and are prepared to pay accordingly.

They try to employ only well-educated, energetic young people with the right attitude, and always to promote from within. The instruction to managers is to hire someone smarter than you are.

This is a world where the chief executive answers his own phone. And his PA's phone if she's away from her desk. He knows if she's not there, because they operate from an open-plan office, as do all Mainfreight people.

MAINFREIGHT'S SUCCESS IS based on two unshakeable beliefs: the only way to keep ahead of their competitors is by the superior performance of their people, and the only measure of that superior performance is how the customers perceive it. It's a way of doing business that is encapsulated in the sayings displayed on their trucks, the source of this book's title and many of its chapter headings.

When it came time to expand they could not afford to buy flourishing, profitable businesses. So, rather than start from scratch, they bought businesses in need of radical surgery. And did it all go smoothly? You had better believe it did not. Initially there were disappointing ventures in Australia and the US, and finally a jaw-dropping moment in Europe when they made their biggest purchase ever only to see much of the profit and turnover walk out the door.

The following chapters will take you on a warts and all exploration of Mainfreight's journey from a small transport company at the very bottom of the world to a highly successful global logistics supply company.

This is the story of how the men and women of Mainfreight did it.

*Keith Davies*
*Auckland*
*July 2013*

# PREFACE

*'The longest journey starts with one small step.'*

MAINFREIGHT'S JOURNEY IS now 35 years long, a path that has led from two people to a team of over 5560 people in eighteen different countries.

Many people who have followed the company's progress, as team members, as shareholders or as customers, may want to know how this came about, the successes and mistakes we made and the development of our culture. That is the purpose of this book.

Perhaps the most surprising thing is how little has changed since the first year. Things like getting the freight through no matter the difficulties — look at the Mainfreight teams' reactions after the Christchurch earthquakes, which you will read about in this book, or Hurricane Sandy in the New York Tri-State area, which ripped the roof off the Mainfreight building and flooded the interior, (and many other natural disasters); eating together; meeting regularly so everyone knows what is happening; the annual and Christmas bonuses based on profit sharing; the endless discussion about business theory and practice; the constant improvement achieved by doing weekly profits and statistical measurement of our performance; clean trucks; treating inwards freight (for delivery) from another city as slightly more important than our own outwards freight; teamwork and aroha amongst us all.

This list could go on and on. What matters is that we have had 35 years honing these standards and adding new ones such as open plan offices; Ready, Fire, Aim; graduate programmes; internal promotion, and owning our own freight buildings.

These are the foundation blocks on which the company is built.

Over our 35 years, there have been thousands of stories (many of which have been either left out of this book or sanitised to protect the guilty) and many hundreds of people (some of whom are no longer with us) who have given all their energy to the company, to the team and to succeeding. This book can't acknowledge all of them, but the company does value their contribution.

Enjoy this book, and be part of our next 100 years.

*Bruce Plested*
*Executive Chairman*

# THE MOM
# OF TRUT

T he Villa Ruimzicht, on the outskirts of Doetinchem, a tiny town on the Netherlands–Germany border. It is Thursday evening, 17 March 2011. In the dining room of the hotel, each table decorated with a single white rose, regulars are enjoying the house speciality of a four-course surprise meal. In the bar, where Norah Jones' 'Don't Know Why' whispers from the speakers, a power play is in full flight.

At the bar sits one man, immaculately dressed in tailored white shirt, trousers pressed to within an inch of their life, shoes reflecting the perfectionist within. Leading business publications had not voted Don Braid best-dressed businessman for nothing. Nor CEO of the year, twice in fact.

Mainfreight's group managing director is playing his part in this drama to the full. He was in town to make a deal: to buy a company that will bring the company's ambition of total global expansion a step closer.

Mainfreight had already come a long way in the 33 years since it all began with one truck, in faraway New Zealand. The transport and logistics business had a global gross turnover of NZ$1.3 billion. It employed more than 3400 people, half of them in New Zealand, with 186 branches worldwide — in Australia, the US, mainland China, Hong Kong and Singapore.

'FUCK HIM. THE deal's off,' Braid said. 'We're going home.'

Further down the bar, in the doorway to the restaurant, stood Mainfreight's suave Indian-born lawyer, Carl Howard-Smith, nodding furiously and saying 'No' to his smartphone. On the other end of the line, 18,000 kilometres away on a private beach on Waiheke Island, off Auckland, New Zealand, was company founder Bruce Plested, staring out to sea as he reiterated: 'No one's ego is to be allowed to get in the way of this deal.'

Howard-Smith, Plested's long-time friend and confidant, glanced down the bar and decided this was not the time to relay such a message to Braid.

Behind the lawyer a tough-looking figure of a man was clearly flustered. Wim Bosman was not used to being told to 'fuck off'. Not in public. Not in front of his team. Here was a man who 48 years before had founded the transport company that bore his name. It had been just him and a single truck he drove himself. Now it ranked as one of the largest and most respected privately owned transport and logistics companies in the Netherlands and Belgium. There were fourteen branches employing close to fifteen hundred people throughout Europe; more than a thousand trucks and trailers, and vast warehouses, some of which were bigger than all the Mainfreight warehouses in New Zealand combined. Bosman ran his empire with an iron fist. People came to work to do as they were told.

The tension was palpable as men strode frantically between bar and restaurant, relaying hushed messages back and forth.

'He means it, the deal is off.'

'But he can't tell Mr Bosman to fuck off.'

'He just did.'

Braid, meanwhile, was explaining to his New Zealand national transport manager Mark Newman, loud enough for all to hear, that Newman would no longer be moving his family to a leafy lane on the outskirts of Amsterdam to run Europe; but not to worry, he could go back and be in charge of the Auckland branch. Braid was playing to the gallery, or at least Newman hoped he was.

Watching all this, but showing no hint of amusement, was Mainfreight's chief financial officer, Tim Williams. Such was the trust and respect with which he was regarded within Mainfreight that he was the only man in the company empowered to say 'No' to both Braid and Plested and have them unwaveringly accept his judgement. And Williams had given a great big tick to this deal. A deal he had stumbled on by mistake.

IT HAD ALL begun with a telephone call he should not have received from a well-placed source at an accountancy practice. Wim Bosman was looking to sell; would Mainfreight be interested?

In any year, Williams dealt with hundreds of time-consuming

'rubbish' proposals that crossed his desk, but this one seemed worth a second look. Then came another call. 'Forget that information, we don't have permission to let it out.'

Williams told Don Braid, who called Bruce Plested, who was on one of his regular sojourns at a language school, Institut de Français in Villefranche-sur-Mer, in the south of France. (He explains this as wanting to be prepared for the day Mainfreight buys a company in France.)

A week later, on a chilly day in September 2010, Plested walked through the arrival gate at Amsterdam's Schiphol Airport to be greeted by Bosman, who was holding aloft a history of the Mainfreight company, published to mark its twenty-fifth anniversary, by way of introduction.

Plested had come to look and listen. He had no intention of entering into negotiations. As he sat with Bosman in the company boardroom in its headquarters in the little town of 's-Heerenberg he asked about the computer system, to be answered with a shrug. 'All I know is they talk to each other.'

Plested assumed from this that the system was old-fashioned. He got that right. Bosman had not been spending on upgrading it. Plested would have loved to have walked around the site to see how the freight was handled, how clean the warehouses and canteens and toilets were, and how the folk on the floor interacted with Bosman — show him these things and Plested has no need of a spreadsheet to tell you how healthy a company is. But Bosman was having none of that. He did not want anyone to know Plested was on site. Did not want him talking to anyone. Did not want anyone to know the company was for sale. That made a sort of sense, although the truth was that hardly a soul in the place did not know the company had been on the market for at least three years.

Plested had been interested in expanding Mainfreight into Europe for some time. He had concerns, however. The European attitude to work bothered him. The emphasis was on a work–life balance that to him seemed to revolve around more and more holidays for fewer and fewer hours of work, and a certain lack of ambition. He saw that as fine for companies trading within Europe, but anyone with global ambitions would be competing against people in New Zealand, Australia, the US and Asia, who were working longer and harder and with more determination than the Europeans.

He compared it to the supporter who stands up at a football

MAKING YOUR LOGISTICS WORK

MAKING YOUR LOGISTICS WORK

The Netherlands

match. He gets a better view than the people behind, so they stand up and then the people behind them stand up, and eventually everyone is standing up. The Chinese and the Americans and the Australians and the New Zealanders were all standing up, and Plested was worried about doing business with people who were sitting down.

There was the example of a driver who had worked for Bosman for 30 years and was entitled to 69 days' holiday a year. If they gave him a week off a month he still would not use up his entitlement. As for firing someone — forget it. To get round the law, everyone seemed to be on short-term contracts, with renewal at the discretion of management. Rather than embracing staff, the law was keeping them at arm's length. It was all very foreign to Plested's Mainfreight, where everyone was considered family.

Despite these reservations, Plested liked what he saw during his visit. He could see that Bosman was sitting on a potentially good business. The Netherlands is often described as the 'gateway to Europe', from which all major economic centres in western Europe can be reached in less than 24 hours. For a start there is Rotterdam, the largest port in Europe, second busiest in the world after Singapore, and Amsterdam's Schiphol Airport, Europe's fourth largest civil aviation hub. Plus an extensive network of road, rail and waterways. To say the Netherlands was an attractive centre for distribution and logistics would be a considerable understatement.

Don Braid also knew that Europe was critical to Mainfreight's long-term success; the missing link that would complement already established businesses in Asia and the US. Without a meaningful presence in Europe, Mainfreight was never going to be a true global force.

Braid's vision had always been to enter Europe by buying one of the company's European agents, but all discussions to that end had proved frustratingly slow. It had dawned on him that they were dealing with owners running what were effectively small lifestyle businesses. He realised, as Plested had done, that their ambition was to support their families, not to be the biggest operation in their home city, let alone country.

But buying Bosman was a very different proposition. By seamlessly merging the Bosman operation with Mainfreight's existing networks in Asia and the US, the company would be well on the way to achieving its ambition of becoming a global transport and logistics business. Bosman was part of both the German-based, Europe-wide *System Plus* and the French-based *Volupal* freight distribution networks. Mainfreight would be able to tell customers in Invercargill, tucked away at the bottom of New Zealand, and as far away from anywhere else in the world as you can get, and those in Sydney and Shanghai and New York, that goods could be delivered to 22 European countries, west and east, without leaving Mainfreight's hands. They were also offering transport and storage of hazardous materials and express delivery. Plus, there was an air and ocean international business that was very underdeveloped and losing money.

So a purchase process swung into action. Don Braid followed up Plested's visit with a trip to the Netherlands in October 2010, and by December there was a heads of agreement, allowing full due diligence to commence in January and February 2011.

Earlier in the week before the Villa Ruimzicht meeting, while Braid and Newman were on a private-jet inspection of the Bosman empire, Carl Howard-Smith had been crunching the numbers with Tim Williams and Simon Cotter of Grant Samuel, the investment and advisory group serving the Australian, New Zealand and Asia-Pacific market. Grant Samuel was a favoured group; Mainfreight had an almost pathological aversion to consultants of any type, but Cotter had proved his worth on a number of previous deals.

They had undertaken a word-by-word page-turn of the agreement that took a full week to complete. Bosman had a financial advisor, Jac van Melick, who had impressed Plested and indeed everyone in the Mainfreight team; a lawyer; and company accountant Henk Messink, his confidant, on the case.

The Bosman deal was by no means perfect. Braid would quietly remind people that while it looked great on paper, there was much work to be done. Yes, there was a large business in the Netherlands and Belgium, strong branches in France and Romania and fledgling operations in Poland and Russia but, with a 2010 turnover of €240 million and earnings before interest, tax, depreciation and amortisation (EBITDA) of €19.4 million, it was actually smaller all-up than either of Mainfreight's Australian or US operations.

That said, for €110 million Mainfreight would be buying a world-class logistics business along with the exceptionally bright young people who made it all tick. There would be a further earn-out payment of up to a maximum of €10 million if the Wim Bosman

Group achieved EBITDA of at least €20 million for the year ending 31 December 2011.

THE DINNER HAD gone well. Fine food and fine wine. As the conversation turned to the deal, Bosman declared he would only accept six times EBITDA. Don Braid had always known that would be a reasonable figure but had been holding out for 5.5, with an earn-out, while he waited for Howard-Smith, Williams and Cotter to tip him the wink that the numbers added up. Now he had that confirmation, Braid publicly conceded the point, agreed to Bosman's demand and stuck out his hand. They had a deal, he thought.

After all the due diligence, flying round Europe, poring over the books and sizing up the potential, the extended hand signified a great deal. At Mainfreight they do not do contracts, they do handshakes. They pride themselves on the fact that there is nothing more binding than a Mainfreight handshake. Yes, they understand other people have need of lawyers and bankers and accountants and documents signed in triplicate, but it was the handshake that mattered.

But then, at the last minute, Bosman pulled away, wanting €5 million in a 'break fee' to compensate them for their trouble if Mainfreight's shareholders failed to approve the deal, as they would have to do. Braid was astounded. He was booked to fly home the next day. This? This was game playing. He stalked off.

Bosman remained at the table with his arms folded. Carl Howard-Smith stepped in to offer €500,000 as a break fee. The Bosman team laughed, which irritated him just a bit. The negotiations dragged on into the evening, when it was agreed to park the fee. Howard-Smith was more than just irritated, he was mystified. After all, Bosman and his right-hand man Messink, the de facto chief executive, had been trying to sell the company for years. They had made much of the need to find a buyer who would not asset-strip the group, make great numbers of their people redundant and change the company name. Bosman wanted to keep the company and its people intact and retain its good reputation. He wanted a buyer with no footprint in Europe, one that would take over the entire operation and see virtue in keeping the name for its brand value.

But his problem was that the existing multinational transport and logistics companies had no need of the Bosman operation, which would merely duplicate what they already had. And there was the small matter of the *System Plus* and *Volupal* networks that provided so much of the Bosman service and hence profit and net worth: networks made up of mirror-image companies of Bosman throughout Europe, companies that would not tolerate a major competitor buying Bosman. These franchises were alliances, a network sending freight backwards and forwards among themselves, and they would frown on Bosman being sold to the likes of DHL or FedEx. And they had muscle. *System Plus* was a €12 billion enterprise, making it collectively bigger than any of the large multinational forwarders. Bosman could only sell to a smaller purchaser, which narrowed the field considerably.

So Howard-Smith could confidently challenge: 'Well, who are you going to sell to? You tell me, who are you going to sell to? We will keep your people, keep your trucks rolling, keep your name. You tell me who you are going to sell to who isn't going to rip this place apart and fire half your people? What are your people going to think of you when you have got 100 or 120 million euro on your boat with your helicopter whizzing about and they are begging on the streets of Amsterdam?' It was tough. Tim Williams winced, even though he had heard it before. Howard-Smith would endlessly challenge the Bosman negotiators with, 'You're giving us nothing!'

Such a lot was at stake. Williams and Howard-Smith and Braid also knew Mainfreight would be welcomed as buyers by the other franchisers. Mainfreight had a relatively small amount of international trade, and at any hint it was setting up its own operation in Europe its agents would take their business and long-held customers to other operators, rather than risk them being taken by Mainfreight/Bosman, with an accompanying loss of commission.

Braid had long been concerned about agents controlling Mainfreight's freight in Europe rather than the company dealing directly with customers and, critically, controlling freight exports from Europe to the US. The existing one-way traffic was highly frustrating. If Mainfreight waited five years for another mid-level freight company purchase opportunity to come along, their sheer volumes and revenue might present an unpalatable gamble as agents fled, taking customers with them.

Despite differing views of whether Europe would be bigger or smaller than the Australian or US operations, Bosman would, dollar-

MAKING YOUR LOGISTICS WORK

WIM BOSMAN

Amsterdam

wise, be Mainfreight's largest acquisition yet. It was their first serious step into Europe, and would be a driver of substantial growth in the coming years. And there would be much to learn. The Europeans made New Zealand freight handling look inferior. The cleanliness and the stock keeping were impeccable, largely because of the number of women they had working on the warehouse floor. If the deal went ahead, Mainfreight's blokey culture would be set for a shake-up.

WHILE HOWARD-SMITH, BRAID and Williams did not know the precise details of Wim Bosman's circumstances, that night at the Villa Ruimzicht they were sure this was a man making a final lunge for the line. They were right. Had the Mainfreight deal not gone through, the plan was to appoint a new managing director and for Bosman and Messink to retire on sensible pensions.

Despite their anxiety and frustration, Bosman's performance was no great surprise to the Mainfreight team. He had visited New Zealand prior to signing the letter of intent that enabled due diligence to commence. Back then, they had put Neil Graham alongside him as a best buddy. Plested's partner from the very earliest days was a master salesman. He understood why Bosman was being stubborn: the figures were so big he thought there must be huge margins at stake in the synergies. During the visit Graham would patiently explain the risk involved for Mainfreight. Bosman was looking for trust, and Mainfreight was looking for that too, along with the right price and margin. Patience ran thin, with Bosman constantly out of the room calling his lawyers in Amsterdam.

As for Mark Newman, he had known the Bosman business was special after his first 130-kilometre drive from Amsterdam to the German border and 's-Heerenberg, where he found a business brimful of intelligence. There he had met a host of friendly, smiling, articulate, energetic English-speakers, keen to get on with business. Now, everything depended on that final handshake.

The pre-negotiation strategy had been for Newman to get along with Bosman, and for Braid not to. Braid had been playing his role to the hilt; now it was time for Newman to earn his keep, to deal with a man who had started his business in 1964, the year Newman was born. Given that his wife Christine had initially burst into tears on being told they and their two sons might be moving to the Netherlands, but was now excited by the prospect,

Newman felt a double responsibility.

Newman was Mainfreight culture through and through. He had been with the company for over twenty years, since his university days, and was currently managing the New Zealand domestic transport operation. And now, maybe, he thought, running the Bosman business. To this day Newman remembers without embarrassment giving Bosman a hug, and then a kiss, as he urged him to reconsider.

So there they were in the bar: Braid feigning anger, Howard-Smith getting telephone instructions from Plested, Cotter bemused, Newman wondering how to break the bad news to his wife, and Bosman's team tip-toeing around them all, clearly wanting to repair the damage.

When Braid looks back on the moment he recalls, 'I just thought he was a rude prick. It made sense to use a private jet to visit all their locations, and he was always asking, "What you think? Aren't we great?" As we flew from Romania to France, halfway through the flight he stuck his hand out across the aisle and said, "Shake hands, let's do it." I told him we would do that when we had the numbers and I thought it was right. Then I would shake his hand. He kept pressing me to do the deal and I kept saying, "Not until we have the numbers, not until we understand this business." Three nights later that's exactly what happened and there he was refusing the handshake.'

HOWARD-SMITH REJOINED HIS group. No mention of the Plested call. 'Just you watch, they'll be out in a minute or two and I'll bring the break fee back to €2.5 million and you already have your six EBITDA on the table.'

And so it went. The advisors agreed to the terms, and at three in the morning a text came through announcing that Wim Bosman was on board; the deal would be done that day, once a few remaining issues had been resolved.

There was a huge sigh of relief all round. Yes, they had bought it relatively cheaply, and it was a good business with a tight culture, but there was a huge 'but'.

Mainfreight knew from the due diligence that the company's logistics division was dependent on a number of large companies. Three of them — Samsung; Ravensburger, the game, toy and puzzle manufacturer; and Sara Lee, the giant food and beverage distributor — had already indicated they would be leaving. This was the reality of the global financial crisis, as even the biggest and the best found demand for their product shrinking and, with it, the need to outsource warehousing. They had more than enough space of their own. That, and the factor of desperate price-slashing by competitors.

To make matters worse, Bosman was retaining ownership of some of the land and those massive warehouses, which would be rented to Mainfreight. Howard-Smith had negotiated the rent to reflect the loss, with no review for the three years it would generally take to replace such customers. Little did they know of the April Fool's joke that was about to be played on them.

WHEN THE MAINFREIGHT team arrived at the Bosman head-quarters later that day, they were ushered into the boardroom to be greeted by a tray of glasses and bottles of champagne. 'Schoolboy error,' whispered Cotter. They were planning a party; the deal was in the bag. The remaining six outstanding 'details' were dealt with in less than 30 minutes, with even Howard-Smith feeling awkward as he once more trotted out his 'You are giving us nothing' line.

That done, it was raised glasses all round, and the new CEO smiled and sent a text to his wife: 'Pack your bags girl.' Mark Newman was two weeks away from taking charge on 1 April 2011 — the day on which he would discover Mainfreight had lost 53 per cent of the Bosman warehouse turnover and profit to match.

But for now, on that beach far away, Bruce Plested took the confirmation call from Carl Howard-Smith. Thirty-three years after it all began, Mainfreight had a beachhead in Europe.

# GO ANYW
# AS LONG
# IT'S FOR

# HERE
# AS
# WARD

New Zealand, just prior to Christmas, 1977. Union power was at its peak. Inflation topped 18 per cent, pushing up production costs. The country had slipped from fourth to twentieth in the list of wealthy OECD nations.

Unemployment soared, and large numbers of skilled people voted with their feet, migrating to Australia. Those who remained found wages falling behind prices. Industrial disputes erupted as workers chased rising prices and the spiral of inflation continued.

Amid this chaos and confusion unions ruled supreme, demanding ever higher wages. And it was in the freight forwarding industry that they struck with dramatic effect: Stop the freight and you stopped the country.

Little surprise then, when news broke of a worker walkout at the Southdown Lane terminal of the freight forwarding company New Zealand Freighters. The real shock came later when it became clear that not just the militants but also normally passive office workers were out on the footpath. They had all put their names to a petition of protest, registering their 'shock and extreme displeasure'.

The source of their displeasure? One of the company's bosses, Bruce Plested, had been sacked. The outraged workforce was demanding the reinstatement of a member of the enemy class — a capitalist. But a capitalist with a difference. Plested had recognised early on that workers saw the union as their family. He had consciously and quite deliberately set out to make the company their family, to replace the union in their affections. He preached that everyone should have a share in the riches. And they knew he meant it.

This was a philosophy Plested would nurture and develop throughout the company he would eventually form: Mainfreight. As a newly qualified accountant he had moved from the dynamic Fisher & Paykel appliance company to join a container-packing company that was then folded into the larger New Zealand Freighters. He

**NEW ZEALAND FREIGHTERS**

Nationwide Rail and Sea Forwarders
Overnight Air Services by Sendair
Trans Tasman Services

NEW ZEALAND NAPIER WELLINGTON FREIGHTERS LIMITED

Telephone ......591-309......

P.O. Box ......12-234......

Town ......Penrose.......

13th December, 1977.

New Zealand Freighters,
P.O. Box 26-260,
EPSOM.
Auckland.

Sirs,

We, the undersigned, being the employees of New Zealand
Freighters located at the Southdown Lane Terminal wish
to hereby register our shock and our extreme displeasure
that the company should have seen fit to terminate the employment
of Bruce Plested.

We feel that his dismissal reflects the inability of this company
to recognize individuality.

We remain,

The Freight Forwarding Division of Brambles Burnett Ltd.

Forty-three New Zealand Freighters workers signed the petition demanding
reinstatement of their boss, Bruce Plested.

became Auckland manager, quickly demonstrating that he was a man light on his feet.

One particular incident serves to demonstrate his initiative. In 1974 the vital north–south Auckland to Wellington rail link was cut when the bridge at Ngaruawahia, just north of Hamilton, was flattened by a train derailment. These were the days when everything moved by rail; trucks were barred by law from competing over long distances with the government-owned New Zealand Railways (NZR). Thinking nimbly, and using air as well as driving around the bridge to load again onto rail, in the first week of the derailment Plested's Auckland branch made NZ$33,000; the second week returned NZ$34,000. And when normal rail service resumed they never dropped below NZ$25,000. Word had gone around that despite the derailment, Plested and his team had delivered, and people were prepared to pay for service — a lesson never forgotten.

Sadly, the greater the profits he returned for his masters, the more they seemed to reject his thinking and methods. For the law of the day prohibited goods being transported further than 40 miles (64 kilometres) by road, later to be increased to 150 kilometres. New Zealand Railways granted an effective monopoly on all inter-city freight transport, allowing just four companies (Alltrans/TNT, Daily Freightways, New Zealand Freighters and Mogal) to have concessional rates, and between them they ran a price cartel. All of these companies were Australian controlled, which infuriated Bruce Plested all the more.

He hated it. Hated the price fixing. Hated the other forwarders. So much so that on 15 October 1976 he wrote to Prime Minister Rob Muldoon complaining about the rail service, union problems and restrictions on offering an alternative road service. The detailed tale of woe provides a telling snapshot of the times.

Dear Sir,

I am Auckland Manager of a freight forwarding company, offering rail services throughout New Zealand, sea services to the South Island and to Australia.

I am a strong supporter of your aims and policies, but would like to catalogue from my diary, the immense problems our industry is suffering.

*June 14* Storemen & Packers had one day off in protest at Government Wage Order.

*June 21* The shunters put a ban on our siding on Monday through to Thursday afternoon. Because of the national rail stoppage in the North and South Island, we were unable to send any wagons of any description.

*June 28* No *Coastal Trader* sailing this week.

*July 5* No empty wagons were supplied either on the Monday or the Tuesday.

*July 8* Railways refused to accept conventional South Island traffic, due to Cook Strait backlog.

*July 12* Out of an allocation of 40 seafreighters [containers], only 26 were actually shipped on the *Coastal Trader* due to Cooks and Stewards dispute. Seven seafreighters followed four days later on the *Maheno* and seven were short-shipped.

*July 19* Heavy rain, high winds and hail. This has been going on since Thursday night. New Zealand Railways reduced all South Island sendings by 33 per cent. Allocated 33 seafreighters on *Coastal Trader* and this later in the week reduced to 26 owing to seven seafreighters short-shipped the previous week. Heavy rain all week until Friday.

*July 24* Saturday. Promised six wagons to clear Washdyke glass — all staff brought in — no wagons supplied.

*July 26* Almost no wagons supplied. Due to Cooks & Stewards dispute, no South Island traffic was allowed to be sent on the Monday or Tuesday. All South Island sendings are still reduced by 33 per cent.

*July 27* NZ Seamen all took a day off in protest of the Government's wage regulation, and to support the drivers' wage application. It is still raining. Heavy rain and hail several days this week.

*August 2* All New Zealand Railways' South Island sendings are still reduced by 33 per cent.

*August 3* Auckland wharfies went home for the day, resulting in wharves being closed.

*August 4* Harbour Board employees went home for the day, resulting in wharves being closed.

*August 5* Tally clerks went home for the day, resulting in wharves being closed. Rained heavily for most of the week and wagon supplies grossly inadequate.

The list continued in similar vein throughout the winter months and into October:

*October 1* Nuclear ship — *Long Beach*, arrived Auckland. Entire waterfront closed for several days, until nuclear ship leaves. Advised by Union Company that *Marama 169* has sailed for Sydney with eight out of our 30 seafreighters for Sydney. Balance of cargo is not due to leave Auckland now until 18.10.76. The *Coastal Trader* ex South Island on 22.9.76 still on the berth and appears unlikely to be discharged before Wednesday 6.10.76.

*October 4* All Auckland wharves remain closed because of *Long Beach*.

*October 5* Five wagons short. *Long Beach* nuclear ship sailed this morning, and all wharves working — queues five hours long on to wharf.

*October 6* Wharf queues five to six hours long.

*October 7* No wagons supplied. Still four hours to get onto the wharf.

*October 8* Auckland Storemen & Packers Union had a stop-work meeting at 8 am, returned to work at 12.30 pm.

*October 11* Supplied only seven wagons.

*October 13* Supplied no wagons. All men stopped work at 8.30 am — went on strike to meet at 7.30 am the following morning. Wharves stop-work meeting 7.30 am–8.30 am.

*October 14* Five wagons short. Men met at 7.30 am. Went home for the day to meet at 8 am on the 15.10.76.

*October 15* Men returned to work at 9.30 am, but they are feeling the strain of outside inadequacies of wagons supplied, and industrial stoppages. Advised by NZ Shipping Corporation that all coastal services on *Coastal Trader* into and out of Timaru, have now been cancelled. Advised nuclear submarine due in Christchurch Wednesday 20th, and highly likely another sailing of the *Coastal Trader* will be missed.

*October 16 Coastal Trader* due to sail for South Island from Auckland, with cargo loaded three weeks ago.

I do not know what action the Government could take to relieve these industrial pressures, or make up for inadequate New Zealand Railways rolling stock. I do know, however, that we are losing some of our best transport workers to industries which are not under such great pressures.

Yours faithfully.

THE REPLY WAS almost immediate and to the point, Muldoon writing: 'It is not a pleasant story and I sympathise with you and other transport operators, as well as the loyal workers in the industry who must be experiencing many frustrations.'

Plested's fate was sealed — his bosses would be furious that he'd written to the prime minister. His future was in jeopardy, for there was a delicious irony here: the good folk who managed commerce and industry in New Zealand understood that an inefficient rail service, further compounded by endless crippling strikes, required regular increases in freight charges — increased costs with no corresponding increase in service. The troublesome branch manager simply did not understand.

Bruce Plested understood all right. He had NZR in his sights as the enemy. At seven o'clock every morning he would call the railway manager responsible for supplying wagons to his freight yard and point out how many were missing. By nine o'clock he would be in the offices of the Transport Licensing Authority.

The law of the day required a special licence to move goods by road, and there had to be a very special reason for such a licence to be issued. NZR's failure to supply wagons should have been a good enough reason, but the Transport Licensing Authority refused to act.

One memorable day, Plested found himself momentarily alone in the tiny Transport Licensing office. There, on the desk, was a complete set of blank licences. In a flash the book was in Plested's pocket, where it remained as he spent the rest of the day arguing for clearance to move his goods by road. The fruitless discussion ended at four o'clock, when the bureaucrats all went home. Plested drove back to his depot, filled out a licence, and scrawled a signature across the bottom.

To this day he makes no apology for this act, which would be repeated many times. 'We just did not regard it as law-breaking. They were stupid, pathetic, bureaucratic morons destroying our country.'

Plested had also fine-tuned his method of dealing with unions. Behind his office door was a well-worn suit he wore for all negotiation meetings. It gave a clear message: the company could not possibly afford to pay another cent.

MEANWHILE THE AUCKLAND branch was making record profits from satisfied customers, yet his senior management were complaining about the size of Plested's telephone bill. He was working round the clock to keep the wheels turning but they steadfastly refused to pay the account, with the result that his home phone was disconnected, for a second time. A furious Plested marched into his office, snatched a heater and, as horrified accountants ducked for cover, swung it about his head by the cord before smashing it into a newly installed and most expensive Italian PABX machine. He then dictated a hasty resignation, matched only by the speed of his sacking.

It was this sacking that led to the walkout at Southdown Lane, but Bruce Plested did not want his men, his friends, out of work so a deal was done that got everyone back to work. A cheque for NZ$7000 was handed over, and he drove away in the company car. Three weeks later — and he remembers the day well, 18 December 1977 — he was painting his house when the idea hit him.

The *Coastal Trader* was a government-owned ship that ran a weekly freight service up and down the coast — a single roll-on, roll-off vessel providing a weekly service between Dunedin, Christchurch and Auckland. The ship operated outside those transport regulations that now imposed a 150-kilometre limit on all land transport bar rail — it was effectively outside the influence of NZR and the dominant forwarders. Following a phone call to long-time friend Graham Eddington, operations manager for the *Coastal Trader*, Plested spent December 26, Boxing Day, in the lounge of Wellington Airport thrashing out a deal. There was typical holiday chaos in the background, with constant final calls for missing passengers, as the country's state servants and their families made a frantic dash from the capital for their summer break. The two men were oblivious to all this as they hunched together in a corner of the bar for a meeting that began just after breakfast and ended late in the evening, with both the worse for wear.

Plested's request was simple enough. A guarantee of space on the *Coastal Trader* for a transport company that did not yet exist. Not so very simple really. There would be howls of protest from the big four. There would be political pressure. Eddington would be on the carpet as his own management felt the combined heat of a well-practised lobby group.

They were about to take a tiger by the tail. What the hell! They shook hands and had another drink. Then it was back to Auckland to make the dream a reality.

While at New Zealand Freighters, Plested had become close friends with the former operations manager, Howard Smith, who had since established a water-blasting business in partnership with another colleague, Robbie Andrews. Together they agreed to set up a company of which Plested would own 52 per cent, with 16 per cent each held by Smith, Andrews and Bryan King, who owned a forklift hire business and would supply one of his machines free for twelve months in return for his shareholding.

FEEL TH
BUT DO I
ANYWAY

E FEAR

T

Plested needed a holiday and set off for Waiheke, the tiny island that was slowly developing from its earliest beginnings as a seat of Maori power and influence to a holiday retreat and hippie haven. Eventually it would mature into a wine-growing paradise, attracting some of the nation's, and indeed the world's, wealthiest people.

Bruce Plested was at this stage a long way off the wealth that awaited him, but he had progressed from his working-class roots. He had been admitted to the prestigious Auckland Grammar School after a personal plea to the headmaster by his mother Elsie, a tailoress-machinist who had struggled alone to bring up Bruce and his younger brother Gerald. Plested remained close to his mother throughout her life, fully aware of how much she had sacrificed to bring up her two boys after their father left. (On her death in 2007, group managing director Don Braid arranged for all Mainfreight flags to be flown at half mast, a gesture that greatly touched Plested.)

After leaving Auckland Grammar the elder Plested boy went to Teachers' Training College, and two years later was in front of a class at Avondale's New Windsor School as a probationary assistant. He hated it. And what the young Bruce Plested hated doing he stopped, exchanging talk and chalk for a labourer's job making concrete slabs and blocks. Employment as a wages clerk followed at Fisher & Paykel, where he went on to qualify as an accountant.

For a time he played a mean piano, six nights a week, with the Feet Beats at the Bel Air coffee bar up the shadier end of Auckland's Queen Street. He had also played in the Satarocks skiffle band, a name inspired by the 1957 Russian Sputnik, sharing the stage with his childhood friend Carl Howard-Smith, who would go on to become a successful lawyer, later playing his part in the Bosman purchase.

On New Year's Day 1978 the young commercial lawyer sat across a trestle table from Plested as the two men nursed hangovers in the noisy garden of a beachside bar at Waiheke's Onetangi Hotel.

Plested was excited as he outlined his plans — a freight forwarding company that would drive a proverbial truck through the protectionist laws that allowed the woefully inefficient rail network to combine with the Australian transport companies' cartel to hold New Zealand commerce and industry to ransom.

Howard-Smith listened intently as his friend laid out his strategy of using the underutilised *Coastal Trader* to cut days, weeks even, off the transfer of goods between New Zealand's North and South Islands. He hesitated momentarily, not wanting to deflate the enthusiastic entrepreneur before him, before asking the obvious question: 'If this is such a good idea, why isn't everyone doing it?'

Plested glanced around before answering; among the festive crowd were some of the country's commercial elite, holidaying on the island. 'Rail have an absolute monopoly and charge what they like no matter how bad their service is. But that's not the real scandal.' Plested was warming to his theme. 'The real scandal is the big forwarders are given huge rail discounts that their customers don't know about.'

Howard-Smith's mind was racing, but Plested had not finished. 'They have a secret agreement not to undercut each other in the market. To never take a client off another cartel member. No one is going to drop their prices. That's the agreement.'

His friend smiled. 'Shame they weren't stupid enough to put it in writing.'

Plested's reply made the normally unflappable lawyer's jaw drop. 'Oh, but they did. And I have a copy of it.'

He went on to explain that he had a handy memento from his days at New Zealand Freighters, where he had been handed the document and told, in no uncertain terms, 'This is how we do things round here.'

The next question came from Plested. Did Howard-Smith know a good commercial lawyer who would be ready and willing to set up the new company? He certainly did — no problem.


SO IT WAS that late in the afternoon of 6 March 1978, at the newly appointed company solicitor's chambers at Lake Road, Takapuna, on Auckland's North Shore, the business was formally incorporated. Howard Smith, Bruce Plested and Carl Howard-Smith set off in search of a pub in which to celebrate. The unlikely trio — the giant, smiling Maori, the powerfully built accountant/trucker, and their brief — adjourned to the Gables pub in Ponsonby. When it came time to pay, the lawyer was saddled with the bill. His trailblazing corporate clients were both broke.

The company started life trading as Mainline Freighters, a name over which the three partners had agonised for weeks only to be told, three weeks into their new operation, that the Companies Office had found an Australian building company named Mainline Dillinger. They would have to find a different name. Bruce Plested caught the next flight to Wellington, fully expecting to have to do battle with the government bureaucrats. He stared at the form, the words 'Mainline' and 'Freighters' blinking back at him.

'What about Mainfreight? Can I have that?'

To his surprise the answer was an immediate 'Yes', and the company that would come to dominate the New Zealand transport industry, and embark on a giddy ride across the planet, was born.

Ironically, the company was initially set up to be a no-frills, low-cost service, but within a few weeks it became obvious that Mainfreight had the most reliable service in the country. The *Coastal Trader* was leaving NZR for dead. The emphasis quickly switched to both service and price. A single startling fact perhaps demonstrates more clearly than anything else the impact they made on the freight forwarding scene: Mainfreight was making a profit within five weeks, and did not borrow money for three years.

They first set up shop as Mainfreight in an Auckland warehouse/office at 135 Morrin Road, Panmure, in a deal in which they paid just half rent for the first six months. On the way home from signing the agreement, Plested was pulled over by a traffic policeman who wanted to know why the speedster was smiling.

'I've just signed to rent a building. I'm going home to tell my wife Maureen; I'm going to start a business.'

The traffic cop removed his sunglasses, glanced at the letter Plested held out, saw the annual figure of NZ$32,000, put his hand through the window and grinned. 'Put it there; best of luck.' No ticket, just an early example of what they refer to as 'Mainfreight Luck'. Three years later they bought the building.

Significantly, when they pitched for business one of their referees would be Don Rowlands, an Olympic representative and winner of a Commonwealth Games gold medal in rowing. Plested had met Rowlands while working for Fisher & Paykel. When Rowlands

N GX44

J/2 COLLECT $1.10 LAMBTONQUAY 3 51P

TED BOX 14038 PANMURE

COLLECT $1-10

DATE STAMP

PANMURE
N Z
13 MAR 1978
TELEGRAM

Serial No.

Sent

To          Checked

Rec'd
By  4·31∩

By

**INLAND** 🛡 **TELEGRAM**

Tel. 142    51449B—35,000 pads/9/74D.

NAME MAINFREIGHT TRANSPORT LIMITED AVAILABLE

REGISTRAR

COL 140362

**It's official. Mainfreight's name is approved.**

was given the task of running a joint venture between Fisher & Paykel and the Champion Spark Plug Company he had selected the 24-year-old Plested as part of the team that would instigate spark-plug manufacturing in New Zealand.

Plested had been identified as a driven man. At one stage he had been working at night as a cleaner in the Fisher & Paykel offices, mowing the Champion lawns, working in a garden centre on Saturdays, concreting on Sundays, and still studying accountancy at night while holding down a day job as assistant accountant.

This was the energy that led the new company director to chase and win business from New Zealand Starch, which regularly sent 44-gallon drums of glucose in containers to South Island sweet manufacturers. It was business perfectly suited to seafreight.

The containers used on the *Coastal Trader* were called seafreighters. The first week there had been one, the second a pair, and the third week saw two pairs leave Auckland. They were in business.

The alacrity with which New Zealand Starch took up the Mainfreight offer was hardly surprising given the service being provided by NZR. It could take weeks and sometimes months to deliver goods from Auckland to the South Island. Unbelievable as it may sound today, it was not uncommon then for companies to order three or four months ahead to get supplies on time. Despite this, the major freight forwarders stuck with NZR and the huge discounts it offered them.

Not that Mainfreight was in the charity business; they were making a healthy margin. And they worked all the hours God gave. This was the world into which Tracey Rickards walked in August 1978.

The 18-year-old typist was a dead ringer for the young woman who would shortly become the people's favourite, the blushing young girlfriend of Prince Charles, later known the world over as Princess Di. When she arrived at the Mainfreight office Tracey was confronted by three men working out of a room that measured all of six metres by four. Bare concrete-block walls, a brown carpet, hardly room for the old manual typewriter, and they all smoked. She was to discover that they expected an extraordinary work ethic. One day when she had the flu they collected her from home to come in and do the accounts at the Morrin Road office in her pyjamas.

In the cramped little room Plested wrote out the invoices by hand

Tracey Rickards at work on the accounts in her pyjamas.

and Tracey would tear a sheet out of an invoice book and type it up. The invoices were all posted on a Friday evening from the central city post office to be sure they arrived by Monday. And on the sixth day she would call . . . 'This is Tracey from Mainfreight, I would like to come and collect the cheque today.' And people paid.

They started as they intended to go on, which included insisting that everything had to look 100 per cent every minute of the day. Thirty-six hour shifts were not uncommon. The freight went, no matter what. And, at the end of every day, it all had to be left tidy for the next.

There would be no division of labour at Mainfreight. Visitors were quite likely to see Tracey Rickards or Bruce Plested driving a forklift. (Even today, all new recruits, graduates included, find themselves working on the floor to start with. In the early days they were expected to do this for up to two years.)

Soon Mainfreight bought a truck, an eight-wheeler Leyland Crusader that had been to the moon and back and was nicknamed *Wonder Wheels*. The truck came with a driver, Gary ('Gazza') Songhurst, who clearly remembers his introduction to the company. Plested informed him, 'We're going to be the biggest freight forwarder in New Zealand in ten years and it will be image and service, not cut rates, that does it.' Songhurst soon came to grips with the Mainfreight way. About to set out on a round trip to Wellington, he was confronted by his new managing director, resplendent in black shorts and singlet, climbing up into the cab. 'We'll need two drivers for this trip.'

And drive Plested did, all over the country, drumming up business. Yet he hated pitching to strangers. One lonely morning in Dunedin he stood in a phone box with the snow falling outside, making the dreaded cold calls to no avail. He realised he needed help. In desperation he called Neil Graham, an old friend from New Zealand Freighters days, who had tipped him off about New Zealand Starch. Graham urged him: 'Call my mate John Edmonds.'

Edmonds ran a firm of building supply merchants in the family name and was a heavy user of fibrolite, which was delivered from manufacturers James Hardie in Auckland. A valuable contact indeed. Emboldened by the knowledge that he had a strong introduction, Plested duly called, used Graham's name, and was granted an interview. He pitched for the business by undercutting the existing forwarder by a full NZ$30 a tonne, and got the contract. Only later

One of Mainfreight's earliest trucks, *Moody Blue*, ready for action.

did Plested learn that Graham had never met John Edmonds. He had merely wanted to give his friend enough confidence to make the call.

The success of pitching for such business lay in knowing how much the opposition was charging. Plested had a guaranteed route to success. Tracey would shamelessly call the opposition transport company and purport to work for one of their clients. 'I have to put together a quick report for our managing director and need the rates you charge us . . . can you let me have them.' Without fail the rates would be read out, and Plested would amaze the prospective Mainfreight client with his highly competitive counter-offer, which still ensured a healthy profit.

For Mainfreight was able to ship goods for less than the competing companies charged for their slower, less efficient rail service. And when the *Coastal Trader* was not operating, Mainfreight would move goods by road, despite the regulations prohibiting it, often with licences they wrote themselves.

When they first started out their rates were 20 to 30 per cent cheaper than the competition, but when the big four started to lower their prices, Mainfreight did not. Service ruled.

Mainfreight might have been lean and hungry, but it was no secret society. Everyone was kept informed of profitability, with weekly figures posted on the office wall. And they knew something else: at the end of the year there would be a bonus, with 10 per cent of profits split equally among the team. The team, always the team.

The remainder of the profits went back into the company for better buildings and carpet and later the lunchroom, where a canteen lady addressed surprised visiting bankers as 'luv' and served storemen and drivers hot meals, just like their mums made. Meals they ate seated beside the managing director.

Soon the tiny office was too small and they moved into a portable Lockwood house alongside the warehouse. Mainfreight now had all of fourteen people on the payroll. Tom Roscoe, a union delegate known as 'Tommy Gun' from New Zealand Freighters days, joined Mainfreight in 1979 as a loader. One day he clumped through the new office in his steel-capped boots, stretched his arms across Plested's desk, leaning very close, and complained, 'This company will never be the same again, Bruce. It's getting too big.'

Little did anyone know quite how big it would become. In the early days of 1978, when they first did NZ$10,000 of sales for the week, the party went on into the wee hours. By 2012 they would be doing NZ$10,000 of sales every two and a half minutes, 24 hours a day, seven days a week.

Meanwhile it was all hands to the pump, with Plested's wife Maureen knocking out debtors' statements on her NCR32 accounting machine, in between landscaping the depot and cooking the Thursday night roast for the entire team. Clean and tidy and beautiful was the motto.

All this did not go unnoticed by the competition. Mainfreight was becoming more than just an irritant. It was time to shut them down. Time to really flex muscle. In fact, all the competition achieved was that Bruce Plested took his old friend Neil Graham fishing and hooked a deal that would forever change Mainfreight. But first, he would read a life-changing book.

# IF OPPO[ ]
# DOESN'T
# BUILD A

# RTUNITY
# KNOCK,
# DOOR

The year 1979 was a terrible one for New Zealand. When an Air New Zealand DC10 ploughed into Antarctica's Mount Erebus 257 people perished and the nation went into mourning. Then, as the oil crisis bit deep, it faced both a ban on weekend petrol sales and the introduction of carless days.

Plested felt the need for a break and took off with Maureen to stay with his brother Gerald, who was living in Singapore. The experience changed his life for a number of reasons.

First he drove into a parking building and found people charging a fee to help him reverse into a space and then to wash his car. There was even a blind old man demanding payment to let the anxious pass into a public toilet. It was a revelation — pure capitalism at work, entrepreneurs making a living.

While in Singapore he also discovered Ayn Rand, the renowned novelist and screenwriter best known for her development of the philosophical system of objectivism that she captured in *Atlas Shrugged*. Plested had been given the book by his mother, with strict instructions to read it. And he met a Malaysian fortune-teller who pronounced, 'It doesn't matter where you go, or what you do, you will always carry the bulk of the responsibility. And you will have luck around you always.'

Bruce Plested at last knew what he was. He was a capitalist. Pure and simple. No question.

Back in New Zealand the reinvigorated entrepreneur was having little luck dealing with the transport cartel, who were applying enormous pressure. They successfully objected every time he applied for a licence to move goods by road. They were also jostling for position on Auckland's Mount Wellington, using binoculars to look down on the Mainfreight depot to see what and whose freight was coming and going. Among them, lying in the dirt, was Kerry Crocker from Plested's old stamping ground, the giant New Zealand Freighters. Once they identified Mainfreight's customers

Mainfreight's first home on Auckland's Morrin Road, Panmure.

they would approach them with a standard offer of a 30 per cent discount. Anything to put Mainfreight out of business.

These were the days when transport companies were only allowed to make a 17 per cent return on assets. By law! An official from the Department of Trade and Industry haunted the company, wanting to know what return Mainfreight made on its assets. 'But we haven't got any assets,' Plested would reply, to which the bureaucrat answered, without so much as flinching, 'Well, you're not allowed to make a profit then.'

'We've just got one trailer and one truck,' Plested explained.

'Well, you're only allowed to make a return of 17 per cent on your assets. How did you decide to sell freight at this price?'

When Plested explained he had plucked the figure out of thin air, he was told, 'Well, you're not allowed to do that. It's got to be a price approved by Industry and Commerce.'

Plested's subsequent suggestion as to what the gentleman might care to do with his regulations is unprintable.

Bizarre as this may sound today this was New Zealand in 1979. It was a country whose bureaucrats would have been equally at home in the Eastern Europe of the day. A country where powerful figures in the cartel were lobbying politicians, who were in turn lobbying their departments. Where word came from friends within the trade union movement that competitors were paying some union members to make trouble for Mainfreight.

Plested was even getting death threats, forcing him to have a private, unlisted telephone number. One New Year's Eve, at a party in Hastings, he was sharing barbecue-cooking duties with a traffic policeman who launched into a tirade of abuse against the company after spotting someone wearing a Mainfreight-branded hat. Bemused, Plested asked why the anger, to be told that they were under instructions to stop Mainfreight trucks, that they were 'bastards' and were being monitored through the national police computer. Another time, Gary Songhurst was stopped in Wellington while driving *Wonder Wheels* and told by the traffic officer, 'We want you bastards.'

Intrigued, Songhurst asked if the officer knew how many trucks Mainfreight owned.

'No.'

'Well, it's one.'

'Can't be!'

Always a clean sweep from Mainfreight. From left: Wally Wright, Ken Leef, Howard Smith, Gazza Songhurst and Tommy Gun Roscoe.

'Yes, just one.'

To this day Plested finds it hard to conceal his anger at what he saw as a concerted campaign of harassment by the government and its bureaucrats who had been so successfully lobbied by the cartel. And the unions were just as determined to make life difficult. One unforgettable day, union delegates had been dispatched from Daily Freightways and Sea Freightways to make trouble. When they arrived Plested was so scared he did not offer them coffee for fear they would see his hands shaking.

'I sat on my hands for the whole time. They demanded that we buy all this safety equipment for handling dangerous goods. We didn't have any dangerous goods but we had to buy respirators. I was frightened of getting smacked. I was frightened of our guys getting smacked. I was frightened of losing the business.'

The tension was unrelenting. Famously, Mainfreight was put under pressure by opposition companies' union delegates to pay higher penal rates to the three men employed to work over the weekend to unpack and load freight that came from Christchurch on the *Coastal Trader* for delivery in Auckland on Monday. Mainfreight was already paying them time and a half for the first three hours on Saturday, then double time for the rest of the weekend. The storemen worked Saturday and Sunday so the trucks could roll out at seven o'clock on Monday morning.

New Zealand had never seen anything that efficient. Freight was pouring in at such volumes that Mainfreight did not dare advertise for fear of the quantity of freight that might be generated. Suddenly, without any warning, Mainfreight found itself blacked at the wharves in both Auckland and Christchurch. Plested was convinced the entire business was in jeopardy 'as union bosses flexed their muscle'.

To the union's surprise, Plested agreed to the demand for additional weekend pay. It amounted to an extra $200 a week each for the three men working that shift. This on top of the overtime they were already being paid. They had asked for the world, and he paid it. It meant that most of the Mainfreight people who worked that shift were paid enough to be able to buy a house. And it was business as usual for the company, which was just $600 a week worse off.

Plested found more ways to make union muscle irrelevant. Mainfreight moved from hourly award rates to monthly salaries

TOP — The Mainfreight team eats together. ABOVE — The first Christchurch depot in 1979.

for its workers, something that continues to apply throughout the company. And it maintained the bonus system, sharing 10 per cent of the profit between everybody each year. The philosophy was simple enough: have your people think like capitalists. You do not go on strike for silly reasons and damage your income potential when you have a car and a house to protect.

There was an extra week's pay at Christmas. And hams. Unheard of. And they all ate together. This was the Maori way that Plested had learned during his childhood and while labouring. Everyone brought something for lunch and shared it around. For the first decade of Mainfreight this was the way. Then came the subsidised cafeterias.

Mainfreight was making a favourable impression with customers and workers alike. Plested would later reflect, 'I don't think any man could have stopped us; we had that head of steam up and success was only a matter of time and degree.'

Then the cartel struck back, convincing the management of the Shipping Corporation that space on the *Coastal Trader* out of Auckland could only be given on the basis of the space taken up south to north. Mainfreight was only shipping up to ten seafreighters north, compared to 25 south. The cartel booked the whole ship out of the South Island, a move aimed at killing Mainfreight.

That was when Plested invited Neil Graham to join him for a weekend's fishing off Waiheke on his 5-metre runabout, *Tuatahi*. Neil Graham was the curly-haired extrovert who had been assistant general manager of New Zealand Freighters. By the age of sixteen he had been expelled from two schools and had amassed 53 driving convictions, with which he papered his bedroom wall. Yet after a succession of jobs he had stumbled into the transport industry, working on a furniture removal truck. He was hooked. He was the boy they always teased by sending him to get a left-handed screwdriver, but he loved the freedom. By the time he had turned eighteen he had his heavy traffic licence, a year later he had leapfrogged into management with McBeth Carriers, and by his early twenties he was overseeing people who had been in the industry since before he was born.

Through a series of company takeovers he had ended up at New Zealand Freighters, where he was when his friend Bruce was fired. By the time he was invited out fishing by his mate he was heartily sick of freight and thinking seriously of a move into tourism. Neil Graham was a transport natural, though, and Bruce Plested knew it.

By two o'clock in the morning a second bottle of rum had been opened as the men watched the moonlight reflecting back across the wavetops where dolphins rose playfully. They had been talking for hours, Plested going over and over his vision for Mainfreight. It was a vision he had put before Graham in the past. Finally he just shrugged and asked, 'Look, are you in or are you out?'

The offer was a shareholding and the position of joint managing director, with Graham returning from Auckland to Christchurch, the city where he had been born and bred. The two men shook hands and finished the rum.

IF THERE WAS a defining moment for Mainfreight, this was it. The cartel, by pressuring the government and the Shipping Corporation, had ensured Mainfreight's future. This was the start of one of those rare but successful business partnerships where one partner is the organisational genius and the other the confident and persuasive frontman.

On 1 June 1979 Neil Graham opened a Mainfreight branch in Tuam Street, Christchurch, with a caravan for an office and his wife Helen as the office junior. Graham's answer to the cartel assault was to book space north, which under newly written rules meant Mainfreight had to be given equal space going south.

Graham had a long association with the New Zealand Wheat Board from his time at New Zealand Freighters. The board received a government transport subsidy to cover the cost of getting flour from subsidised South Island flourmills to the profitable Auckland market — subsidy upon subsidy. It all made perfect sense in the New Zealand of the day. And Mainfreight certainly was not complaining as the company shipped wheat north.

Memories were starting to fade of their earlier ambition to earn NZ$50,000 a year. The reality that they could become seriously rich was starting to dawn. One memorable night, as Bruce Plested and Howard Smith, the original founding partners, were yet again discussing their needs and aims, Plested suggested they should adopt a twenty- or even 50-year vision. To which Smith, emboldened by the beer in his hand, replied, 'Why not think of ourselves as a 100-year company?'

It was an empowering moment. In years to come, this philosophy would give them enormous freedom and flexibility in decision-making. Now they were no longer worried about this week or this month or even this year. They were a 100-year company.

THEY WERE STILL very much a transport company, however, with Plested and Graham both being fans of the high-profile Mack truck. In 1981 a trip was arranged to the US, the home of Macks. The joint managing directors were instructed to present themselves at New York's Pan Am Heliport, where the Mack Truck executive helicopter would be waiting. It was a freezing day, with driving snow, and it was with some relief that they welcomed the arrival of a chopper and its courteous pilot, who ushered them both on board.

When the pilot heard that this was their first visit to Manhattan, he treated them to a close-up fly-past of the Statue of Liberty before heading off to Pennsylvania and Allentown, headquarters of the mighty Mack Truck empire.

The two New Zealanders were somewhat bemused when the pilot set the chopper down in an empty field. 'They'll come and get you in a minute,' he said, and with that he was gone. A van duly arrived, and Plested and Graham were whisked away to be greeted by the somewhat confused management team of a baking powder factory.

The mistake explained, they were soon once more aboard the helicopter. The pilot had lost all sense of reverential service, let alone humour, and repeated the same phrase, endlessly, throughout the return trip to New York: 'I'm so pissed with you guys.' His mood was not improved on being forced to land beside a beautiful Mack helicopter that dwarfed his baking powder machine and came complete with two pilots and a red-jacketed major-domo who served breakfast on what was a mirror of the Presidential helicopter.

Once more they were treated to a Statue of Liberty tour before being deposited outside the world famous factory, from which flew a banner declaring 'Welcome to Bruce and Neil from Mainfreight, New Zealand'. There to greet them was the company president, who also happened to be the local mayor. He presented his valued guests with keys to the freedom of Allentown.

Factory tour completed, it was off to the golf club for lunch, where the visitors were sworn to secrecy after being told that their hosts had just landed an order from the Indonesian army for 140 Mack trucks. There were speeches and then the vice-president rose to ask, 'Now tell us, Neil, how many Mack units do you and Bruce currently have operating in your corporation?'

At this point Plested rose to head for the bathroom as Graham announced to his expectant audience: 'We have three.'

Without so much as a flinch, the vice-president replied, 'And let's hope that when you're with us next year, let's hope it's four . . .'

BY THE EARLY 1980s Mainfreight had grouped its forces around the ports of Auckland, Wellington, Christchurch and Dunedin. Through a combination of coastal shipping and a cavalier approach to road restrictions, they were driving an enormous wedge through the abundance of regulations that led to New Zealand being described as a Polish shipyard. In Mainfreight's book, overly officious bureaucrats were to be defied. Absurd, ill-advised laws were made to be broken.

Mainfreight's novel approach was attracting both customers and top men from within the industry. In November 1980 Kerry Crocker, the very man who had spent so many hours peering down on Mainfreight from his mountain hideaway, arrived from New Zealand Freighters. He was taken on as a sales manager, and found that having got the freight business he was then expected to load it. (He remains with the company to this day.) Crocker found the company still writing its own licences when necessary to move freight by road, with the growing confidence to fabricate their own, previously unheard of, two-way licences to ensure trucks did not return empty.

Mainfreight's rather chequered history of dabbling with what were, quite simply, forged licences would in time become a subject of mild embarrassment as it grew from maverick to mainstream to respected public company with worldwide interests. That said, the company's founders consistently argue that they were merely circumventing laws that were squeezing the life out of the commercial heartbeat of the nation.

Strangely, they took their inspiration from the enemy camp. Trevor Farmer, the legendary former chippie who had almost single-handedly introduced containerisation to New Zealand and built the mighty Daily Freightways, was regarded with awe by Bruce Plested.

Mainfreight's early shareholders. From left: Bruce Plested, Howard Smith, Terry Cunneen, Neil Graham and Robbie Andrews.

These were tough times that called for tough men, and they did not come any tougher than Farmer. The two men might have been bitter rivals but they were long-time friends. It was a friendship that would even survive all of the conflicts that lay ahead. When Plested was worn to a frazzle he would join Farmer and his cohorts for a Friday night drink, just to soak up the vitality. Farmer seemed impervious to the pressure; Plested watched and learned and absorbed the energy.

The competition was still watching Mainfreight. New Zealand Freighters sent a young salesman named Bryan Curtis out into the market to target selected Mainfreight customers with an offer of NZ$68 a tonne, Auckland to Christchurch. This was a staggering reduction on the standard price of between NZ$160 and NZ$190. One such customer was Ipsco, a specialist dust extraction manufacturer, which happened to be managed by Gerald Plested, younger brother of Bruce. He was not taking his business anywhere, but he did take the sensible precaution of getting the remarkable offer in writing.

Bruce Plested awaited his moment with the signed document in his bottom drawer. The moment came when New Zealand Freighters went to Mainfreight's prized customer, James Hardie, brandishing an offer of NZ$100 a tonne to Dunedin. It was an offer James Hardie could not refuse. The account was lost. The very next day a beaming Plested presented himself at the James Hardie headquarters to wish them well with their new freight forwarder.

'No hard feelings, these things happen, but just for old time's sake, I feel there's something you should know.' The NZ$68 a tonne offer was put on the table.

New Zealand Freighters were summoned to a meeting with James Hardie, where they were confronted with the document and forced to offer the same rate to their new customer. The move cost the company NZ$27,000 a week. These would prove to be unbearable losses. Three months later the parent company, Brambles, sold out to the Owens Group and retreated to Australia. The word was out: Mainfreight played for keeps. As for Owens, they would play a significant role in the Mainfreight story to come.

Mainfreight was clearly making its presence felt, with the chairman of one major competitor threatening Plested, warning that he should toe the line. 'We can make life very difficult for you.' Plested, in turn, intimated that he would make public the cartel's monopoly agreement, one paragraph a week for three months.

'Is that blackmail?' he was asked.

'Call it what you will . . .'

The agreement contained fourteen quite unambiguous and clearly defined conditions. Specifically, no member of the cartel could underquote to another member's client. The threatening phone calls stopped.

Mainfreight had further wins. The giant Marsden Point oil refinery, which was being built on New Zealand's north-east coast, required formidable amounts of freight. By rights, all this should have been sent north by rail to Whangarei, which was outside the 150-kilometre radius, and then by road to the refinery site. Common sense prevailed though, and Mainfreight was granted a special licence to cart by road direct to Marsden Point from Auckland.

Mainfreight was successfully arguing the sheer stupidity of protecting NZR to the detriment of the nation's economic growth. And all the while Plested was developing his company philosophy, based on Professor William Ouchi's *Theory Z*, which he had established after studying Japanese methods of business management. Put simply, you treat people as if they are going to stay with the company for 40 years. In addition, you slow down promotion, rather than moving them from job to job every six months. And you always promote from within. The theory is that when the managing director dies you just employ a new storeman and everybody moves up one. Throw in a dash of passion, and you're there.

IN 1982 PLESTED determined to do something to bolster Mainfreight's board. They needed some outside muscle. Not a white knight exactly, but someone who could add a new perspective, some additional wisdom born of wider experience than merely dealing with freight and truckies.

He found his answer in, of all places, the *New Zealand Woman's Weekly*. Flicking aimlessly through the magazine one day, he found a familiar face staring back at him: the rowing ace, Don Rowlands, his mentor from Fisher & Paykel days. Rowlands was a man Plested continued to rely on for regular advice, catching up with him most weeks. It was a eureka moment. The managing director of Fisher &

Paykel was just the figurehead Mainfreight needed.

Throughout his long career Rowlands encouraged self-management while hiring people who would challenge him. Constantly. He did not stifle people; he let them breathe. He was a man in business to have fun and make money, in that order, with the credit going to those who did the work, not the boss. He was a man who took joy in the success of others and lived by the creed that if you do what is right you will please some people and astonish the rest.

While running Fisher & Paykel, Rowlands had brought in William Edwards Deming, the American widely credited with assisting Japanese manufacturers to develop unheard-of levels of quality and productivity along with lower costs, all of which created vast international demand for Japanese products.

Don Rowlands, clearly a man ahead of his time, was known as the 'working-class managing director'. When Fisher & Paykel workers staged a one-day strike following concern about how a proposed productivity bonus might be calculated, Rowlands accepted responsibility for the communication breakdown and paid them for the day. He said he understood the concern, and suggested the union appoint an independent auditor to examine the books and report back that all was in order.

No one had heard anything like it. A trade union being allowed into the holy of holies to examine a company's books and check the bottom line? Labour Prime Minister David Lange, a man renowned for his caustic wit, once greeted Rowlands with the words, 'I know who you are. You're the guy who tries to make capitalism respectable.' Rowlands correctly took that as a compliment.

Long before the rest of the world cottoned on to the notion, Rowlands was tearing down walls and breaking down barriers in his constant demand for open, frank and transparent communication. It was an approach that took Fisher & Paykel to the leading edge of technology, research, development and manufacturing.

Here was an engineer with a logical approach to everything from productivity improvements and cost efficiencies to eliminating waste. From assistant production manager he had risen to take total control of Fisher & Paykel, with time off to become managing director of Champion. Even after his retirement from Fisher & Paykel he remained a board member for a further eleven years. He also served on the boards of Henderson & Pollard, the New

Zealand Naval Dockyard, Progressive Enterprises Group, Nestlé, CWF Hamilton and, of course, Mainfreight.

He was president of both the Auckland and New Zealand Manufacturers Federation, with a business career that was matched stroke for stroke in the sporting world as a rower. Rowlands won nine New Zealand rowing championships, a silver medal in the eights at the 1950 Empire Games and gold four years later in the single-scull event at the Commonwealth Games. He then served as an administrator in the sport he loved so much, making an outstanding contribution to national and international rowing and, more recently, acting as patron of the 2010 World Rowing Championships, held in New Zealand.

Years earlier Bruce Plested had asked Rowlands whether he might have a future with Fisher & Paykel. The reply was brutally honest: 'I don't think you have one. You have enough horsepower to be the finance director of F&P one day, and maybe even managing director, but there's a logjam in front of you, too many guys with seniority over you.'

That was the turning point for Plested, who confided that he had an opportunity to get into the transport business. Rowlands had developed a rule of thumb that if someone looked as though they should be in a job then they should be. The man across the desk from him was solidly built, square-jawed. Yes, he looked like a truckie. 'Go do it,' was his advice.


ONE MONDAY NIGHT in September 1982 Rowlands sat in Plested's office, as he had done many times before, and listened as the branch managers called in their crucial weekly profits. He marvelled at the encouragement handed out by Plested. That was Plested's skill, getting people motivated.

Plested had concluded early on that far too much time was spent preparing budgets that were then invariably altered as a result of unforeseen circumstances. What was important at Mainfreight was making more money than they had the previous year, on a week-by-week and month-by-month basis. The policy of checking weekly profits allowed them to tell at a glance if they were ahead of or behind the game. Further analysis could reveal why. With such high-quality information to hand, who needed budgets?

Business taken care of, Plested refilled his guest's glass and then made a startling approach: 'You've been offering advice for a long time, and I'd like to make it official; I want you to be chairman of the company.'

A public announcement was made the very next day, setting in motion a remarkable chain reaction. The trade unions suddenly viewed Mainfreight in a totally different light. So, too, did the competition. The little trucking company, with branches in Auckland, Hamilton, Christchurch and Dunedin, employing 140 people, was now linked through Rowlands to the mighty Fisher & Paykel. Mainfreight had been embraced, endorsed even, and the impact was immediate. The bureaucratic pressure eased as it dawned on the 'system', from union delegate to Cabinet minister, that little Mainfreight had grown up and was to be taken seriously.

Don Rowlands now sees his chairmanship as a clever move by Plested, who in turn regards it as a natural progression by a company in dire need of some added professionalism. In truth, Don Rowlands, *Theory Z* and *Atlas Shrugged* might *all* have had their influence on the evolution of the company, as has encouraging workers to be capitalists who own their own homes and have agreeable cars alongside the promise of an annual bonus. But those who have made it their business to analyse Mainfreight's success have difficulty going past the Bruce Plested/Neil Graham relationship as the key ingredient, certainly in the company's first quarter-century.

It would become an extraordinary partnership. Plested was the serious one, while Graham was one of the boys, charming and disarming, with a mind like a steel trap. Plested took care of the nuts and bolts while Graham worked his charm on the customers. Together they sold Mainfreight's ability to get the job done. Customers loved them. They were a breath of fresh air. They had passion.

They sold on the basis of a simple proposition: 'We have challenged the New Zealand Railways monopoly, we have challenged the price fixers. If we go out of business you will be back to the bad old days and the rates will increase again. We'll love your freight to death and get the job done for you.'

It was only logical that the two men should concur that treating their workforce well would eradicate union firepower. There was more to Mainfreight than just regular salaries. There was a sense of caring, epitomised by those hot meals each day in the canteen.

Their uniforms were better. Their boots were better. Their pride in themselves was better. Mainfreight cared for its team. Not its staff, its *team*. In short, Plested and Graham built a company in their own image — a company where mate looks after mate.

They might have been looking after each other, but the system was still against them every step of the way. NZR was right to be concerned but could not respond with better service. Its management reacted the only way they knew, with discount upon discount, handing out massive rate cuts to the favoured few in the form of taxpayer-funded subsidies to destroy a private enterprise competitor.

ONE OF THE Mainfreight team who met the *Coastal Trader* in Auckland was a student earning extra money while studying for his commerce degree. In 1984 Mark Newman was the dogsbody's assistant, handling 72-kilogram bags of flour and 50-kilogram bags of bran and pollard, its by-products. He earned NZ$24,000 that year while studying full-time at university. It was phenomenal money for a student.

Two years into the degree, Plested suggested to young Newman that he continue studying part-time and join the company. He went from part-time loader to full-time assistant accountant, dropping NZ$10,000 a year in the process. His first day in the office was an eye-popping experience. While most companies were starting to come to terms with computers, here was a world devoid of them. Mainfreight was using manual NCR32 accounting machines. It took all day Friday to balance the debtors' ledger. Every month Newman would collate all the information from four branches and painstakingly write out the ledger, which then had to be hand-balanced. The assistant accountant was personally writing 1000 cheques a month. It was not the future he had been dreaming of at university.

However, its incredibly labour-intensive nature made it totally effective. 'I'd passed every exam but had never truly understood accounting, until I did it the Mainfreight way,' Newman says.

But while Newman was learning he also realised that he was only going to achieve part-time success with his BCom, so he decided to return to full-time study. All his weekend work materialised again — and the money! It was a decision that would bear eventual

TOP — Tommy Gun Roscoe at the end of a 24-hour shift. ABOVE — Mark Newman the graduate accountant at work.

The 1985 Wellington branch opening. From left: (back row) local kaumatua, Dennis McLean, Andy Melrose, (second row) Bill Chandler, Howard Smith, Wally Wright, (third row) Bruce Plested and Don Rowlands, (front) Richard Prebble and Neil Graham.

fruit for Mainfreight, with Newman playing a significant role in its global expansion.

Meanwhile, in 1985 Mainfreight established a new Wellington branch, which was opened by Cabinet minister Richard Prebble. Little did he know it but, like Newman, the lawyer politician had just signed on for a long-term relationship with Mainfreight.

BY THE MID-EIGHTIES the Christchurch branch had 211 active customers, with the number growing by the week. Neil Graham reported back to Bruce Plested that they were in a position to survive the potential loss of their biggest account, the NZ$3 million Wheat Board business, and still make an overall profit in the South Island. They were prophetic words indeed.

The sheer absurdity of the flour subsidy had also finally dawned, and flour movement from Dunedin and Christchurch to Auckland stopped dead in its tracks. No more Wheat Board account.

There was still the dreaded Unit Freight Rebate Scheme to deal with. This had been introduced in 1973, and gave South Island manufacturers a 10 per cent subsidy on freight costs for goods sent to the North Island. The rebate applied to rail but not sea, meaning the *Coastal Trader* traffic did not qualify.

That was bad enough, but NZR turned the screw further in 1982 by publicly increasing its rates by 15 per cent while at the same time offering its favoured customers a full 20 per cent discount for additional freight. The motive was simple enough: kill off the *Coastal Trader* with massive hidden discounts, at the same time driving the troublesome Mainfreight out of business.

This was a direct assault on both a government-owned shipping line *and* the only New Zealand-owned freight forwarder offering a serious challenge to the four major Australian-controlled companies. To make matters worse, when Mainfreight shipped to Dunedin they were faced with crippling rail charges to move goods on to Invercargill, just outside the 150-kilometre limit. They were being charged the same price for the short hop as Alltrans was paying for a wagon to travel from Auckland to Invercargill, the length of both islands. And then there were the strenuous objections to all applications for a road licence, which were denied. Mainfreight and the *Coastal Trader* were under serious threat as a viable economic alternative to the big players, who were so dependent on their cosy relationship with rail.

The government finally saw sense, and in the mid-eighties began scrapping the protective legislation that prevented goods being moved more than 150 kilometres by road. This allowed Mainfreight to shift its sights inland, where it set up a string of new branches and was able to offer a more comprehensive service. It was a big call. New Zealand was at the time crippled by high inflation, interest rates for domestic borrowing were at a staggering 23 per cent, and companies were able to earn unprecedented interest overnight on their funds.

Mainfreight came up with a cunning plan. They slipped their annual tax cheque into a hand-addressed, tatty old recycled envelope that was then driven out to a rural post box for posting on 7 March, tax day. It took the tax department ten days to get round to opening the nondescript envelope and banking the cheque. During that time Mainfreight was earning interest on the tax money, making a memorable NZ$33,000. These were irrational days, with no end of 'sure fire' deals on offer. But some deals, as Mainfreight was to discover, were just too good to be true. 'We were,' in Plested's words, 'about to get our arses burnt.'

Deer farming was all the rage. Venison was in demand, but the real profit came from deer antlers, which were ground up and sold to Asian gentlemen convinced of its magical arousal powers. This was Viagra on the hoof. That was where the smart money of the day was, and that was where Plested and Graham were advised to put their hard-earned cash. Then an unscrupulous Asian trader began mixing pig blood with the crushed velvet to increase volume and profit but not necessarily performance. Word got out, and confidence in the enhancing powers of ground-up deer antlers collapsed throughout Asia. Proof positive that what goes up doesn't always stay up. Mainfreight lost NZ$450,000.

More significantly, from Plested's perspective, 'We should not have been involved in an enterprise that did not produce monthly profit and loss accounts, and balance sheets on a regular basis. I would commend that lesson to everyone in all their business dealings.'

THAT RESOLVED, THEY placed an advertisement for a computer accountant. It was time to get someone with real experience in integrating computer and accounting systems. Kevin Drinkwater

The Morrin Road team in 1983. From left: (back row) Dennis McLean, Tom Makaware, Kerry Crocker, James Plested, Terry Cunneen, Mark Newman, Lloyd Lawless, Bruce Plested, (front row) Wayne Milner, Ken Leef, Bryan Curtis, Vern Wright, Tommy Gun Roscoe, Howard Smith, Geoff Unsworth.

spotted the notice, applied, and was granted a five o'clock interview. He had just the right sort of experience, having spent time contracting to companies in the UK.

It was ten o'clock by the time Drinkwater got home. He was never late home, and by eight o'clock his wife was ringing the hospitals and police. The following day Plested and Graham took him to the obscenely expensive Bonaparte's, their preferred restaurant when they wanted to make a good impression, where he was promised a car of his choice and a generous salary package.

Still Drinkwater hesitated. Apart from anything else, he worried that given where he lived he would be driving home into the sun every night. His father-in-law knew enough to say, 'If you're working for Bruce Plested, the only thing you'll have to worry about is the moonlight.' So Drinkwater agreed, the deal was signed, and Plested rang soon after with the exciting news that he could collect the car of his choice from the Avis second-hand car yard.

Other companies had computers and fax machines; Mainfreight had a ledger book and now a computer expert. They put Drinkwater to work loading freight. The first person with a university degree to work at Mainfreight, the first person to wear a suit every day, loaded freight all around the country. And he absorbed everything there was to know about the company and its needs. He fitted in: during a year off before going to university, Drinkwater had cut scrub, dug graves and worked at the Marsden B power station.

He and Mark Newman swept the floors and learned the Mainfreight philosophy. It was the team that won, not the individual. He soon came to love Mainfreight; the energy was electric, the vibes phenomenal. This was a true family culture.

Drinkwater was a runner who liked to exercise during his lunch break. Unbeknown to him, Plested issued a special dispensation: Drinkwater could run and swim during the day, but woe betide anyone else who thought they could take time off. Drinkwater was a thinker; he was working while he exercised, Plested declared.

While he was loading freight and thinking, Drinkwater was fast taking in the fact that despite its primitive accounting systems and handwritten general ledger the company was making money, huge money for the day: NZ$5 million a year before tax. He knew they were cowboys who bent the rules and broke down fences. But these were rules that needed to be broken. These were quality cowboys.

And he learned valuable lessons from these practical men. If you can't do it right manually, you can't computerise it correctly. To this day Drinkwater runs through projects manually to achieve the final result. Then, and only then is the process automated.

In June 1986, when he finally computerised the general ledger system, Drinkwater found another Mainfreight surprise. Mark Newman had been balancing the books by hand; he was good, they always balanced. Drinkwater was impressed, until he discovered that the young Bachelor of Commerce student was simply altering inconvenient figures to ensure his success. Drinkwater was horrified. In fact, when the books were computerised they were found to be out by just NZ$126.

The computer operating system they chose was ideally suited to Mainfreight. It was simplicity itself. The PICK *Reality* system had been invented by Dick Pick during the Vietnam War for the Pentagon, after the US Army had complained they spent months training people to operate computers only to have them killed after a week in the field. Dick Pick built a system that involved computers communicating in a language for which they had never been programmed before: English. Plested and Graham liked the sound of that and bought it with no further discussion.

They were going to need just such a system, as Mainfreight was about to get very busy indeed. When it was first installed there were 2500 consignments being entered each week. Come time for replacement, thirteen years later, it was handling 50,000 consignments a week without any modification to the basic design.

The computer had at least solved the problem of how to consume some of the vast profits they were generating. What to do with the rest? The Mainfreight men were about to be made an offer they could not refuse.

# CREATIV
# THINKIN
# INSPIRE
# LIMITED

E

G IS

D BY

FUNDS

Business was booming in 1986. It was time to make all that money work for itself. Enter Ian Johnstone, a financial whizz-kid. Did he have a deal for Bruce Plested and Neil Graham!

As he explained it, Mainfreight would buy non-deliverable foreign exchange contracts in US dollars for 24 hours, and if the value of those dollars went up in that period they could sell them and take the profit. If they went down, no need to panic: Johnstone would simply roll over the 'investment', and keep rolling it over until said dollars were worth more than their purchase price. This was a licence to print money. He just needed Mainfreight's balance sheet to show they could sustain the potential losses of him playing with NZ$2 million. Not that there would be any losses, of course. This was bombproof.

And who would not have believed that, for the scheme had been developed by and was being channelled through the Development Finance Corporation (DFC), a government-owned finance house. What could be safer or more proper than that? It was the closest thing Plested and Graham had seen to a money-printing machine.

This was all part of the madness of the 1980s. There were fast-buck deals to be had everywhere. It was all perfectly legal. Everyone was making money. Why should Mainfreight be excluded? Hell, even the government was involved in this one.

All went well to start with. Johnstone brought them a cheque for NZ$400,000 and in return took his cut of NZ$40,000. Then the exchange rate against the US dollar tumbled from 58 cents to 42 cents and DFC came under review. New management was appointed, and a decree was issued that there be no more non-deliverable foreign exchange contracts. Mainfreight was asked to pay NZ$3.5 million to DFC.

Plested and Graham were faced with having to sell valuable Mainfreight real estate to pay the debt and stay afloat; their newly established branch network was threatened. Time to visit Wellington and talk with the bankers. Not that they were real bankers, they just behaved as though they were. DFC was not a registered bank; it was a 'specified institution', an authorised dealer in foreign exchange. Later it would apply for bank status, by which stage the full extent of its financial woes would become clear to inspectors and the sorry saga would end with DFC in statutory management.

In Wellington, Plested and Graham felt as though they had walked into a Walt Disney set. Everything in the DFC office was silver, from the carpet and the walls to the 5-metre-high ceiling. Even the trees growing in the foyer were silver, and it was a platinum blonde who ushered them into a glass-tiled meeting room, where they were kept waiting for twenty minutes. It took less than twenty seconds for the Mainfreight men to decide it was time to play good cop, bad cop.

Graham: 'Yes, we have liability here and we'll deal through it as best we can, but we're a small company in lean times.'

Plested: 'Fuck that, you start suing us, you'll have a real scrap on your hands.'

The bankers were dealing with two men who had a 100-year vision. This was just a blip. The bankers didn't stand a chance.

Faced with the DFC debacle, Graham and Plested did not panic. They dragged it out for months on end, and finally the exchange rate started wandering up from 42 cents to 52 cents. By this time they were only down about a million. But it was a terrible year, weighed down by heavy debt because the men from the silver room had changed the rules.

At one stage the debt was down to NZ$300,000 and the bankers said, 'Make us an offer.' Plested offered NZ$1000 a year for 300 years. Eventually it got down to NZ$150,000, and on the last day of the financial year, 31 March 1989, a message arrived: 'Pay us NZ$150,000 today or we'll sue you for the whole NZ$3.5 million.' The men from the silver room got their cheque by return mail.

Carl Howard-Smith says he learned a valuable lesson from this experience. 'If you don't know what they're talking about, ask. It doesn't matter if you are sitting with 100 people and to everyone else you are a fuckwit, ask. Ian Johnstone taught me that lesson. Never nod wisely when you don't understand.' From that point on, no one was to be allowed to forget deer velvet or the men from the silver room.

DESPITE SUCH SIGNIFICANT setbacks, Mainfreight continued its meteoric sales and profit growth through 1986. They were reporting sales up 33 per cent, margin up 32 per cent, and after-tax profit up 27 per cent. This evolving expansion was recognised by NZR, which now gave Mainfreight the same preferential rates as other major forwarders. Recognition indeed. Mainfreight had arrived.

Mainfreight also remained the biggest shipper on the *Coastal Trader*, but the writing was on the wall for its continued use. The company was now able to truck goods the length and breadth of the country without the need for questionable licences. They were developing an expanding network of branches nationwide.

The *Coastal Trader*'s future was further threatened by NZR rising from its lethargic, complacent state to deliver from Christchurch to Auckland in three days. By the turn of the century that was down to 24 hours. Rail could speed up, but the ship simply could not go any faster.

In the midst of all this, Mainfreight International, a 50–50 partnership with Plested's brother Gerald, had been established. This would later become a fractious bone of contention between the two men. For now, though, Gerald was making valuable contacts, none more so than as New Zealand agent for the export ocean services offered by Carolina Freight Carriers, a gigantic, predominantly domestic trucking operation in the US.

While Kevin Drinkwater was loading freight, sweeping the floor and assessing Mainfreight's computer and accounting needs, the joint managing directors took off to inspect Carolina Freight. It was a company with amazing similarities to Mainfreight. It had been established in 1932 when Grier Beam bought a one-year-old Chevrolet on credit and began hauling coal to Lincoln County schools. In 1938 Grier was joined by his brother Dewey, and they set about building one of America's most innovative trucking companies. They had revolutionary technology that helped build revenues to US$1 billion by the time Bruce Plested and Neil Graham stepped through the doors of the company's headquarters in Cherryville, North Carolina. The town had a population of 5000, most of whom worked for the trucking company.

They stared wide-eyed as they were given a conducted tour. They saw computers that could track and trace freight. And they saw dock-handling equipment that was so much more efficient than anything in New Zealand. They watched, they listened, and they

Kevin Drinkwater uses Mainfreight's early computer system.

learned. And they asked, 'Would you mind if our computer man came to have a look at this?'

'Shucks, no,' came the reply. 'We'll share with you anything you want to know.'

By November 1989 Kevin Drinkwater was on his way to computer buff's heaven. He was given unlimited access to Carolina Freight's computer programs and freight-tracking system. He found himself a favoured guest in North Carolina, where he was treated to a privileged tour of a massive, tornado- and bomb-proof computer room, given a detailed insight into the freight-tracking system, and received answers to all his questions.

This experience enabled Drinkwater to blend Mainfreight's original ideas with those he picked up in Carolina to create a system suited to New Zealand conditions, a system that automatically enters and prints consignment notes. He called the system *Freman*, a name that reflects both the term 'freight management' and the consequent freeing up of a man from the warehouse.

Within months of Drinkwater's visit to North Carolina, Mainfreight had gone from no freight tracking to having pick-up and delivery information at their fingertips. Drivers were equipped with electronic wands that they could swipe over a bar code to record delivery, and then download the day's activity back at the depot. (Mainfreight went halves with the printer Wickcliffe in buying the barcode printing machine.) Mainfreight would be the first New Zealand company to transmit data over a radio telephone, and later the first in Australia to download information from a vehicle in the field using cellular technology.

Drinkwater had also been introduced to *Sally*, an interactive voice-response computer system that would tell customers precisely where a delivery was in the system. This was timely, as back in New Zealand Mainfreight's customers were increasingly asking for up-to-the-minute information on where their freight was. What followed was typically Mainfreight. They found a computer boffin, Eden Shields, who, working from a farm at Wellsford, just north of Auckland, had developed a prototype of a voice-response system. Kevin Drinkwater bought the rights to its use for Mainfreight.

A few months later, Neil Graham happened to be visiting Auckland and was with Bruce Plested when Drinkwater put his head round the corner. 'You got five minutes? Have a little demonstration for you. Pick up the phone, dial this number.'

The two men flicked on the speaker phone and dialled. 'Welcome to Mainfreight's freight-tracking system; please enter your consignment note number . . .' They entered a number and the system told them where the freight was.

Their response was immediate: 'We want it, we want it!'

Drinkwater was somewhat taken aback, given Plested and Graham's usual conservative approach. 'But you don't even know how much it's going to cost!'

'We don't care. We want to have it.'

*Tracey* was on her way. Once again the name had a dual meaning: a reference to Princess Di lookalike Tracey Rickards, and the more prosaic 'trace your freight'.

Now, not only did Mainfreight have a tracking system that was so good it blew the socks off everybody, but just three months later they had also introduced an interactive voice-response system. Customers could talk to the system 24 hours a day and get up-to-the-minute reports on the status of their freight.

*Tracey* had one drawback, though. She was designed never to tell a lie. Customers punched in their consignment note number and were given whatever information was on the database at that particular moment. If Mainfreight had failed to dispatch the goods, *Tracey* revealed all. Customers loved it. Four telephone lines were going non-stop as they called in to check on the status of their deliveries. There was an interesting twist to this as well. In the past there had been endless queries about whether a consignment had been delivered, requiring time-consuming checks through the paper work. Now, if *Tracey* said it had been delivered then everyone accepted that as gospel. Payment was speeded up all round. It was a breakthrough.

The prototype had been developed, using Eden Shield's operating system, by Sean Dick of Designertech who, along with Sandfield Associates, has a twenty-year history of doing development work for Mainfreight. Not that Mainfreight has embraced every piece of new technology. Voicemail and answerphones were, and remain taboo. Even in 2013, all internal phones ring until they're answered, preferably within three rings.

While the rest of the industry was still trying to come to grips with freight tracking, *Freman* became indispensable to Mainfreight's customers. Soon, the company's and its customers' computers were talking directly to each other. It would be eight years before the rest of New Zealand caught up.

One memorable day, Kevin Drinkwater took a disbeliever to see the system in operation at the television distributor Philips. Following a conducted tour, the doubtful one asked the Philips logistics chief, 'So tell me, what's the benefit?'

'Listen,' came the reply.

'I can't hear anything.'

'My point exactly; here we are in the freight-dispatch area and the phones aren't ringing. Nobody from sales is calling to find out where their freight is.'


THE AMERICANS AT Carolina Freight had recognised a similar heritage and philosophy to their own in the New Zealanders, and more than a decade later Mainfreight would, as we shall see, execute an extraordinary coup by buying a slice of the very company that had helped with and inspired so many of their technological advances. But that was very much in the future. For now, Mainfreight was about to embark on another of its non-core business, money-losing ventures.

On 1 September 1986 Mainfreight had NZ$964,000 on call deposit with Auckland-based merchant bank AIC Securities Limited. The very same day the bank was put into liquidation by National Mutual Trustees.

Plested and Graham were having dinner when the news came through. Unfortunately there was not a great deal they could do at the time, as they were in Banff, Canada, on a trip arranged by BP for favoured customers. The two men went back to their motel, sat on the floor and drank. Whiskey for Graham, rum for Plested. And they talked. They talked until dawn, and concluded the loss would not put them under. They were a 100-year company. They wrote it off in their minds.

Lesson learned. Mainfreight would never again hold more than NZ$500,000 in any individual merchant bank. What they did do was notch up the machine a couple of gears, allowing Plested to report the following year, 'We appear to be heading for a profit before dividends in excess of NZ$2.5 million for the year ended March 1987.' It was a remarkable performance given the AIC and foreign exchange losses. What might have brought most companies to their knees had merely spurred Mainfreight to greater efforts.

Bruce Plested (left), in the US to visit Carolina Freight, got on the job immediately.

The market was depressed, their competitors feeling the pinch, yet Mainfreight had emerged with healthy and steadily rising profits.

Not that the picture was universally rosy. The newly opened Napier branch had lost close to NZ$100,000 in its first seven months. Drastic action was called for. Bruce Plested headed south to take control. He sacked the branch manager then sat behind the desk, feeling rather alone in the world, wondering what to do next.

Clearly, he needed a fix-it man. He was in the process of writing an advertisement for a replacement manager when through the door walked 23-year-old Craig Evans, who had popped in for a chat with his old friend, the recently departed branch manager. The timing could not have been better.

Evans needed a job. He had just been made redundant after six years' service with Freightways Express; he had been about to leave on his honeymoon when he was given the news. Plested offered him the job of storeman, but Evans turned it down. The next day Plested was on the phone offering him the job of branch manager.

'How much does that pay?' came the question.

'Same as a storeman,' came the reply.

Evans joined that day. Plested had recognised in him someone who really knew his stuff, and Evans had a foot on a ladder he correctly judged would take him places.

Plested, meanwhile, had other matters to deal with. Expansion was very much top of mind, but he knew that organic growth would be a long and tedious process. Merely opening a new branch every year was not the answer. Mainfreight needed to be in the takeover game. But who and how? Plested and Graham decided on a practice run.

Craig Evans had a swift learning curve when he joined Mainfreight.

# THE ONL
# WORSE T
# LOSING I
# GIVING U

Y THING

HAN

S

P

I n March 1987 Mainfreight spent NZ$85,000 buying Alternative Freight, a company with an annual turnover of approximately NZ$2.5 million and a margin of 25 per cent. Mainfreight promptly lost half the business as concerned customers fled. It proved to be yet another invaluable exercise.

As they wrote down everything that had gone wrong, the realisation dawned that customers who relied on a small operator such as Alternative were there because they wanted to be. When a larger operator came along and took over, those customers were inclined to jump ship and find yet another small operator. They did so for a number of reasons. Some believed small operators offered the cheapest prices; others were convinced they would get a more personalised service, while yet others feared their business was too small and insignificant for a major operator.

Plested and Graham also learned that when the business was taken over Alternative's freight became lost in the Mainfreight pool. It could not be identified anymore, and the bigger outfit was not able to treat Alternative's customers with the same kid gloves. Most crucially, though, they discovered that companies that are for sale tend not to be in good shape; they tend to have terrible debtors, customers who expect, as of right, to pay in two or three months, customers who make life difficult. These were all lessons well learned.

Meanwhile, their friend Graham Eddington, with whom they had set up the original *Coastal Trader* deal, had left. Under new management, the *Coastal Trader* was no longer treating Mainfreight as a valued customer. Their freight was being left on the wharf and, in an ironic twist, preference was being given to smaller forwarders — the same little outfits for whom Mainfreight had opened the door by smashing the power of the price-fixing freight companies and driving a wedge through the protection given to New Zealand Railways.

It was open slather, with new companies seeming to open by the day. Mainfreight could not afford to take this development lightly. They were looking at a 50 per cent drop in profits on the previous year as a direct consequence of aggressive price-cutting from the plethora of new freight forwarders.

As it happened Mainfreight and NZR were pushed further into bed together when Neil Graham received a telephone call from Mervyn Bennett, sales director of Comalco, the giant aluminium smelter at Bluff. Comalco was a freight forwarder's dream client. In addition, Graham was anxious to land the Comalco account as it would replace the Wheat Board and allow him to continue matching the tonnages being sent from the North Island. Alltrans had long held the account, with word around the industry traps that they had just slapped a rate increase on Comalco.

Bennett was now asking Mainfreight for a tonne rate indicative. Graham had been courting the sales director for months, and gave a verbal response on the spot. He could tell from the silence down the phone that his price had hit the mark. The courting dance was over; they were into serious discussions.

Mainfreight was on a roller coaster. Back in Auckland, Plested was focused on buying the freight forwarding company Mogal, which had taken over New Zealand Freighters, after itself being taken over by the Owens Group. The freight forwarding arm of Owens was suffering under both the new regime of transport deregulation and its own poor management, and was in terminal trouble. It was running huge losses, paying the cost of a debilitating battle with militant unionists. Mogal was a company of similar size to Mainfreight, and in late 1987 its emissaries had come to declare: 'We know you can't afford to buy us, but we want to find a way that you can.' Plested had been handed a terrific negotiating position on a plate in the first minute of discussion.

The timing of the Mogal and Comalco opportunities could not have been better. Mainfreight did not have the rail facilities to handle the amount of aluminium that would come from Comalco, certainly not in Auckland. A new terminal was urgently required as Mainfreight was in the process of negotiating with its new-found friends at NZR to purchase a six-hectare site on which to build a terminal, complete with undercover rail line. It was a necessary development but it would not come cheap.

The Mogal approach solved a number of problems at a stroke. The deal included its Southdown rail-serviced depot on two hectares of sealed land. There were also rail-serviced depots in Christchurch and Dunedin.

The purpose-built facility at Southdown Lane in Auckland was essential if they were to handle the massive loads generated by Comalco. They would be moving from a mere 2000-square-metre terminal to one with over 8000 square metres. Plested did the numbers. They would be taking over a company of equal size, doubling their sales, and would be out of debt within the year. Must do.

The deal went through only after hard bargaining in which Plested insisted on virtual vacant possession. 'Your people have been destroyed with bad morale and unionism,' he told the Mogal negotiators. 'We don't want to take on any of them.' To ensure continuity with customers, however, they did inherit a number of owner-drivers and a sales force that appalled Plested with their attitude, clothing and, a Plested pet hate, brown shoes.

A meeting was called, with the promise that it would be a social affair with a few drinks to break the ice. Plested and his team were there but the disgruntled Mogal sales force failed to appear. Again they were summoned, and this time they turned up but in a resentful, uncooperative mood. The next morning they were summarily informed, 'We've made a mistake, a terrible mistake. You're fired. We'll pay you redundancy.'

These were clearly not 'Mainfreight' people. As for the cost of the redundancies, Plested did not even ask. He just knew what it would cost to keep them in terms of poor returns. The one Mogal employee they did keep was Phil Massey, engineer for the Auckland branch bulk flour silo. He was 80 years old, and stayed with them a further seven years before eventually retiring, and only then because the flour business went.

The entire Mogal deal added up to NZ$1.7 million — Plested threw in an extra NZ$1 for the goodwill. It was quite a leap from their earlier practice run. And it was all done with a minimum of publicity after Plested's mother, who had a great deal of influence on him, advised him to keep his head down.

Mainfreight moved in on 18 December 1987, with Kerry Crocker, Mark Newman and friends armed with water blasters and spray-paint guns. It took them nine days to clean and paint the Southdown depot to Mainfreight standards. Christchurch was much the same. When they opened the kitchen cupboards they were so dirty they simply could not clean them. Plested issued instructions to paint

TOP — The Mogal name comes down in Christchurch following the 1987 takeover. ABOVE — Kerry Crocker (right) and his son Stephen bring a touch of Mainfreight blue following the Mogal takeover.

over the filth: 'We'll buy new cupboards later.' Up in the ceilings they found dead rats too large to be sucked down the industrial vacuum cleaners they brought in.

This was the first test of imposing Mainfreight culture rather than just shoe-horning in people from one small branch. This was a whole company on a major scale. It proved easier than anyone had imagined. The owner-drivers embraced Mainfreight as they now had a clean and tidy workplace. And they had access to senior management.

Bruce Plested was shocked when he was told that Mogal did not hold meetings because the former management believed all they produced was 'crap'. That was about to change; Plested's door was always open. He answered his own phone. He'd talk to anyone about any problem. And they were paid on time, every month, regular as clockwork.

As for the customers, the lesson learned from Alternative Freight was not to simply push up rates with a 'take it or leave it' attitude. All Mogal customers were told that Mainfreight would commit to their existing low rates for three months. Mainfreight was able to identify all former Mogal customers by giving them consignment note numbers beginning at eleven million. Five years later they could still tell who was an ex-Mogal customer.

Mainfreight had given itself breathing space in which to prove its worth to Mogal's customers, demonstrate its superior service, then put up their rates. Not everyone approved, but virtually every company stayed.

As if the Mogal deal did not create enough excitement, in the midst of all this came confirmation that they had indeed landed the contract to move all Comalco aluminium throughout New Zealand from January 1988. What would be the biggest freight contract in the country involved up to 30,000 tonnes of aluminium ingots each year.

Pitching for Comalco had an interesting side effect: it opened further dialogue with the enemy. NZR was now more than interested in Mainfreight, and quickly agreed to a special rate in return for all the business. This was a major windfall, as Mainfreight had already quoted to freight by rail without expecting to get a special rate. Now they were looking at serious profits.

The 1988 Comalco contract involved 30,000 tonnes of aluminium each year. It was the biggest freight contract in the country at the time.

MAINFREIGHT MIGHT HAVE been expanding but these were also lean years. The effects of the October 1987 financial crash really began to bite the following year, when 70 of Mainfreight's customers went into receivership in a six-month period.

In testing times Mainfreight's ultimate strength lay in its people. Opposition companies were chasing their employees in search of the Mainfreight way. Four of the sales team were approached by opposition companies and offered increments of between NZ$6000 and NZ$13,000, massive increases for the day. Plested talked the situation over with his chairman, Don Rowlands, who flicked through the pay cheques and pronounced them too low. Almost immediately everyone received an increase of 10 per cent, while branch managers and other high-performing senior people had their salaries increased by between 20 and 40 per cent.

To add to the pressure, the Comalco business was not running as well as anticipated. Mainfreight was being introduced to the harsh reality that aluminium is just another world commodity, with the ups and downs that entails.

And there were other changes as a result of the government's deregulation of import and export controls. With a new emphasis on international trade, Mainfreight began asking searching questions of itself. Their competitors were not actually Alltrans or Daily Freightways. Rather, they were the most efficient transport operators, wherever they might be in the world.

Plested and Graham were increasingly asking their team to deliver more than some of them expected. This was certainly the case when they opened the Tauranga branch on 5 April 1987. Chris Knuth was in charge, operating from an uncovered rail siding with an old container as an office. He had been a storeman, loading freight for Crockett and Watts, when Mainfreight took over the Hamilton company two years earlier. He had been working for a demoralised company that was losing money hand over fist, and he did not see what difference Mainfreight could possibly make. Then one Sunday a bus arrived to take the entire 30-strong Hamilton crew for a trip to Auckland. Rather than the new management simply arriving and telling them, 'We're taking you over and this is how it'll be', they were introduced first hand to the Mainfreight way. In Auckland there was a barbecue, with the bosses on hand to answer any questions they might have. And cook the sausages.

Then there were the premises. Theirs were filthy, these were spotless. And there were the trucks. Theirs were Japanese, dirty, old and under-powered. Mainfreight's were brand-new and gleaming. And they heard about being paid on time, and about canteens and bonuses.

Two years of this and you would have thought the message might have sunk in. But on being sent to run the new branch, one of the first things Knuth did was call his managing director in Auckland and suggest he pay his troops extra to work in the rain. It did not take Plested long to get to Tauranga, where the doctrine of Ayn Rand was patiently explained. Capitalism was about everyone working for maximum return and then sharing in the profit. It would be a turning point in Knuth's life. 'I don't think I've asked for anything so stupid in all my life,' he says.

Knuth would spend five years in Tauranga, followed by stints in Hamilton and Auckland as branch manager, before eventually moving to Australia when Mainfreight crossed the Tasman.

# THE WAY
# LEARN I
# BEGIN

TO

TO

By 1989 there were Mainfreight branches the length of the country, and further new initiatives began to appear as the year came to a close. Bruce Plested had been reading again. This time it was Tom Peters' book *Thriving on Chaos*, a publication that argued it really was not necessary to spend millions of dollars to improve efficiency.

And they learned great customer service from Australia's Ansett airline, which had crossed the Tasman to fly New Zealand skies in competition with the national carrier, Air New Zealand. After leaving an umbrella on board an Ansett plane Plested called the airline from his Wellington hotel, to be told which seat he had occupied, on which flight, where the umbrella had been found, and that it would be waiting for him in the corporate lounge. Lesson learned — the service you don't expect is the service you remember.

So began the Mainfreight tradition of sending birthday cards to customers, followed up with a call on the day. It was all about how to be noticed and appreciated for little cost. There was even a short-lived suggestion that women on the sales team should send Valentine cards to their customers. 'Brilliant! We have enough trouble keeping their hands off us, without sending them Valentine cards,' was the response.

Then came the Easter tradition of hot cross buns. These buns were not sent anonymously in elegant boxes, they went the Mainfreight way, delivered by hand, then buttered and spread with jam on the spot. Do that in the middle of an office and you tend to get noticed. Just as they were when a Mainfreight truck turned up to a client's premises with a portable barbecue and the sales team prepared a feast for all the staff.

And there were apples: another tradition that continues to this day. Once a year everybody, team and customers, receives a 9-litre bucket of apples. The impact of this seemingly innocuous gesture has to be seen to be believed. Mainfreight people talk about it in the same breath as the annual bonus. The idea would spread

Mainfreight apples for all.

from New Zealand to Australia and the US in years to come, with similar results.

Apples were all well and good, but if Mainfreight needed a more substantial novelty to boost enthusiasm and morale, it came when they began operations in Australia in 1989, as Mainline Distribution. The move was made primarily to help out a major client, Fisher & Paykel, which was facing storage and distribution problems in New South Wales.

Why Mainline? Businessman Peter Uren had already registered the name Mainfreight in all the states of Australia and started an international freight business, claiming the name in the hope of using Mainfreight as his New Zealand agents, although his real sights were on Asia. He also registered and then franchised the name, or did dual shareholdings, in Korea, Singapore, Taiwan and Hong Kong. Later, Uren's business would collapse and in August 1993 Mainfreight was able to buy its own name in Australia back from him for A$30,000.

One of those who had joined Uren's operation was New Zealander John Hepworth, who later broke away to form a company named ISS, which he would expand from Australia into Asia. This was a fortuitous move for Mainfreight which, close to a decade later, in 1998, would take over ISS and so inherit all its Asian agents and dual shareholdings. They would then operate under the rebranded Mainfreight International.

Mainfreight had a philosophy in those early days of never having more than one branch at a time running at a loss. Within months of opening their Sydney branch it was in profit, so they opened Melbourne in 1990, followed by Brisbane in 1991.

Bryan Curtis, Dennis McLean and Judy Davies were running the Melbourne operation, and Dave Kingdon was in charge of Brisbane. Curtis had joined New Zealand Freighters in 1980, at the age of seventeen, and later joined East West Transport before pitching up at Mainfreight's door hoping for a top job. Plested put the tall, slim Fijian on the loading floor for five years, where he earned huge sums working the weekend shift. Then he was sent on the road selling, before being promoted to branch manager and finally the posting to Melbourne as general manager of Australia. He was being groomed for senior management.

McLean had joined the company ten years earlier as a sales rep, and had been the initial frontman for Mainfreight when they first

TOP — Mainfreight began trading as Mainline in Sydney in 1989. ABOVE — Judy Davies taught herself accounting before taking on Australia.

opened in Australia. Davies had also started as a sales rep, in the Morrin Road branch in Auckland, before transferring to Australia where she taught herself accounting and effectively ran the financial side of the business.

Success breeds the expectation of reward, and Plested and Graham were feeling the need to spread the shareholding among senior team members. These included Kerry Crocker, Dennis McLean, Kevin Drinkwater and Judy Davies, who were each rewarded with 10 per cent shareholdings in Mainline, which almost immediately started losing money, serious amounts of money. The losses often reached A$15,000 a week, with the total annual loss for 1991 rising to A$380,000.

The tide of red ink was a direct result of the failure to convince their Australian customers of Mainfreight's traditional pitch that quality service was worth paying a little extra for. Australian businesses were just happy to have their goods delivered. Union problems, with endless demands and stopworks, were accepted as par for the course, as was sloppy handling of their products. That was something you learned to live with in Australia. No one wanted to hear the Mainfreight story of quality, perfection and service. 'Pull the other one, cobber. Give us your cheapest price and then take 10 per cent off that.'

Australia was looking like a big mistake and, in mid-1992, Plested spelt it out for his board: 'We are putting a lot of effort into trying to achieve profit in Australia, and if our New Zealand profits hold up, and we can see some light in the distance, then we can hold on for perhaps another twelve months. If not, we plan to close down Australia in November 1992, once the Sydney lease expires.'

In the years ahead Plested would change his tune quite dramatically, at times being a distinctly lone voice advocating the absorption of loss after loss in his determination to make a success of Australia as a launching pad to the world. But for now nothing he could see indicated that anything was about to improve.

Then, a major blow: Fisher & Paykel began manufacturing in Brisbane and took its distribution in-house, a loss that instantly knocked the Sydney operation for six. Mainline limped on, but in mid-1993 Plested called a meeting in Melbourne. The glum message was that the board had tired of the whole sorry affair and that Mainfreight was pulling the plug. Time to pack up and head home.

Curtis and Davies were not so easily moved. They pleaded for more time, talked of the teams who depended on them, of the breakthrough they were sure lay ahead. Plested gave them a year to get their act together, with one condition: everyone had to take a 10 per cent pay cut. He would later insist that this was merely to get them focused on the task, and that he never had any intention of pulling out of Australia.

The pressure prompted a return to Mainfreight basics, from which Plested felt they'd strayed, and the purchase of a struggling company they could fix, rather than establishing a new one. Premier VIP Distributors was a Sydney-based warehousing company that had one major asset, Carter Holt's business. Mainfreight had acquired the Carter Holt account in Melbourne and Brisbane, but not Sydney, where Premier delivered good service at a good price.

The purchase did the trick. By the mid-nineties, Mainfreight's Sydney branch was sometimes making A$20,000 a week, Melbourne A$5000, and Brisbane was breaking even. It was time to focus on the home front.

MAINFREIGHT HAD ENTERED the 1990s with the most successful year in its twelve-year history, despite the difficulties associated with the Mogal takeover and the Comalco contract. But the pressure to improve and innovate was inexorable. Plested and Graham had returned from their 1989 visit to Carolina Freight shocked at how far behind the US they were on the high-tech front. They might have been ahead of the game by New Zealand standards, but not by those of the US.

Drinkwater had learned the Americans were moving freight more efficiently and therefore less expensively than anyone in New Zealand. Part of that was utilising docks, which enable smaller terminals with lower ceilings to be used: the trucks park outside, alongside a raised dock platform for convenient loading and unloading.

Drinkwater came back with training manuals that set out how jobs should be executed, creating the platform on which Mainfreight built its standards of excellence. Training had always been important to Plested. When he was at Champion, Don Rowlands had put him through the Training Within Industry (TWI) programme, which had been designed during the Second World War to teach quite

THE AUCKLAND TEAM
MARCH 1988

TOP — The 1988 Auckland team. ABOVE — Howard Smith (left), Bruce Plested and Don Rowlands celebrate Mainfreight's tenth anniversary, 1988, (in the background is a Mainfreight rug hand-made by Bruce's mother, Elsie).

complicated tasks by using a step-by-step guide. Plested had been sold for life.

And nothing was simpler than Mainfreight's marketing policy of providing a high-quality service with the objective of attracting only those customers who appreciated added value and who were prepared to pay accordingly.

While the sales teams all knew what they were looking for, Plested would pore over those crucial weekly returns seeking a new advantage. In March 1990 he spotted an interesting anomaly between Dunedin and Napier. The two branches were generating approximately the same amount of sales, with identical revenues. The difference lay in the bottom line. Dunedin was losing NZ$300,000 a year, while Napier made that much.

It was an intriguing comparison, as the two branches engaged the same number of people. The difference lay in how they were engaged. Napier employed five workers and had six owner-drivers, while Dunedin employed eleven in its team. Two months after Plested's discovery, with a little financial help from Mainfreight, and no resistance, the Dunedin drivers happily became owner-drivers. In one year Mainfreight went from losing NZ$300,000 a year in Dunedin to making NZ$280,000.

The logic was stunningly simple, as explained by Bruce Plested. 'When we owned the trucks, if we had a light bulb go out the driver would come in and say, "Light bulb doesn't go in the truck." We would have to phone up the auto-electrician to come down and put in a new bulb and he would charge us NZ$70. Whereas an owner-driver always carries some bulbs in the glovebox; it's easy, he whips one out and screws it in. And you don't even know it's happened.'

The impact was extraordinary. Suddenly, when a truck needed a grease and service it happened during downtime over a weekend, not when it was needed on the road.

The fixation with open plan was another bold break with tradition. In Auckland, Mainfreight's Southdown operation was expanding apace, requiring additional office room. Enter Don Rowlands with a the gentle enquiry: 'Have you considered open plan?'

Plested harboured the traditional belief that everyone required an office. An invitation to revisit Fisher & Paykel followed, and his conversion was instant. Plested saw 80 engineers working in one room, each aware of what the others were doing. There was constant exchange of information.

Neil Roberts (in hat) directs Mainfreight's ground-breaking television commercial featuring the Mainfreight truck *Shadow Dancer*.

The very next day the instruction was given for walls to begin coming down at the Mainfreight Auckland branch. Open plan is now an integral part of Mainfreight culture the world over. Open-plan offices, with no partitions at all, resulted in people working more quietly and more efficiently. The company had prided itself on having a team atmosphere where anyone could talk to anyone else. Now the final barrier had come down. Plested is convinced that profits rise and fall with and without open plan as sure as day follows night.

MAINFREIGHT MIGHT HAVE been growing, taking over the opposition, operating computer systems ahead of most others in the world and delivering unmatchable service for extraordinary profits — but no one knew about it. Mainfreight was New Zealand's best-kept secret. Now that, too, was about to change. In 1990 the company made a television commercial.

It began with a call from Plested to Neil Roberts, the flamboyant founder of video production company Communicado.

During the filming Plested and Roberts, the wild man of New Zealand television, hit it off. It was hardly surprising. Roberts, a former television reporter, had founded Communicado in 1984 with one camera and a smattering of clients, and had built it into a multimillion-dollar operation. The company began by making corporate videos before developing into a full-scale television and movie production company, with Roberts never far from the headlines. The tabloid media loved the Ferrari, loved the Rolls-Royce with the straight-through exhaust. And they loved it when Roberts reacted to being banned from driving, yet again, by splashing out on not one but two Russian MiG 21 fighter planes capable of 1400 mph. A lovable rogue in the Mainfreight mould, he would die tragically early of cancer.

The commercial Comunicado made largely consisted of Bruce Plested, Neil Graham and Howard Smith standing in front of some large trucks while a voice-over advised that they covered the country. The commercial was judged to be directly responsible for landing accounts including Fletcher Wood Panels and New Zealand Wire, in all worth NZ$6 million a year. New Zealand Wire, which supplied high-tensile galvanised wire to New Zealand farmers, was an interesting gain, as it had been the first account they pitched for — thirteen years later it had finally been landed, with the help of that one TV commercial. It was simple yet stunningly effective. Deliberately avoiding any hint of a hard sell, it took the theme 'Special People, Special Company' and successfully implanted it in the subconscious of New Zealand.


MAINFREIGHT'S RELATIONSHIP WITH Carolina Freight was growing and goods could now be delivered door-to-door — picked up anywhere in the US and shipped through to New Zealand on the original pick-up consignment note, and traceable on the tracking system. At home, however, the economic slowdown, along with a financial crisis in Asia, was having an impact on the New Zealand economy. Mainfreight was feeling the pinch. Group profits were down NZ$1 million from just over NZ$5 million in 1990.

The joint managing directors were in no mood to accept failure. At a branch managers' meeting held on 9 August 1991, Plested laid it on the line: 'The margins are down and Mainfreight is going into survival mode.'

Added Graham, 'Many of you have attended these meetings before and agreed to implement the decisions made, yet returned to your branches and taken no action. This will be your last chance. Fail to act now and you are likely to get the bullet.'

The branch managers were sent away with orders to question every cost, including rates, insurance and electricity. Ringing in their ears was advice that the key to a zero spending regime was to stop unnecessary expenses before they occurred. It was too late once you received the invoice.

Their farewell message was, 'Everyone must go away with fire in their belly to do better than ever before!'

There was growing concern that the company was not hiring future leaders. 'They just couldn't and wouldn't grasp that they needed to train replacements for themselves, which most people don't want to do because they feel they're cutting their own throats. That's absolute crap, of course. If they don't train their successor we can't promote them,' remembers Graham.

The danger was clear. Given the policy of only promoting from within, if the branch managers failed to pick winners, and were afraid to employ people who were better than they were, then Mainfreight's very survival was in question.

AS MAINFREIGHT MOVED into 1992 it faced a second consecutive year of declining profits. And the company was to learn another valuable but expensive lesson when it started a road service between Wellington and Christchurch. This involved truckloads of freight crossing the water divide of Cook Strait on ferries between New Zealand's North and South Islands.

Yes, the trucks were making money, but not as much profit as would have been made had the freight gone all the way by sea. It took six months to accept and address the problem and pull the pin on a bad decision. The exercise was watched with intense interest by the Freightways opposition, whose South Island operation was under the management of a young Don Braid.

Bruce Plested had developed a personal mantra that 'margin is what matters, not revenue'. The Warehouse account would have been top of mind as he constantly hammered the message, 'If you are undercharging customers, then you're just a busy fool. Each account must produce a satisfactory margin.'

The Warehouse and Plested had first crossed paths in December 1987, when the giant retailer rented Mainfreight premises that they subsequently left in a poor state of repair, requiring a NZ$50,000 refit. When they failed to pay, Plested threatened to stop their imports coming across the wharf. Warehouse founder Stephen Tindall delivered the cheque in person, climbing the stairs to Plested's office despite having a torn achilles tendon in plaster. He apologised for the delay as he handed over the cheque, with never a mention of the threat that Plested was ready to explain had only been made to get his attention.

Tindall's determination to hobble up Plested's stairs was a grand gesture with a purpose. He was en route to becoming New Zealand's second richest man and unquestionably the country's most generous philanthropist. He was on a roll, seeming to open a new Warehouse store every week — cut-price stores with the slogan 'Where Everyone Gets A Bargain'. At the time he was importing endless container-loads of cheap goods from Asia. Later there would be a far greater emphasis on New Zealand-made goods, but meanwhile he had a cartage, warehousing and delivery problem of some magnitude.

The cheque handed over, commiserations about the injured leg taken care of, the two men turned their attention to more important matters. When Tindall finally hobbled back down the stairs, he had an agreement for Mainfreight to handle all his warehousing, together with unloading all those containers, sorting the goods, then distributing them to his nationwide chain of stores.

That was when Plested uncovered one of Stephen Tindall's secrets for making money. He would tour Asia, visiting factories that were in trouble. Plested recalls eleven containers filled with shoes in a confusing shambles of type, colour and size, which Mainfreight was then expected to distribute, correctly matched and paired, by colour and size, to stores the length and breadth of the country. As for being paid more to sort out the shambles, forget it.

Plested was determined to do a good job, thinking that Tindall would be reasonable at the next round of negotiations. Unfortunately, they were negotiations from which Mainfreight inevitably emerged with even lower prices. For Tindall was a master negotiator; Plested says Mainfreight did not make a single dollar out of The Warehouse for the first three or four years. 'They pushed so much freight into the system at Christmas time, from October onwards, it wrecked our own operation.' Mainfreight even bought a building at a cost of NZ$1.2 million to handle the troublesome client's warehousing needs. And still they lost money.

Mainfreight held the account for five years, and every year it grew enormously. Finally there were 55 Warehouse stores, and each one would receive a predetermined percentage of a container-load of goods, which Mainfreight dutifully sorted and delivered.

By 1992/93 The Warehouse was generating over NZ$3 million of revenue per annum and Mainfreight was employing eleven staff in Auckland who were dedicated to the task. All for a profit of just NZ$14,000 for the year.

Finally Plested and Graham went to negotiate the price up with Tindall. They walked out not speaking to each other, without any price increase at all, after being outmanoeuvred by the Warehouse man in his corporate red shirt.

Plested was furious. 'It was one of Neil's and my blackest moments.'

They were negotiating with a man who had started by personally delivering stock to his new stores in the back of a Cortina, and he was not shy about going for the best price. The way Tindall recalls it, 'Bruce seemed to take exception to the process of negotiation. We were the customer, and we don't accept the first price that people put up. The best way to negotiate a very good price is to actually offer something way lower and come back to a middle ground; everyone knows that's the way you negotiate something. They ask for three dollars, you offer a dollar, and meet somewhere in the middle.

'Bruce took it pretty hard when I suggested his service was worth a dollar not three. He was personally affronted and did not seem to appreciate it was a negotiating technique. He choked up, got red in the face, and said, "That's an insult." He absolutely lost it and I could see he was ready to get up and punch me.' Tindall had managed to expose the passionate side of the normally dispassionate Plested.

Tindall would eventually set up his own warehousing and distribution system, and to this day Bruce Plested will not shop at The Warehouse, although Neil Graham and even Don Rowlands will still sneak in for the occasional bargain without ever letting on.

It was a bitter experience, and another timely reminder that it is margin that matters, not revenue. Not only that, but it was also a reminder of the need to be careful that pressure from large accounts did not impact on service to smaller customers.

# SUCCESS

# JOURNE

# A DESTI

# IS A
# NOT
# IATION

In 1993 came a remarkable development that had the potential to change the face of New Zealand transport forever. The government ordered 'scoping studies' on the ownership of the railways. It was planning to sell. Enter Chris Dunphy.

Dunphy's father had run a trucking company in the Bay of Plenty, and the youngster had a fascination with transport. His mother would spend weekends driving him round industrial parks so he could photograph his beloved trucks. Not that he neglected his studies. At the age of sixteen he was enrolled at Auckland University, paying his way by driving trucks. At nineteen, with his BA completed, he headed to Wellington to do an honours degree in transport economics.

Dunphy then ventured into merchant banking, and at Buttle Wilson worked on the Telecom privatisation, collecting a bonus equivalent to three years' salary when the NZ$4.25 billion deal went through. The high flyer was with Ord Minnett Securities, the wholly owned sharebroking arm of Westpac, when he came armed with the proposition that Mainfreight could become the minority New Zealand shareholder in a US rail company takeover of New Zealand Rail.

On the face of it New Zealand Rail was not a pretty sight. It had 20,000 employees, as the government effectively used the operation as a 'work for the dole' scheme.

Dunphy stood before the Mainfreight team explaining, with the help of a whiteboard, how they could be part of a consortium to buy their former foe. This involved Railroad Development Corporation and General Electric from the US; Brierley Investments, at the time New Zealand-based; and possibly the Ports of Wellington and Auckland. Soon after, a representative of the Pittsburgh-based Railroad Development Corporation arrived in Plested's office in the form of Henry Posner III, who took *Atlas Shrugged* from the bookshelf and asked, 'You like Ayn Rand?' It was a meeting of minds.

Even combined, the two companies could not afford to purchase New Zealand Rail's stock of spare parts, let alone the whole infrastructure, but together they did have the ability to understand and manage the operation. The Mainfreight team was welcomed into the consortium and found themselves being introduced to terms they had never heard of, such as subordinated and mezzanine debt, which all boiled down to massively inflated borrowing and high interest. And real risk. This was a venture built entirely on borrowed money.

The American rail men were bringing expertise, General Electric would supply much-needed engines, and Mainfreight brought New Zealand credibility to the table. And they put up NZ$10 million in cash. Mainfreight was in fact the only partner to put its own money on the line. Plested and Graham were conscious of this, but had plans to make a dramatic lunge for a greater shareholding at the final hour, rather than risk derailing the project early on.

Putting in a competing bid were glamour local merchant bankers Fay Richwhite, who had earlier been advising both New Zealand Rail and the telecommunications company Clear, which had an interest in the sale as it used a fibre-optic cable that ran the length of NZR's north–south route. The merchant bankers and their rail partners, Wisconsin Central, had no need of due diligence — they already knew all the secrets. This gave them a huge advantage over the Mainfreight team, who had no one who understood what that fibre-optic cable was worth or what Clear would be prepared to pay for it.

In the final analysis that would be the value gap. Mainfreight eventually put the value at somewhere between NZ$10 million and NZ$15 million. Fay Richwhite, with its inside knowledge, bid far more and would flick on the fibre-optic cable for NZ$75 million.

Mainfreight made a video spelling out how they would use the rail network to improve the nation's infrastructure and benefit commerce and industry. They wanted everyone to know what Mainfreight stood for. No one watched it. Bruce Plested and Neil Graham went to Wellington and asked a nameless bureaucrat from the Reserve Bank what their reaction would be if the Mainfreight bid was just a little short. They were bluntly informed: 'If you are five dollars less than the others, they will get it.'

So it was that in July 1993 the Fay Richwhite-led consortium paid NZ$328.3 million for a company that had minimal debt, borrowing most of the purchase price against the assets acquired.

There was minimal debt because the merchant bankers, in their capacity as government advisors, had suggested that the company's debt of NZ$1.2 billion be forgiven. And the government had contributed NZ$360 million of new equity, on the basis that a new owner, free of debt, would be able to spend money fixing up a company that was so vital to the country's infrastructure.

And what did the Fay Richwhite/Wisconsin Central consortium do? Between buying the company and having to pay for it, they borrowed NZ$223.3 million that was paid to the shareholders — Fay Richwhite and Co included — as capital distribution. Money that was then used to pay the government for the railway.

First they rebranded the system 'Tranz Rail', then they embarked on a slash and burn process to extract maximum profit and capital gain. Passenger services were cut and lines closed. Two years later, Tranz Rail was listed on the New Zealand stock exchange. This is when the original shareholders, estimated to have paid no more than 20 cents a share when all the various financial arrangements were taken into account, began selling. They variously sold out for sums as high at NZ$8, and no lower than NZ$3.60 a share — tens of millions of shares.

The four main original investors, including Fay Richwhite and Wisconsin Central, reportedly made total profits of NZ$370 million, mainly tax-free, from the sale of their Tranz Rail shares. These shares were soon virtually worthless, prompting, as we shall see, more government intervention and yet more privatisation.

The Mainfreight consortium would have taken a radically different approach. The money would have been left in the business, which would have concentrated on servicing the needs of bulk customers such as the forestry, coal and dairy industries. The number of massive trucks on New Zealand's roads would have diminished hugely.

Under Mainfreight, the rail system would have provided an enhanced service to the tourism industry, and improved the dreadful commuter rail services in both Wellington and Auckland. There would have been new ships on Cook Strait. A long-term objective of restructuring the rail network to create a well-managed national strategic asset. And then, and only then, would profit be taken. As history has proven, the complete opposite transpired. Mainfreight licked its wounds and sat back to ponder. At least they now

Mainfreight's new facility built on KiwiRail land in downtown Wellington in 2011; road and rail together.

understood what was involved in conducting due diligence. That would be most useful in the years ahead.

And there were major changes at the top of the management team. In 1993 Howard Smith sold out of Mainfreight to follow his passion for farming. Ironically, some eight years later he would be headhunted by Tranz Rail to bring his special brand of management magic to bear — they certainly needed it. (Smith is now retired and living in Otahuhu.)

Chris Dunphy joined the Mainfreight team as its acquisitions dynamo, becoming New Zealand marketing and strategy manager. And Neil Graham's health began to deteriorate. Heart problems that would trouble him for years to come were diagnosed, requiring Bruce Plested to take a greater role in the day-to-day running of the company. A daunting challenge loomed.


BUYING MOGAL HAD doubled the size of Mainfreight. Buying arch-competitor Daily Freightways in 1994 would double it again. This was a big deal.

It was not that Mainfreight really wanted to buy the competing company — they certainly did not need to. Daily Freightways — known as the 'Orange Roughy' — was in trouble. The influence of its dynamic managing director, Trevor Farmer, was on the wane as he cast about for fresh challenges.

Farmer had a long history with the company. In 1985 he and his business partner Alan Gibbs had mounted a management buy-out of half the publicly listed Freightways Group, taking full control in 1993. They would eventually sell the entire group, but for now Farmer was convinced that freight forwarding was in terminal decline. He and Gibbs had put in their own bid to buy New Zealand Rail, only to see the Fay Richwhite offer succeed. Now they were looking to sell the Daily Freightways branch of their business. Farmer was quitting the freight game to focus on new investments in communications and Sky Television.

A nationwide freight forwarder with a comprehensive distribution chain, Daily Freightways was one of Mainfreight's major competitors. Plested believed the business had been wrecked by poor labour relations and equally poor management, with one outstanding exception, its general manager, Don Braid. But the last thing Mainfreight wanted was for the business, and Braid, to be snapped up by Tranz Rail, which was also rumoured to be in the market.

There was another significant consideration. Chris Dunphy had been urging Plested to take the company public, with the qualification that they would first need to be making NZ$10 million from turnover of NZ$100 million for the market to consider them an attractive proposition. The acquisition of Daily Freightways would provide a useful way forward.

They entered discussions with Farmer and his team. Don Braid made a presentation in which he painted a more than healthy picture of a company they knew was on its knees. The Mainfreight people were impressed: Braid was good. Plested only had to look at Daily Freightways' trucks and buildings to know what a basket case the company really was. The buildings were run down and poorly maintained, and the trucks were dirty, all anathema to the Mainfreight culture of spotless buildings, surroundings and, above all, trucks.

But in playing hardball Plested risked missing the jewel in the crown of thorns: Chemcouriers, the division of Daily Freightways that handled dangerous goods. The Mainfreight team assumed Chemcouriers was another lame duck.

During the negotiations involving senior managers from both companies, Plested and Farmer had just called time on an uncomfortable discussion about tax liabilities when Chemcouriers came up for debate. Plested left no one in any doubt of his inclination to walk away from what he saw as an additional irritant. Farmer, attempting to impress upon them how keen he was for them not to miss out on the Chemcouriers opportunity, dragged Plested and Dunphy outside for a private word.

Plested knew he was up against a master negotiator, and rushed to get the first word in. 'We'll give you two hundred and fifty thousand and that's it.'

Farmer was in no mood to see the sale falter at this late stage, but nor was he inclined to totally give Chemcouriers away. 'Look, this business is a beauty — give us a million for it.'

Plested glanced across at an impassive Dunphy and replied with his straightest face, 'Seven hundred and fifty thousand.'

'Done,' Farmer snapped and they shook hands.

They signed the deal that night in the high-rise offices of lawyers Buddle Findlay, with a view of the Auckland Harbour Bridge. The sun was setting when Don Braid arrived, elegantly attired in a blue suit with blue and yellow striped tie. He sat down across the desk from the Mainfreight team and came straight to the point. 'What do you want of me? Do you want my resignation, to continue — what do you want of me?'

Carl Howard-Smith glanced sideways, expecting Plested to suggest they sleep on it. Instead there came the bluntest of replies. 'I don't know if you are going to be with us or not.' Howard-Smith, like others in the room, was embarrassed by this typical display of Plested honesty. Braid merely shrugged. 'I'm comfortable with you running the business,' he told Plested, 'and I am available for a period of time to bed it down, to do what needs to be done to ensure the sale process is successful.' Then he left.

What no one else in the room knew was that Braid was seriously evaluating his future in transport. Unbeknown to the Mainfreight team, the man handling the sale process had been trying to buy the business himself.

Braid was, in his own words, 'gutted' by Farmer's decision to sell Daily Freightways. For the man from Timaru this was the end of an extraordinary journey. When he left school at sixteen there was a choice of three jobs: apprentice electrician, policeman or a job with the Shipping Corporation. The third, working for the government shipping company, which acted as an agent for P&O and also owned the *Coastal Trader*, seemed 'the most exciting' prospect. He joined as a clerk, and would spend two years filling in manifests for ships loading meat and wool destined for the UK and Europe. He then joined Sea Freightways, progressing through the Freightways Group until he eventually took control of Daily Freightways in 1991, aged 30.

Braid knew what needed to be done at Daily Freightways. He formulated plans to increase morale, levels of service and margin. He was in the process of achieving his aims when word came down from above: 'Ready it for sale.'

By then Braid had been trying to knock Daily Freightways into shape for three years. When he took over there was a senior management culture of going for lunch every day at noon and not coming back. When he called a meeting of all the branch managers there were people who had not shaken hands with each other for thirteen years; they never got together to talk shop, to talk anything. He really did believe he was on a roll, but the For Sale sign was up.

Once the message had sunk in, Braid began to look at buying

the business himself. Why not? He had worked hard for three years to put it on the right track. He was assured by a business analyst that the numbers stacked up and that he would be able to borrow the money he needed. When he confided in the branch managers, they were all behind him. By day Braid was putting together a presentation for the market. By night he was preparing his own bid. He was a driven man, then as now.

In the end, Trevor Farmer was faced with an offer of NZ$7 million from his own right-hand man and one of NZ$6.2 million from his friend Bruce Plested. What swung the sale was that Farmer wanted a quick, clean, uncomplicated deal, which Mainfreight was offering. Daily Freightways had NZ$2 million of debtors — debtors that Mainfreight was offering to take over at a discount of 5 per cent. It was a masterstroke: they knew full well the debts would almost all be instantly retrievable, and they knew Farmer wanted to sweep the decks clean.

Braid left the Mainfreight team and the lawyers to their celebrations, aware that he now had to explain this turn of events to the carefully selected team of loyal branch managers who were fired up to follow him as the new owner of Daily Freightways. His next task was to urge them all to switch their loyalty to Mainfreight, for so many years their sworn enemy. To a man they would.

Quite a day. Plested had just paid over NZ$6 million for a megacompany he had been battling for decades. When he called home to break the exciting news to his second wife, Nancie, she replied, 'That's wonderful, that's great. Would you get some green-top milk on your way home please?'

THE DEAL INCLUDED another brand and a separate operation. Daily Freightways focused on the rail moving business, while subbranches concentrated on the inter-island shipping service between Auckland, Christchurch and Dunedin using the *Coastal Trader*. In addition, Freightways Express had 40 owner-drivers delivering freight throughout the country, with branches in places Mainfreight had never been before.

While the new acquisition had its problems, Plested knew it was fixable. And one man would be critical to that. A matter of weeks later, Don Braid was invited to become a major part of the enlarged company. Seventy people had to be made redundant as he closed

**Don Braid**

or merged all the Daily Freightways branches except Auckland, Wellington and Christchurch, where they continued to operate as the renamed Daily Freight. Throughout the rest of the country the two companies were simply merged. The whole process was carried out with no negative publicity. Braid remembers the experience of making so many people redundant as particularly distressing, and resolved never to be placed in such a position again.

With the Daily Freightways purchase came the concept of having two large freight facilities in each major city: too much freight in one, and it is simply moved across to the other, an approach that continued as Mainfreight expanded in Australia and the US.

The Mainfreight team also remembered the lessons from the past while merging with the Daily Freightways operation. Crucially, there was the decision not to put up rates. Daily Freightways customers were given time to assess the new owners. Mostly they found themselves dealing with a rechristened company, and in the case of Daily Freight practically the same name as before, using the same coloured trucks, driven by the same men, and managed by the same team, with Don Braid at the helm.

After much thought came the realisation that a company could run multiple brands in a small market, whereas bigger markets tend to favour a single brand. Smaller populations are more fussy and brand-loyal than larger ones. Braid and the team never fathomed why this was, it was just a fact. There would now be a deliberate policy of competition between the Daily Freight and Mainfreight brands in New Zealand. A dissatisfied customer could always leave and take their business to the other brand.

Once the takeover was complete, Mainfreight could see the real story behind Daily Freightways. They were operating at a 24 per cent margin, against the 40 per cent it would become. It was a classic case of a company in trouble, delivering poor service, faced with customers threatening to leave, and having to lower prices again and again. As Plested would thunder repeatedly, 'Everything goes downhill if you give poor service.'

It wasn't the first time Mainfreight had bought an underperforming company for next to nothing, picking up the odd good executive on the way through and then moving on. But this time they realised they had another ace in their pocket: they could take the Mainfreight culture, the Mainfreight attitude, and plant those philosophies in a completely different company — even a company as culturally different as Daily Freightways.

Today Plested is of the view that the purchase of Daily Freightways was one of the most significant events in Mainfreight's history, if not *the* most significant. It gave Mainfreight the springboard to go forward, and the knowledge that they could transplant their unique culture to such a different environment gave them enormous encouragement and confidence.

For the morale at Daily Freightways had been truly appalling. On one branch visit, when Plested complained that the workers' toilets were not very clean, he was told that they were washed down every Sunday night with a fire hose. That soon stopped. Plested was fanatical about providing individual, splash-proof porcelain urinals in the gents' toilets. This had involved a major battle over many years with the country's bureaucrats who favoured the traditional method of men standing shoulder to shoulder in front of a stainless steel wall and trough. Plested was convinced that men who were treated with respect would return it in bucket-loads. Soon there were smart toilets, freshly painted buildings with open-plan offices, and a spotless canteen serving delicious food that was eaten with everyone sitting together at one long table. And the holes in the walls where striking workers had, over the years, hurled bricks at the building were repaired. Morale went through the roof, and with it those profits. The word went out that more owner-drivers were required, and they appeared in droves.

Weekly wages were converted to monthly fixed salaries, time clocks were thrown out, and weekly Positive Action Team (PAT) meetings were started in all areas of the business. Throughout Mainfreight these meetings are held at the same time each week, typically with no more than six or seven people, with the aim of trying to work out how to do a better job next week than last week.

The Mainfreight system of inter-branch allowances was also introduced. This allows branches to be adequately rewarded for deliveries they do on behalf of another branch. The receiving branch is allocated a fixed amount of revenue based on the weight and size of the freight. If the freight is sold cheaply for any reason, the receiving branch still receives the full allowance, ensuring that no branch can 'buy' business by offering cheap rates and expect another branch to carry the cost.

And no one who was there will forget the Christmas of 1994. The Daily Freightways business was not yet in profit, but Plested and Graham turned up to hand out Christmas bonuses. Hard men, grown-up hard men, cried that day.

As for Don Braid and his chief finance man, Tim Williams, they could not believe their first board meeting. They had arrived weighed down with detailed financial reports and budgets.

Williams soon realised he had entered a new world. At Daily Freightways they had been expected to present graphical detail of key performance indicators and financials. The two weeks prior to each board meeting would be spent putting together graphs and overheads for a presentation made standing on a podium before the full board.

Now, no sooner had Braid begun his presentation to the Mainfreight board than Plested interrupted. 'Just tell us in your own words how things are going.' That done, the discussion turned to what hats they should give children at the upcoming Christmas party. Braid and Williams looked at each other in total amazement. At Daily Freightways, three months of every year had been spent preparing budgets. Braid just had to ask: 'Don't you want us to present budgets?' Plested's reply rings in his ears to this day. 'We don't do budgets here, mate. Just make us more money than we made last year.'

Neil Graham explained to the startled men, 'An outside influence as tiny as the Reserve Bank changing a fraction of a percentage point for borrowed money, or a war, or you lose a major customer, and it's all gone out the window. We measure ourselves against last year. An actual figure of last year.' Simple.

Budgets are typically justified as necessary in order to prevent expenditure blowouts. Mainfreight just asks everyone to be sensible. 'If we do this, will it make the company money? If not, why are we doing it?'

And making money they were. Within a year the combined operations of Daily Freight, Chemcouriers and Mainfreight created a domestic business with revenue that rose from NZ$77 million in the March 1994 year to NZ$131 million in 1995.


OTHER RAMIFICATIONS OF the merger would resonate for years to come. Mainfreight International was now working closely with Brambles International in Australia, providing international coverage that managing director Gerald Plested considered 'very good for our future development in these regions'.

The truth was, however, the antagonism between Mainfreight International and the rest of the Mainfreight people was immense, to the point of being unworkable. There was a widespread belief among the rank and file that Mainfreight International was not pulling its weight. There was internal pressure to sell Mainfreight's 50 per cent share to Gerald Plested for a dollar and move on. Cooler heads argued that the brand had to be protected.

Braid was amazed at the bad blood between International and Mainfreight. It was as if they were two separate companies, and it hadn't helped that the Daily Freight team preferred to use another international forwarder, LEP, which was at that stage still part of the Freightways Group, from whence the bulk of the Daily Freight people had come. There was also a totally different attitude toward the Australian business. Braid and his Daily Freight team saw Australia as part of their expanded domestic operation, an aspiration to which LEP was more attuned compared to Gerald Plested's determined international focus. A painful experience lay ahead as Mainfreight realised to its cost the difficulties associated with mixing family — two brothers in particular — and business, and entering into a 50–50 partnership without a controlling hand. It was a problem that would only be resolved after much heartbreak.

However, with the Daily Freight purchase bedded in, Plested had every reason to be pleased but he remained concerned about falling into the trap of 'Big Company Syndrome'. He could spot it a mile off: arrogance, using consultants, bringing in outside cleaners to sweep the depots, hiring pictures and plants and, another personal hatred (up there with brown shoes), putting blue rinse in the toilets. He wanted none of that. He insisted there would never be any substitute for 'working hard'.

If arrogance was a symptom of 'Big Company Syndrome', then the new Tranz Rail was, in Mainfreight's view, riddled with it. Deeming the time appropriate to put up their prices, they arranged a meeting so they could break the news to Bruce Plested and Neil Graham in person. And they were not just going for any old increase. They were going for the doctor — a 50 per cent increase.

They arrived half an hour late, without any apologies, so Plested ushered them into a windowless meeting room rather than the airy office with its comfortable couches. He sensed their mood and dispensed with any pleasantries, insisting they get straight to the point. Once the increased rates had been put rather clumsily on the table, the Mainfreight pair swung into their well-practised good cop, bad cop routine.

Graham: 'You have to understand we are vulnerable to such increases.'

Plested, butting in: 'Hell will freeze over before we'll pay that. If you want a fight, you're really buying a fight. This is unfair in every respect; we'll move our freight by other methods.'

Graham, calm as ever: 'Our customers could never withstand such an increase; this would be very bad for the nation's economy.'

Plested, to the point: 'What part of "fuck off" don't you understand?'

The Tranz Rail men left without their increase.

# A HOME W
# BOOKS I
# HOUSE W
# WINDOW

ITHOUT

LIKE A

THOUT

One evening when he was at home watching television, Plested saw writer Alan Duff being interviewed. He was talking of Maori being in crisis. The following day Plested rang Duff to ask if there was anything he or Mainfreight could do to help. At the time, Duff was just starting a programme called Books in Homes. Mainfreight gave NZ$10,000 to the programme in its first year, and now supports over 50 schools, ensuring 10,000 children have access to books they might not otherwise have. Overall the scheme helps 540 schools and 170 early childhood education centres, each child gets about seven books a year, to own and take home. While Mainfreight does not reveal its total contribution to Books in Homes, it is believed to be well over NZ$1 million.

It's a gesture that embraces the Mainfreight philosophy. In Plested's words: 'Honestly, we do it because New Zealand needs a bigger economic pie packed with skilled people. The world is a diminishing place for people who are not educated. People in underdeveloped countries will work for one dollar an hour making widgets, so we're not going to be able to make widgets here unless we make them for one dollar an hour. And we don't want our people earning one dollar an hour. They must have a skill level that enables them to earn twenty dollars an hour.

'So we are just fanatical about education and specially fanatical about education for the poor, because we think the poor produce more entrepreneurs as a percentage of the population than the so-called middle classes. The poor have got hunger in their bellies, and if they can get an idea, plus an education, then they can go ahead and put it together. It's the poor beginning that gives them the incentive to keep going.

'Educating the poor is one of the most important things we can do. If we force education into them we'll get a bigger bang for our buck in terms of growing the economy than by developing any other sector of society.'

TOP — The tiny Bairds Mainfreight Primary School in South Auckland had a computer suite the richest schools in the land would have been proud of. LEFT — Bruce Plested put Mainfreight at the very heart of education in New Zealand. Also shown is Mainfreight owner-driver, Fred Kalman.

TOP — Bruce Plested with his secretary Carol Selwyn. RIGHT — Bruce Plested visits the Bairds Mainfreight Primary School computer suite in March 2013, the twentieth anniversary of the company's relationship with the school.

And supporting Duffy Books in Homes, as it is now known, is not purely a charitable act on Mainfreight's part. Plested is the consummate capitalist. 'We're hopeful that because of books and education some of these kids are going to hit the workforce in a position to look upon Mainfreight as a desirable company to do business with or work for,' he says. 'I have a real expectation that we are going to get repaid for this. Putting books in the hands of poor kids will not entirely be without return for us.'

Mainfreight was already directly involved in the classroom before Duffy Books in Homes was set up. When the company had some unwanted softball gear, left over from a time when it used to stage inter-branch games, Plested's secretary, Carol Selwyn, thought of giving it to a school. Looking through the phone book, the first school she came across in the poorer area of South Auckland was Bairds Road Primary School in Otara. She rang to offer them the gear. There was one small problem, however: she hadn't realised that Plested had other plans for it. She was instructed to offer NZ$1000 instead. The school's gratitude was overwhelming. A deputation turned up to thank Plested in person, followed by letters, then details of how they were spending the money, on new sports uniforms that featured the Mainfreight logo.

The little Otara school knew a thing or two about relationship-building, inviting Bruce Plested, Carol Selwyn and Kevin Drinkwater to numerous functions. Plested soon found himself asking if there was anything else Mainfreight could do for Bairds Road — perhaps helping them with a project that was currently too ambitious and costly for the school, but which might become a long-term undertaking for Mainfreight. 'A computer,' was the instant reply.

Soon Drinkwater was arranging a demonstration of two computers for the benefit of school staff, to establish what was needed and what might be achieved. When the demonstration was over Drinkwater uttered words that would become part of the school's folklore: 'Oh, look, it's too much trouble to pack them all up again. You may as well keep them.'

Little did the tearful principal, Kerry Crossman, and the chair of the school's board of trustees, Pat Kake, know but this was just the start, a test. At the time the only person at the school with real computer skills was Deirdre Cummings, who worked in the office. She patiently began to train students and teachers alike to use the computers.

If the school was to have a computer in every classroom, then clearly every teacher would need the appropriate training. Drinkwater arranged a visit for Kerry Crossman and some of his staff to the department of computer studies at the Auckland College of Education, as it was then called, and a preliminary training session. Drinkwater asked if it would be possible for the teachers to be trained on-site, at Bairds Road School.

'How many computers does the school have?' a tutor asked.

Crossman was just about to explain that unfortunately they only had two when Drinkwater butted in. 'They have one for every classroom,' he said.

The staff were stunned. There were 25 classrooms at Bairds Road School, and they had been told Mainfreight was planning to install a computer in each at the rate of three a year. Now Mainfreight sent a truck around with another 23 computers. They had the whole lot in one hit, a computer for every classroom.

Next, it was the Mainfreight people who were surprised. There came a whisper that the board of trustees was planning to rename the school after its benefactor — the school was keen to show its gratitude, and to continue to build its relationship with the company. The move led to a debate with a shocked Ministry of Education, and some parents who were opposed to losing the name Bairds. In the end a compromise was reached, and in June 1997 up went the sign: Bairds Mainfreight Primary School.

By July 1997 the little South Auckland school, with its predominantly Maori and Pacific Island roll, not only had a computer in every classroom but a suite of twenty of the very latest state-of-the-art computers as well. They were as well equipped as most private schools. It was the start of an extraordinary relationship as more computers arrived, followed by laptops and printers, and later a complete update of all the equipment. Over the following twenty years, to 2013, Mainfreight would contribute NZ$750,000 in technology and other benefits to Bairds.

Mainfreight's fanatical belief in the ability of education to help poor children overcome seemingly impossible odds gave the transport company a whole new image. Now they were no longer 'the jokers with the clean trucks'. Now they were 'the jokers with a school named after them'.

As for Duffy Books in Homes, it would continue to grow, giving away more than eight million books to more than one million New

Zealand children. It is a sadly needed service in a land where OECD research shows that nearly half the workforce cannot read well enough to work effectively in a modern economy. The impact of the Duffy Books in Homes programme was revealed in a New Zealand study of a cross-section of 500 children, which showed that those who received books were a massive 35 per cent ahead in reading achievement compared to children from similar backgrounds who were not in the scheme.

In New Zealand the Duffy Books in Homes scheme has attracted government assistance of some NZ$1.3 million, while other sponsors have chipped in a further NZ$2.5 million. Later, as Mainfreight expanded into the US — a country where they estimate tomorrow's prison population based on today's literacy rates — they would again be a major sponsor of the reading message. Sadly, in the United Sates there is no government contribution; Mainfreight is the sole backer of Duffy Books in Homes in the US. The company has invested US$80,000 a year over the past four years and has given away a total of 140,000 books.

Not that it has been easy. The Mainfreight team would ring US schools, announce their desire to give away free books, and have the phone go dead as disbelieving and suspicious teachers hung up on them. They would not even reply to emails. Then Kevin Drinkwater heard the tale of an American boy, born into poverty, who became a neurosurgeon. Ben Carson's mother was illiterate but she saw the importance of having books at home and encouraged her son to read. He would become a director of paediatric neurosurgery at Johns Hopkins Hospital in Baltimore, and the first surgeon to separate twins joined at the head. (Dr Carson's story is recounted in the film *Gifted Hands*.)

In the US, Dr Carson runs a foundation that helps re-establish libraries in schools that have lost them through funding cuts. When Drinkwater called to offer him US$10,000 the surgeon did not hang up, and they have been working together ever since. In 2012 Dr Carson visited New Zealand to promote Duffy Books in Homes and to spread the message of how reading helped him to climb out of extreme poverty.

Ask Bruce Plested why Mainfreight is involved and he shrugs.

'Someone has to do it.'

# IF YOU F
# TO PLAN
# ARE PLA
# TO FAIL

AIL
YOU
NNING

**B**y 1995 both Bruce Plested and Neil Graham sensed a degree of arrogance creeping into the company's culture. Despite their vigilance it seemed that Big Company Syndrome had somehow infected the business. Complacency was evident. They were concerned enough to feel the need for a shake-up right across the board in terms of presentation, dress code, and all the considerations that had been so important in the early culture. As Carl Howard-Smith saw it, it was almost like Mao unleashing the Red Guard.

Mainfreight was still feeling the lingering pain of the crash of 1987. The New Zealand economy remained stagnant. No one had received a pay rise for at least two years, and while the business was in good shape, overall margin control was less than perfect and overhead costs were considered out of control. Bruce Plested imposed a limit on the number of pens people might have and, to make the point that no one was exempt, went down on bended knee in the office to beg a biro from a secretary.

As Kevin Drinkwater recalls it, 'Not all branches were at fault, but Bruce's approach is to use a shotgun so he hits low-hanging fruit everywhere.'

Plested was in such a mood when he chose Flock House, a former agricultural college near Bulls, for a branch managers' meeting to launch his New Beginning. This proved to be a no-punches-pulled affair. Attendees got the message even before they arrived: they were to drive, not fly. When they got there they found themselves sleeping on uncomfortable bunks in spartan barracks.

For Don Braid it was an illuminating experience. First he was called up to the top table to sit alongside Plested and Graham, signalling to the troops that here was a man destined for more than merely running Daily Freight. And the theme intrigued him. Plested was soon onto his hobby horse of combating mediocrity.

The message was simple enough: if you mean to profit, learn to please. He fumed and raged at what he labelled the arrogance of

Mainfreight. There was an attitude that losing a customer was of no consequence — there would always be another. Mainfreight was so much better than the next guy that it did not matter; Mainfreight was the biggest and the best, no one could touch them.

Here was a managing director out to kick arse, and none too particular about who he upset in the process. And upset some he most certainly did. Some took it so personally that on their return to Southdown there were mumblings about asking the board chairman, Don Rowlands, to approach Plested and get him to calm down. Chris Dunphy put his hand up and declared he would do it. 'I'll talk to Bruce. Best I do it.'

Dunphy was the new boy on the block. He had no history with Plested; there was no baggage. There was general agreement it would be best for Dunphy to do it. In truth they all admired his courage.

Plested listened in silence as Dunphy detailed the concern 'below stairs'. His eventual response was, 'I welcome the revolution.' He had got his desired reaction; he knew they understood his concerns, even if they had not liked the way he spelt it out.

Mainfreight would change. It was time to spread responsibility more evenly. Kevin Drinkwater was appointed general manager, warehousing and distribution, and Don Braid was elevated to general manager of all freight forwarding, This moved him into Plested's domain. Little did he know what a powerful omen this was.

Reflecting on this period several years later, Plested would explain his anger as frustration with the speed of decision-making, and the need to get people's attention. It certainly worked, and heralded a new style. Branch manager meetings were run by Braid and Dunphy, who introduced a more relaxed dress code, from shirt and tie to smart casual. If there was fear of anything, it was the prospect of the whitewater rafting trips that accompanied the new-wave meetings.

The Flock House experience had left a lasting impression on Braid. He, too, shared a passion for detail and quality; he recognised how that extra 2 per cent was the difference between being average and being the best. Anyone who is in any doubt that Braid shares the Plested passion should hear him reflect years later on that meeting. 'If we don't rant and rave we don't get change. I didn't disagree with what he said at Flock House. I could see the level of arrogance that existed. They had just bought one of their biggest competitors and they looked down their noses at us.

'And it showed in the way they dealt with customers, and frankly, we have to fight that all the time. Despite all our efforts not to, Mainfreight can get ahead of itself, think it is better than sliced bread, and we need to keep our feet on the ground all the time. You are only as good as your last consignment, and that's what Bruce went on and on about. Perhaps I didn't agree with some of the personal attacks that went on in the meeting, but the wake-up call was there and I liked the toughness Bruce had about what we were doing. A toughness about quality and detail and mediocrity. At that stage it was all about getting New Zealand right, and today we have that same attitude about growth around the world and how big we can be, and we fight mediocrity the same as Bruce fought it then.'

Braid might have been a bit embarrassed about being invited to the top table, and he knows there were bruised egos in the room, but he notes that the most bruised are no longer with the company. Why? 'They were not good enough. Those who were good enough are still with us.' He takes the same attitude to growth. 'We still do not tolerate the inability of people to accept what we can become.'

Braid acknowledges that he was just as capable as Plested of becoming tyrannical and laying the charge that mediocrity, not caring enough about every customer, every consignment, was destroying the business. Accepting this, he would later step aside from running the branch manager meetings in 2001, allowing Mark Newman and Craig Evans to take over.

Plested changed too, playing the role of father figure while the young Turks dealt with the daily grind of running the extraordinary company he and Neil Graham had built. The newfound freedom of expression was to be called upon almost immediately, as Tranz Rail chose this moment to declare itself, none too subtly, to be Mainfreight's major competitor.

PLESTED COULD ONLY watch and wonder. The new company appeared to have no profit motive, despite being privately owned. It quoted way below market rates to attract business. Numerous small customers were paying less than Mainfreight, a major client, was being charged. And Tranz Rail was competing on the road with its own fleet of trucks. There was even talk of expanding the reach it offered freight customers by linking with Australian railway companies and shippers to provide a trans-Tasman service. Its vision for the future increasingly appeared to be a mirror image of Mainfreight's.

There was distrust on both sides, with Mainfreight being given graphic proof that Tranz Rail was indeed positioning itself as a major competitor. The company offered to cut a full NZ$500,000 off the annual fee Mainfreight charged Carter Holt Harvey for moving wood panels out of Christchurch, even though Mainfreight was moving it via rail. The mighty manufacturer reluctantly stayed with Mainfreight, but made it clear that had Tranz Rail's performance not been so inadequate the business would have been lost.

Plested reported to his board, 'The price difference clearly indicates their intention to take us head on and force us to downsize to a position they are comfortable with.'

Mainfreight's spend on rail dropped dramatically. At the time of the Freightways purchase, the combined Mainfreight and Daily Freight annual spend was NZ$25 million. This would drop by more than half, with Tranz Rail insisting that all freight be delivered in containers to its yards. There would be no more shunting trains off the main line onto railway sidings constructed at Mainfreight branches, where they would hook up wagons that were already loaded and ready to roll.

Tranz Rail invested heavily in electronic commerce to position itself as a fully integrated transport operator rather than just a rail company. The company even embarked on a major poaching exercise to lure away Mainfreight people. The threat was not lost on Plested, who reminded everyone: 'Our strategy to counter Tranz Rail is clear. We must retain and build our customer base by ensuring that everybody lives and breathes the Mainfreight belief in superior performance.'

Rail might have been causing problems but there was some good news. Firestone signed a deal for Mainfreight to handle all its warehousing and distribution nationally from January 1996. The entire output of the tyremaker's Christchurch plant would be channelled through a purpose-built distribution centre on Mainfreight's Sockburn site for distribution throughout New Zealand.


WHILE ALL THIS was going on, Plested and Dunphy were planning the company's next big move. Mainfreight listed on the New

Zealand stock exchange on 14 June 1996, at 96 cents per share. On offer was New Zealand's largest freight forwarder, with daily services by road, rail and sea to over 250 towns and cities in New Zealand, and a fledgling Australian business.

Investors were looking at an impressive track record. The company had doubled in size twice, through the 1987 purchase of Mogal and the more recent acquisition of Daily Freightways, which took turnover in 1995 to NZ$131 million. Mainfreight was forecasting earnings after tax of NZ$4.7 million from a network any competitor would struggle to replicate.

Together Neil Graham and Bruce Plested still owned approximately 50 per cent of the company, with Plested holding 38 per cent. The remainder was held by financial institutions, in New Zealand and overseas, together with more than a thousand private New Zealand investors.

The board took on a new look. Kevin Drinkwater and Kerry Crocker stepped aside, and those who owned shares in the Australian operation were bought out, all to present a tidy package for the float. Rowlands, Plested, Graham and Howard-Smith were joined by two new directors: John Fernyhough, a prominent former lawyer and businessman, and Richard Prebble, a former minister in the Labour government, responsible for transport, railways and civil aviation, and associate finance minister.

There was an irony behind the Prebble appointment. To this day many New Zealanders believe he was responsible for deregulation of the transport industry and the privatisation of New Zealand Rail, which he was not; and that he introduced road user charges, which he did not. A National government did all of the above.

And it was now that a young Mark Newman returned to New Zealand after five years in Europe. Plested called, and suddenly Newman was in the logistics business as manager of Freight Place, a warehousing operation purchased in August 1995, that was dependent on a single client, Black & Decker, for 80 per cent of its business. The client was not paying its way, so Newman upped the rates, with an ultimatum that the company pay or leave. They left.

Almost immediately Newman was summoned to a meeting with Plested. He feared the worst, but was told that he had been promoted to branch manager in Wellington. He would have charge of approximately 140 people in the combined Mainfreight, Daily Freight and Chemcouriers operation, in a newly refurbished facility

TOP — Plested and Dunphy celebrate the public listing of Mainfreight. MIDDLE — New director Richard Prebble. ABOVE — Bruce Plested and Neil Graham.

to be opened on 5 December 1996.

Newman was more than a little nervous when offered this opportunity, not about the job, although he had never done anything like it in his life, but because his wife Christine, an accountant, had just landed a position with a salary of NZ$85,000. His own NZ$50,000 salary was not going to change much when he took on the new job. Fortunately, Christine was savvy enough to back his belief in both Mainfreight and himself. They moved to Wellington.

A PUBLIC COMPANY, a new board, a team for the future, and now the words 'supply-chain management' were being heard at Mainfreight.

Mainfreight's belief in managed warehousing was borne out by the facts. In the US, 70 per cent of all manufactured products were warehoused by third-party contractors. In Australia, 30 per cent of consumer durables were warehoused under contract. By contrast, in New Zealand only 11 per cent of goods were warehoused using third parties. It was fitting, then, that the company should next turn its attention to LEP, a global forwarder with a long history in international trade.

The company's origins go back to 1849 when two Swiss entrepreneurs, Langstaff and Ehrenburg, set up a transportation business in the French port of Le Havre. They were later joined by an Englishman, Pollack, and it was from this partnership that the name LEP came. By the late twentieth century LEP offered delivery of virtually any kind of goods, from anywhere to anywhere in the world. And the original Freightways Group, which owned 75 per cent of LEP's New Zealand operation, was continuing its policy of selling down company assets.

Mainfreight saw in LEP New Zealand a business with a NZ$60 million turnover that could be purchased for NZ$2.6 million. Further, LEP and Mainfreight International would be able to co-operate to mutual advantage, right down to sharing containers.

The other 25 per cent of LEP New Zealand was held by the Public Warehousing Company (PWC), which owned LEP worldwide. This was seen as a bonus given that Mainfreight was looking to achieve additional growth from international as well as domestic business.

LEP had always been a pioneering company, in 1919 establishing the world's first airfreight forwarding office at what was then Hounslow Airport, London. It had developed into a world leader when it came to initiatives in the field of logistics management and internet technology. Unfortunately, the New Zealand leg of this operation was tired, rundown and bouncing in and out of profit. The Freightways management who were handling the sale had been candid enough to admit that they really did not understand the business and had no idea why its profit varied so much from year to year.

For Mainfreight, though, LEP New Zealand proved to be a happy purchase. Not only did it make money and provide work for other Mainfreight divisions, but there was also the bonus of those valuable international contacts. LEP had branches in 450 cities throughout the world.

The LEP investment seemed a perfect match. And the attraction soon grew significantly, when LEP New Zealand acquired LEP Australia, in February 1998 for what was termed a 'nominal consideration' of A$1. This was again for a 75 per cent interest, with LEP New Zealand agreeing to pick up debts of some A$2.5 million. In return Mainfreight gained a branded branch network with operations in Brisbane, Sydney, Melbourne, Adelaide and Perth; a wholesale airfreight forwarding operation, Air-freight Consolidators International (ACI), with operations in both Melbourne and Sydney; premises in Sydney and Melbourne with market values in excess of A$2.5 million; and approximately A$3 million of outsourced work that then became available to Mainfreight.

The purchase had a defensive strategic objective as there was growing unease with the way Mainfreight International operated. It was too conservative, its profits too fragile. It was not considered big enough to have real traction. There was also concern at the growing dependence on Brambles, which serviced Mainfreight International's needs in Australia. Brambles was showing real signs of losing interest in the international business. Mainfreight required an insurance policy, a vehicle in Australia, in the event that Brambles was to sell out or close down.

LEP was the answer, and it worked because when Brambles did eventually sell, to Tranz Rail, the move decimated Mainfreight International. Brambles had been its biggest customer, and all the freight now went into Tranz Rail's own international freight set-up. In hindsight this was of no real consequence as the trans-Tasman seafreight business quickly became marginally profitable for all, beaten to death by small forwarders, in New Zealand and Australia, competing at the lowest possible price.

Mainfreight International, with its emphasis on wholesale forwarding, worked alongside LEP, which focused almost exclusively on the retail market. Mainfreight International operated on low margins for other forwarders, while LEP dealt directly with individual import and export companies requiring a specialist service. That said, LEP Australia was a business that had not made a profit in five years, and was further hampered by low morale and decrepit facilities.

LEP International worldwide had a chequered past. It had been badly caught in the 1987 sharemarket crash, was in statutory receivership by 1990, and then left seriously short of money two years later by a highly leveraged management buy-out. After that came a number of ownership reshuffles followed by a worldwide name change to GEO Logistics, with the exception of Australia and New Zealand; by that time Mainfreight had its 75 per cent ownership, and insisted on retaining the name LEP for its brand value.

Mainfreight International had long been a concern, with a feeling at board level that Mainfreight's 50 per cent shareholding was restricting its ability to drive the company as a true member of the group. The half share had been a further irritant at the public float: such subsidiaries are frowned upon by analysts. The problem was, of course, that the other 50 per cent was owned by Bruce Plested's brother Gerald, who was driving a hard bargain.

Prior to the float, Carl Howard-Smith had been sent to negotiate a deal with Gerald, with whom he had a longstanding friendship. Earlier Bruce Plested had asked his brother what he believed the business was worth, to be told Gerald wanted to quit with NZ$1 million in his hand. Chris Dunphy subsequently valued Gerald's share of the business at NZ$1.2 million, and that was the offer Howard-Smith made. It was rejected out of hand. Bruce Plested has since learned that his brother had been encouraged by Mainfreight's bankers, Westpac, to believe Mainfreight International was worth NZ$6 million. So it was that Mainfreight went public still owning 50 per cent of the international business.

Since no one within the original 'family' grouping was having any success in getting Gerald Plested to the table, they now sent the 'just fix it' man, Chris Dunphy, with instructions to tidy up the anomaly, no matter what. The two men met for lunch in a steak house. That was as civilised as it got, with Dunphy's opening gambit setting the tone.

'You don't like me and I don't like you but I am empowered to do a deal. What do you want?'

Gerald Plested walked away with a tenanted building valued at NZ$2.6 million and a tax-free dividend worth a further NZ$400,000. The deal was not pretty, but it was functional.

MAINFREIGHT WAS STARTING to look more than attractive: publicly listed, record sales and record profits. Managed warehousing operating from nine sites in New Zealand and three in Australia. It was time to sign on another twenty young university graduates to work right across the business, double the previous intakes.

Plested explains, 'This is not a business of rocket science. It's not as if we have to understand nuclear physics to be able to do it. But we are significantly advantaged if we have a lot of well-educated people questioning the way we do things and coming up with smarter solutions than we might have come up with in the past.'

One of their brightest and most questioning young people was Craig Evans, who, by the close of 1997, was growing increasingly frustrated about the way the company was being managed and about his own career path. What happened next provides an extraordinary insight into the workings of Mainfreight and the Bruce Plested mind in particular.

By this time Craig Evans was manager of the Christchurch branch in the newly enlarged publicly listed company. They were no longer a private boutique operation. Previously, there had been Bruce Plested and Neil Graham and the team. Now Chris Dunphy was advising that the business needed structure or there would be nowhere for high-energy people to go. Mainfreight was in danger of losing people like Craig Evans. It was prophetic.

In late 1997 Bruce Plested visited the Christchurch branch. By this time Plested was probably stretching himself too far, and was unable to give enough attention to his ever-expanding team of bright young managers. He spent his day talking to customers and left without so much as a word to Evans, who was starting to feel increasingly isolated, lonely and unwanted. A call from Neil Graham to ask how the visit had gone prompted the reply, 'My career at Mainfreight just came to a close.' Evans had decided to resign.

The next morning Evans was at his desk bright and early,

preparing to wind up his job and wondering whether it was too late to do something with his life. At eight o'clock sharp, Plested walked through the door. He had caught the red-eye flight from Auckland and wanted to talk. The two men took off to Neil Graham's country home in the beautiful Hoon Hay valley on the outskirts of Christchurch. They sat in the sun and talked. Or rather, Evans talked and Plested listened.

The message was to the point. A branch visit from Bruce Plested should be an occasion to celebrate success and talk positively of the future. Evans pulled no punches as he told Plested that everyone understood the need to rule with an iron fist in the early days, but those days were over.

'I grew up in the world of hard knocks, I'm thick-skinned. But it wears you down when all you get is criticism. We want someone we can take our problems to without being chastised.'

By now Neil Graham had effectively retired, and Bruce Plested was listening to his most senior man in the South Island spelling out real concerns about both the company's direction and the style of its managing director. Evans felt the business was being managed 'through binoculars' from Auckland. He was talking of Plested's 'controlling' approach to management, which brooked only limited discussion.

The disheartened branch manager could see morale crumbling. Young, spirited, entrepreneurial people, the future of Mainfreight, were questioning whether they wanted to be part of it anymore.

Evans was in full stride. 'Our decision-makers are too functional. They are so busy fighting in the trenches, they don't have time to do the planning.'

Plested sat there in the sun, deep in thought, as Evans went on.

'You don't know the power of your own mouth. When you say things, people take it for gospel, that's it. People love you coming to their branch. You're the biggest motivation tool this business has. You are it. But when you come in as the hit man, you actually destroy the culture. The very culture you built.'

That night Craig Evans went home and told his wife he was not resigning after all. He was Mainfreight's new business development manager. Now he was doing something he enjoyed — planning for real growth.

WHERE OTHERS MIGHT have responded with rage to such unrestrained criticism, Bruce Plested began a subtle transformation. 'I do try to listen when people criticise me, and while I don't always necessarily change, I do try.'

Plested became a mentor, Mainfreight's motivator extraordinaire, as he set about ensuring the company became more focused on its 'three pillars': culture, family and philosophy.

The three pillars grew out of the occasional Saturday morning meetings Plested and Braid would hold with senior team members in Auckland. This was Mainfreight culture in operation: no complaints about giving up family time; this was about the management team getting together to share McDonald's, which Braid would bring, and talk as they could not during the week. Today they get everyone together on the phone every month or so, but back then they would sit around the table and talk.

Braid remembers, 'We'd ask — what are the non-negotiables? What makes us different to the other guys? And we wrote them down. It's not business school language but it's what we feel about the business, it's what matters. We just wrote down what we believed in under three headings, and they became pillars. It comes down to the way we do things around here.'

# Culture
- Under-promise, over-deliver
- Keep reinventing ourselves with time and growth
- Education is optional, learning is compulsory
- Let the individuals decide
- Keep it simple
- Tear down the walls of bureaucracy, hierarchy and superiority
- Avoid mediocrity — maintain standards and beat them
- Look after our assets
- Immaculate image and presentation
- Promote from within
- Integrity — how it affects other people
- No job descriptions

# Family
- Eat together — use mealtimes as a discussion time

- Listen to each other
- Share the profits and the successes
- Openly discuss problems and openly solve them
- Don't beat up your brothers and sisters
- Have respect — seek it from others and show it by actions

# Philosophy

- 100-year company
- Profit comes from hard work, not talk
- We are driven by margin, not revenue
- Train successors, so that you may advance
- An enduring company is built by many good people, not a few
- We are here to make a positive difference, as well as a dollar
- We 'care' for our customers, environment and community
- Total quality management base

THIS WAS 1998. Mainfreight was twenty years old and prospering, in an era when half the world's economies were facing varying degrees of difficulty. When New Zealand's sharemarket and exchange rate went into free fall, Mainfreight sales exceeded NZ$200 million for the first time and net profit increased by almost 22 per cent. They were still very much a New Zealand company, with branches throughout the country, plus a small business in Australia with a turnover of A$7 million.

Then Mainfreight found they had made a mistake. In late 1997 they bought Trade Air, an Auckland-based air and sea international freight forwarder. The idea was to boost the flagging Mainfreight International by merging it into the new acquisition. The enlarged international division, together with LEP, would ensure that Mainfreight ranked among the largest forwarders in the sea and air market. They put Trade Air's management in the pound seats, a move based on the assumption that since the company was lucrative, showing profits in excess of NZ$1 million, it must be well managed.

Mainfreight has endlessly analysed this mistake. At the time there was a negative attitude within the larger company toward Mainfreight International. The mistake was not recognising that they had some good people — good people who left when the new Trade Air team was put in over them. And, in buying Trade Air, they failed to identify its dependence on a few key accounts. Two of these, Dress for Less and Levenes, went into receivership only months after the acquisition.

Mainfreight International was having a year from hell. And just when it seemed things could not get any worse its largest agent, Brambles International Australia, was sold to the enemy, Tranz Rail. If it could go wrong, it did, and the division was increasingly being regarded as a basket case.

Fortunately, they did get it right when they purchased ISS, the international freight forwarding company that would be rebranded as Mainfreight International Australia. Here was a takeover with a difference. Mainfreight was not buying a dog in need of training. ISS was not only a successful company, it was also run on similar philosophical lines to Mainfreight. John Hepworth and his Sydney manager, Michael Lofaro, thought the same way when it came to the treatment of people, the creation of teams and business ethics.

Lofaro had first encountered the transport industry when still at school, loading and unloading trucks as a summer holiday job. At the University of New South Wales he studied electrical engineering before dropping out to join the airfreight division of Freight Management International, part of the giant Mayne Nickless Group. He quickly rose through the company, becoming an assistant branch manager in his mid-twenties, and just as quickly tired of the office politics. He then found his way to the door of Peter Uren, the man who had registered and was using the Mainfreight name in Australia. Lofaro was hired as a Sydney salesman for Mainfreight International Australia in 1987.

It was there that he teamed up with the tall New Zealander John Hepworth, who quickly determined that Lofaro was better suited to the operational area than to sales. A strong friendship developed and two years later, in 1989, Lofaro and Hepworth would start up their own freight company, ISS Express Lines. It was this business that, nearly a decade later, would be sold to Mainfreight, with both men included as part of the deal.

ISS looked and felt like a Mainfreight operation, right down to the open-plan, flat-management and open-door policy. It had offices in Brisbane, Sydney, Melbourne, Adelaide and Perth. Hepworth had recently signed an agency agreement with US company CaroTrans, which had in turn also arranged representation in Europe by the Ziegler Group of Brussels. At the same time, ISS was shipping goods from Asia to Australia through their agent and partner David Shiau in Taiwan (just to add to the confusion, Shiau was trading under the name Mainfreight Taiwan). The Taiwan trade was so successful that in 1996 Hepworth went to Hong Kong seeking a partner.

Hepworth had known that business in any port is usually dominated by three good agents. It did not take him long to identify Norman Lock as the man he needed. Lock was a legend in the city. He was reputed to have a fixed routine that involved massage in the morning, followed by lunch, and later a move to the city's nightclubs, where he was said to spend US$1 million a year entertaining clients.

The deal with Lock's Vincent Shipping led to major expansion of the ISS business, and the Hong Kong trade was soon bigger than Taiwan. Manufacturing was flourishing in South China, and Hong Kong was the export boom town. Hepworth did the sums and knew he and David Shiau needed to set up their own business in Hong Kong. Sylvia Tsai was brought in from Shiau's Taiwan business to run it.

ISS opened in Hong Kong on 1 August 1998. Two months later Mainfreight bought ISS, and took control of its 25 per cent interest in the Hong Kong business. The Asian business was arranging air and sea cargo on behalf of customers in Australia and France, with Australia as its main market. At one stage ISS was the largest handler of giftware out of Hong Kong and Taiwan into Australia — items like cups, plates, crockery, serving dishes, cutlery and statues. It was also dominant in the bicycle export trade from China to Australia. Then came the personal-computer boom, and it was shipping desktops and hard drives made in Taiwan and China.

Within two years the market was shifting more to Shanghai, and Linda Huang, who had previously worked for the Australian shipping agent Burns Philp and the Chinese company Cosco, was brought on board to set up shop there. Plested and Braid were at pains to ensure they had a 50 per cent shareholding in the Asia operation, with Shiau, Sylvia Tsai and Linda Huang holding the balance between them.

The business performed satisfactorily for ten years, at which time Mainfreight bought out its Chinese partners in a carefully thought out acquisition. To begin with, Mainfreight had focused on learning the intricacies of trading in Asia with what was a small joint venture, while at the same time their new partners came to terms with having to supply and meet weekly profits, targets and bonuses. Once both sides were comfortable, and with the necessary trust and loyalty of the shareholders in place, Mainfreight was able to buy it 100 per cent.

As they came to terms with Asia, Mainfreight's determination to be recognised as a committed trans-Tasman operator was reflected in its purchase of three hectares of industrial land in Melbourne. This was to be the site of a substantial freight warehousing facility to ensure continued service for the growing number of New Zealand companies that were relocating to Australia.

This was becoming increasingly important as the Tasman, once considered the most expensive stretch of water on earth after Cook Strait, was now seeing much lower freight rates. When the cost of sending a single container in either direction was between NZ$2000 and NZ$3000 it made economic sense to manufacture on both sides of the Tasman. Once the price dropped to below NZ$1000 this effectively removed the barrier to trans-Tasman trade. Large numbers of Mainfreight's manufacturing customers were now concentrating production in Australia alone; it made sense for Mainfreight to position itself at the end of those assembly lines.

Back in New Zealand a vision of the future was also starting to emerge, with the purchase of around six hectares of rail-serviced land in Railway Lane, Otahuhu. This was to be the site of a major freight forwarding and integrated warehousing facility for South Auckland.

Around the board table, though, there was an increasing aware-ness that a strong presence in Australia was essential to protect the business. Some might have seen this as a defensive move, but Braid insisted it be treated as an offensive strategy.

Braid was always on the offensive, thinking of New Zealand and Australia as one. The question was, how to get everyone thinking like that?

# IF YOU L
# QUESTIO
# YOU DON
# FORWAR

VE IN A

N MARK

T GO

O

Mainfreight had begun with a policy of never hiring anyone who did not have the potential to become a branch manager. Now they wanted thinkers with the potential to be not so much branch managers as managing director. The brief was simple enough: 'Find people for the future — people who will fit into the team, have a cultural fit. Achievers who are going to be able to take the company to another level. People able to grow and develop themselves and Mainfreight.'

Christine Meyer had worked with Mainfreight in the mid-eighties when it owned the courier company, Castle. When Castle was sold to the Freightways Group, Meyer went with it, working for Freightways for two years before returning to Mainfreight to run its forkhire business. In 1989 she left to continue what had been part-time university education, and to complete a psychology major. Five years later she was back at Mainfreight as quality and training manager, a role that would develop into human resources and the all-important employment of graduates.

She would hire business and law graduates, and then have to explain to these young men and women with a BCom/LLB, whose friends were sitting in plush high-rise offices working for major law firms, that they would be spending the next two years driving forklift trucks, loading containers, and sweeping the depot floor at day's end. For when graduates are employed at Mainfreight there is never a promise of a particular role. The understanding is that they come into the business for a career that will unfold as they learn and show their potential.

Over the years, time spent on the floor has been reduced, but the theory remains the same: these are likely to be the men and women who will be running the company one day. They are encouraged to make both suggestions and decisions from day one, on the basis that they know the business from the floor up.

Today Meyer feels great satisfaction when she sees people she took on as graduates holding senior positions.

One of the greatest issues facing employers of talented young New Zealanders is the tendency they have to save for a couple of years and then leave for a world trip, from which many do not return. This was talent that Mainfreight recognised it could not afford to lose, so Meyer began finding work for them within the Mainfreight family throughout Asia, Australia, the UK and the US. When overseas, Don Braid would try to track these young people down and buy them a drink. Treat them like family and they stay in the family.

Potential managers, or those who 'have what it takes', are exposed to both internal and external leadership courses. One example is an Outward Bound leadership course that is tailor-made for Mainfreight, with an emphasis on pushing participants out of their comfort zones: up at six for a run, breakfast, climb a mountain and sleep out overnight. The only promise? Tomorrow will be tougher.

The aim is to test people in a completely different environment, forcing them to rely on others to get things done. It is about forming informal relationships and lifelong friendships with Mainfreight people from all over the world, while linking decision-making to what might happen in a branch. People change, some quite dramatically, leaving the course with a greater sense of confidence and a real understanding that team playing is not a cliché, it is critical to survival in life and business. Wherever you go in the world of Mainfreight it is not long before someone mentions that they have been on the Outward Bound course or are waiting to go.

In what was an industry-first in New Zealand, in August 2004 Mainfreight opened a training centre with an intensive five-day course that focused on skills but also on learning about the company's history, culture and expectations. Every new member of the Mainfreight family was expected to complete the course, as were all existing team members. Similar programmes would be run around the world as the company expanded. It was like an in-house university, right down to having a mock depot, where people learn why Mainfreight does things a certain way. Always there's the need to understand *why*. Why do we recycle? Because we want to be a good corporate citizen and look after the environment. Why don't we have job descriptions? Because it makes sense; we are a team. Give people a job description and that's all they do. In a team everyone does whatever it takes to get the job done. That is the culture.

An illustration of the Mainfreight training and culture is the fluorescent vest issue. Occupational health and safety law, in both New Zealand and Australia, states that people working in areas where there is moving heavy machinery must wear a fluorescent vest. Braid saw this as a politically correct fad. Good training is the best safety measure anyone could have. He would argue the vests might keep the bureaucrats happy but do not necessarily save lives. The health and safety people were told in no uncertain terms what they could do with their vests, and Mainfreight invested instead in training.

Braid explained his thinking to endless bureaucrats: 'Safety is about training and investing in people to enable them to be as responsible as they need to be. A vest doesn't do that.' Eventually the New Zealand Department of Labour relented, acknowledging that they were impressed by the Mainfreight culture and attitude, and a compromise was agreed — a reflective strip would be placed on uniforms.

Braid saw this as a lesson: Never let bureaucrats run a business. When a forklift went off the dock in Sydney the labour inspector's first question was: 'Was he wearing a fluorescent vest?'

Braid was incredulous. 'What difference would that have made? What matters is better training, not the colour of the vest. Training and everybody being safety conscious is what saves lives.'

Again, the Australians eventually allowed a compromise, with fluorescent stripes being put onto the Mainfreight shirt while they spent the serious money on training and instilling the right attitude into people working on the dock.

Braid's attitude to the fluorescent vests also reinforced the determination to get every single new recruit to challenge bureau-cracy. Christine Meyer would be frustrated by young people who came into the business and immediately wanted to complicate it. For years Mainfreight had no form of employment contract, but after mounting pressure Meyer introduced a 'Welcome' letter that covered a few employment details. She was then approached by graduates offering to develop a more sophisticated contract. Meyer explained that she did know how to create a more complex contract, but it was not what was wanted.

'They see how simple everything is and just can't help themselves, wanting to complicate it with more process. I would have to explain over and over again that it works because it is simple; simple is best. If you want to change it, try to make it simpler; that's why we hire smart young people like you. To make it simple.'

Braid would stress to new recruits, 'It's about making decisions and not letting the bureaucracy hold you up. There is no red tape here, no memos. Remember, simple is best; it's about not making anything too difficult.' He would use their accounting as an example: it was almost as simple as a domestic household budget. 'Hey, did we spend that much on electricity this month? Who hasn't been turning off the lights?'

THE GRADUATE PROGRAMME didn't meet with universal approval. Meyer was confronted by branch managers who complained that they did not have a degree, so why did the company need to employ people who did? Plested solved that problem. Branches that did not employ graduates found themselves out of the bonus pool, and one year a branch lost out on the 'Branch of the Year' award for failing in this one regard.

A fair degree of baiting went on: 'You may have a degree, son, but here's a broom — start sweeping the floor.'

Martin Devereux joined in May 2000 with not one but two degrees, in law and management. Meyer was in 'hire people for the future' mode the day she took Devereux on. Ten years later, in March 2010, he would replace her when she retired.

His friends were working for top law and accountancy firms while he swept the floor of a warehouse in South Auckland and drove a forklift. Today it is he who interviews graduates, and he is always at pains to give them the hard facts. It was not always like that; Devereux admits that the company did tend to oversell, with talk of travelling the world when in reality very few of them got to do that. Now he urges new employees to drive out to where the branches are, and to note that there are truck stops and petrol stations and pie carts where you can grab a bite to eat, not smart cafes and restaurants.

But he also tells them of his first day in the open-plan executive area, when he watched the managing director answer his PA's phone and explain that she was away from her desk, but 'could he help?' And he leaves them in no doubt that promotion from

Mainfreight's policy of finding people for the future drives the successful graduate employment programme.

within is more than just a sign on the wall; it is deeply embedded in the business ethic of the company.

Don Braid takes the hiring seriously, too. He wants people who are anti-bureaucratic and, critically, willing and able to make decisions. 'We don't live in question marks. We require a "yes" or a "no". Make the decision, and if it's a mistake learn from it and don't make it again.

'If you live in a question mark you don't go forward, in fact you go backwards. So make decisions. And that's not just the executive team and branch managers, it applies to everyone in the business. The message to everyone is simple. We need decisions made as close to the customers as possible. You decide: "Yes" or "No".'

This can be daunting for senior managers, let alone people down the chain, something Braid recognises. 'Yes, but hopefully we are creating a culture among our people so it doesn't frighten them. We want them to know that behind them is the Mainfreight team supporting them.'

Finding leaders is always an issue at Mainfreight, and for Braid in particular.

'One of the disappointments Bruce and I have is that some of our managers have employed less than quality people, and that's where the danger lies. It's lazy employing just whoever they can get their hands on rather than the very best people, and that's what we have to get back to so we have leaders everywhere with the potential to run this business.'

The determination to promote from within might suffer when they don't hire the best people in the first place, but acquiring new companies helps, as Braid has found.

'Within the Bosman business are some very good people, and we will promote them through the business. Buying companies allows us to refresh the talent pool from within.

'People ask what keeps us awake at night. The answer is simple; it is finding people capable of running the business as we expand and into the future. With more than 220 operations around the world, you have to have the comfort of knowing you have the right people in each of those operations. And, as we continue to grow, who is going to run South America, South Africa, India? We have to have those people ready, and if we don't we are in trouble.'

Finding people with the right attitude also niggles at Braid constantly.

'I heard this woman on the radio. She ran a media empire and had just laid off 180 people. She was calling them "FTEs". Then she explained that meant full-time equivalents. Not once, not once did she personalise it and talk about them being real people, human beings who had lost their jobs. They were just a statistic. It was a depersonalised numbers game. How does a person like that get a team to go down a different, difficult path during tough economic times? Why would you follow someone like that?'

That said, Braid is quick to admit Mainfreight doesn't get it right all the time. 'There is a failure rate, and that's down to the branch managers. Our decentralised approach to employment means we expect our young branch managers to pick the people who will eventually be promoted through the business. If they don't get that right, there is a double risk.

'It is a black mark against our people, the branch managers and executive team, and of course myself, if they don't have people to promote from within. That is the start of the slippery slope, because not only do we not have the leaders for the future, but if you employ people who don't care, with no intelligence, no passion and no energy, you also need two for every good one that you have, and that comes with a cost.'

In Meyer's book, finding the right people comes down to finding team players. She looked for people with a background of team culture, admitting to being wary of people who were overly individualistic, such as the highly academic, or violinists, piano players or even golf players, believing they would struggle because of the need for a team culture. She looked favourably on people with a rural background.

As the business has become, in her words, 'more sophisticated', the ability to take people who did not initially fit the mould has grown. Now the emphasis is on hiring people smarter, brighter than yourself.

Bruce Plested puts it more simply. 'I look for three things in potential new team members: intelligence, energy, and do I like them.'

Most companies have human relations people who talk about treating their staff with respect, but few match the Mainfreight emphasis on the team and caring for each other. There's a good illustration of this from the early days of Mainfreight, when a Christchurch customer was rude to the Mainfreight receptionist.

The branch manager, Wally Wright, found her in tears, established what had happened and sacked the customer. Word quickly spread throughout Mainfreight: 'They mean what they say about caring for each other.' It happened a long time ago, but it's now part of company folklore.

That caring has stretched to awarding scholarships to the children of team members, who receive NZ$3000 a year for the first three years of their university education. This being Mainfreight, though, it is a performance-driven scholarship. They must pass all their papers. Fail at any stage and the cheques stop coming.

THE NEW MILLENNIUM now loomed, and with it came expansion into North America and Australia. In the US, Arkansas Best Corporation (ABC) had taken over a domestic trucking company, Clipper, which had in turn taken over a similar operation, Carolina Freight, which was well-known to Mainfreight. Carolina Freight just happened to have an international freight forwarding business named CaroTrans 'tucked away in the basement'.

CaroTrans came with a colourful past. The company had been hurriedly put together on 1 April 1994, on the eve of a threatened strike by the mighty Teamsters' Union, which had an all-pervasive presence through the vast majority of American trucking companies. Carolina Freight, which at this time was struggling to survive, was anxious to reduce the exposure of its international business to union pressure. The company had two small international operations, one unionised, the other not. The solution seemed simple enough; they folded both companies under the umbrella of the newly created CaroTrans, which deftly inherited non-union status. But because it was created in a rush, to beat the looming strike, CaroTrans was poorly structured from day one, from both an accounting and a management standpoint.

CaroTrans struggled for two years as an add-on, until 1996 when ABC snapped up Carolina Freight and in doing so inherited CaroTrans. It was bolted onto yet another non-union operation and promptly forgotten. ABC did eventually find a use for CaroTrans, as a convenient company in which to park the corporate jet out of sight. The analysts, though, were whispering in ABC's ear that they should divest some of their diverse 26 companies and focus on their core business.

So it was that CaroTrans management, wanting to protect their people, went looking for a sympathetic buyer who would not be hell-bent on winding the company up and merging the business into its own. Enter Mainfreight and the European agent Ziegler Corp from Brussels. Mainfreight also had an agency agreement with CaroTrans, which meant its potential sale was a development Mainfreight could not ignore. Should CaroTrans be sold to a competitor, Mainfreight would lose all its established trade with the US. Overall, Mainfreight stood to lose business in Australia and New Zealand worth a combined NZ$1.6 million in pre-tax profit. Ziegler stood to lose a further NZ$2 million.

CaroTrans was a non-vessel-owning common-carrier, or NVOCC. In other words, it purchased wholesale container space from shipping lines and then on-sold it to individual freight forwarders. It was on track to become the third largest such carrier in the US, providing a tremendous opportunity for Mainfreight to gain a competitive edge over other freight forwarders.

Mainfreight had to move, and move quickly, as there was another potential buyer in the wind — another New Zealander as it happened, although he had made his fortune in the US. Owen Glenn owned NACA, the world's biggest NVOCC business. Mainfreight knew that if NACA snapped up CaroTrans then along with it would go all their hard-won business between New Zealand, Australia and the US.

CaroTrans was a complex set-up. Its CEO, Wayne Schmidt, lived in New York, its head office was in Chicago, and most of its 150 employees were based in the southern and southeastern states. There were eight branches: Los Angeles, Chicago, Houston, New York (New Jersey), Baltimore, Charleston, Atlanta and Miami. There were sales offices in New Orleans and Charlotte.

Mainfreight began due diligence, which revealed that CaroTrans was losing money. There was an internal assumption that the business made a healthy 32 per cent operating margin, but that is all it was — an assumption. The truth would be revealed as more like 22 per cent.

It was not until Mainfreight had completed the purchase, and finalised the accounts for March 2000, that the full extent of the company's losses was revealed as being close to US$3.5 million, not the US$2.2 million they had been expecting.

To outsiders that might seem a major loss, but Mainfreight had gone into the deal with its eyes open. To establish such a business there are but two choices: buy an existing one or start from scratch. Mainfreight estimated it would be looking at between US$15 million and US$20 million to build a proper non-vessel-owning business of its own. Even with the unanticipated losses, CaroTrans was a bargain.

CaroTrans certainly looked a good deal on paper. Ziegler, a highly respected international freight forwarder, took a 40 per cent stake. Ziegler was a substantial organisation, with revenues exceeding US$1 billion and offices throughout Western Europe. And it was privately owned. As CaroTrans' European agent, Ziegler was concerned that if the business was sold to other than a neutral party it would lose all its freight business from the US into Europe. Mainfreight's similar concerns made this an ideal partnership.

During negotiations, Bruce Plested and Chris Dunphy travelled to Brussels to meet Arthur Ziegler at his offices in Rue d'Ordanne. They were surrounded by a thousand years of history, in the very heart of Europe. A moment of pure theatre followed as the colonials waited for an audience with *le patron*. He did not disappoint, being precisely one hour late for the meeting, which was followed by lunch at his personal restaurant.

Dunphy's mastery of French, a gift from his mother, a language teacher, eased the way and lunch ended with a deal. The expectation was for Ziegler to pay US$l million for its 40 per cent stake and get board representation. It was the first time they had taken a minority shareholding, and it led to much soul-searching and prevarication.

Meanwhile the ABC management was determined that CaroTrans would be sold intact, rather than being broken up by a US-based conglomerate. Mainfreight's negotiators, Dunphy in particular, were quick to seize on this, providing an assurance that CaroTrans and its people would be safe in their hands. The final deal saw Mainfreight financed into the purchase with vendor money — the perfect arrangement. This was vintage Dunphy: first agree a favourable price, then casually mention, 'We're not going to pay you upfront, we're going to pay you off over two or three years.'

John Hepworth, who had come with the ISS purchase and had been running Mainfreight International in Australia, was transferred to New Jersey in late 2000 to replace Wayne Schmidt and to join forces with Greg Howard, an executive vice-president of the company at the time of its purchase. Greg Howard also had history with Mainfreight.

He had joined Carolina Freight from university in 1984, spending two years in sales for the domestic operation before being transferred to the international division in Holland. The fact he was issued with a one-way ticket might have alerted him to the fact this was not to be the short-term posting he had been promised. Six and a half years later he returned to the US from an assignment that eventually expanded to include South Africa, Asia and Oceania. During a visit to New Zealand he met the Mainfreight crew, signing them up as agents.

A few years later, in 1996, Howard was in Australia negotiating with John Hepworth as they arranged for ISS and CaroTrans to join forces. Hepworth convinced Howard to drop Mainfreight in favour of the ISS agent in New Zealand. Howard flew to Auckland to deliver the bad news in person to Plested, with his new agent sitting outside listening to the car radio. The meeting went on and on — for so long, in fact, that when Howard finally emerged the waiting car had a flat battery. A smiling Bruce Plested appeared carrying jumper leads, to give his departing former partner a jump start.

Greg Howard says he will never forget the call he received in 1998 from John Hepworth, informing him that he had sold his ISS business to Mainfreight. Or the call in 2000 to say that Mainfreight had bought the business of which he was vice-president.

John Hepworth (left) and Bruce Plested on the ABC corporate jet.

# LEARNIN
# HARD WA

G THE

Y IN OZ

Could Mainfreight match the CaroTrans purchase with an acquisition in Australia? They did so on 3 April 2000, when K&S Express came on the market. Mainfreight paid A$9.4 million, on paper improving their existing A$10 million revenue domestic Australian operation to one of almost A$70 million revenue. The reality was somewhat different.

Again, they were buying a small piece of a big company. K&S Freighters was a substantial trucking and logistics company that operated throughout Australia. K&S Express was its 'less than container load' (LCL) division.

The question that was asked by analysts, the media and indeed Mainfreight's bankers was, 'Why did they buy it?' The answer was that they needed to be in Australia for their customers in New Zealand, and it was a reasonably sized deal that gave them a team of 385 people across all the major centres.

Mainfreight could not credibly tender for any major freight work in Australia without an efficient and effective network. They had been in Australia for close to ten years and were still seen as a small company scratching around looking for work, struggling to make a buck. They needed the K&S acquisition, which overnight delivered major terminal facilities in Brisbane, Sydney, Melbourne, Adelaide, Ballarat and Perth, plus agents in a number of smaller outlying areas; a fleet of 186 pick-up and delivery vehicles and forklifts; and that team.

However the business media were soon reporting 'a horror time in Australia', with Mainfreight's total profit for the year to March 2001 slashed to NZ$2.4 million, 73 per cent down on the previous year's NZ$8.9 million. All of which prompted Plested's famous observation: 'We knew it was a dog, we just didn't know how big a dog it was.'

It was a dog that would take four years to train, with Mainfreight pouring countless millions into the correction process. Introducing

Chris Dunphy (left) and Chris Knuth had their work cut out when it came to getting to the bottom of the K&S business.

an untried computer system, questionable due diligence, aggressive trade unionists, appalling service from Telecom, and the attempt to force New Zealand culture on deeply suspicious Australians all had a part to play in the miserable process.

During those four years Bruce Plested fought a lonely battle with his own nervous board. The purchase put immense pressure on the rest of the global enterprise, with the very survival of CaroTrans in the US threatened. The Mainfreight due diligence team had been confronted with what were termed 'normalised' accounts, which showed that the company was a profitable operation when in fact K&S Express had been paying exorbitant fuel and rent costs to the parent company. In crude terms, K&S Freighters had stripped out and was then in the process of flogging its LCL freight division.

The Mainfreight team was not completely fooled — they correctly gauged it was probably losing about A$4 million a year. The purchase was a calculated investment, and they knew Mainfreight would suffer quite substantial losses for a period. They got that right. Restructuring the business quickly drove that loss to A$8 million, with more to follow.

Mainfreight talks persuasively of how it is cheaper to buy 'dogs' that need fixing than to start from scratch in a new country. The company's purchasing history shows that such companies have almost always come with hidden surprises. So how effective is the due diligence process? No one, least of all Don Braid, denies that it's a problematic process with small companies that are struggling, and whose owners have every reason to hide unpalatable details.

'The point with due diligence is that if you find stuff you can't stomach, then you need the balls to walk away. I think there will be more of that in the future.

'As we learn more what to ask, and what not to ask, we have become more savvy. But we will always miss some stuff and will never be told all the truth, as [the companies] of course come wrapped up like a Christmas present.'

To this day the K&S deal remains a sensitive issue among some of Mainfreight's most senior players. Questions abound about the efficiency of the due diligence process, and whether they should have purchased K&S in the first place, rather than waiting for a more suitable opportunity. And there would be endless debate about the decision to install an untried computer system.

This was *Maintrak*, a new operating system that was being

developed at the time for Mainfreight. While it was not yet functioning in New Zealand, the decision was made to launch the new platform in Australia. There were enormous problems from day one.

Director Richard Prebble looks back on this as 'one of the biggest mistakes we have made in the company's history'. With the benefit of hindsight, he regrets not more rigorously challenging assurances that the new system would work. 'I questioned it, I was incredulous about it, and I was persuaded by the answers.'

Kevin Drinkwater had been in the US working on the CaroTrans issue when *Maintrak* went off the rails. To this day, though, he argues that the technology was not at fault. Yes, they went early, and more time would have been useful. But when the same system was installed in New Zealand two years later no further modification was required, saving a fortune in licence fees. The software was, he argues, 90 per cent right. The people operating it were the problem.

The bottom line is that they effectively bought a bad business, and made it worse as a consequence of feeding incorrect data into a new, unproven IT system, which resulted in inaccurate and inflated rates being charged to customers. The initial figures were fantastic, the returns beyond all expectations. Everyone was convinced they had once more worked the Mainfreight magic and turned around a basket-case company. Then customers started screaming about being overcharged — and they took their anger with them as they left. For more than six months Mainfreight was faced with paying back overcharged money, damaging the team spirit, which initially had been quite high.

Computers aside, Australia advanced apace. Chris Knuth, the former Hamilton loader who had steadily risen through the company ranks, had initially been sent to Australia to get Mainfreight, LEP and Mainfreight International working together, to create momentum between the various divisions. Plested had once again repeated his well-worn message of the past decade: 'If you fail, we run the risk of having to pack up and leave Australia.'

Later, during the negotiations with K&S, Mainfreight was denied the access it needed to the branches. Knuth was perfect for the job, going undercover, signing himself in as representing a range of high-profile clients. 'It was easy,' he said later. 'They signed me in and I was shown around. It's amazing what can be seen by just looking and keeping your mouth shut.'

Like the rest of the Mainfreight team, Knuth knew they were

buying a dysfunctional business. But they would be going from a business that employed 50 people, with a few million in sales, to a company with a nationwide network and A\$70 million in sales. They knew the network was in need of costly repairs, but the A\$9.4 million price tag was still regarded as a great deal cheaper than growing such a business from nothing.

It was not a dissimilar argument to the case for buying CaroTrans. Australia was a mountain Mainfreight had to climb. Fail in Australia and they were unlikely to remain successful in New Zealand; they would, in Bruce Plested's words, 'shrivel and become mediocre'.

IT WAS NOW or never for Mainfreight in Australia. Their New Zealand customers, winemakers in particular, increasingly saw their future as dependent on Australia. Their success was contingent on getting their products into and around Australia efficiently.

Plested maintains he has never had a minute's regret about buying K&S. As with CaroTrans, they knew that buying part of a business exposed them to normalised accounts that would be, in Plested's words, 'bullshit'. 'We wanted their sales and the branch network and that's what we bought. I doubt they knew how much it was losing.'

K&S fixed their rates per pallet, not by weight and cubic capacity, which is how the rest of the world prices freight. It was little wonder that the new computer system struggled and so many mistakes were made. In addition, Telecom's trans-Tasman link — the Southern Cross Cable — could not cope with the congestion, and it took Mainfreight staff three minutes to enter each consignment note. The cable had plenty of capacity but the speed allocated by Telecom was inadequate.

Telecom's chief executive, Theresa Gattung, did not return Plested's calls when he called her to complain. 'My calls were blocked continually by her personal assistant,' he remembers. 'It was unbelievably bad. I was ringing all the time but they would not let me through, saying she was aware of our problem and they were doing all they could to assist. I just wanted to talk to her and they refused to put me through.'

That was probably a good thing, given what he might have said. 'Angry' doesn't begin to describe how Plested felt; customers were being overcharged some A\$80,000 a week, and Telecom was not helping.

Back at the coalface, the former K&S staffers were coming to terms with being on the Mainfreight team. Leading hand Ossie Osman had started with K&S five years earlier in Melbourne. He had watched managers come and go on average every six months as he progressed from the parcels department to leading hand in a world where time-and-a-half and double-time wages were the rule of the day. Then Mainfreight arrived, and with them the notion of a monthly salary and the instruction 'Kindly do whatever is necessary to get the job done.' No more overtime. Union power was threatened, and it was quickly a case of 'everyone out'.

Osman stood on the street and thought of his new wife and their young baby and the house he was building for them and the mortgage, and after ten hours he walked back in. As he walked into the warehouse his jaw dropped. He had known Chris Knuth was hands-on, but he hadn't expected to see him driving a forklift. Knuth raised an eyebrow. Osman explained that he wanted to get back to work, and was pointed at a forklift. Threats followed, but Osman knew the company was losing A\$60,000 a week, and there was that mortgage to pay. He was now a capitalist, Mainfreight through and through.

When Chris Dunphy was parachuted in to work his magic on the K&S deal, the merchant banker found himself in truly foreign territory. It was never the intention that Dunphy should be in the driving seat, but once the enormity of the task was grasped he moved in as general manager. The plan was to bed it down and move on, a task that was expected to take a year, but in fact took the better part of three years.

No sooner had he stepped into his K&S management role than the phone calls started: 'We know where you live and we know what your kids look like.'

Dunphy found himself confronted by good old-fashioned blackmail. Simply, if he did not want strikes he should pay off the union official. 'That's how it works here, cobber.'

Mainfreight did not pay bribes, but they did pay redundancy to people who had to leave. It took a heavy toll on the bank balance and on the management team's morale. They were coming to terms with the fact that they had acquired a business that was more dysfunctional than it was functional.

Again the question arises — could they have done more due diligence? To this day Chris Dunphy, who is now running his own business, doesn't have the answer to that. His most significant recollection is underestimating the amount of management needed and grossly underestimating the amount of bandwidth required to run the IT systems. This had a huge impact on Mainfreight, as Dunphy was being lined up to take on joint overall management of the company with Don Braid.

MAINFREIGHT HELD ITS twenty-second board meeting as a public company on Thursday 15 March 2001, in its Melbourne boardroom. It was a landmark meeting: Bruce Plested moved that Don Braid and Chris Dunphy become joint managing directors. Chris Dunphy surprised everyone by turning the offer down. He had yet to get the new Australian venture into profit. That was his main responsibility, and he took the view that Braid should be appointed sole managing director.

No one was more surprised than Braid, as the two men had previously agreed to just such an arrangement. It had been Dunphy who had effectively bulldozed Plested into publicly signalling his intention of establishing the joint succession. Now it had been openly declared before the board, and without any consultation Dunphy had pulled out of the deal. Braid was 'gutted', his trust sorely tested.

Dunphy shrugged at Braid's outrage, an outrage made all the more intense by the fact that Braid had often acted as peacemaker, smoothing over feathers ruffled by Dunphy, who seemed capable of generating extraordinary and conflicting emotions among Mainfreight's senior management.

He was certainly good at making waves and raising eyebrows, at one stage urging them to bid for the floundering Air New Zealand. There were those in the company who had watched how smoothly he had asset-stripped parts of CaroTrans, selling a shipping business that was operating between the US and Puerto Rico to help pay for the business. Might the financial whizz-kid have similar plans for Mainfreight itself one day?

Dunphy had made no secret of the fact that he was interested in creating a Fortune 500 company, and was critical of Plested's continuing ambition to develop and nurture a 100-year company.

Dunphy was happy to play high-stakes poker, while Plested sought the comfort of long-term, considered, proven strategies.

Never was the clash of temperaments clearer than in 2001 when, with the share price languishing, Dunphy suggested a management buy-back of the company. Plested was vehemently opposed to the idea and it went no further. Several months later, a deputation of bankers from Westpac requested an appointment with Plested. He agreed to the meeting on the condition it had nothing whatsoever to do with a management buy-back. The meeting lasted less than fifteen minutes before the bankers were shown the door. They had indeed been interested in discussing a management buy-back, and it was a buy-back with an additional twist. They were offering NZ$1.70 for each of his 21 million shares — Plested could take a cheque for more than NZ$35 million and walk away from the business he had founded.

Before suggesting, in his inimitable fashion, that they should leave, Plested noted with some disgust that the bankers were to take a fee of NZ$3 million for putting the deal together. Plested maintains that they did not tell him who was behind the buy-back, and is equally emphatic that he did not ask.

Dunphy, who was in Melbourne at the time, was not a party to the approach, but he did know who was behind it. 'Yes, [it was] a tumultuous time: the share price was languishing and the analysts just weren't understanding either the expansion story, or the fact that we had a long-term view of acquisitions in overseas markets. We had one international shareholder, Mike McConnell, who ran money for Roy Disney [brother of Walt] who was as close to an activist shareholder as existed back then. Mike was keen to privatise Mainfreight.'

Dunphy had moved away from his enthusiasm for privatisation, but he remained convinced there should be more active capital management, such as a share buy-back, as a means of getting the share price above the book value. He recalls the buy-back discussion getting little traction at a Mainfreight board meeting and leaving it there. Then, unbeknownst to him, McConnell had engaged Westpac, and from that had followed the request for an audience with Bruce Plested.

Dunphy recalls the aftermath: 'Bruce saw it as "the night of the long knives", with the result that things were frosty between us for some time! However, I think Bruce knows that I wouldn't do something involving the business without both his consultation and blessing. The privatisation of Mainfreight had neither, and accordingly was not ever going to occur.'

TWO MONTHS LATER, toward the middle of 2001, Don Braid and Bruce Plested flew to Las Vegas to meet the CaroTrans branch managers. Exhausted after the flight, they exchanged greetings with the CaroTrans people then fled downstairs to the Flamingo Casino coffee shop. Plested was in a pensive mood, and Braid could tell there was something in the air.

Over soup and toasted sandwiches, to the accompaniment of the trill of slot machines, the Mainfreight founder laid out his succession plans. Don Braid was to step up from the position of New Zealand managing director to assume the role of group managing director, with full responsibility for all the company's businesses and shared businesses in New Zealand, Australia, the US, Hong Kong and China.

Bruce Plested would assume the role of executive chairman, with Don Rowlands, the current chairman, remaining as a director. Chris Dunphy would continue to manage the Australian division, with a clear brief to return it to profitability. John Hepworth would persevere with his mission to drive the international business from his base in the US. And Kevin Drinkwater would have global responsibility for IT.

The two men shook hands in the glitzy Flamingo gambling den, and Braid knew he had a deal cast in stone. Both men were at a turning point in their lives.

Bruce Plested was a great believer in playing to the strengths of the individual, of making the job fit the man, not the man fit the job. In the early days he had confided to Neil Graham that he felt guilty about not being active enough in the front line. His partner had responded, 'You can't have everybody running up the beach into machine guns; we need someone to sneak around the back and drop a hand grenade into the bunker. That's what you do.'

Plested knew his grenade-throwing days were numbered. He needed to play to his other strengths. This is a man who can drive past a Mainfreight branch on a Sunday afternoon and tell you whether it is profitable and has a good manager by the length of the lawn and the general cleanliness of the property. The time had come to put his age and experience to work, to do more handshaking and less shouting about the state of the toilets.

As for Braid, he maintains he was not 'gagging' to run the business, but if they thought he was capable, then fine. Did he ask what authority he would have, and what an executive chairman might do?

'I didn't have to ask that. I knew what an executive chairman does. Put another way, I knew what Bruce would do. He started the business, he had a passion for it and would interfere whenever he bloody wanted. Why not?'

Braid concedes that the chain of command is frustrating at times, but, he says, 'We are a better business for it. Leadership is two up and two down. The executive team must get irritated with us going direct to branch managers, helping them make decisions or urging them to do other things, without them being in the meetings. It's an approach that reduces the number of layers in the management structure; all part of a determination for open-door meetings and speed of decision-making.

'We visit all the branches, and that must piss off Greg Howard and John Hepworth in the US and Michael Lofaro in Asia, but it's about creating momentum. It's not about interfering; we don't have the hierarchical red-tape process, it's as flat as it possibly can be.

'The same exists with me. Bruce will ring one of the executive several times a week. Fuck knows what they talk about but it doesn't worry me. If we are a better business for it then so be it.'

That is what the handshake sealed.

# ALWAYS
# YOUR WO

KEEP

RD

**B**ack in New Zealand, Bruce Plested was still fending off critics among financial analysts, sharebrokers and the business media. He would not be deterred. He was determined to establish Mainfreight firmly in Australia, which had an economy seven times the size of New Zealand.

The talk was now of creating a global business exclusively from the profits earned in the New Zealand marketplace over the past 23 years. 'Imagine the growth we will be capable of globally in the next five to ten years,' Plested would say, 'as we build off the profits available from both countries.'

The media were still picking up on the Australia issue, though. New Zealand's leading business newspaper, *The National Business Review*, pointed out in its 29 June 2001 edition that an Australian-driven profit collapse for the March year had seen the transport operator's share price fall to 100 cents, 'just a flea's breath' above the 96 cents at which they were issued when Mainfreight had floated five years earlier.

Since the float the shares had twice reached 200 cents and twice halved again, but the ups and downs did not seem to bear any relation to profitability, which had, until the latest year, grown steadily with the exception of a small slip in 1999. What investors seemed to have missed in the general gloom was that Mainfreight had bought loss-making companies before, both in Australia and elsewhere, and turned them around. In fact, buying loss-making companies and turning them around was the company's stated strategy.

*NBR* helpfully pointed out that LEP Australia, which Mainfreight had bought for A$1 in February 1998, had lost A$330,000 in its first year, made a A$592,000 profit in the second, returned A$609,000 in its third, and just kept growing. The newspaper suspected the market's pessimism was driven by a simplistic assumption that Kiwi businesses that tried to cross the Tasman would always end up failing. As a company likely to turn over NZ$500 million that year, Mainfreight deserved more attention, and better analysis, *NBR* commented.

They could have been referring to Fisher Funds. A specialist sharemarket investor with an eye for quality growing businesses, it had only been operating for three years but had bought Mainfreight stock to the maximum allowed by its internal regulations. Fisher Funds was small at the time, with around NZ$300 million invested, but it attracted attention because of the personality and high profile of its founder, Carmel Fisher.

She in turn could not help but notice the 73 per cent drop in Mainfreight's profit. While she admired Plested's enormous self-belief, Fisher knew that Australia was littered with the remains of New Zealand companies that had gone there and failed because they did not understand the difference between the two countries. She saw Mainfreight as guilty of that, and over eighteen months had expressed her concerns to Don Braid: 'You are stuffing up; pull back, rethink.'

There was real frustration at Mainfreight that no one seemed to understand they were in this for the long haul. As Fisher explained, 'The hundred-year vision is completely foreign to most fund managers, who don't even have the luxury of thinking in terms of a year. Our investment decisions are published every single day, and every month or quarter we are compared with each other, determining who is going to win the mandate for the next million dollars or hundred million dollars that comes up for investment. The investment community is far shorter in terms of its focus than Mainfreight. I'm sure every listed company out there gets frustrated with the market and our short-termism.'

That said, Fisher Funds have a longer-term view than many, with just 25 per cent of its portfolio turned over most years against the 100 per cent of many other fund managers. Carmel Fisher maintains, 'We only sell if there is a fundamental change in the investment case, not the share price, and the Australia issue was fundamental with Mainfreight.'

Braid's response was to the point. 'If you don't like it, sell your shares.'

Fisher did — she sold right out, every last share. 'From our perspective, they had taken a strong domestic operation and stuffed it up. Australia was taking management time and attention and not making any money, and I had expressed these concerns over a period of a year or so. It wasn't a surprise when we sold.'

Was Fisher Funds responsible for the subsequent dramatic drop in the Mainfreight share price? 'We did not lead the charge, but we told our investors, and it might have had a knock-on effect.'

For the record, Fisher Funds is now back into Mainfreight, again to the maximum allowed by their own in-house rules.

If pressed on the issue, Plested would stress the importance of shareholders understanding that the profitable development of the business was going to take time and they were not yet in a position to predict when that would be.

This did beg the question of why they were investing so much in Australia. Plested would explain endlessly that they had tried to expand the business organically for twelve years but they could not satisfy the requirements of customers, so they needed to buy a medium to large business they could develop.

Australia was New Zealand's largest export market for manufactured goods, while New Zealand was Australia's third largest market. Many companies operated branches on both sides of the Tasman, so Mainfreight had to respond in kind and regard the two countries as one business area. After all, the US, Europe and Asia all thought of New Zealand and Australia as one marketplace.

Braid and Plested both knew that multinationals, usually based in Europe or the US, increasingly engaged a global freight company to provide all their freighting and warehousing services throughout the world. If Mainfreight were merely to operate in New Zealand, they would be reduced to moving freight from the Auckland wharf to a global freight company's warehouse in the city, work they would have to tender for against perhaps six trucking companies. This was not an area where Mainfreight sought to operate. If the analysts did not understand that then Plested and Braid certainly did.

The strategy was to focus on transport and warehousing opportunities, together with demands from New Zealand customers who were already in Australia, or were developing the Australian market. To take advantage of these conditions it was vital to increase Mainfreight's capability and network in the vastly larger Australian domestic market.

Director Richard Prebble was ambivalent about Australia too. While the board had bought into Plested's vision of going to Australia, he says, 'With the benefit of hindsight we bought K&S without enough thought, but that applies to every purchase we make and after every new purchase we talk of doing better due diligence next time round.'

The boardroom was starting to become a lonely place for

Plested, with even Graham privately urging his friend to pull out of Australia. Plested was having none of it. 'No, we've got to hang in there, we've just got to keep pounding away at it.' Back in the 1980s he had wanted out. Now, it was the persistence of his own people on the ground, agreeing to those pay cuts in the process, that made him persevere.

Rumours swirled around the Australian operation: a sale to Toll, the giant Australasian transport and logistics company, was on the cards; Plested and Dunphy were planning to buy TNT, another giant Australian global freight company specialising in express delivery; Dunphy was setting up a business of his own, and had plans to leave. Dunphy was in fact telling Plested that he would remain with Mainfreight until the Australian distribution business was in profit, and hinting at his desire to retain an interest through a future consultancy role.

Eventually, through grit and hard slog, Dunphy and his right-hand man, Chris Knuth, turned the business round. It may have taken more than three years, but when they were finished it looked and felt like a Mainfreight business. Not only did it have blue trucks and freight terminals with docks in them, but it was also underpinned by margin and reporting systems and, critically, they were no longer losing money.

The luxury of hindsight shows they were perhaps in too much of a hurry. They did not pause to consider the fact that the history of Australia was radically different to that of New Zealand. Dunphy and Knuth would eventually grasp that Irish Catholics with bitter experience of the oppressor Protestant Englishman had settled Australia. Outlaw bushranger Ned Kelly? He was not a criminal who had run around shooting people; he was a decent Catholic standing up to the Protestant constabulary. From such thinking came the essential premise of the Australian union movement — all bosses are bastards.

This was a land where workers had a certain number of days off on the roster to do personal things or nothing at all. At Mainfreight, if you needed to go to your child's school or see the bank manager, you went and made up the time later. In Australia you could cash in your guaranteed sick days for money. At Mainfreight if you were sick you were paid and if you were not you worked — extra hard.

The Mainfreight bosses naively thought that ensuring a neat and tidy workplace, installing subsidised canteens where everyone

Christian Aliste, Mainfreight
Sydney, one of a new
breed of owner-drivers
in Australia.

ate together, putting all the company's financial secrets up on the wall, paying bonuses, and treating everyone like family would make all that union nonsense go away. They did not understand. The union was there to actively ensure disharmony between worker and employer. Conflict was essential to make their role meaningful.

Mainfreight cast all its bread on the water at once. This was treated with outright hostility and suspicion from a workforce who demanded to know, 'How much are you making out of this — mate?'

Taking care of quality freight required quality trucks and drivers. Dunphy put Mainfreight's money on the line. Drivers who bought their own trucks had an absolute guarantee that if it did not work out, Mainfreight would buy the truck from them and pay back the bank. They were called upon to bail out just one owner-driver, and soon the truck was taken up by another.

When a supervisor drove a forklift, 100 men walked out. And Knuth found himself in court after an altercation with a worker. The incident cost Mainfreight A\$20,000. And there were other payouts too as the powerful Transport Workers Union stepped up the pressure.

And the losses just would not go away. In 2001 they lost A\$7.5 million in Australia. Westpac was starting to flex its muscle, insisting they sell assets to reduce exposure. The suggestion was that two properties, which had been hard to buy — the Brisbane terminal, a purpose-built warehouse and freight facility, and a 3-hectare block of land and warehouse in Melbourne — had to go.

David McLean, the head of Westpac's Institutional Bank in New Zealand, recalls Plested's reaction. 'We felt they should sell property to reduce debt but Bruce was adamant he did not want to be held to ransom by landlords and stuck to his guns. They were right and we were wrong.'

'Westpac brought pressure to bear but were firmly put in their place,' remembers Tim Williams. '"Get fucked" springs to mind.'

Interestingly, the properties were subsequently sold, a decision made and controlled by Mainfreight. Despite the tension of this period, Mainfreight's relationship with Westpac continues, and in 2007 the bank determined to release all security it held over the company and move its relationship to an unsecured negative pledge basis. In other words, the company's financial strength was such that the bank did not require a bond anymore.

Something was called for to recognise the momentous occasion. McLean decided a set of handcuffs would be a suitable gift to celebrate the 'release'. But where to find them? A friendly policeman pointed the banker in the direction of a sex shop, which he entered with a nervous backward glance. Once inside he found bondage equipment for every occasion and selected the largest, most solid pair of handcuffs on show. Mainfreight's reaction? The handcuffs are still on display in its boardroom.

MEANWHILE, BACK IN that same boardroom, the torrid Australian experience was not going down well, with John Fernyhough in particular adamant they should pull out altogether. The other directors had huge respect for Fernyhough, who was one of New Zealand's most influential businessmen of the 1980s and 1990s. He was a director of several major companies including Lion Corporation, in which he was also a substantial shareholder. With an estimated personal fortune of NZ$30 million, he was the first chairman of the state-owned Electricorp, and a champion of privatising state enterprises. His wife Christine also had a connection with Mainfreight through her tireless work for Duffy Books in Homes, working out of the company's office on Auckland's Great South Road.

Matters came to a head during a dramatic board meeting at the Southdown branch in Auckland. A furious Fernyhough argued it was time to admit they had got it wrong, cut the substantial losses and pull out. An equally angry Plested fumed that he never had a doubt that Australia was their future. They had to be strong. 'I don't care if it takes ten years to get established there. If we crumble back to New Zealand we'll go nowhere.' Both men were visibly upset but it was Plested who won the day, arguing the merit of taking a long-term view.

The truth is, he had been surprised by the passion with which Chris Dunphy and Chris Knuth had set about de-unionising Australia and installing owner-drivers. It would take a decade, but Melbourne was to become the most profitable Mainfreight branch anywhere in the world.

At a key tipping point the Mainfreight team philosophy had become infectious. Customers could sense it as they walked through the door. Mainfreight only wanted quality customers who valued their high-end product and being cared for with kid gloves, and who would pay on time. That was not an easy conversion. They had bought a business based on low-value freight and cheap rates. The first thing they did was up the rates by some 15 per cent. Chris Dunphy took the no-nonsense approach of, 'Take it or leave it.'

Price-sensitive customers fled in their droves, taking A$20 million in turnover with them in the first year. Dunphy drew a line in the sand, waving goodbye to customers they did not want, and focused on the freight they did want. High value was the name of the game.

This was certainly different. This was a branch-orientated business with owner-drivers, some of whom would have up to A$300,000 invested in their vehicles. They were no longer relying on a union for security; now they put their faith in Mainfreight.

The fact that total profits were slashed by some 73 per cent could to some degree be put down to the brutality of Dunphy and Knuth when it came to the parcel business that came with K&S. The A$16 million business was selling at prices well below cost. They bit the bullet and established a A$15 per consignment minimum charge for inter-city parcels. Take it or leave it. Within six months of the purchase in 2000 the parcel business had fled too.

They were tough times indeed. Not a week went by without industrial action or the need to go to court. On one occasion Knuth went to a bar instead. Eighty loaders and drivers had walked out over yet another trivial matter. Across the road in the local pub Knuth found Kiwi and Irish drivers who were happy to break the picket line and shift his freight. He paid them cash. In a paper bag.

It would take several years for Dunphy and Knuth to defeat the unions and have the 'blue blood' of Mainfreight running through the veins of all who worked there. For Knuth in particular this was a mission. He was one of the first to grasp the Plested belief that their culture was a competitive advantage.

But it was a business strategy that was constantly analysed and reviewed. Knuth would sound warnings the very culture that made Mainfreight special was in danger of being diluted because not enough people understood it. And those who did were being stretched too thin as they moved out across the world to manage the constantly expanding company. In the years to come, Plested, Braid and the entire board would come to share this view.

As Don Braid explained to John Hepworth, 'Just accept the

culture, and once you do that you will love this company. It's not bullshit; they won't put up with anyone who doesn't want to be part of it.'

AN ERA WAS ending with the changing of the guard. Bruce Plested might have been executive chairman, but Don Braid was now running the show on a day-to-day basis. He was the one calling the shots and, more importantly, taking the weekly calls as branch and country managers reeled off their results. Plested had never been afraid of letting his displeasure be known, but any cross words tended to be tempered with a word of encouragement. Braid was not always inclined to be quite so considerate. If he was not happy he said so in no uncertain terms, leaving the caller in no doubt of his expectations.

Chris Dunphy stepped down from the Mainfreight board early in 2003 to set up his own shipping business. The merchant banker argued it was clear Don Braid was better suited to taking Mainfreight forward in the image of Bruce Plested, and it was time to move on.

His departure coincided with the untimely death of John Fernyhough. Two new directors, Emmet Hobbs and Bryan Mogridge, both of whom had impressive business backgrounds, were appointed. Hobbs had begun his career as a journalist but soon found his niche in business at the Union Steam Ship Company, followed by Pacifica Shipping, ABC Containerline, Australian Airlines, Qantas, and as executive director at Brambles, the Australian industrial services company. Bryan Mogridge held chairmanships of Rakon, Pyne Gould, BUPA Care Services, UBS and the Starship Foundation.

Dunphy left Mainfreight emotionally shattered by the K&S deal. He was also sceptical about the 100-year vision, and the view that transport companies evolved into different businesses. He would give the example of Brambles, which started in Australia as a transport company and developed into waste management, landfill and records management. Dunphy put this down to new management seeing transport as not making the margin of the spin-off companies, and finally taking the decision to sell. (Brambles is now a pallet company, with no transport arm anywhere in the world.)

He believed that Mainfreight's challenge would be to resist what every other expanding transport organisation had found irresistible. And while he concedes the power of the culture, he worries that 'it could easily develop myopia, with people who can finish each others' sentences that always end with "it is the Mainfreight way, we have always done it this way". You innovate, you re-engineer or you die.'

No such fears for Bruce Plested, who suggested to Knuth that he take over Australia.

'No,' was the simple answer. 'I'm not the sort of person you need.'

Knuth did not relish having to report in person to the board of directors. He liked to speak his mind. He had, quite literally, fought unionists toe-to-toe. He did not want to 'pussyfoot about'; it was not his style. He had enjoyed the day-to-day contact with Bruce Plested and he did not favour the take-no-prisoners approach of the new management — and for that read Don Braid. Knuth left to set up his own business in October 2003.

They were four years into the K&S venture and just starting to break even. Did Plested have concerns that his new group managing director might have been a touch tough on the senior troops?

'No. People have to adjust to new regimes. Some can't.'

# THE MAN
# TOP OF T
# MOUNTAI
# FALL TH

ON

HE

N DIDN'T

RE

While the 'Mainfreight culture' is integral to the company's success, it made much of not imposing a culture on the US, rather, allowing an American version to emerge in its own time. The fact is, they really did not understand Americans. Yes, they spoke the same language, but it might as well have been Russian for all the real comprehension that occurred.

They needed a catalyst, a defining moment, a flash of inspiration. In short, they needed help, help that would come from an unlikely source on the morning of Tuesday 11 September 2001.

John Hepworth, now running CaroTrans in the US, was at Newark Airport on the outskirts of New York. He was boarding a small charter flight to Charleston when he heard a fellow passenger gasp, 'The tower! One of the towers is on fire.'

Hepworth had been in the US long enough to know what she was talking about — there were only two towers, the Twin Towers. He had often admired the New York landmark from the tarmac at Newark. He did not even look up — it couldn't be, not one of the towers on fire? Never.

But everyone was shouting and pointing and he finally looked and, yes, there was smoke billowing from one of the towers. The passengers completed boarding, and the pilot kept the radio open so they could listen to the confusion. As Hepworth looked out of the window he saw the second red flash.

'Oh my God, it's a terrorist attack.' Those were the last words the passengers heard from the traffic controllers before they shut down the radio.

Hepworth tried calling his wife, but he could not get through. Looking round the plane he saw frustrated faces everywhere as his fellow passengers punched numbers into their phones — just as countless millions of other Americans were doing at that very moment. Realising that the American mobile-to-mobile network was jammed and would be down for hours, Hepworth called his son Daniel's landline number in Australia.

'Call your mother on a landline and tell her I'm okay but on the runway at Newark. Tell her she needs to get supplies . . . tell her to get some money out and some groceries . . . if we are under attack we need to be prepared . . . cash and food.'

Back inside the terminal Hepworth managed to get through to Greg Howard, his number two at CaroTrans, with a request to collect him from the airport. It was now swarming with panic-stricken passengers, and policemen who had gone from lightly to heavily armed in what seemed like a matter of seconds.

On the way back to the office they became stalled in a traffic jam on the freeway and watched in disbelief as the first tower collapsed. Howard was crying, pinching himself, thinking he had walked onto a movie set. This just could not be happening. The human cost hit home when they arrived at the office — three of the women team members had daughters who worked in the towers. There were also radio predictions of an imminent chemical attack. People were urged to take refuge in their cellars and to tape doors and windows. Hepworth called his wife. This time he got through. He added tape to her list of cash and food.

By now came some relief: the news that two of the women's daughters were safe. However the third was still unaccounted for. Hepworth closed the office, sent everyone home to their loved ones, and arranged support for those with family members caught up in the disaster. Then he headed home. His wife arrived at the same time. When he went to the boot of her car to collect the supplies he found four boxes of Diet Coke and two cartons of cigarettes. They were all set up to survive the war.

He was soon to discover two things: how patriotic Americans were, and how angry he himself could become. Soon there was an American and a New Zealand flag flying from the Hepworth home in Walnut Circle, in the suburb of Basking Ridge. Three homes in the community were missing husbands who would never come home. A cooking roster was organised, and every Thursday for three months the Hepworths would deliver a cooked meal to one of the families. Hepworth says he was so angry he would have donned an American uniform and gone to war had he been asked — angry, shocked and full of respect for the patriotic fervour he saw all around him.

There was such a strong sense of being and culture that Hepworth's understanding of the US and its people changed overnight. He took one of the first trains into Manhattan and found himself misty-eyed as people demonstrated their patriotism by singing old Civil War songs. Back at work, with the good news that all three of the women's daughters were safe, there was a new bonding. 'We became more than just friends in the team after that,' he remembers.


MAINFREIGHT WAS IN pretty good shape at the time too. The business had 82 branches throughout Australasia, Asia and North America, sales revenue of nearly half a billion dollars — or NZ$1.67 million for every day of the year — and employed over 2000 people. Now was the perfect time to grow the US business; to see how the country operated; to see what opportunities existed. And lo and behold, the domestic freight operations would prove just as profitable as the international operations.

There was growing trade development within the Asian region, and a further increase in trade with the New Zealand and Australian operations. These were the early days of trade between China and the US, opening up huge opportunities for CaroTrans. Braid let everyone know it was a question of when, not if, they would open more branches. The plan, though, was always to establish an independent retail operation in the US under the Mainfreight brand, while using the services of CaroTrans to get its freight to any market around the world, thus retaining profit from collection to delivery.

The great benefit of the wholesale operation was that as a booking service, rather than actually handling freight, it had the ability to double profit without doubling the people or the costs to the business. It was perfect for what is traditionally a very low margin business, and helped by Mainfreight's decentralised management style that allows its branch managers to take whatever decisions are necessary to maximise margin, and consequently increase profits.

The CaroTrans case was further helped by the mega-mergers of a number of shipping lines around the world. Customers who had previously dealt directly with shippers were looking to freight forwarders as their volumes became too small for the larger shipping lines to service. They were also helped by smarter, value-adding technology, including new voice-activated software for logistics. Critically, they were licensed in the US to operate as an international freight forwarder, and approved by the Federal Maritime Commission to act as an ocean freight forwarder.

Braid summed it up for everyone: 'We have our USA business Green Card.'

THE NEW CENTURY had brought with it an emphasis on being faster, quicker, cheaper. Australia might have been bleeding red ink but in New Zealand the domestic forwarding market had increased sales by 8 per cent, with operating profits up 18 per cent to NZ$14.9 million. This was despite significant losses at the turn of the century resulting from Comalco's decision to drop Mainfreight in favour of a cheap offer from an international shipping company to move aluminium from the Bluff smelter to the upper North Island. And there was the decision of Firestone in Christchurch to take back warehousing that had previously been done by Mainfreight in a dedicated, purpose-built facility.

The Comalco loss was taken with a shrug. This was the account Neil Graham had landed in the early days, and even as they walked away the aluminium manufacturer was singing Mainfreight's praises. The international shippers were charging nearly NZ$100 a tonne less than rail. No one could match that, and Mainfreight could not blame them for taking it.

The alternative was for Mainfreight to buy a ship, and they did consider the option, for a few seconds. There is a postscript though. Four years later, Comalco was calling. 'The international shipping line is pulling out; can you help?' There would be a two-week tender process before Mainfreight won the business back, then another two weeks for the railways to restore their line to the Invercargill depot, then the first tonne of aluminium was on its way. The relationship continues, although the aluminium business does struggle.

Firestone was quite another matter, and Mainfreight's challenges with this account revealed how dependent the company was on its big customers, and how vulnerable this made it. Mainfreight had made a huge commitment to Firestone in both Christchurch and Auckland, setting up massive warehouses. The thinking had been that once a customer committed to their stock being stored and distributed by a third party, they would not lightly change their decision.

Not so. As Mainfreight was to learn, if the customer chooses to change, for whatever reason, be it strategic or competitive, then change they will. In Firestone's case it was a change of ownership, when the Japanese-based Bridgestone took over the American

Firestone worldwide. Bridgestone had a global mandate not to outsource its warehousing or logistics. Plus, there was the cultural divide. Whatever the Americans had been doing had to be wrong, hence the decision to use Mainfreight was wrong.

Craig Evans, today Mainfreight's general manager of the group supply chain, was running logistics at the time. He remembers it as a turning point that showed the company it had to be more contractual. 'The Firestone loss was the best thing that happened to us. It made us become a true logistics company with a far more sophisticated warehousing operation with pick-and-pack, rather than relying on big bulky customers. We were forced to be more scientific in the inventory we managed; more science, more detail, better at what we did.'

The same would happen in Australia, where Mainfreight set up a so-called logistics service in 2000 on the back of timber-merchant client Carter Holt Harvey. The warehouses were little more than big timber stores, but when the business was lost they switched to high-quality customers with high-quality product who were demanding high-quality service — a genuine logistics service.

They might have had the infrastructure, but performance was anything but perfect. Analysis showed that Mainfreight's logistics and warehousing was performing at 98 per cent. Put another way, there was a 2 per cent error rate on delivery times and general handling. Most companies would accept such a low error rate from their own people, but not from outside suppliers. There is a zero tolerance for error within a warehouse environment, where customers have a sense of ownership that borders on the emotional.

Having put itself in the supply-chain cycle, Mainfreight was faced with customers who demanded nothing less than 100 per cent efficiency. Bruce Plested responded to this increased expectation by reminding everyone that the 2 per cent failure rate was often not the result of weather, mechanical malfunction or computer failure, but, he would thunder, 'The failure of a person to care enough to complete a function as if their life depended on it.'

Lest anyone doubt the seriousness of such a small shortfall, he stressed, 'Think, if we were only 98 per cent efficient at crossing the road. After 49 crossings we would be run over and maybe killed. What if our water contained 2 per cent sewage?'

To understand Mainfreight thinking at the time you just have to listen to the new group managing director, Don Braid, speaking as the company turned 25 in 2003: 'God knows where we're going to end up. We don't know yet. We are quite critical of businesses that have these specific strategic plans of what they're going to be in ten years' time, and how they're going to get there. That said, it is becoming very clear that this will be an international business supplying global freight solutions and services for customers everywhere.

'All the businesses we own are starting to really work together. That's where the future is, that's where the growth is. Our man in Chicago is now thinking not just of sending freight to Auckland or Melbourne, he is thinking into our warehouse and out for distribution to the end user, selling the total supply-chain philosophy, the ability to use every business we have to supply a service to that one customer.

'It's taken a while but now our individual business units think as the group, as total service solution providers. The trick is for each unit to be able to think that way, act as a group, and yet still be selfish enough to go and make money in their own business unit or branch.

'The key to ensuring they have sales in the business is to ensure the entire group has that business. We do that by trusting each other, for that's the key. Trust each other, believe in each other.'

Mainfreight's immediate targets included opening further branches in China and the US; expanding into Europe, South America and elsewhere in Asia; and radically enlarging its Australian operation. Don Braid looked confidently to the future. 'This is a very special company full of very special people and it's not arrogant to think of yourself as being part of something special, something different, something that has a passion. If you have that desire to be different, to be special, then you will be.'

AS MAINFREIGHT APPROACHED its first quarter century in 2003, it was clearly emerging as a leader in global supply-chain management in New Zealand. The company was no longer merely about trucks and transport; it was about providing intelligent end-to-end solutions.

They had bought that 50 per cent shareholding in CaroTrans at a time when the business was losing in excess of US$3 million a year. Now those losses were in check, creditors were being paid on time, and with an improved reputation on the international freight scene, offers of work at volumes that once they could only dream of began to come in. This in turn created additional work for the Australia and New Zealand operations, while the part-owned businesses in

Hong Kong and Shanghai were firming relationships with agents in both Europe and Asia. In short, there was an international spin-off from the success of CaroTrans in the US in a way they had not previously conceived. They could negotiate shipping space and rates on a global basis and build an international business with CaroTrans in the US as the hub, rather than Australia and New Zealand.

CaroTrans had soaked up around US$5 million, which was still considerably less than the US$25 million it was estimated it would have taken to set up their own infrastructure from scratch. A fifth the size of NACA, CaroTrans was showing signs of recovery, actually picking up clients, including some from NACA itself, and both Ziegler and Mainfreight were determined to support their new joint venture into profitable times. Well, that is a slight exaggeration. Mainfreight was determined; Ziegler was hesitant, making them a poor partner in Mainfreight's eyes. For CaroTrans still needed money from its owners to stay afloat. Mainfreight was making regular top-ups, a million here and a million there. Ziegler, however, with its massive trucking, warehousing and forwarding operations throughout Europe, with over 5000 employees, was financially stretched, struggling at home in Europe and not coughing up its share.

Finally Plested and the board tired of waiting. Matters came to a head on 14 January 2003, when Ziegler and its bankers ABN Amro refused to renew a letter of credit. Braid sensed the need to end the relationship. The timing could not have been better.

Plested took on the role of dealmaker with relish. He went to the table with a figure in mind and came away having written a cheque for US$1.845 million — a cool half a million more than he had intended. Plested acknowledges there was criticism of the amount he paid, but argues, 'It was the sort of deal you have to do.

'It was a critical turning point, and if we paid half a million more than we should have who cares. We still ate the same; the share price remained the same. There are times when you just have to get on with it. Too many people don't do deals because of pride. You can't hope to always go back with a smart deal, mostly you pay 10 per cent more than you had hoped, but it makes no difference. The seller always thinks he was too soft.'

CaroTrans would become the cornerstone of the Mainfreight International business. Now they could set about aggressively targeting new business without the inhibitions of their former partner when it came to Europe.

By October 2004, eighteen months after the takeover, John Hepworth, with the 9/11 lessons in his bag, was heading back to Melbourne to head up the group's international divisions. Greg Howard, who had been inherited with the initial purchase, replaced Hepworth as leader in New Jersey after spending two years in New Zealand, at his own request, for what was described as an injection of 'blue blood'. Howard described it as a 'prisoner exchange'. They would meet up again in 2008 when Hepworth returned to the States, this time to Los Angeles, to run Mainfreight US.

THE ZIEGLER EXIT behind it, CaroTrans might still have had problems, but there was a lot to be happy about. The company was exporting to more than 230 destinations, it had opened an office in Cleveland, and it was soon making over US$1 million a year from one of the largest manufacturing areas in the US. This fitted nicely into its sales strategy of developing a strong import programme from Asia. They were now focused on the long-term objective of creating a truly global company and recognised the critical importance of the Asia/US trade links.

The growing threat posed by CaroTrans was not lost on Owen Glenn's NACA. Following the terrible events of 11 September 2001, airlines and shipping companies had imposed surcharges because of increased insurance premiums. Owen Glenn went after CaroTrans customers, offering to waive the surcharge if they switched to his company. It was his way of saying, 'Don't think you can mess with me.'

Greg Howard had admitted to struggling with the enormity of it all and, to his credit, had said he needed to be refreshed. Hence the request for a transfer to New Zealand, where he would revitalise the international business between 2002 and 2004. Where Howard had been strong on detail, Hepworth was the motivator and culture fanatic. It was he who brought the passion that would within a couple of years see CaroTrans turning a profit.

Plested was quick to warn Hepworth, 'When you turn round a bad business and come into profit you often slump as you start patting yourself on the back and stop focusing.' Braid would be less subtle, 'That's just the start; we expect much more.'

It was a timely warning as NACA became increasingly aggressive, absorbing the insurance surcharges and going after CaroTrans customers. It was a strategy that cost CaroTrans US$850,000 a year as they, too, were forced to drop fuel surcharges or face losing all their business. Plested and Braid urged their US team to go into attack mode. The message was simple enough. Rather than lowering their own prices they should go after Glenn's customers, forcing him to pull his salespeople out of the market to defend his own position.

The Plested message was clear: 'Report back every night who you have seen, what you quoted, and then follow up. Know a week ahead who you will be calling on next Monday, Tuesday and Wednesday, otherwise those big bastards will get you.'

The scuffle cost Mainfreight, but NACA would lose too, US$4 million a year by Mainfreight's estimation. And here was the lesson. Freight forwarding is a people business. When the people they had been dealing with left, customers felt abandoned and began looking round for someone who would care for them and their freight. They wanted familiar faces — faces like NACA's Michael Forkenbrock.

In 2004 Hepworth hired Forkenbrock as a salesman, at Howard's urging. It was an inspired choice for which Hepworth and Mainfreight have forever been grateful. Plested quickly identified the salesman as a gung-ho entrepreneur, and told Hepworth, 'Let him run wild and free, just give him an occasional yank.' NACA customers, who recognised a familar face, fell into CaroTrans' lap. Owen Glenn would later tell Plested and Braid that he wanted to buy their business just so he could fire the salesman.

Customers were looking at a good business backed by a publicly listed company. Had Glenn made his surcharge attack two years earlier, when CaroTrans was truly struggling, it might have been a very different story. Even so, CaroTrans was still having trouble paying its bills. One memorable night a call came from MSC, the Mediterranean Shipping Company — the world's largest shipping line — with a blunt warning: deposit US$250,000 into their account immediately or they would effectively shut CaroTrans down.

When Mainfreight bought out Ziegler they had a bank overdraft of US$3.5 million. Not anymore. Hepworth phoned Plested to ask that he send more money. 'I have no more money to give you,' Plested replied. 'You need to show me you are an entrepreneurial manager. I have just put NZ$4 million of my own money into Mainfreight New Zealand because K&S is taking so much. I repeat, I have no more money to pay you.'

Hepworth was shocked to the core. 'Bruce, I have people at my front door asking for money and I don't even know if I can pay the salaries this week.'

Plested hung up. From that moment CaroTrans dug deep. Hepworth never missed a salary payment for the team as he started a rebuild programme that took nine months. He had to delay payments to suppliers, so customers who were slow to pay found their freight being put on hold. In the process the genial Hepworth discovered that as he became aggressive people started paying faster and faster. And then he discovered the Yellow Roadway Corporation, courtesy of Forkenbrock. Quite simply, Yellow operated a transport management system that was a true lifesaver.

CaroTrans used hundreds of truckers to deliver freight all over America. The bills were pouring in, the small finance team could not cope, and there was not the cash to pay the truckers, who were getting more than a little annoyed. There was a real threat that CaroTrans would be blacklisted by the very people who made their business tick. Yellow was in the business of paying truckers. They managed all the invoices and, for a cut of the margin, made sure everyone was paid. Most important of all, the truckers of America trusted Yellow. Yellow changed everything, and to this day Hepworth considers the Plested call one of the absolute turning points in his career. It was certainly a turning point for CaroTrans.

At the same time Braid was pushing for CaroTrans branches to pack freight into containers in their home cities and hand over to shipping companies at that point. This dispensed with the cost of moving that freight across the US to a port such as Los Angeles, to be loaded into a container there before being sent to New Zealand or wherever in the world. Now the shipping lines were bearing the cost of getting the loaded containers to port. Loading direct containers eliminated considerable cost, improved margins, and helped sales as customers had the confidence of knowing their freight was being loaded into a container out of their home city. It was a strategy that definitely beefed up CaroTrans.

The culture was changing, too. In the early days Mainfreight had been careful not to impose its thinking on its new American team, but slowly they began to adapt. The New Jersey and Charleston branches threw out answering machines and began taking each other's phone calls, to be greeted with compliments from customers. The Los Angeles branch no longer had a time clock for people to record when they arrived and left. The last two offices, Houston and Charleston, were going open plan.

# KINDLY
# YOUR EG
# THE DOO

Chapter
15

LEAVE
TO AT
R

Bruce Plested and Don Braid were determined that the unique Mainfreight culture would not be jeopardised or diluted by growth. They knew it was people who made the difference. Their competitors now had clean trucks and polite drivers and smart IT systems and even warehouses. What they did not have was the Mainfreight attitude. What had begun as a natural way to motivate the team was now regarded as a competitive advantage, a business strategy to be improved upon at every opportunity.

If they needed further encouragement it came in 2005 when they happened upon *Good to Great*, the inspirational book by Jim Collins, a specialist in management strategy. Collins' messages were pure Mainfreight, and the book was adopted as a bible. Its critical message was 'forget your ego' — the company comes first.

From now on the emphasis would be on encouraging not merely debate, but *fierce* debate, with everyone then rallying round and supporting the final decision. There could be no room for personal agendas, only what was good for the company, the team. It was the team, always the team, Braid and Plested emphasised over and over. Never seeking to blame, but always searching for understanding so that they all emerged wiser from an experience.

There were but three questions: What are you best at? What delivers the best return? What are you passionate about? Then, combine all three and just do it.

Mainfreight was seeking to adopt what Collins refers to as 'Level 5' management: lack of ego combined with a passionate, ferocious, unwavering resolve to achieve success for the company. Such managers demand lack of bureaucracy, consistency, culture, people with a farmer work ethic, the right people in management positions, simple structure and — one more time — lack of bureaucracy!

Hearing Braid and Plested talking of a lack of ego can elicit the odd wry smile. Neither man is exactly consumed by self-doubt. But their uniform response is that ego is permissible when it is used

The *Maintrak* computer system in action.

for the good of the company, not the individual. This means the freedom to talk and debate vigorously.

'Understanding ego is the most important thing we have learned in the last ten years,' Plested says. 'If people are playing for themselves we can't have them in the team. That simple.

'When people say "I", we are on instant alert. It has to be "We want", not "I want".'

This was everything Don Rowlands had been preaching, with a modern twist. They were to hire only the smartest and the best, take responsibility when anything went wrong and give credit to others when it went well. And make sure everyone in the company understands that each and every one of them has been taken on board because of a genuine belief they have the potential to one day rise to the very top. Mainfreight was not in the business of hiring people who came to work to be told what to do. They wanted the 'right' people, not just people.

There might have been doubters in the marketplace, and even on the board, but Plested and Braid sensed they had a tiger by the tail. They were going global and nothing would stop them. They had just two questions: Where is the margin? And where are the people who can make it all happen?

Braid was determined that Mainfreight would tick all the boxes. He knew that all their competitors had the technology and they had the infrastructure, but he was equally sure they did not have the culture — they did not have the Mainfreight people.

DON BRAID WAS also determined to follow the Mainfreight mantra of not allowing technology to override culture — to resist at all costs the danger of becoming technology obsessed. While there would be a cautious 'Yes' to using carefully selected technologies, there would be an emphatic 'No' to climbing on the technology bandwagon.

Braid puts it this way: 'I think the lesson is, don't dumb down the workforce. Technology makes us efficient, but we want everyone thinking about what they are doing and what decisions have to be made. We want people making decisions as close to the customer as possible.'

There can be little argument that in the early days Mainfreight led the way with its information technology. Today, though, IT solutions are standard; everyone uses automatic scanners to register collection and delivery, and voice-activated hand-held devices to ensure the correct item is picked and packed from the shelves of warehouses, wherever they may be in the world. Everyone has, and expects to have, access to information 24/7. Even at the turn of the century, if the systems went down the company could survive for a day or two. Five years later, such was their dependence on an ever more complex IT system, they could survive no more than three or four hours without a lasting snarl-up that might reach from New Zealand through Australia to Asia, the US and Europe.

Today the IT department has specialist niche areas requiring skills that others in the overall group have no idea about. Like the customers, they just expect everything to work perfectly, and never question how. So much is taken for granted. There's so much information, so much technology, but do people really need to know where their parcel is at any given nanosecond?

The answer to that comes from IT manager Anthony Barrett: 'No, they don't need it, but they have been conditioned to expect this sort of service, and will ask what sort of tracking we provide and how accurate it is and how often we provide status reports, even though no one in their company is checking them.

'What matters is that we tell them when there is a problem and what we are doing about it. Everything is just peace of mind really. The bottom line is, customers just want to know it will be picked up, cared for and delivered correctly and on time.'

Not so long ago, in some companies, when a parcel had to be delivered a receptionist would simply call her favourite courier company — her favourite being the one that looked after her with gifts and even, if her company was big enough, the occasional holiday. If people complained because parcels were not being delivered efficiently or something went wrong, she would call another courier company and it started all over again.

Today, companies have logistics divisions, and the person in charge there is the one who will be yelled at if no advance warning is given of a problem. As Kevin Drinkwater says, 'We are about providing information to customers that will make them more efficient and effective on a daily basis.'

The Mainfreight systems had to become proactive, alerting customers ahead of time to any change in their profile — quite simply, giving them the information they needed to store and move the minimum amount of freight. Or to put it another way, the information to ensure they were efficient, made money and kept their costs down. What customers wouldn't thank you for that?

For years Drinkwater had been preaching, 'Information about freight is almost as important as delivering freight.' Plested hated it; to him, Mainfreight's competitive advantage was that they got the freight there on time and in one piece. But even Plested had to concede that where once the delivery of freight was very much a lottery, now everyone was getting it there pretty much on time. Information was becoming critical; customers needed to be forewarned of what was happening down the supply chain so they could implement just-in-case strategies if there was a problem. Yes, they required the confidence of regular on-time deliveries, but if their forwarder kept them fully informed it allowed much tighter stock control and reduced costs.

During the global recession, customers who had left in search of cheaper prices came back for just such a service, in what is known as 'flight to quality'. Big, medium and even small customers came back because they needed reliability and predictability — predictability being the operative word, as customers showed less and less interest in tracking their freight from their office computers or mobile devices. There was a growing awareness that Mainfreight did that for them, and would sound the alarm if any action was required.

There were huge expectations on the part of customers the world over, and with it came pressure from Drinkwater to upgrade the system constantly. He saw this part of the service as a distinct competitive advantage, and complained bitterly at the small amount of time devoted to Mainfreight's IT capability during sales pitches. Braid would counter that the company's IT department was bigger than IBM, and was dismissive of reports that similar companies spent 3 to 4 per cent of revenue on IT while Mainfreight was spending just 1.8 per cent. Ernst & Young was asked for an opinion, and reported back that in the US they would expect a company of similar size to have 99 people running its IT team, with a further 109 in Europe. Mainfreight had a total of 35 people. The advice was: 'You are under-investing.' Braid was again dismissive, retaining the eighteen IT people the company had in New Zealand until revenue doubled, when the number was allowed to increase to 20.

Braid's reaction reflects a deeply rooted and enduring fear that IT can get in the way of the culture. An example of this is his concern over letting the raters — who set the price for collecting,

Mainfreight's people are its greatest strength.

storing and delivering a customer's freight — punch the relevant information into a computer and allow the machine to determine the price. Mainfreight operates NZ$1 million worth of software, but even so Braid is emphatic: 'Too many bells and whistles can stuff the system. Rating is about quoting. Quoting is about sales, about understanding schedule, margin and our business. You can't have a machine in a back room do that.

'A computer will only do what it is told and won't pick up mistakes, while a good rater will pick up those things. And these quite complicated areas where we earn our money are great training grounds. A sales rep should work there before going on the road, to learn what a schedule is and how to rate a consignment note and what to charge a customer. Skills that are then taken out onto the road and then applied to running a branch.

'There is a place for technology to make you efficient, but not to dumb the business down, or dumb your people down.'


AS MAINFREIGHT SURGED ahead with its Australian and US endeavours, at home the rail issue had been bubbling away. Rumours continued that Toll, firmly entrenched as Australia's largest general freight carrier, was set to establish itself in the New Zealand domestic market, either as a road transport operator or, possibly, even as an owner of rail. Toll and Mainfreight had been very close in the mid-1990s when Toll was acquiring Brambles. Its people had visited New Zealand for a tour of Mainfreight, with a view to buying its computer systems. They loved what they saw, then went away and came up with a cheaper option. When they approached the software suppliers directly, Mainfreight was tipped off, stopped the move in its tracks, and the relationship soured.

Mainfreight had further reason to be concerned. The privatised Tranz Rail was diverting rail freight to its own trucking operation, and rail freight volumes gradually fell away. As a result of this extraordinary diversification, by 2003 the Tranz Rail share price dropped to its lowest levels ever, with the company accused of deliberately running down some lines through lack of maintenance. The government was then rumoured to be considering various schemes for bailing it out and regaining control of the critical infrastructure. They were even citing one of their reasons as providing a 'level playing field' for freight movement.

Even as this was happening, unbelievably, Tranz Rail management were actively looking for partners and thought Mainfreight might actually be interested. The first overture had come from Tranz Rail boss Michael Beard, who approached Plested about a 'friendly takeover' of Mainfreight. Plested refused, making it clear that any such deal had no place in his 100-year plan for the company. A war of words broke out. Plested criticised Tranz Rail publicly for running down its network in favour of road, while Beard accused road transport firms of lacking the commercial focus of rail and shipping.

Bruce Plested and Don Braid were asking publicly why a rail company wanted to run so many road vehicles and required an international freight forwarding business. And why were they closing rail lines between towns and cities that had manufacturing industries dependent on a rail infrastructure for their very global competitiveness and survival? They accused Tranz Rail of destroying a valuable asset with unrealistic business strategies, in direct contrast to Mainfreight's own ambition to provide customers with a highly competitive, quality-driven, long-term transport network — a network that was now under threat.

Then came another approach, this time from a group of Tranz Rail's senior people, bent on their own management buy-out and seeking a partner. Plested ignored their overtures. Not that he was uninterested in rail; far from it.

Mainfreight knew the importance of rail as a national asset but saw the need to compete with the rail company aggressively, with the aim of lowering the shareholders' expectations of its worth.

By the same token, it was accepted that any association with Tranz Rail would involve inheriting clients who were there for cheap rates and would not appreciate Mainfreight putting up prices with the justification of better service. Plus, there was the small matter of the Commerce Commission and any concerns it might harbour about such a perceived monopoly.

All the while Tranz Rail continued its slide into mediocrity. This was an operation so woeful that it would win the Roger Award — an award established by the anti-foreign-investment campaigners CAFCA, for worst transnational corporation operating in New Zealand — on no fewer than three occasions.

Like Plested, Don Braid was anything but anti-rail, arguing constantly, 'Mainfreight is not a trucking company; we are a logistics company; we are a multi-modal user; we will use whatever form of transport suits our needs and the needs of our customers. And in this country rail is the most logical means of transport. We would put more on rail if we possibly could.'

Mainfreight also needed the coastal shipping service to survive, to provide competition for rail and keep them both honest. New Zealand's coastal shipping services were not protected from competition by visiting foreign vessels plying for trade while in New Zealand waters. Such protection is offered by a system known as cabotage, which is enforced the world over — but not in New Zealand — in recognition of the fact that giant ocean-going cargo ships could pick off the most profitable aspects of local trade while in their waters, at highly reduced rates, just to cover costs. (Witness how the aluminium business had been taken off Mainfreight by international shippers.) Domestic coastal shipping could be left with the crumbs and forced out of business. Braid argued that this lack of protection jeopardised the competitiveness and viability of the entire domestic transport structure.

By early 2004 the seriousness of the Tranz Rail situation was beginning to dawn on the Labour government, which began buying back the critical national asset. Mainfreight came up with a proposal to run the struggling operation for five years, longer if necessary, and then return it in proper running order to the government, which might then have arranged a full public float. Don Braid's intention was to develop a working relationship between Tranz Rail, the shipping companies and the ports, something that had proved impossible to that point. Bruce Plested even had a plan to shake hands with every Tranz Rail employee to let them know they were valued and get them to care about the freight they were responsible for. This was to be a fully integrated rail system that also had a determined focus on the tourism business.

All seemed to be going well, with the finance minister, Dr Michael Cullen, making soothing noises about the Mainfreight approach. Then, in July 2004, without warning, he dropped the government's bid for a controlling stake, stepping aside to allow Toll to buy just under 90 per cent of the operation for NZ$231 million. The government agreed to plough in a further NZ$200 million for track upgrades. The deal, in which the rail operation was renamed Toll New Zealand, gave the Australian company a monopoly of rail, with the added advantage of having its own freight forwarding business.

Mainfreight now had a major freight competitor controlling the rail service while also competing on the road — a competitor who had been given 'free rent' on rail land and facilities for six years. The government did eventually buy the operation back from Toll in 2008, for NZ$690 million, and renamed it KiwiRail. Fortunately they had the wit not to buy Toll's road transport business, which would effectively have seen Mainfreight in competition with the state.

# OWENS –
# THE HOS
# TAKEOVE

TILE

R

A s if the rail debacle wasn't enough of a challenge, in the midst of all that Don Braid was dealing with a takeover that would transform Mainfreight.

In early 2003 Braid went to visit Bruce Plested, who was now housed in a separate office in Auckland's Great South Road. Coming out of the office was high-profile director Norman Geary, a past chairman of Air New Zealand, Television New Zealand and the Tourism Board. At the time he was a director of the National Bank and the giant appliance manufacturer Fisher & Paykel. Critically, he was also chairman of Owens Group, Mainfreight's largest competitor and listed on the New Zealand stock exchange.

'What did he want?' Braid asked Plested as he sat down in his office.

'He just suggested a merger of our two companies. A merger they would control.'

Braid did not need to ask what the response had been. Plested would have been too polite to deliver Braid's two-word dismissal, but it was obvious from the look on Geary's face that the message had been blunt enough. The good news was that they now knew what they had long suspected — Owens was in trouble.

The Owens Group consisted of a New Zealand domestic freight forwarding company that included a tanker fleet; an Australian transport operation that was mainly a wharf cartage operation in Sydney and Brisbane; a logistics warehousing operation in both New Zealand and Australia; international freight forwarding companies with offices throughout New Zealand, Australia and the Pacific Islands and an office in England; refrigerated services (Cooltainers and CoolAir) that included a refrigerated seafreight container fleet operating the Tasman and South Pacific trade lanes; a container maintenance division; two shipping agencies (Seatrans and McArthur Shipping) for shipping lines without physical representation in New Zealand or Australia; and the equipment hire business Hirepool, of which Owens owned 25 per cent.

Owens looked terrific on paper, but it was little more than an equipment hire business with a decidedly unprofitable transport operation. This would be discovered later, but for the moment Mainfreight could glean little; full due diligence of the publicly listed company was not possible.

They knew something of Bob Owens, though. He had been born in Manchester, England, and went to sea when he was sixteen, served in the Royal Navy during the second World War before emigrating to New Zealand, and in 1953 started a shipping agency that was the foundation of the Owens Group. It was based at the port of Tauranga, a town where Owens served as mayor for three terms, and where he also became chairman and longest-serving member of the Bay of Plenty Harbour Board.

His business was initially built on shipping logs to Japan, then in 1975 the Owens Group bought the transport operator Mogal, which had domestic freight forwarding services and had pioneered the trans-Tasman trade. A decade later came a much bigger takeover with the purchase of the Brambles freight company, New Zealand Freighters. Further growth and acquisition followed, including the takeover of Universal Transport and McArthur Shipping in Australia, the basis for the company's Australian expansion. Owens had retired in 1995, and died four years later.

At first glance it seemed a highly complementary business to Mainfreight, and one that could add real value to the group as it grew, providing more logistics and supply-chain services around the world. They were looking at an international business that would merge seamlessly into Mainfreight; a passable airfreight perishable business; and Owens Transport in New Zealand. But what was it worth?

In the winter of 2003, Plested and Braid were watching rugby at Auckland's Eden Park with Tim Preston, the managing director of ASB Securities, who mentioned he had private clients who might be interested in selling their shares in Owens. His clients were Robyn and Wendy Owens, daughters of the founder, who held 11 per cent of the shares between them — shares that were languishing at 72 cents. The two women were concerned enough to attend an Owens board meeting and enquire what the learned gentlemen thought the shares might sensibly be worth.

'Oh, at least a dollar.'

'Fine, we'll take a dollar. Who will buy our shares?'

Not one director put his hand up.

Preston advised that Owens might be worth a look; it was considered to be a company that had lost its way, spent a lot of money on a computer business, a security company, even the fashion house Suzanne Grae.

'Hell, at the right price you could buy it, sell off the non-performing bits and get the company for next to nothing.'

If only life were that simple.

First Mainfreight bought the daughters' shares, then they bought more on the open market, to the point where they had 15 per cent, requiring a public declaration of their intention. This was now effectively a hostile takeover. They could not pry into the company's deepest secrets, so they were standing in the marketplace without really knowing what they were buying.

It was time to make a call on Owens. They thought they were going to a freight company, but found themselves at a building with a hundred cars outside and not a truck in sight. They climbed a set of marble stairs to plush corporate offices where they explained their intentions, promised to be back, and left.

AMP, the wealth management company, held 12 per cent of the shares, and gave an assurance they would sell to Mainfreight. There was no contract, since under their company protocol AMP could not do that until the deal was about to close. But there was a verbal assurance and there was a handshake — a cast-iron deal in Mainfreight's world. On the strength of the deal they went to the open market, buying Owens' shares in earnest.

What Mainfreight had not reckoned on was how mischievous Toll might be. The night before the deal should have closed, with Mainfreight within sight of holding 90 per cent of the shares, which meant they would be able to compulsorily purchase the remainder, Toll struck. They had been sitting round their board table, so the story goes, having a few beers, when a thought occurred. A hurried phone call to AMP followed, with an offer of 5 cents a share more than Mainfreight was offering. Done deal. For a comparatively small investment of NZ$7.7 million Toll had bought 12 per cent of Owens and stalled the expansion plans of a significant competitor. Drinks all round.

Mainfreight was faced with taking an 80 per cent holding in what would have to remain a public company complete with outside directors. Should they or shouldn't they? Plested said 'Yes' to a deal done on 1 November 2003, and Braid took care of the rest.

When the dust finally settled Mainfreight had paid NZ$63.5 million for Owens, with Hirepool valued at NZ$4.25 million. They would eventually offload Hirepool for close to half the entire purchase price. Indeed, they would divest themselves of a range of Owens business interests for a total of NZ$67 million. They would come out of the deal NZ$3.5 million in the black. Ahead, though, lay a protracted negotiation with Toll.

The day Mainfreight assumed control with their 80 per cent majority, the full board was summoned to a special meeting to be held at the Owens International offices. Within twenty minutes all but two of the Owens directors were dismissed. A day later the CEO and most of his senior managers were clearing their desks.

Carl Howard-Smith admits to having been slightly taken aback by the speed with which Braid moved. The fact was, Braid had a plan. He knew what he was going to keep and what he was going to sell.

Then came a call from Mark Rowsthorn, a Toll director. Toll wanted a seat on the Owens board. Braid took the call and uttered his standard two-word response to any request he deemed unacceptable to Mainfreight.

'You can't say that to me.'

'I just did. We don't want you on the board.'

The next day the *Business Herald* called, wanting to know what Braid had said to Toll. Braid told them and they published it, all two words, albeit with judiciously placed asterisks.

Braid was incredulous. Toll was a major competitor. Why on earth would Mainfreight want them on their board, privy to all their secrets and strategies?

Not only would there be no seat at the board table, but Owens would be paying no dividends either. Toll had a 12 per cent stake in a company they had no say in and that paid no return. It was only a question of when, not if, they sold their shares.

Had they been at the table, Toll would have heard Plested's brutal assessment of Owens. In his view it was a company without quality leadership, with no succession plan, and with customers drifting away from a rudderless concern that was diversifying itself out of business.

The Toll situation meant a full takeover was delayed, and frustrated Mainfreight's wish to merge the businesses as quickly as

TOP — Tim Williams has
developed Mainfreight's
accounting systems to be
simple and practical.
LEFT — Bryan Curtis led
the turnaround at Owens.

possible. Plested, who had encountered many poorly run companies, says he had seen nothing as bad as Owens. He was appalled to find inflated salaries, and directors who were eligible for substantial exit packages; some of them chose not to exercise that right but others did. The Mainfreight view was that the directors had not been close enough to the business to assist the company through difficult times. Payment seemed unwarranted. There were directors with no transport experience, and one who was getting extra fees for making the Australian business successful when it was the least profitable part of the group. Another was entitled to NZ$120,000 on leaving — three times his annual fee. Initially Mainfreight refused to pay: 'Sue us, and see what happens to your reputation then.' Undeterred, the director publicly challenged the new owner in an airport business-class lounge. The reply was pure Braid.

There would be payments, and perhaps Mainfreight paid more than it should have, but in the end it was something they needed off their plate. Plested and Braid decided to take the loss and move on.

Owens was centralised, with a massive shared services division for IT, accounting and administration, whereas Mainfreight was largely decentralised and handled such matters on a branch basis, in the belief that head office could not be expected to understand the intricacies of individual branches. In New Zealand there were, and still are, just three people working for other countries: Don Braid, Tim Williams and Kevin Drinkwater. And if they could make that centralised team smaller they would.

There was no such logic at Owens, which had a complex structure of 48 different companies around New Zealand and Australia. Owens also had a complex legal structure, mainly for tax reasons, while Williams had learned not to go for short-term tax gains. The reasoning is simple. You end up with financial advisors driving the structure of the business purely for tax reasons, not commercial reasons. Williams' view is that 'sooner or later the tax guys will catch up with you'.

Williams is a great believer in keeping everything simple. He does not do currency hedging, on the premise that if you overcomplicate a business the board will not have a clue how it is structured. If they buy a business in Europe he borrows in Europe, so creating a natural hedge. 'If I have an asset and a liability in euros then they move the same. It's not rocket science. You can't get everything perfect, but do nothing that's going to bite you in the arse basically.'

He learned the approach from Plested, and now argues, 'If the economy is going well, interest rates are going to be higher as governments try to dampen down inflation but we will be earning more money as we will be going well and can afford to pay that higher interest rate. Whereas, when things are tough you have very low interest rates and we can afford to pay those.'

After qualifying as an accountant, Tim Williams had spent three years working for the Inland Revenue Department before joining Daily Freightways in 1984, rising through the group, then stepping away for a two-year stint at the security services division Armourguard before returning to help ready Daily Freightways for eventual sale in 1994. He had another job lined up but was offered financial control of Daily Freight and Chemcouriers, and a year later became chief financial officer of Mainfreight itself.

As for his reputation as the only person entitled to say 'No' to Braid and Plested, Williams laughs that off. 'I don't say "No" to stop them doing what they are doing but to see if there's a smarter way of reaching our goal. To encourage discussion.'

The big issue with Owens, however, wasn't its complexity; it was Toll, named 'the scorpions' by Mainfreight in a reference to the story in which a scorpion persuades a frog to give it a ride across a flooding river, with endless assurances, only to go back on its word and deliver a fatal sting to the trusting frog. Mainfreight trucks were soon bearing the legend *Scorpion Hunters*.


IT WAS TIME to put the top guns in charge of the new acquisition. Bryan Curtis, who had returned from Australia and had been running New Zealand Daily Freight, was now given the task of turning round the Owens transport operation. It would eventually be run as a separate brand with branches in Auckland, Wellington and Christchurch. Curtis was seen as a leading revenue generator with an ability to inspire the team and deal with any union hiccups. He was also customer-friendly, which would be needed in the coming months, as there were plans to increase rates quite significantly.

But first there was the culture to deal with. Owens' Auckland head office had that marble staircase, while its main depot was the 'dingiest, darkest terminal' Curtis had ever seen in his life. He set about painting the place inside and out, laid carpet where it had never been seen before, installed skylights, brought in new furniture, knocked down the office walls, and went from losing money to being profitable. Curtis managed an extraordinary 211 per cent turnaround in profit from the previous year when they were losing NZ$50,000 a week, achieved by magnificent teamwork and dedication, with Curtis telling customers, 'We ain't the cheapest but we have the best service.'

The logistics divisions in both New Zealand and Australia were totally merged with the Mainfreight operations and came under the wing of Craig Evans, who lived and breathed the business.

Greg Howard, on his secondment to New Zealand from CaroTrans in the US for that injection of blue blood, oversaw the merger of Owens International into Mainfreight International. And Rodd Morgan, as the newly appointed head of Mainfreight Distribution in Australia, had responsibility for all that country's domestic operations. Morgan's appointment had come from the earlier realisation that promotion from within was fine in principle but there were times when exceptions were essential. Australians, it just had to be said, were different.

Plested had been pushing for yet another Kiwi to be given the task, but Braid insisted: 'Trying to do deals in Aussie, every which way you looked, if you were a Kiwi they were going to dork you, they are out to exploit you all the time. They are a tough, tough business race. Nothing wrong with that, in fact we admire the way they do business, you just have to be as good as them and the Rodd Morgans of this world are just like that so they can get on with it.'

The Morgan appointment had happened by accident. He had been a referee for a Toll manager who had applied for a job at Mainfreight, got it, and had then been talked out of accepting it by his current employer. Six weeks later Braid was on the phone to Morgan, then Victorian sales manager for McPhee Transport in Melbourne. Morgan was offered the job and accepted on the spot in what was a leap of faith for both men.

Morgan knew nothing about the Mainfreight operation — did not ask, did not care — he was just excited at the challenge it presented. Little did he know what a challenge it would be. On his first day, he checked the books and called Braid: 'Is this a mistake?' Well, it was 1 April 2003.

There was no hint of humour in the reply: 'No.'

Morgan was looking at a loss for the week of A$190,000, and staring down an eventual loss for that first year of A$4.8 million.

Dunphy and Knuth had improved matters but there was still much to be done. He would later describe his mood as 'mildly bemused and a little bit concerned'. He quickly established that they were chasing business by promising service that did not exist, and set about finding customers he had a hope of delivering value to rather than creating bad blood through lack of capability.

With the purchase deal done, Braid toured the Owens operations in Australia preaching the message of keeping feet firmly planted on the ground, managing each branch as a small business with a focus on quality and margin control, and never believing more is better without the profit that comes from being quality focused, efficient and cost conscious. If ever there was a man fully prepared for the Braid message it was Greg Giarratana, Mainfreight's Melbourne-based national development manager. He had joined Owens CoolAir on 18 August 2003, a date that remains etched in his memory. His friends all laughed, 'Don't you know they are being taken over?' Despite outright denials, that proved to be the case within a matter of months.

Giarratana, an industry veteran, had been in forwarding since the mid-seventies and knew a joke company when he saw one. He walked into a warehouse devoid of freight and was promptly hit on the head by a cricket ball. This was 10.30 in the morning and they were playing cricket.

'What the hell do you think you're doing?'

'Nothing else to do.'

A senior Owens executive he met didn't even know what CoolAir did, let alone that it was number one in New Zealand for handling perishables. There was no process, and the accounting system was run from Auckland. Giarratana was appalled. 'It was a bloody mess. I would ask why some of the people were even employed and be told they were someone's relative. I had been sold a lemon.'

Then Mainfreight arrived in the shape of Don Braid.

'Where's all the freight?'

'There isn't any.'

'Can you fix it?'

'Yes.'

'Great.'

And with that Braid left, not to be seen again for six months, by which time it was well and truly fixed.

Giarratana quickly grasped the Mainfreight approach to running

Greg Giarratana: precise engineering receives appropriately precise handling.

a big business. Don't. The principle was simply that each branch should operate as an independent unit. Oh, and hire people smarter than you are; and consider the three pillars non-negotiable; and never forget that the Mainfreight culture is your competitive advantage.

Braid is a believer in management by walking about. 'The more you walk around the more you learn about your business. When you are on the floor with people they can't help but tell you what is going on. You don't get that in the corporate office. I don't understand what stops management doing this; it's the corporate bullshit thing. "I've got an office. I have a desk. I am too busy."

'The greater the promotion, the more you have to immerse yourself in the business; the more it has to become part of your daily life. Frankly, people who don't understand the logic of getting around more when they are at the top just shouldn't be there. They shouldn't want to employ or surround themselves with sycophants. That's when you have real trouble.'

Braid's management approach is reflected in his attitude toward ties, which follows the Don Rowlands path: 'I used to be a fan of the tie, an office, a car park, but that just divides us from the others. If you isolate yourself, you may as well sit in that office with your tie and hang yourself with it.'

Giarratana was certainly not about to do that. What he did do was go looking for niche products. Australia is an island that imports and exports horticultural products. Flowers, whether they are entering or leaving the country, need to be fumigated. Mainfreight was the first licensed fumigator, a one-stop shop for forwarding, customs clearance and fumigating. Others would follow but never overtake Mainfreight's lead position.

Giarratana believes he was given a transfusion of Mainfreight blue blood, and now makes a point of inviting prospective customers to visit so they can experience it too. This was a man who was used to having his own office and a personal assistant or two, who now has the three pillars displayed on the wall of his open-plan area. He is always delighted when clients read them and ask incredulously, 'Is that true, is that what you do?'

Always the same reply: 'Look around you.'

MICHAEL LOFARO IS another who has totally absorbed the Mainfreight culture. Lofaro had taken over as national manager in

Australia for Mainfreight International when John Hepworth moved to the US to run CaroTrans. Later still, in 2007, Lofaro would move to Hong Kong as general manager of the Asian operation.

At the time of the Owens takeover he was based in Sydney. He, Rodd Morgan and Mick Turnbull, the manager of LEP Australia, were summoned to a meeting at the Owens headquarters overlooking Botany Bay. Don Braid had got there first and sacked the existing senior management, then he divvied up the business between the three Mainfreight men. Braid explained that while he sensed there was a great team and a sound customer base, there was no direction and certainly no leadership. It was a black hole.

Lofaro spoke for them all: 'What do you want us to do?'

'Fix it,' said Braid, then he left for the airport — no point in hanging around.

'It's Mainfreight's style,' Braid explains. 'It's the way we feel about giving responsibility to people. Here's the job, get on and do it.

'We had met for a morning prior to the takeover and outlined what the business was, what we were going to keep, what we were going to sell off, how we expected it to be run and who would have the responsibility. There were no surprises. My turning up was just a tick in the box to get under way.'

Rodd Morgan calculated, correctly, that they would make losses of some A$30 million before things began to break even, so the focus was on customers with high-value product and an express need to move it quickly around the country, while also understanding the value of technology. These would be small to medium customers rather than the large ones who were already using Toll or Linfox, another giant supply-chain provider, at very competitive prices.

There was a real determination to ensure first-rate service and delivery on time, every time. There was a small problem, though. While everyone talks about clients who appreciate quality and are prepared to pay for it, they are not that thick on the ground. The trick was to find clients from whom they could make a reasonable margin, have them so delighted by the service that they stayed, and then later, maybe, address the small matter of renegotiating the price.

Mainfreight quickly sold anything it did not need from the Owens acquisition, anything it did not understand, and anything that didn't fit its jigsaw, including the Container Services Division, Cooltainer Rural Transport Services and the shipping agencies. They retained Owens Transport and Owens International in

New Zealand. CoolAir and the Pacific Island freight forwarding operations of Pan Orient, based in Brisbane, Noumea and Papua New Guinea, would later be absorbed by LEP, a move that would add enormous value to the division and make possible much of the Mainfreight acquisition programme in the future.

The Australian and New Zealand international operations, including Owens, were merged to create a larger, more profitable business with improved market share over a number of international trade lanes, particularly the trans-Tasman trade. There were painful times ahead, but within five years Mainfreight's Australian business would consist of three main activities: International, with a full array of importing and exporting freight services across the world; Logistics, managing the products of over 100 customers in eight warehouses across the country; and Transport, which included Chemcouriers (specialising in hazardous goods), FTL (full loads), Metro (local), and Owens Transport, focusing on carting shipping containers from the wharf to customers and back.

Morgan was fast coming to terms with the Mainfreight culture, which he combined with a healthy dose of Australian cynicism. 'It is the customers who decide, and we had to get people who understood it was their performance that determined their careers and our success. There are plenty of companies that have canteens and promote from within and profit share and all that bloody stuff. It is all very well having it written down on a piece of paper but it is doing it and living it that matters, and we are.

'That's what I say to people who want to come and work here — and analysts or investors and customers for that matter — if you are hooked up with an organisation that genuinely believes these things then you are pretty much on the right horse.'

Soon Morgan would have a Melbourne-based transport training facility to ensure every team member grasped the Mainfreight history, culture and quality expectations. It was imperative to inject quality thinking and change the balance back to the key people who deal with customers and handle their freight. Morgan puts it bluntly: 'We are better than our competitors but we are the best of a bad bunch — a better network with better people with better IT.'

This would have been music to the ears of Kevin Drinkwater, who inherited an Owens system that had cost NZ$13 million. He switched all Owens operations onto the Mainfreight system, at a cost of NZ$25,000, and within two months it was functioning perfectly. Then he got rid of all the consultants and reduced the number of people in accounts from 50 to just four.


FINALLY, IN 2005, Toll tired of the situation. They had endured eighteen months with no dividend, and they needed to get out. A price was agreed over various telephone calls to Don Braid, and he and Bruce Plested were invited to a private meeting in a Melbourne restaurant with Toll CEO Paul Little. They would shake hands on a deal that saw Toll selling for NZ$1.17, 2 cents more than they paid AMP when they bought their 12 per cent. Mainfreight then acquired the remaining shares and the company was delisted from the New Zealand stock exchange in July 2005.

There would be a further twist in the tail for AMP when they subsequently deemed Mainfreight shares worthy of buying. AMP's in-house rules demand a company briefing before purchases over a certain level. However, they have been told in no uncertain terms by Braid that they are not welcome in the boardroom for market briefings until they apologise publicly for breaking their word and also donate the NZ$250,000 profit they made to Duffy Books in Homes. To this day AMP has felt unable to meet Mainfreight's request.

When this ultimatum, along with suggestions of 'deplorable business ethics', became public, AMP protested that they were committed, strong supporters of New Zealand business, only to be told in writing by Bruce Plested: 'What a manifest lie. What bullshit. You completely sold Mainfreight, a passionate New Zealand company, down the drain to Toll Australia.'

As for Toll, they made that meagre profit of 2 cents a share and received not one dividend. On the other hand, they had managed to cause a major competitor some aggravation. And while Braid might have been fuming at AMP, he felt no antagonism toward Toll. He knew they had been as surprised as anyone when AMP sold.

For the third time, Mainfreight had nearly doubled its revenue through acquisition. They had done it in 1987 with the purchase of Mogal, which took annual revenue from NZ$20 million to NZ$40 million. Then the Daily Freightways purchase in 1994 increased revenue from NZ$77 million to NZ$131 million. The Owens purchase would take revenue from NZ$516 million to close to NZ$900 million in the year to March 2005.

The domestic and international operations of New Zealand

and Australia all showed signs of ongoing growth and profitability under 100 per cent Mainfreight ownership.

BY 2005 PLESTED and his team had reason to be slightly relieved that their rail proposal had not gone ahead. The management deal would unquestionably have taken Plested out of Mainfreight to run a business where he would have been obliged to squeeze the best, highest prices out of his own company to move freight by rail.

Meanwhile, the dream to grow a worldwide business from Mainfreight's strength in New Zealand was becoming a reality. The global profile was impressive. They had substantial operations in Australia and the US, and a presence in Hong Kong and Shanghai. The association with agents in Southeast Asia gave Mainfreight access to 400 personnel in twenty offices in Singapore, Indonesia, Pakistan, Malaysia, India, Bangladesh, Thailand, the Philippines and Nepal. And in Europe there were still those valuable links to Ziegler. New Zealand and Australian importers and exporters could be assured of delivery of their product to or from just about anywhere in the world, along with storage backed by some of the most advanced inventory technology available.

All the various strands of Mainfreight were being marketed as a single supply-chain solution. Pulling all this together was the responsibility of Craig Evans, who constantly argued, 'He who creates the most value wins. That's the business we're in, creating value.'

There was growing awareness that the logistics operation, together with high-tech warehouses, was what attracted customers and then cemented them in place.

Mainfreight's timing could not have been better. Many of their clients were migrating to Australia. Not that they were leaving town entirely — they still wanted a presence in New Zealand. They just did not want an expensive and labour-intensive infrastructure on both sides of the Tasman. Increasing numbers of customers were asking about Mainfreight's ability to manage inventory — to warehouse goods with technology that would instantly identify when specific items were required and deliver them on time, every time.

The term 'logistics' may be one of the most misunderstood in the language of freight forwarding. Early in the piece it was little more than a posh word for warehousing, pure and simple. Then, after the US invasion of Iraq in 2001, everything changed — logistics became the buzzword, a military term that would be adopted by the commercial sector.

Logistics was now all about how you got troops and supplies to the front line in order to feed the war machine. The definition was quickly seized upon and adapted to mean storing and moving supplies to the right place at the right time to win the market war. Now there was a single word that embraced the critical ingredients of transport, IT and warehousing. Logistics refers to the tangible life cycle of goods from production to consumption. 'Supply chain' is a broader term, encompassing accounting systems and intangibles such as cost-effective sourcing, supply of raw material and wharf cartage.

This was a defining moment for the industry, as little carriers were now seen as too one-dimensional; the requirement was now far more than simply transporting goods from A to B. In Craig Evans' words, 'The key to selling logistics is to become a trusted advisor, and the way you get there is by always being proactive. The world is changing at such a pace, if we are not giving confidence to our customers that they are at the leading edge the whole time, then we are out of business.'

Don Braid, meanwhile, was continually calling for sales, sales, sales. Just 42 per cent of Mainfreight's top 100 customers traded with two or more of the group's operations. Braid complained, 'We are growing the business but not across all the modes and branches and products we have. It's an old saying, but the best sale is with your established customer; we have lots more to do with customers who already trust us in one or two lanes. We have to think across the whole world. It's about globalisation. Our large competitors pick up worldwide deals; so must we.'

None of this was lost on Evans, who understood the high-value pick-and-pack niche market well. 'When a new customer walks in it's like a mother taking her baby to a crèche. She looks at the environment she is about to hand her baby into, how safe it is, how nice the people are, what equipment there is, what the playground looks like. All those things are critical to her as she is about to entrust you with her baby.

'Our warehouse is no different to a crèche; our customers see their goods as their baby, and if we do not provide the right environment we are going out of business. They are making emotional decisions, so cleaner, safer, more sophisticated, more organised, more professional warehouses are the order of the day.'

As for the people, Evans had a simple rule. 'We're as hip as anyone else. We don't care if people have nose piercings and are unshaven. The only difference is, they don't work for us.'

Potential customers were invited to visit, to walk about and feel the attitude, then offered a gentle challenge: 'Now go visit everyone else who is asking for your business and feel the difference.'

In the years to come the emphasis was on bigger and better warehouses with smooth, crack-free floors to ensure a safe environment for food, pharmaceuticals and other high-value products. The tin sheds of old were replaced by high-spec, dust-free, vermin-proof, high-security facilities. They would have much to learn in this regard from the Bosman purchase.

Evans knew the pressure to perform was high; time was no longer their friend, as the transparency of their improving technology placed enormous pressure on the team. Everyone had technology, so it was essential to keep raising the bar, and in doing so they created customers who were less and less tolerant. That said, the rewards were there.

A good example of this was Mitre 10, the home hardware business that supplied everything from garden tools to kitchens, bathrooms, plumbing and outdoor furniture. In 2008 they were having trouble getting goods to their stores so Mainfreight suggested setting up a joint venture company, Pride Logistics. They began with a leased warehouse in Auckland that held 10,000 pallets. Three years down the track it was just 4000 pallets, such was the efficiency of the Mainfreight system. The saving in held stock was enormous, and the cheaper, faster and better service that developed meant less damage, less pillage and more accountability. Before long Mitre 10 dissolved the joint venture and handed the entire business over to Mainfreight. Point proved.

The better you get, of course, the greater the expectations. Evans would constantly remind his team, 'We are caring for goods they made, that they love and cherish. It's like a bank; if you went to a bank to withdraw your money and some of it wasn't there, how would you feel? We are a trust centre; logistics is a bank in which we hold people's inventory, and you had better care for it and dispatch it when they give you the order to do so. Let us never forget — zero tolerance for error.'

The Manu Street warehouse in Auckland offers a specialised environment for food, pharmaceutical and high-value products.

In the freight environment bumps and bruises are accepted as par for the course when goods are being moved on trucks and planes and boats. Damage is an unfortunate but acceptable reality. But there is no such acceptance when the goods are in a warehouse.

Evans gleefully admits he operated behind his own iron curtain. There were contractor service level agreements that spelled out the expectations of both parties — risk, tenure term, rates and how they might be reviewed. It was all there in the agreement. Once the agreement was signed, then and only then would they shake hands and have a pie and a beer. This was the new reality, the new world of Mainfreight.

When the earthquakes rocked Christchurch in late 2010 and early 2011 the first thing customers and insurance companies wanted to see was the contract. Who held the risk and what were the obligations between the parties? With only 50 per cent of customers covered by formal and written contracts, Mainfreight realised just how exposed it was to customer misinterpretation of where risk lay. It became obvious the business would have to be much more formal in its approach. Mainfreight's proud tradition of the handshake deal was about to become redundant when it came to customer agreements.

Evans then stressed to everyone from the board down: 'We are in the business of buying risk. We must think of ourselves as an insurance company. We need to understand what risk we are buying. How expensive is the product? How damage prone is it? How theft attractive it is? Stop thinking freight. Think bank. Think insurance.'

While logistics was high risk, it could also be high gain in terms of return on investment, but that was dependent on having a full warehouse. Achieving that throughout the year was nigh on impossible as stock levels ebbed and flowed, with ups and downs in the economy having a direct impact on consumer buying and hence demand. There was the added irony that while movement to and from the warehouse generated work for the freight business, the logistics operation, with higher fixed overheads, made smaller profits. How to share the profits of war would prompt endless debate. The warehouse works just as hard, just as many hours, moves just as much freight — it just doesn't load it on trucks.

There was always a danger, too, when a customer appointed a new decision-maker. As Evans points out, 'There is always the risk that the new broom is going to dislike you because the guy before him engaged you, or he may have come from another company that had a relationship with another logistics company that regularly took him for lunch.'

While the personal relationship was important, they now required a scientific relationship that was both contractual and offered a service differential so entwined in the customer's business that it could not be matched by anyone else. Evans was already thinking quite strategically when it came to new relationships. He had little choice, as increasingly the decision-makers were no longer in New Zealand, but in head offices that were now based in Australia and beyond. Now the talk was less of how well they got on with individuals and more about key performance indicators (KPIs). Everyone's expectations were edging up, with that emphasis on faster, quicker, cheaper.

'That was fantastic — what are you going to do for us next year?'

'How are you going to take costs out?'

'What do you mean you can get it there in an hour? I want it to be there in half an hour.'

Where once upon a time a wait of half an hour in a restaurant for a hamburger was tolerated, now irritation set in if a customer was delayed in a drive-through for more than a minute.

Mainfreight's world was changing in other ways too. The internet was starting to change how and from where people sourced their goods.

# BIG PROI
# SIGNAL I
# OPPORTU

BLEMS

BIG

NITIES

The recession of 2008 called for innovative thinking. Five years earlier Mainfreight Precision had been established in New Zealand specifically to service the needs of the Farmers chain of retail stores. Current New Zealand manager Carl George remembers the day well. It was a week before Christmas 2003, and Farmers was in trouble. Mainfreight had been due to take over the business three months later, but suddenly the existing contractor could not deliver. There was a crisis call to Mainfreight, and within 24 hours Carl George had bought 30 vehicles from the defunct carrier so the deliveries could be made nationally. Every spare hand in Auckland, from sales reps to managers, was working past midnight through to the early hours of Christmas Eve, loading containers of lounge suites for stores nationwide.

From there it was a short step for Mainfreight Precision to start delivering furniture and appliances to the homes of Farmers' customers, a business they've kept. After a twenty-year absence, Fisher & Paykel also returned to the fold for just such a service for its appliances.

Now it was time to capitalise on the opportunity presented by the large amount of product being sold on the internet by individuals using sites such as Trade Me, the online auction site. Mark Newman was running the New Zealand domestic operation, which was getting increasing numbers of enquiries about moving dear departed grandma's sewing machine or chair, which had been sold over the internet to someone at the other end of the country. People would arrive with chandeliers in open-top cardboard boxes, expecting service from the freight forwarder: 'Isn't that what you people do?'

Newman remembers it as 'a disaster'. 'I started resisting and put onerous rules in place, making it at owner's risk every step of the way, payment up front from the origin not the destination. We were a freight forwarding business and these people were turning up at

TOP — Carl George.
LEFT — Craig Evans.

branches all over the country with stuff they had sold, expecting us to deliver it because nobody else did.

'It was a real nuisance — lose a piece of business freight and it can be dealt with, but lose someone's prized possession that they have just bought on Trade Me, and it is a different story. They get very emotional about it and it was just a pain in the arse.'

What was worse, while the new business was adding 10 per cent to the amount of freight they handled, they were not making any money on it. Newman would have killed the business dead if he could have, and he did everything he could to get out of it. Then, during one memorable board meeting, Plested leaned forward from his position at the head of the table: 'Big problems signal big opportunity. Get on with it.'

Soon, anyone who sold something on Trade Me could click directly to the Mainfreight website, punch in the dimensions of their item, get a price, order a truck, pay online, and the next day two nice men would turn up and deliver the item to the person who had bought it. Many of the branches even have people who will pack the items. Practically all of this business, consigned to the too-hard basket by the rest of the industry, is still referred to Mainfreight.

The operation would be housed in the new Otahuhu flagship site, which had opened in 2006 as a template for future large depots. With a rail line right into the middle of the building, they had the ability to load and unload wagons at all hours, in all weather, as well as line haul and local pick-up and delivery trucks.

As that site opened they were planning an even larger facility in Sydney. Such was the difference in the size of the two markets that it had taken nearly 30 years to justify a facility of such size in Auckland and just ten years for a bigger, purpose-designed operation in Sydney to be deemed necessary, with another on the drawing board in Melbourne.

The internet business remains a demanding field, dealing with one-off customers who want excellent service they do not have to pay too much for. But the 'click of the mouse' service is all part of a strategy to maximise use of the Mainfreight infrastructure. And with the advent of online shopping, the business of delivering from shops to homes was increasingly moving toward delivering direct from warehouse to home.

Online shopping was starting to pose a threat to the traditional retail outlets as people increasingly shopped from their computers and even their smartphones. In August 2012 Mainfreight rebranded Precision as 2Home, billing it as a door-to-door service not only for individuals with one-off goods to move, but also for manufacturers, retailers, distributors and online businesses. Braid is keen to stress that the business is designed to deal with large, bulky items — even cars and boats and the like — not the courier business of parcels or clothing.

The 2Home service proved a hit in the one-off, too-big-for-a-courier market. There is no need to open an account — just book online using your credit card. 2Home will telephone the customer to arrange delivery at a time that suits, with a two-person delivery service to unpack and assemble if required.

This is the changing face of retail, as bricks and mortar stores feel the heat of internet sales. As Bruce Plested endlessly affirms: Big problems signal big opportunities.


THE EMPHASIS ON being a global supply-chain enterprise had coincided with Greg Howard's return from New Zealand to take control of CaroTrans in the US, with John Hepworth returning to Australia to control the group's international divisions.

Howard held his first branch managers' meeting in December 2004. He reminded everyone that they had but US$35 million in sales and were, to put it bluntly, struggling to make a profit. And that, a fired-up Howard announced, was not good enough. But he had a vision. As his stunned audience looked on, he began writing furiously on the whiteboard. In five years they would have US$100 million in sales, 6 per cent return on revenue, and be US$6 million in profit.

Howard could see the doubt on the managers' faces as they wondered what had happened to him in New Zealand. But he stared them down, and soon began what is remembered as one of the most invigorating CaroTrans sessions ever.

There was no problem with the figures on the whiteboard — they were totally accepted — the problem was how to get there. Listening as the managers planned a major sales drive, Howard suddenly realised he could have put up a target of US$10 million in profit and they probably would have gone for it. As it was, they reached his US$6 million in three years.

For the first time as a team they saw what was possible. It was

Mainfreight beginning to make its presence felt in the US.

a defining moment in making CaroTrans a cornerstone of the international business. In less than a decade they would be setting their sights on being a US$250 million business with profits of US$17.5 million.

Howard was intrigued by how the Mainfreight culture became accepted in the US. He knew how foreign open plan was in a country where an office denoted status, but now they were not only throwing open the offices but they were also holding PAT (Positive Action Team) meetings and having lunch together. They saw the bonus scheme was transparent. And they made the culture their own, not something imposed on them. It became American. When they opened a new branch, two or three people would transfer from an existing branch with the culture in their backpack. And so it spread.

The experience of taking Howard to New Zealand for his injection of 'blue blood' convinced Braid of both its value and the need for such transfers not to be short lived. He argues that two years involves the first six months of settling in, and the last six preparing to leave. He now insists on much more flexibility when it comes to overseas transfers — they must be for as long as it takes.

CaroTrans expanded its services to Ireland, South Africa and Hong Kong, complementing the existing operations in Australia and New Zealand. And it became the very first company of its sort to offer live internet bookings for customers.

Leaping ahead a little, the New Jersey branch, with New York on its doorstep, was servicing one of the most demanding and largest gateways for both imports and exports to and from the US. By 2006 there were direct services to Greece and Turkey plus the ports of Shanghai and Tianjin Xingang, with plans to expand this China service to Ningbo, Qingdao and Dalian. The key objective now was the transformation of CaroTrans into a sales and marketing organisation.

To achieve this, sales manager Michael Forkenbrock established a team of high-level, elite sales professionals in Atlanta, Chicago, New York and Los Angeles. They were his 'Green Berets Delta Force' sales team. Howard told the team: 'Nothing happens until you sell something. And what we are selling is trust. That is our competitive advantage.

'We will deliver your product to Turkey and it will look just as it did when it came off your production line. The other guy may be

US$10 cheaper but is that worth questionable peace of mind?

'And you can tell them they are dealing with decision-makers, not someone in some far-off land. We are local, that's a big difference. Local problems, local solutions by local people.'

This was critical, as both Howard and Forkenbrock knew that on less than a container load the price variance was typically not more than US$5 between the major forwarders, and just US$50 on a full container. These were not deal-breaking sums; there was precious little difference between quotes. What mattered was service, under-promising and over-delivering. They would not sell on price — margin was everything.

CaroTrans was on a roller coaster of success, and Braid was effusive in his praise as profitability and revenue grew year on year in the region of 30 per cent, and more on margins that hovered around the 20 per cent mark.

They were thinking expansion at every turn. Greg Howard assumed a global role for CaroTrans, while Michael Forkenbrock took on national responsibility for CaroTrans USA. They quickly became one of the eight major import operations feeding into the American market. CaroTrans was suddenly being treated with true respect by a worldwide network of agents with whom they were developing a two-way trade. Mutual trust and reliance grew.

Then, just when they thought it could not get better, it did. Their major competitors, NACA and Shipco, who had previously relied on agents in Europe, simultaneously decided to open in that market on their own account. The agents they had been using now needed another partner in the US. Almost overnight, in 2008, Howard was talking of revenue growth of 47 per cent with an expanded range of agents. He was in a position to handpick the best agents in Europe, as well as Southeast Asia and South America.

CaroTrans joined forces with the agent in Holland, and saw cargo volumes double, consolidating their market position within Europe. The talk was of offering the most comprehensive coverage between the US and Europe, with a greater annual container volume and market share than anyone else servicing the NVOCC trans-Atlantic route. They also moved to extend direct service coverage into the central European countries of Austria, the Czech Republic, Hungary and Romania. Europe had long been the largest trading bloc for CaroTrans USA, but now they were uniquely positioned for the tough times that lay ahead.

CaroTrans was given the green light to expand around the world, with new branches opening in San Francisco and Boston and gateway branches in New York, Los Angeles and Miami, bringing the total number of American branches to twelve. Each branch developed its own network of trade lanes, offering customers a direct service, rather than their freight being trans-shipped all around the US.

Such was the success of the CaroTrans wholesale brand that they felt confident enough to launch it in New Zealand and Australia, offering a neutral non-vessel-owning shipping service for the freight forwarding market. In other words, CaroTrans was big enough in its own right not to be confused with Mainfreight, and other freight forwarders felt they could use the services of CaroTrans, as indeed did Mainfreight itself. Perfect.

NOT THAT BRAID was happy. Of course not. He was disappointed with growth on the US–China trade lane, considering the size of those markets, and was talking of an acquisition in either Southeast Asia or China to help develop those trade lanes.

Does this mean he is too tough on his people? Braid doesn't think so.

'We have something special here and we do the company a disservice by not growing it to its ultimate capability. Small incremental gains are not good enough.'

He has a rather blunt message for those who disagree: 'The business has the potential to be really special on the global stage. You are lucky enough to be part of it, but if you don't have the energy or the passion or the wherewithal to do it then move aside.

'If that's unremittingly tough then we make no apologies. We have to believe and we have to deliver. Coming from New Zealand, with four million people, we hone our skills scratching, fighting, kicking, spilling blood for small amounts of business. That's how we grew up and now we go to the big markets and see freight on every street corner. The big companies get lazy around the freight volume that is available to them. They don't have a similar passionate energetic approach to the business that we have and they are leaving crumbs on the table that are bigger than the New Zealand economy.

'We should be snaffling those crumbs off the table and into our pockets. That's what we want for Mainfreight. If that's not what the job is about then we probably don't want it.'

TOP — Greg Howard.
LEFT — Michael Forkenbrock.

MAINFREIGHT WANTED TO be recognised by more than just its customers and the team who worked for it. They wanted to do their bit for the country and the environment. And so a recycling programme began in 1988.

The green awakening started when Bruce Plested began pondering risk: What might go wrong, how it might impact on the business and, specifically, what he might do to prevent it. Inevitably the day would come when a Mainfreight truck would be involved in a serious accident. That one of his owner-drivers might be injured was worry enough, but supposing the truck was carrying dangerous chemicals that found their way into one of New Zealand's pristine rivers? What would that do to Mainfreight's reputation? What would the environmental watchdog Greenpeace have to say about it?

Plested was thinking about this one day as he took rubbish to the transfer station on Waiheke. The little island community was leading the way in recycling, with separate areas for glass, compost, paper and aluminium. A local trust was looking after the environment and getting favourable media coverage for their efforts.

In another of his eureka moments, Plested declared that Mainfreight would do likewise. He began with Auckland's Southdown branch, recycling and encouraging the team to bring their bottles and other waste from home to the depot for disposal. Plested, being the man he is, sold the glass for NZ$40 a tonne with a handy return on the paper too. In truth, though, he would confess that initially the effort was neither to save the planet nor to make money. This began as an exercise in reputation management. One day there would be payback. He was sure of that.

That same year Auckland suffered a major drought, with water restrictions that prevented Mainfreight washing its trucks. This was serious. Their reputation for having the cleanest trucks in the land was at risk. Returning from a business trip to Northland, Plested drove by the Moerewa freezing works, then in the process of being decommissioned. A 20,000-gallon stainless steel tank lay discarded by the roadside. Plested bought it on the spot for NZ$5,000 and had it shipped to Southdown, where what little rain that did fall was channelled from the depot roof into the tank and used for washing trucks and to keep lawns and trees alive. Soon every terminal in the country was self-sufficient in water. In Auckland alone they were saving NZ$600 a month in water rates.

Mainfreight was now years ahead of its time, using collected water to wash trucks, irrigate its grounds and even flush the toilets. And then the accident happened.

They had collected twenty drums full of oil from an engineering company in Christchurch for shipment to a disposal plant in Auckland. The drums were duly consigned to New Zealand Rail. They had been handed over to Mainfreight without any dangerous goods classification, and no one realised that they'd been sitting outside for several years and were rusting with a deadly pollutant inside. The obligation was on the consignor, but Mainfreight should also have checked. The drums had made it halfway up the North Island when an alert member of the public saw dirty liquid sluicing out of the wagon at the Taihape railway yards. The train was stopped and soon the army, fire brigade, air force and police were swarming all over it, with Greenpeace not far behind.

A commission of inquiry followed, with Greenpeace publicly lambasting Mainfreight, which is when Plested hauled out his newsletters about recycling, arranged a conducted tour, explained how an inexperienced dispatcher had accepted the drums, and how fussy the company usually was. Greenpeace concluded this was not a company to make an example of. On a later occasion when paint was spilled after an accident into the Waikato River, a similar conclusion would be reached.

What had begun as a piece of reputation protection developed into a full-scale environmental programme. In 2006, when they opened their new transport and logistics depot in Otahuhu, Auckland, with 25,000 square metres of freight and warehousing operations and a further 2700 square metres of office, cafeteria and museum facilities, it was 'green' all the way. There were solar panels for hot water supply; roof water collection for truck washing and grey water for toilet flushing; increased insulation specifications; energy-efficient air-conditioning systems, and rain-gardens to reduce groundwater run-off.

By then Mainfreight was making no secret of its passion for making a contribution to a better world, with pressure on the US and Australian teams to focus on recycling in each of their branches. Critically, the sustainability initiatives resulted in reduced costs, so both the bottom line and the environment were winning.

Mainfreight also accepted that its business was based on an activity that generates carbon emissions. This had an ironic twist, since it would bring them closer still to the rail service. The simple fact, according to reputable experts, is that trucks emit 4.6 times more $CO_2$ than trains. To reduce transportation by road they were building more freight facilities on rail-served land, and were pushing for more investment in rail infrastructure and coastal shipping. Great effort went into route planning and the use of GPS in congested international cities; using smaller trucks for distribution within and larger trucks between cities; driving with fuel efficiency a priority, and converting from gas- and diesel-powered forklifts to electric.

Even the IT division was not immune, with data centres in New Zealand, Australia and the US minimising computer-room space to reduce cooling requirements and using energy-efficient hardware while running their software on a needs-must basis.

Braid began telling anyone who would listen that to achieve successful reductions in carbon emissions governments must trust businesses to measure, identify and reduce the process. The last thing the world needed was overly bureaucratic and aggressive regulatory policies. He knew he was dreaming, but it was worth a try.

# SELLING SILVER

# THE

I n 2005 Don Braid could justifiably have felt reasonably pleased. The combined revenue of Mainfreight's offshore businesses was finally more than half of the group's total sales. The time was right to sell off some non-core assests.

First on the block was Hirepool, the equipment hire company they had acquired as part of the Owens purchase. They owned a fraction under 25 per cent, Owens having previously sold the majority share to private equity interests. Mainfreight had very nearly not taken Hirepool as part of the deal. Plested had been sceptical, but sent director Emmet Hobbs in to have a look. With his industrial background Hobbs was perfectly suited to fathoming what Hirepool was all about. Hobbs reported back that his cursory look at the books suggested they should both take and retain Hirepool.

They did just that, and it made money from day one. In fact, they quickly came to realise that the company, which rented out everything from tarpaulins to portable toilets to earth-moving equipment, was the jewel in the crown, the most valuable part of the Owens company. Hobbs was drafted onto the Hirepool board as the Mainfreight representative, and it is a credit to his approach that, when the Mainfreight shares were sold, he was retained as a director.

Mainfreight had paid NZ$63.5 million for Owens, with Hirepool valued at NZ$4.25 million. They sold Hirepool to venture capitalists for nearly NZ$29 million. Little wonder that Hobbs argues Owens should have kept Hirepool and sold the rest of the business for NZ$1.

While everyone was watching Hobbs pull off the Hirepool deal, Hobbs had his eye on Braid, who he saw had become an international chief executive that any company would seek. As Hobbs observed, 'He unleashed enormous intellectual capacity. Very fast. Very sure.' Those qualities would be on display in abundance as Braid set about disposing of LEP, the Australia and New Zealand international freight forwarder they had bought in 1996.

LEP was an odd fit, often operating in direct competition with Mainfreight International. That said, Braid knew LEP was a better operation than Mainfreight's own international business. But they only owned 75 per cent, the balance being in the hands of PWC, owned by the Sultan Al-Essa family. PWC, based in Kuwait, was the largest logistics provider in the Middle East. The company was in the process of pursuing an aggressive merger strategy, acquiring many global brands, seamlessly absorbing them into a global network under the Agility brand. They were buying logistics companies in the United Arab Emirates, Singapore, Switzerland, Saudi Arabia, China, Kenya and the US, and in the process they were becoming a global player, named in the Boston Consulting Group's list of 'global challengers' from emerging markets. PWC was not far off annual revenues of close to US$6 billion. And they were letting it be known they wanted an Australian connection — one they owned 100 per cent. A minority share in LEP did not suit their aspirations at all.

Owning LEP outright was doubly attractive to the expansionist Arabs thanks to an earlier move by Braid. The Owens business had a loss-making projects division, the Pan Orient Group. Braid had pondered how to get rid of it, but in the end had wisely decided to keep it, deftly folding it into LEP under the control of Mick Turnbull. Almost immediately it started making money. Braid and Turnbull would have liked to have taken all the credit, but would openly concede there was more than a little luck involved.

The project business specialised in one-off big jobs, moving machinery, gas pipes, drilling rigs and mining equipment for major projects in the Pacific and beyond. This involved chartering ships and planes, and often up to eighteen months of planning before the deal went ahead and specialist teams went into action. A succession of deals that had been years in the planning started to come on line, with Mick Turnbull bullishly declaring 'What a year!' in 2003. Growth in revenue was in excess of 30 per cent and profitability was up 48 per cent.

And it just kept going. In 2005 revenue doubled, with profits outstripping all Mainfreight's other international divisions. There was a team of 40 freight specialists based in Brisbane; a further 50 in Papua New Guinea servicing the mining industry; and a growing presence in New Caledonia handling a three-year logistics project for the major nickel miner Goro. And the projects division was now working more closely with Agility, bidding jointly on a number of major projects in Australia and other parts of the world.

So it was no surprise when Braid received a call from Agility, expressing a desire to visit New Zealand to discuss acquiring LEP. Braid threw out the welcome mat without indicating he was a willing seller. During the initial discussions Agility was seeking a 50–50 partnership, which did not appeal to Braid. He stalled for time, predicting they would come back with an offer for total control. It was an offer he would have little option but to accept, as there was the underlying threat that Agility would buy a major competitor on its home patch and then throw its global might behind it.

The New Zealand visit ended in stalemate and was memorable only for a visit to Plested's Waiheke Island home, where one of Agility's negotiators took a quad bike for a ride and failed to negotiate a rather steep hillside, tumbling dangerously close to a precipitous cliff face. He survived, there was nervous laughter all round, but no deal.

There followed a visit to Dubai, where 75 per cent of the world's construction cranes were hard at work, and then Kuwait, where Agility had the contract to supply food to the US Army in Iraq, from a 100,000-square-metre warehouse. There was clearly money to be made here, and Plested and Braid came home with A$67 million for their 75 per cent share in LEP.

They had the money to go forward and make substantial purchases, as indeed they would, but Plested was not a happy man. Yes, they had been paid a more than fair price, no argument there, but LEP was a profitable business that was returning close to A$6 million a year. Plested knew he could have borrowed the A$67 million and more than covered the resulting interest with the LEP returns. But Agility had made no secret of their aggressive global expansion plans, with the likelihood that they would acquire a strong New Zealand and Australian operation. The question was, would they put their weight behind a 25 per cent shareholding in LEP or a new acquisition they owned outright? And if the latter, what would that do to LEP's viability?

Plested knew they had to take the money. Braid had another way of looking at the numbers. They had just sold LEP for a staggering profit after earning handsome returns over ten years. Plus, they had the freedom to expand around the world, without having to concern themselves with respecting their joint shareholder in LEP. Plus, the balance sheet was cash positive to fund that international expansion.

There were those at the board table, Rowlands in particular, who noted the exchange between the two men with interest. Plested made no secret of his acceptance of the case for selling, but it was the determination of Braid that impressed. Here was a man clearly fixed in his view — a man for the moment. As for Plested, he had already determined that there should be a smooth transition of power and authority to Braid. He knew that if the company was to survive him then professional management was essential. Later he would talk of how 'beautifully it evolved'.

Mainfreight was finally in a position to actively pursue acquisition opportunities in the US, and to increase its shareholding in the businesses in China and Hong Kong. The policy was now 100 per cent ownership.

Time to go shopping.

MAINFREIGHT HAD SUCCESSFULLY opened in Shanghai with Linda Huang at the helm and was spreading further afield. Shenzhen, across the border from Hong Kong in South China, was the first port in China to have a free trade zone for international trading, and by 2003 it was handling more than ten million containers. It ranked as the fourth largest port in the world, with direct shipping services to Australia, offering huge opportunities for Mainfreight.

It was similar in northern China where Ningbo, then a four-hour drive southeast of Shanghai, was quickly establishing itself as the world's third largest port, handling more than a quarter of all China's exports. Again, there were direct services to Australia, along with Europe and the US. Later would come Xiamen, a major port city on the southeastern coastline; this was an historically important trading gateway for the Fujian region, with strong links to Taiwan.

For Mainfreight it was a question of when, not if, it would open more branches, with CaroTrans in the US looking for such opportunities. John Hepworth was becoming increasingly aware of the cultural divide between China and the US, with the Americans seeing themselves as the global power to whom everyone else should be submissive. Worse, there was the notion that each posed some sort of international threat to the other. While the Chinese wanted to build friendship and relationships, the Americans just wanted to get the business done, which could lead to tensions on both sides. New Zealanders, on the other hand, were seen as far less of a threat.

TOP — Linda Huang: opening up China. RIGHT — Michael Lofaro: piloting Mainfreight Asia's growth in one of the most dynamic regions of the world.

Kiwis tend to get up in the morning with the aim of both working hard and having fun, something the Chinese understood.

There was still concern within Mainfreight about China, however. They had a relatively small business there, making profits of around NZ$2 million. The business needed a major shake-up, but the Mainfreight board was loath to push for a full takeover in a country they still knew little about.

Chinese companies were often set up by people with the sole objective of ensuring their families lived a better life. Few wanted to take on the world. So it was for Mainfreight's Chinese partners, who considered trading between China, Australia and France more than enough, thank you. Comprehending that the US trade route had the potential to be their biggest and most profitable was proving too big a leap of faith for the local management. It was time for Mainfreight to buy out the other shareholders.

On 1 August 2007 their former partners — David Shiau, Sylvia Tsai and Linda Huang — sold their shares while choosing to remain with the company. This development was coupled with the appointment of Michael Lofaro, who moved from Australia to base himself in Hong Kong with overall responsibility for Mainfreight Asia. The implicit message was that Asia was the key to developing a worldwide logistics network. With Lofaro driving the development of Southeast Asia, Linda Huang and her team were left the freedom to grow China.

Huang had been a less than willing seller. Back in 1993 she had been working for the Australian shipping agent Burns Philp as a secretary; when the general manager asked what her ambition was, he was told, 'I want to be the manager.' In a blink Huang was moved into the operations division, learning from the floor up the importance of communication, keeping customers informed, knowing what the options were when problems arose, and the associated costs.

She stayed with Burns Philp for seven years until the business was sold to Cosco, the giant Chinese container shipping company. The change was dramatic; Huang did not like the internal politics and was soon talking with Mainfreight, who asked if she would care to open an office for them in China. She and Suzy Zhou, a colleague from Burns Philp, opened the Shanghai office in July 2000; Huang had a baby two months later.

Outsiders can make the mistake of believing Chinese women

to be meek and submissive. Nothing could be further from the truth, especially in Shanghai, where more women own their own businesses than men and where there are certainly more women in middle management than men. In short, Shanghai businesswomen are as tough as they come, and Suzy Zhou and Linda Huang are up there with the best. Joan Ji, the Shanghai branch manager for CaroTrans, and a leading player in driving the business, is equally strong-minded.

When Huang was asked by Don Braid if she was happy about selling her shares, her blunt reply was 'No'. Left with little option, however, she went along with the others. As it turned out it was a happy development, with the sale allowing her to buy shares in Mainfreight itself.

After the Mainfreight takeover, when Huang and Zhou went looking for new office space in Shanghai, they did a deal on premises with twice the space they needed. They had a plan — to double the size of the business in five years. They had taken on board Braid's simple instruction to put the past behind them and convert everyone to acting and thinking with profit and growth as their focus.

Many companies that go into China think the answer is to have their own management teams run their enterprise. Mainfreight was determined to make no such mistake. Lofaro would be the only non-Chinese member of the team. Even he, who had been dealing with Asia for the past twenty years, still found it daunting to be confronted by a population of 1.3 billion people. There were Chinese cities with populations that exceeded those of New Zealand and Australia combined.

His first move was to hire only bright young locals; he wanted Chinese people calling on Chinese customers. He ruffled a few feathers as he set about introducing the Mainfreight culture. When he went looking for larger premises he rejected the first ones he looked at because the toilets were not up to scratch. And he tore down the walls: open plan was the order of the day, with bigger desks for everyone, and the figures up on the wall for all to see.

He found himself dealing with a well-run boutique business driven by the 'Emperor' syndrome, where if the boss says do something everyone just does it. At the first few branch managers' meetings he found himself becoming hoarse because he was the only one speaking. So, gently, he introduced the favoured PAT meetings, empowering everyone on the team to make decisions, creating a business with structure and team leaders, and letting it be known that promotion from within was no mere company slogan.

Everyone was encouraged to challenge and question and make suggestions. He knew he was getting his message across when they all blamed him for the global financial crisis that struck within three months of his arrival, causing east-bound trans-Pacific trade to drop 30 per cent.

Branch development in China continued, though, and within six months of Lofaro's arrival, in January 2008, the Guangzhou branch was opened. This gave them five branches throughout China and Hong Kong, with a service expanded to include the trade lanes to South America and the UK, with the European and intra-Asian trade lanes a high priority.

The global crisis showed they had to expand the product mix and trade lane structures, so in September 2008 Lofaro called a branch managers' meeting. It was quite a radical meeting: not only did he invite the branch managers, but he also asked them to bring their top guns, their best team members, no matter what their position.

These were interesting times in China as the once dominant position of Hong Kong had been eroded. It had been the decision-making hub of the region, but following the Chinese takeover from the British in 1997 there had been a gradual decline as the mainland Chinese asserted themselves more. This was reflected throughout the Mainfreight operation as more authority was devolved to the branches. They in turn were conscious of their ability to be part of a supply chain geared to feeding and clothing the emerging middle class of a nation that in 30 years had achieved in development terms what had taken the West well over 150 years. The Mao suit was being replaced by a snugly fitting Armani. It was becoming a country of high-rises and gated communities, a country where the government knew it must enrich the lives of the average citizen if it was to retain its power base, a country just like the US, without the vote.

The 'Shanghai ladies', as they call themselves, were well aware of the commercial realities of the new China. They knew they had to have their own trucks and warehouses, and quality training for their team, and they were on the lookout for high-value clients who were prepared to pay for the Mainfreight service.

When Lofaro called his September meeting they gathered in the city of Guangzhou. As Lofaro looked out at the seventeen team members in the room he could see true excitement. Many had never left their home cities before, never been on a plane, most certainly never attended such a meeting as this where they were being asked to question, challenge and make a contribution to the future direction of a company of which they were effectively being given ownership. They were being invited to run the business. It was a totally new concept.

They sat and talked for a day and a half, and they created five-year goals that they then wrote up and put on the wall of every Mainfreight Asia branch. And they adopted a Mainfreight Asia culture that was all about the removal of the 'Emperor' syndrome and empowering people. Everyone left the meeting knowing they were permitted to make mistakes, with the understanding that only people who do things make mistakes.

This was a huge turning point. The growth of China as a nation has been led by the provinces, with their strong local government structure ensuring construction of railways and airports while also developing industry. Central government may give the impression of running everything but in reality it is provincial government that drives the country. Now provincial Mainfreight was taking responsibility for its own destiny.

Lofaro left the meeting with a new view of life too. The passion with which the team grasped the opportunity made him realise he had been travelling to Asia for all those years and had never met a die-hard communist. They might well exist in theory but, in Lofaro's words, 'Day-to-day Chinese are the most business-oriented capitalist people you could imagine.' He believes that since the country opened its doors to the world in 1978, China has been the land of the entrepreneur, be it boiling up noodles at the side of the road or building skyscrapers.

As the West put its collective credit card to one side in the midst of economic turmoil, China set about replacing one market with another, a domestic consumption model for its own burgeoning middle class that numbers in the hundreds of millions. From what had once been a predominantly export market, the trade balance was becoming almost 50–50 as Lofaro and his team contemplated the future of Mainfreight Asia. Where once Taiwan and Hong Kong had been the economic and commercial heart of the business, the world was now dealing directly with mainland China, with all its diversity and cultural differences.

Lofaro had a team that spoke many languages and dialects. Many were multilingual, not only speaking Mandarin, but also Cantonese — the language most prevalent in Hong Kong and Guangdong Province in southern China — and English. They knew Europe presented a huge opportunity, and they were also looking to Thailand, Vietnam and Cambodia to feed the consumption monster in China.

The pace of change was extraordinary. Just months prior to Lofaro's meeting, China had been known for producing cheap goods that it exported to the rest of the world. Suddenly, even as the global financial crisis struck, China was importing cars, bathroom wares and clothing as Chinese consumers became increasingly discerning, with a developing taste for name brands. Hong Kong was their favoured shopping city as it was easy to get entry visas, with hordes of Chinese tourists, weighed down with money, to be found every weekend lined up outside the Louis Vuitton shop.

In other words, Hong Kong was no longer an export port. Mainfreight needed to understand the import business and everything that went with that, from warehousing even as far as having blue trucks on the streets of China's great cities. And what this team talked about, they did. Nowhere did the mantra of Mainfreight being a 100-year company sit more comfortably than in China. People with a history dating back many thousands of years have little difficulty accepting the importance of longevity.

As they planned for the future, China was surpassing the US as the world's largest manufacturing power, and would soon account for a fifth of global manufacturing. China was the largest sovereign fund in the world; the only country that was spending on major infrastructure. Best not to forget the US, though.

REACH F
THE HIG
APPLES

OR
H
FIRST

While Mainfreight was now an emerging global brand, a retail freight forwarder that dealt directly with the customer, in one of the biggest markets in the world it was only represented by CaroTrans, a wholesaler that was also servicing Mainfreight's competitors. It was time to establish Mainfreight in its own right in the US by acquiring a company that would specialise in international freight forwarding.

And it was perfectly positioned to do just that. It had NZ$100 million from selling its shareholdings in LEP and Hirepool. Of that, NZ$12 million had been spent buying its Asian partners' shares. There was plenty left to buy a suitable concern in the US.

The first step was to create a company to do the buying, and for that they needed a local who knew the ropes. John Hepworth headhunted Tom Donahue, an industry veteran and CaroTrans customer. He flew into New Zealand on a Friday; on Saturday they showed him the Auckland operation; on Sunday came the offer to help get Mainfreight USA started; on Monday Braid shook his hand, and he flew home that night.

On 1 November 2006 Donahue started Mainfreight International Inc, USA, as a freight forwarder/customs broker, and began looking at companies to buy the very same day, working from the kitchen table of his home in Costa Mesa, California. Mainfreight was again operating on the principle that it is better to acquire an existing company, even if it is a 'dog', than to start from scratch. They brought in advisers Grant Samuel and began wading through the list that Donahue had drawn up. They started with 3000 different businesses, which Grant Samuel helped whittle down to 100, and then ten that were finally considered worthy of a serious look. Most were quickly dismissed as overvalued. One memorable Los Angeles concern is remembered for the surfboards out front and the outright refusal of the owners to meet because the surf was up.

In everyone's minds they were looking for an international

freight forwarding business. People would ask whether they would have trucks on the road in the US, and Braid would answer that he 'didn't think so', reminding them of what Mainfreight was doing in China and in the the US through CaroTrans, and how that would drive their global aspirations. The combination of international and domestic freight, along with warehousing and logistics, was purely a New Zealand and Australia focus.

And then they discovered Target. It was a publicly listed company with three Baltimore shareholders holding 60 per cent of the shares while the original founder and CEO, Chris Coppersmith, held 10 per cent. Touted as an international freight forwarder, it employed 256 people in fourteen branches and twenty franchises spread throughout the US and had sales revenues of US$180 million for the past year.

On paper it looked a perfect match, a retailer that would complement CaroTrans the wholesaler. It was just what they needed. John Hepworth was part of the due diligence team. He understood the US, realised their freight forwarders do both domestic and international business, knew from CaroTrans that they could pay a margin of 35 per cent to Yellow and make as much again from customers happy to pay for prompt service — and was to discover that all is not what it seems in the land of the free.

Target certainly looked like an international business. Hepworth visited the operation in China, saw nameplates, and went to an agency meeting in Malaysia where he met people from all over the region. It looked terrific, until he realised he was looking at a freight bulk partner that was moving goods from country to country for an agent's handling fee, with no real profit share and certainly no real control of customers. Just a handling service, pure and simple. It got worse; some US$10 million of the so-called international freight was to Canada or Mexico — not exactly boat or plane territory. Hepworth concluded that if the Mexican and Canadian businesses were included, Target was a 90 per cent domestic enterprise.

Michael Lofaro took a look at the Asian leg of the Target business. If the deal went ahead, he would have the task of merging it with Mainfreight Asia, which he was about to take over. Lofaro reported back to Braid that there was nothing to merge. While it was registered in Hong Kong, Target was a dormant business left over from previous owners, a series of franchises with local forwarders. It was designed to give the impression of being a global

TOP — Long-time
Mainfreight director
and legal counsel, Carl
Howard-Smith. LEFT —
John Hepworth has guided
Mainfreight USA through
significant structural and
strategic change.

company when it was really no more than a shingle on the wall. Lofaro remembers telling Braid, 'There's nothing here; it's smoke and mirrors.'

So the Mainfreight board knew, even before the ink was dry, what it was buying. But they did not have a billion dollars to buy a fully functioning company that met every desired requirement. It would be cheaper to buy a domestic business and run international through it than to start from scratch. So that's what they did, in November 2007. It was a full takeover.

This was Mainfreight's biggest acquisition to date, costing US$56 million, or NZ$75 million at the current exchange rates. Finding an international business that would satisfy all its requirements for growth and global domination for the money Mainfreight had available was always going to be incredibly hard. Finding one that ticked all the boxes and had no skeletons in the cupboard — impossible. Simon Cotter of Grant Samuel put it in perspective: 'They were looking to buy a US$50 million business, and for that you get a rich person's ski lodge.'

At pains not to make the mistake Mainfreight had made in Australia by installing Kiwi management hell-bent on introducing a New Zealand culture, they retained Chris Coppersmith as CEO. Tom Donahue was named vice president. In Chicago Donahue faced a revolt by Target people who wanted to keep using their current wholesaler and not CaroTrans. He pushed and pushed until one day they walked out en masse, thinking he would succumb. Donahue accepted their resignations and booked himself into a hotel, from where he ran the operation for the five weeks it took him to find the right people to drive the business.

During a period of constant change and challenge, Donahue's stand-out memory is of the day that Braid informed Coppersmith that the company's name would be changed to Mainfreight. Target was a well-known chain of stores in the US, so there was confusion enough there, and the logo was, in Braid's opinion, pure 'rubbish'. Coppersmith's response was, 'Okay Don, I'll talk to my people and we'll come back to you with our decision on that.'

'Don handled it well; he didn't hit him,' remembers Donahue.

Well, not exactly. A meeting for all Target's branch managers, agents, franchisers and suppliers was set up in San Diego. As it happened, that same week the Mainfreight board was meeting in Los Angeles, and the directors decided to take a bus down to San

Diego for a close-up look at their new acquisition of three months' standing. Braid was invited to address the gathering and, after a few low-key words about the inevitable need for change, he was asked directly from the floor whether the name was to be changed. His answer was an emphatic 'Yes'.

The next question was, when might this happen?

'Within 90 days.'

It was one of those you-could-have-heard-a-pin-drop moments. Then Target's public relations man said, 'If you change . . .' But before he could complete the sentence Braid butted in, 'Excuse me. You didn't listen to what I said. It is not *if*. We are. And I've just worked out that by July 1 the name will be Mainfreight.' The group managing director was making his presence felt.

Change was indeed required. Target was not just a domestic operator, it was also a domestic airfreight forwarder, and there is a big difference between a trucking company and an airfreight forwarder. They would fly goods from Los Angeles to Chicago for customers who were prepared to pay 40 to 45 per cent margins to have them delivered the next day.

Today Hepworth admits, 'I hate to say this, will probably get my arse kicked, but it's true, I don't think we did a really good job of due diligence.'

Plested has never lost a moment's sleep over the matter ('Or any other!' he laughs). 'Due diligence is something you do when you have made up your mind to buy a business. All that's up for discussion is how much you are going to pay.' He is quick to stress that he is in no way casual about due diligence, but says, 'There are always issues you find afterwards, especially with an international business where clients are forever coming and going.'

For that reason he sees the infrastructure and the people as mattering more than the customers. 'What I look for is how the business can be merged into the overall scheme of things.'

Due diligence is always a ticklish issue, and nowhere more so than at Mainfreight with its overriding desire to make quick decisions and be seen to be acting on them. The fact is that it operates in a business environment that is incredibly sensitive to customer confidentiality. Sellers, no matter how keen they are to clinch a deal, are extremely reluctant to reveal who their customers are, let alone the terms under which they operate. Typically, this information is kept in what is referred to as the 'black box' right up to the moment when the deal is ready for signing. The last thing anyone wants is a competitor, posing as a buyer, gaining access to customer information they can then use to lure away the business.

Hepworth's major concern was the fact that they did not appreciate that one office, Atlanta, was producing most of Target's profit. They had clients such as JVC, the consumer electronics specialists, who were at the time dominant in the big game field, in particular with *Guitar Hero*. It made millions, and Target was shipping it to homes throughout the US.

And there were huge software clients such as Sandisk, the world's largest supplier of memory sticks, the gaming company Arrow, and the Bank of America. These companies made up 60 per cent of the business, but on the Target books they appeared to provide less than 20 per cent of the turnover. This was because the accounting for JVC, for example, appeared in five separate codes, while Sandisk had three or four different names. In other words, they were splitting revenue streams in the ledger under different accounting codes, at the customer's request.

Then, to make matters even worse, within a year of the takeover the global financial crisis struck and Target lost five Fortune 500 companies who were no longer happy to pay a 45 per cent margin for airfreight. Stock was no longer flying off the shelf, there was no need to have it there the next day. 'Put it on a truck. Next week will do.'

Mainfreight nosedived into an overnight US$6 million loss. A business it had bought thinking it would make US$3 million in the first year, yet had only made US$1 million, had now made a US$6 million loss.

Braid flew into town and Coppersmith left, to be replaced by John Hepworth. There would be no further problems rolling out the culture. Hepworth set himself up in an open-plan office and began talking to people, with Plested and Braid making regular visits to do the same.

Another problem was the fact that Target had significant warehouse space around the US — terrific in boom times when customers are desperate for space; not so when the economy comes to a sudden halt. Hepworth's task was to build the business and the culture from scratch, restructuring the warehouses to create a genuine logistics business while creating clearly defined transport and international divisions, just as they had in Australia.

The fact that it took them more than a year to replace Coppersmith with Hepworth is accepted as a misjudgement by Braid and the entire board. They'd held back, determined not to make the mistake they'd made in Australia of imposing their New Zealand management style on reluctant staff. They learned a valuable lesson with Target: keeping senior management is one thing, letting the previous owner have a say in things is quite another. In their view, Coppersmith had enormous difficulty accepting the New Zealand company, and Braid in particular, calling the shots.

Hepworth had been at the helm for mere days when one of the sales team remarked, 'Oh, now we know who is in control.'

THE MAINFREIGHT TEAM knows all too well the moment the 2008 recession started. A great swathe of the overnight airfreight business involved shipping top-brand, top-price fashion garments from Los Angeles to the boutiques of New York. The women of Fifth Avenue were ahead of the game, and stopped buying some weeks before the term 'subprime' was first heard. A business that had grown at 10 per cent every year for ten years stopped dead in its tracks. Coppersmith had been requested repeatedly to reduce the company's dependence on this part of its business, and now they were awash with red ink. It was one of the things that had made Braid's decision to move Hepworth back to the US all the easier.

Then the banks concluded they did not need replacement computers delivered in such a hurry, geeks stopped playing computer games, and the rest, as they say, is history.

It was time for Braid to take a long hard look at the fundamentals of the business. Yes, it was all about supply chain and wanting to be in at every step of the process, running customers through as many aspects of the business as possible. But what they really needed were customers with built-in protection against economic upturns and downturns.

By now, Mainfreight had been developing a relationship with John Deere, the tractor and mower manufacturer, which had a global reputation for unmatched excellence. It was explained to the Mainfreight team that while John Deere built tractors, they actually regarded themselves as in the food and construction business. That was their core market. Their customers grew and built things, and continued to do so, recession or not.

So it was with another visionary customer in Australia: Bunnings, the do-it-yourself, cheapest price, everything you need for your home, warehouse chain. While retailers the world over were shedding staff and profit, Bunnings was opening more and more stores throughout New Zealand and Australia, and by 2011 Mainfreight would be one of its logistics suppliers. Bunnings was recession-proofed: people put off selling their homes when the market collapsed, choosing to renovate instead. Rather than trading up, people were repainting their homes and fitting new kitchens and bathrooms, and Bunnings had everything they needed. For Don Braid, being asked to tender for such a significant customer, along with other major operators, was a defining moment for Mainfreight Distribution, a coming of age.

Meanwhile Braid was driving the message: 'No matter how tough things get, people need to eat and drink. We want to be part of that market. Chase customers in the food- and drink-related business. Oh, and don't forget construction.'

The global financial crisis delivered a jaw-dropping 35 per cent drop in revenue for the US business. The same crisis forced a New Zealand and Australian revenue drop of 10 per cent, which was bad enough, but they had been set up as variably costed businesses, with running expenses that rose and fell as the business either expanded or contracted, and consequently they could cope by making adjustments. But with a 35 per cent reduction, no matter how variably structured, any business is going to struggle without slashing and burning and destroying itself in the process. Mainfreight USA determined to absorb the losses, and began the rebuild.

TARGET HAD TOLD the Mainfreight team that there was a recession in the US as the fashionistas of New York put their purses away. On the other side of the world, in New Zealand, there were bankers spelling it out. Tim Williams was about to get a letter from Westpac, informing him they might have to invoke the market disruption clause. He did not have a clue what they were talking about, but had it patiently explained to him.

Every bank contract written contains such a clause, covering the bank's back in the event it cannot come up with the money. Fail to pay them and there are penalties aplenty. But, if the bankers find themselves short, and fail to supply the loan a company might depend on for its very survival, then no penalties, no comeback, you are on your own. Williams was bemused.

'Why are you telling me this?'

'Well, some of your borrowing is in US dollars and if things keep going the way they are we may have trouble supplying them.'

Williams quickly concluded matters were a great deal tougher than they appeared in the financial pages. He spread their risk with a second bank. That was October 2008.

Director Bryan Mogridge came up with the idea of a badge with the simple slogan — *Mainfreight doesn't do recessions*. It would prove to be easier said than done.

In the US Hepworth was coming to terms with the fact they might just have paid rather too much for a business supposedly making US\$3 million a year or more, a business on track to losing that US\$6 million. Forty per cent of his freight volumes had gone in just one month. These were dramatic times, with people fearful of losing their jobs. Something more than a slogan was called for.

The message throughout the Mainfreight world was simple enough. No one would lose their job, but when people left they would not be replaced. And no bonuses and no wage increases. But, repeat, no one would lose their job.

They went back to basics: people were asked to turn off the lights, those with cars and even cellphones not essential to their jobs had them taken back. If they were needed, 'Yes'; if not, 'No'.

The belt-tightening would be slightly harder for the CaroTrans folk to bite on as they were busy increasing sales by 45 per cent and profit by 48 per cent. Some recession they were having. CaroTrans was the stand-out. When acquired it was losing over US\$2 million per annum. Nine years on, CaroTrans had established itself and opened offices in China, Hong Kong, Australia and New Zealand. And, despite the recession, it was continuing to expand.

CaroTrans was buying space on ships for containers that they then filled with cargo from customers who did not have enough freight to fill a container of their own. Recession meant there were more and more people wanting less than a container load. CaroTrans was in business thanks to an aggressive sales marketing pitch of their service. Greg Howard reminded people they had but 0.001 per cent of the transport market, and if they went to 0.002 they would have doubled the business. That was the message everywhere as Braid hammered the need for sales, sales, sales.

In New Zealand, young managers from around the world turned

up to the first board meeting of the recession expecting the worst. They knew about the freeze on hiring and bonuses and wages, but they expected more. They were confronted by a beaming Bruce Plested. Director Richard Prebble remembers Plested's words as if it was yesterday. 'This is great, this is wonderful; I have been waiting for this for ages, this is our opportunity.'

Plested was soon in full flight: 'We need recessions, the capitalist system needs recessions, they weed out the weeds and leave only the good trees behind. Every single one of you knows there are things in your branch that you could do better but you haven't been able to because when you are making such good money it's not easy to persuade people to make difficult changes.

'Well, you go home and think of that list of things you have been wanting to do and now can because everyone knows we have to be leaner and meaner and more efficient if we are to survive as a company and keep our jobs.'

The room was silent, all eyes on the chairman. You could have heard the proverbial drop.

'There are a lot of desperate transport companies out there that will make some crazy offers for our freight, and we're going to have to be just as crazy, because it is better to be running full trucks than empty ones.'

And then the inevitable twist from the keen business brain. 'I'm hoping this recession lasts a while, and my gut feeling is this should be a beauty, as the other guys are going to fall over.'

He then reminded his audience of a stunning truth: 'During every single recession Mainfreight has grown its market share. This is going to be the making of this company; it is fantastic news.'

They went back to their branches to take on low-margin, high-volume accounts such as Coca-Cola and to make them profitable by introducing efficiencies. They also took on fast-moving food items. Like Don Braid, Plested had a simple message: 'Even when times are tough, people are reluctant to stop eating. This is how we recession-proof our business, our family.'

One of those watching all this from the sidelines was Carmel Fisher, whose investment fund was once more backing Mainfreight. She never saw their competitive advantage as clean trucks and polite drivers and great IT. She saw the culture as the biggest competitive advantage.

'It's an attitude. You can feel it; it is a tangible attitude. And in tough times you don't want to be a market darling, because a slight stumble and people think you are overpriced. No such thing as loyalty among the investment community because of our short-termism. The fact is Mainfreight cut bonuses, and I know how heart-wrenching that must have been, but they positioned the company for hard times ahead. I knew that. I'm not a financial analyst, I am a believer in people. And Mainfreight people believe in the company. I saw that when they cut the bonuses.'

CARL HOWARD-SMITH ALSO saw the recession as good news, providing an opportunity to do something about the bad habits the company had slipped into despite its vigilance. 'We had become too bureaucratic. We had to refocus on employment and spending. Do we need that new coffee cup?'

The fact that Mainfreight was able to cut back to survive the recession begs the question of whether they had become too fat in the first place. Tim Williams, who watched the numbers on a daily basis, argues that the intention was never to be too lean and mean, as that would have jeopardised their ability to build for the future. They cut NZ$32 million in costs and could have gone much further. They could have slashed their graduate hiring programme but chose not to. Those graduates were the future.

CaroTrans was looking to the future, too, as it continued its amazing resurgence through the recession. Additional branches opened as Greg Howard pushed a programme of decentralisation while introducing new IT initiatives, with plans for a completely redesigned 'virtual network' concept to offer to clients.

The US might have been gripped by recession; their revenues there were down by a massive 30 per cent, but Mainfreight was busy expanding services across the country, to and from all the major US cities, and expanding the trans-border service into Canada. At the same time, they were developing a stronger common overseas agent network throughout Europe and Asia, and establishing LCL air- and seafreight services to and from the US. And they were expanding their customs brokerage services to the east coast cities of New York, Albany and Charlotte.

There were also frustrations, especially in opening a service from Monterrey in Mexico to Dallas, Texas. While there would be an office for international freight in Mexico City, developing the cross-border trade proved difficult. In Braid's words, 'We don't always get it all right.'

Plested would admit to great satisfaction in battling through the recession. Not only had they survived, but they had also improved market position and increased profits, albeit by just NZ$1 million. He would remind shareholders that the company's targets had always been deliberately challenging, and drawn criticism as such. In 2002, with revenue of NZ$401 million, the target had been to reach NZ$1 billion for the year ending March 2007. Plested would grudgingly concede that they only reached NZ$968 million that year, but in the 2009 financial year they hit NZ$1.265 billion.

Then, as the world spluttered and gasped its way through what many were calling another Great Depression, Braid was at it again: setting a revenue target of NZ$2 billion to be achieved by 2015; the US operations to earn more profit than Australia and New Zealand; to have in excess of 300 branches around the world; to be located in six European and three South American countries, and to have a branch network throughout Asia, including India.

As 2010 loomed Mainfreight took the brakes off. There would be an allocation of NZ$3 million for bonuses in the 55 branches that had improved their profit. Not a full bonus as they knew it, but a welcome return to profit-sharing. In a typical year each branch divides 10 per cent of profit between all team members on an equal basis, and there is also discretion to pay more to those judged to have performed above and beyond. On this occasion the bonus was based on 5 per cent of profit, with no discretion for additional reward.

Was Braid happy? No. But he had the badge — *Mainfreight doesn't do recessions*.

RECESSION OR NOT, there was a determination to expand the Australian business. In 2008 Mainfreight judged the timing right to launch a nationwide hazardous goods service under the Chemcouriers brand.

Rodd Morgan admits to being dragged 'kicking and screaming' to the dangerous goods business. He understood the high standards required and worried that Mainfreight did not have the expertise. He was also concerned about how food customers might react to having their produce being moved about by a 'dangerous goods' company. His solution was to keep his head down and hope Braid and Plested would forget about the idea. They didn't, and Morgan was duly accused of 'gradualism' by Plested.

Soon there would be a liquid logistics division with a dedicated fleet of tanks for food-grade products and a separate fleet for chemicals. It began as an Australian service, then trans-Tasman, and eventually a full supply-chain solution for international customers. They were also continuing to develop Mainfreight's Australian trade lanes to and from Europe and Southeast Asia in both seafreight and airfreight. The weak link was airfreight.

Mainfreight went looking for the solution and found an actual 100-year-old company, Halford International, a business well respected in the Australian freight forwarding and customs brokerage market — perfect, it would seem, to strengthen the worldwide international freight network. Mainfreight was very much sea-focused, with an in-house resistance to air from people more accustomed to road and sea. They needed to get into the largely airborne perishables business in Australia, which is to say the critical food-related products, just as they had in New Zealand.

So, once more, they dug into the LEP-funded piggy bank and A\$21.6 million later, in July 2008, Halford was theirs. They held back 20 per cent for payment later, which was fortuitous because to describe the deal as bad timing would be a slight understatement.

They had been looking at a business that was making A\$8 million profit. No sooner had they bought it than that profit slumped to A\$6 million. This resulted from a combination of the recession and, to put it mildly, things not being exactly as presented by the previous owners. Little did Braid know it, but he and his due diligence team were being confronted with a dummy run of what was to come in Europe with the Bosman purchase.

The customs brokerage business is almost solely about who the owner of the business knows, which golf club and which societies he belongs to, and which agents he deals with. 'You send us freight and we'll send you freight.' That is how it works.

Mainfreight had looked at Halford's overall volume and customer base, and its supposedly good team, and concluded it would be the perfect fit. The truth is, they had thought they were buying a business that would deliver more airfreight product, when in reality Halford was mainly a customs broker not an international freight forwarder. They were the WACO (World Air Cargo Organisation) member for Australia, with freight forwarders in Europe and Japan controlling all the freight coming down to Australia from their markets, thus inflating the airfreight volume on the Halford books.

There was worse to come. The Perth operation was small, with a weak team; Adelaide relied on two customers; Brisbane was a loss-maker locked into leases, and Melbourne also had excessive land and property leases and was in the process of losing sizeable customers. They closed the Brisbane branch, merged the Sydney, Melbourne, Adelaide and Perth operations, and scrapped the Halford IT system.

Within months Don Braid was reporting to his board that integration was moving slowly and benefits had yet to be seen. In the first month they had lost A$32,172, and it was his intention 'to revisit this result before any further settlement payments are made'. The Halford directors were in full denial mode; lawyers were engaged. Finally, it was agreed Mainfreight should reduce the outstanding A$4.3 million by A$1 million.

In the view of the Mainfreight board Halford's key director stayed on too long — ten months too long — the hope being that he would assist in holding on to customers. As is so common in such circumstances, the effect of that was to slow progress towards a smooth transition. Lesson learned, again. And an additional lesson for Braid was that no matter what the acquisition, big or small, they all come with their own set of problems. A small one such as Halford has as many problems as an Owens or even, as he was to discover, a big deal like the Bosman transaction.

He would tell his board, 'The lesson is we probably don't want to be buying little businesses when we can buy a bigger business and have a greater return for the same amount of problems.'

TO UNDERSTAND MAINFREIGHT and its extraordinary culture is to jump forward in time to Christchurch in the early hours of 4 September 2010, when a 7.1 magnitude earthquake struck.

There were not the mass fatalities that would come when a second major shake hit the city five months later, killing 185 people, but it was severe enough to cause massive damage and shake everyone from their beds. Mark Ritchie included.

The branch manager for five of Mainfreight's six Christchurch warehouses was asleep in his home just 2 kilometres from the epicentre when the quake struck at 4.35 am. He woke to no power, no phone, and the certain knowledge that this was serious. Not wanting to take the risk of driving in the dark, he waited for first light and then set off, taking his wife Sandra and her mother Dawn, as they did not want to be left on their own.

Ritchie drew up at the main branch, which housed three warehouses, just as the first of the aftershocks started. His main concern was for the dangerous goods warehouse, but the first one he came to housed not chemicals but wine. He was met with a torrent of water: the sprinkler system had been ripped from the wall and a million litres of water had already been pumped through the warehouse. Prising open the door, he clambered over broken shelving and a mass of shattered wine crates and broken bottles to reach the back of the warehouse and turn the water pump off. That exercise alone took half an hour, with further aftershocks bringing down more shelving and preventing him returning the way he had come. After forcing open a rear door Ritchie set off for the second warehouse, where acids and corrosive cleaning products were stored.

Peering through the window, he was relieved to see that very little of the shelving had collapsed. But then he saw that 30 drums were leaking liquid. Each drum contained 20 litres of acid and various corrosives. Worse, as in the first warehouse, the hoses had been torn from the wall and water was pouring forth to mix with the chemicals, creating a deadly concoction that would soon be flowing over the safety bunds designed to contain a chemical spill. The bunds could hold 240,000 litres, but the spill was on the verge of creeping over the top. What to do?

Ritchie waded through the chemical mix toward the sump that housed the water valve. First he dipped his finger in, and then, when that did not sting too much he plunged his arm down and turned off the water. Then the itching and burning started. He headed for the next warehouse to find water to wash his arm. This was the warehouse where all the truly dangerous goods, including poisons, acids and alkalis, were stored. He could not get near the door, so horrendous was the smell. Through a window Ritchie could see that 80 per cent of the racking had collapsed. Acids and poisons that had been stacked seven pallets high were running free on the floor of the warehouse. This time there was not even water to dilute it.

Fortunately, this was a warehouse that was designed to contain spills, and he knew nothing would escape. A phone call to the fire brigade, just three minutes away, told him how serious the quake had been. They told him if the spill was contained they had more important things to attend to; the entire city was in a state of collapse. He was instructed to block off the street so no one could get near, and told that the brigade would come when it had time.

It was not long before the rest of the Mainfreight team arrived, forming a human chain to clear customer stock from the damaged warehouses. Two working days later, despite all the aftershocks, some of which measured 5-plus on the Richter scale, bringing down more shelving and pallets, they were up and running again and servicing clients. Experts in full chemical suits and breathing apparatus would eventually take weeks to clean out the warehouses.

All over Christchurch warehouses were in disarray, and a not atypical response at some was to order up a front-end loader that would then shovel all the stock, whatever it might be, ready to be trucked to a waste disposal dump once the insurance assessors had ticked it off. Stock and warehouse equipment worth tens of millions of dollars was disposed of in this way.

Mainfreight's long-time insurance broker Murray Calder shouldn't have been surprised but even he admits to a degree of amazement at what happened next; the same went for the insurance company assessors when they finally reached the Mainfreight warehouses some weeks later and began asking where all the stock was. They fully expected to be pointed to where the front-end loader had done its work. Instead they were shown to the bays in which every single piece of salvageable stock had been arranged.

This did not go unnoticed by the insurance companies. In Calder's words, 'They were like stunned mullets!' Even in early 2013 major disputes were continuing over earthquake claims in Christchurch. Mainfreight received a NZ$1 million payout for new racking within two weeks.

Christchurch was in ruins, restoration work all but halted, as insurance companies declined cover to building contractors while the aftershocks continued. That was when Mainfreight decided to show its faith in the city and build a new terminal. The contractor was duly turned down for construction cover but the insurance company dealt directly with Mainfreight, awarding them NZ$30 million in cover, cover not available to others, cover awarded within 48 hours of Calder asking for it.

As he explains, 'They minimised loss to customers and hence insurance claims. It's a two-way trade.'

As for Mark Ritchie's arm, 'It was just a rash. No one died.'

# MOST PE
# ARE STO
# BY THEM

# OPLE PPED SELVES

The three pillars — culture, family and philosophy — that had embodied Mainfreight's principles for a decade or more came under scrutiny following the recessions and the financial crisis of 2008. Braid decided they needed to take a more bullish approach.

'If you make decisions then people will respect you for standing up and making them. We had to do that.' To ensure everyone understood, they added a new line to the philosophy column of their three pillars: Ready, Fire, Aim.

Question whether this might be the most appropriate image for a publicly listed, globally expansive company, and Braid is quickly on the defensive. 'What it means is we are taking steps forward; we are not sitting back strategically planning and waiting for an opportunity. It's about energy and momentum. It doesn't mean do it and worry about it later. It means make a decision.

'That's not to say we don't think it through. We think it through and then just do it. And if it is the wrong decision we shape it up and get it right. Of course we think it through, there is debate and discussion. But, we don't get caught up in paralysis by analysis, that's not Mainfreight.

'And if we can do that at board level and at executive level it is providing a direction and a style for all our people to follow so they do the same thing in everyday freight. They don't sit in a question mark about whether they do this or that for a customer. They make a decision. And, if you have people in the business making decisions for you, taking responsibility, you have a healthy business. You are enhancing the business and the individual. They are better for taking that decision and we are better for it as the whole business moves forward.

'I can't say this often enough. Sitting in question marks is not what we are about.'

Bruce Plested, by now 66, and increasingly stepping to one side to allow a seamless devolution of power and authority, welcomed the approach. He had become concerned about Braid's ability to drive everything himself as the company grew in size, and there was frustration that managers were not moving at the required pace.

With each acquisition they made, local management were instructed to adapt the Mainfreight way to suit their own culture. Some things would of course be non-negotiable, such as weekly profit and loss reports; open plan offices; lack of bureaucracy, and talking to each other rather than relying on email.

Plested was now asking, 'How long can we keep running our operation from New Zealand?' In any business day Auckland would communicate with offices from Hong Kong, Shanghai and Perth in the west to New York in the east. Soon, it was hoped, Europe would add another direction. Plested made no secret of the fact that the notion of one day basing the international freight business in the US had crossed his mind.

Don Braid was wrestling with this idea too. But with country managers in Australia (Rodd Morgan), the US (John Hepworth, and Greg Howard in CaroTrans) and Asia (Michael Lofaro), and later Mark Newman in Europe, all backed by their senior management teams, he could see no point in taking the headquarters anywhere else.

He compared it to the argument from analysts and the media that they needed fresh directors. Around the board table were Neil Graham, Emmet Hobbs, Bryan Mogridge, Richard Prebble and Don Rowlands, not to mention Bruce Plested, Carl Howard-Smith and Don Braid, all with vast business experience. But they were frequently told that they needed to change the make-up of the board, which was judged too old and too male.

Don Braid sees a stable and experienced board as the foundation of the 100-year vision. 'The board and the company must have commitment to each other. Short-term boards make weak, short-term decisions. Instead of buying property, they lease. Instead of getting the very best person, you end up with the next-best person. Whereas, if you are never thinking about selling and making your money that way, you are focused on making it a good business. You make a different style of decision, you make long-term decisions. And you treat your people as if they are going to be with you for a long period of time.'

Braid says the same argument applies to chief executives, most of whom know full well they have a lifespan of just three years in

Mainfreight's Board of Directors in 2010. From left: Neil Graham, Don Rowlands, Emmet Hobbs, Richard Prebble, Don Braid, Carl Howard-Smith, Bruce Plested and Bryan Mogridge.

the job. 'They know from day one that they have a short space of time to get their bonus and share options and farewell payment sorted. That's the focus. A big chunk of their time is short term, thinking about their own issues, their own self-interest, not that of the company.

'We have directors who after six or seven years are only truly coming to grips with the company. Men like Hobbs and Mogridge. Why move them on? Directors should be people who understand the business and have been there for years and will be for years into the future. We need longevity.

'Sure, if you don't perform you are gone, but we don't have a policy of a short-term CEO or board member. The hundred-year philosophy gives you that, as it encourages promotion from within. Long-term thinking has long-term returns.'

Neil Graham and Don Rowlands retired from the board in 2011 but there are still directors who, when dealing with an issue, admit to asking, 'What would Neil have done?' or, 'What would Don have said?' Plested, who is now in his seventies, is equally sensitive to criticism that the board might be on the old side: 'Experience, that's what we want, experience.'


AND, AS THE first decade of the new century closed, the 'old' board had approved expansion of the home operation. Owens Auckland had moved into the revamped Mainfreight site at Southdown; a new facility had opened in New Plymouth; there was a new Daily Freight facility in Christchurch; there were plans to make substantial alterations to the operation in Palmerston North; there was a new facility in Whangarei, and new warehouses were commissioned in Wellington and Auckland. All of this was to accommodate the changing style of customer, with more pick-and-pack, and products such as toys, food and pharmaceuticals. Mainfreight International and Owens International were merged to establish a more efficient network with branches in Auckland, Tauranga, Napier, Wellington and Christchurch. This also involved a complete rebranding to exclude the Owens name, creating the sole brand of Mainfreight International.

Another major development was the incorporation of a purpose-built data centre into Mainfreight's new Auckland site at Otahuhu, to house critical computing infrastructure that ran virtually all the systems for Australia and New Zealand. Customers could now be given delivery information within seconds, any time from anywhere via the internet. Mainfreight was moving into the virtual world.

SO MANY SMALL companies had warehouses and warehousemen and computer systems, all to manage small amounts of stock. What they required was that Mainfreight supply a full warehousing service and allow the little company owner to visit a 'virtual' warehouse on his laptop from anywhere in the world and see his business at a glance. Mainfreight would accept goods, store and in turn deliver to order, allowing their customers to manage everything electronically. There would be no need for them ever to visit the warehouse.

It was a virtual future of which Richard Prebble became a great fan after Mainfreight's experience with a couple of enterprising New Zealanders whose business, Kiwi Shipping, imported American cars and spare parts from Los Angeles into New Zealand. They may have been good at buying cars, but they rather lacked shipping know-how and approached a Mainfreight that was in a downturn after the Target acquisition and the recession. Mainfreight had an empty yard in Los Angeles, where the branch manager was Jason Braid, son of Don. Such was the success of their collaboration with Kiwi Shipping that Mainfreight now owns the business. Buyers can now go to the Kiwi Shipping website, find the car of their choice, and have everything from shipping to customs clearance and delivery taken care of.

The young Braid, like his twin brother Corey, had worked for Mainfreight while studying business at university in Christchurch. Today Corey runs Mainfreight Air & Ocean in Sydney. After university, Jason worked for Owens International in London before joining CaroTrans Chicago in 2006. These were the fun, pre-recession years as the young branch manager hung on for a three-year ride in which Chicago made annual profits of US$1.2 to US$2.5 to US$3.5 million. Even as the recession bit they still made US$3 million.

The move to Los Angeles turned Jason Braid's world upside down. He went from being a golden boy to counting grey hairs in a branch that was losing well over US$1 million a year. It would take him two years to get it back into the black — just. Then came the decision to split Mainfreight's American business into domestic and international divisions.

There were fears this would complicate the business, but in fact the split helped Mainfreight identify where problems and opportunities were, and to decide how to resource the various strands accordingly. On the domestic front they were delivering door to door, city to city. They were now exposed to a whole new world. When Don Braid visited the giant shoe company Skechers, he found himself standing in a warehouse so large he could not see the end of it. The warehouse was deemed too small for the company, which had a freight account worth more than Mainfreight's entire revenue from its New Zealand operation.

ACROSS THE OTHER side of the country another young Mainfreight manager was about to get grey hairs too. Shane Michalick had been appointed branch manager for Mainfreight's Newark office. He arrived at ten o'clock on the evening of 5 January 2011 from his home in Wellington to New York's biggest snowstorm in living memory. There was a rental car waiting but no GPS; someone had decided it would be cheaper if, rather than renting, he bought a GPS the next day. Somehow he found his way to his hotel, and the next morning presented himself at an office where everyone insisted on calling him 'Sir'.

This was a man with true blue blood in his veins. He had started with Mainfreight as a seventeen-year-old back in 1985 at the Morrin Road branch in Auckland. During an interview with founder Howard Smith, who was at the same time polishing a rifle, Michalick asked no questions but took the job. He mowed the lawns, made the tea and loaded containers for two years before launching a stellar 25-year career in the Auckland, Rotorua, Palmerston North and finally the Wellington branch, which he turned into a chart-topper. Then they handed him the keys to New Jersey. He knew he was being set a challenge — what he didn't know was how big it would be.

Michalick had the management skills, but this was unknown territory. In New Zealand, freight forwarding operates on a single level: get it there the next day, get a signature and get paid. In the US there is a charge every step of the way, such as for using the lift gate on a truck or taking the freight inside, and there are multi-levels of service from overnight to two-, three- or five-day delivery. And every delivery is charged according to its zip code within the city or

TOP — When Hurricane Sandy devastated the Mainfreight New Jersey facility, branch manager Shane Michalick led from his bucket seat. With no electricity or heating, the team picked orders by flashlight. ABOVE — The refurbished offices offer much greater comfort!

state — and there are 43,000 different zip codes, each with its own delivery charge.

It was no surprise that Newark was losing money; the rent alone was US$17,000 a week, and it was locked in for ten full years, with no escape clause, a legacy of the Target acquisition. Certainly, the office was in a prime location, a nice building, close to Newark airport and New York. But US$17,000 a week! No wonder they were losing US$1.8 million a year across international and domestic traffic. Michalick had just inherited the biggest losing branch in the Mainfreight world.

Elsewhere in the country it was not just Los Angeles that was on the back foot; Chicago and Atlanta were also losing money. It was all down to a lack of sales. Don Braid reminded the team of some home truths. They were earning a couple of hundred million in revenue from a market worth US$30 billion. 'Rather than being daunted by the size of this market, and the competition, we have to see it as an opportunity. We have to have belief in our systems and style and functionality and ability to satisfy customers. Like Australia, it will take time and require energy and passion and clear strategic direction. Just don't make too many mistakes doing it.'

Yet the 2011 year had started so well. Greg Howard was on an upward trajectory with CaroTrans in the US, the first international division to break the NZ$10 million profit mark, and they opened the Group's first branch on the South American continent in Santiago, Chile. Export volumes rebounded to record levels as exporters shifted more volume to the non-vessel-owning companies instead of committing all their business to the shipping companies. Building on the momentum, Mainfreight expanded the Asia network, opening branches in Tianjin, the major seaport entry point for cargo feeding Beijing, and Shenzhen. The fourteenth US branch opened in Seattle, and there were also offices in Singapore.

Mainfreight might have been opening more and more branches and returning those record-breaking results, but the US economy was continuing its slide through 2011 to 2012. Michalick could complain about the rent, but he knew the real issue came down to lack of sales. And he had slightly more competition than in Wellington. Within a 20-square-mile radius of his depot there were no fewer than 500 other freight forwarders. They were all competing for a dwindling market in an area that was shedding manufacturing, with thousands of businesses going under or shifting overseas or to the Midwest, driven out of New Jersey by restrictive laws and high wages. Those that remained were fleeing to forwarders that were undercutting Mainfreight with crazy prices.

Michalick did not hesitate. He hired seven reps and put them on the road. Their instruction was to sell the Mainfreight network, but there were much bigger companies offering just such a network and more. Then, the day they were actually truly busy, he introduced them to the Mainfreight way by donning overalls and loading freight. They had never seen anything like it. And they stopped calling him 'Sir'.

# BOSMAN
# COMPLE
# THE JIGS

The Bosman purchase was a strategic step, not one transacted just for growth. It was an exceptional fit with the existing business and culture of Mainfreight, which now had the opportunity to serve a larger market with more customers than ever before.

At the time of the purchase, the Mainfreight team thought it would pretty much leave the Bosman operation to its own devices, let it earn an EBITDA of €20 million a year, pay down some loans and everyone would be happy. They should have known better.

When Mark Newman finally got his feet under the table at Wim Bosman he found it being run, as indeed it had been for the past ten years, by its chief financial officer, Henk Messink, on behalf of a most autocratic owner. On the surface, Bosman was strikingly similar to Mainfreight, with an emphasis on customers, teamwork and quality; a company that cared for and treated its people just as Mainfreight did. Scratch that surface, though, and a financially focused and centrally controlled company was exposed.

Remember, they had paid €110 million, with a further €10 million payable if the Wim Bosman Group achieved EBITDA of at least €20 million for the year ending 31 December 2011.

They had known that three of Bosman's biggest clients — Samsung, the electronics appliance supplier; Sara Lee, worldwide distributor of frozen and packaged foods; and Ravensburger, the global games and puzzle distributor — were leaving. That had been factored into the sale price and the lease on some of the land and warehouses. What they had not realised was that the gem in the pack, Giant Bikes, the world's largest bicycle manufacturer, with facilities in Taiwan, the Netherlands and mainland China, with sales in over 50 countries and 10,000 retail stores, was also on the move. The news that this blue-chip account was leaving broke the first day Mark Newman turned up for work at Bosman, that momentous 1 April 2011.

As Wim Bosman tells it, Giant's logistics director had left,

TOP — Mark Newman. ABOVE — Liane
Philipsen. LEFT — Jon Gundy.

and the financial manager had taken over, demanding a better price. Bosman had resisted. As others tell it, Giant wanted a new approach, with more investment from Bosman in infrastructure. This had been greeted with a corresponding demand for a lengthy contract to ensure the investment was repaid. There was apparently no mention that these discussions had reached stalemate at the time of Don Braid's stand-off with Wim Bosman in the Villa Ruimzicht.

On his first day in charge, Newman had been seated across the desk from Henk Messink for ten minutes when the phone rang. He watched as the accountant's countenance changed from concerned to alarmed before, hand over phone, he whispered the news: 'Giant Bikes have called to say they are leaving.'

They were moving 100 metres down the road, back to the people they had left three years previously because of the bad service they were getting. They were going back for price.

Did the Bosman team know this was on the cards? Newman was of the view there was profit protection going on during the sale process. This would have repercussions later with Bosman's final payout not being made. And how did Braid cope? Were there questions about how diligent the due diligence had been? Were the asterisks flying?

Braid is pragmatic. 'Giant leaving hurt. Had we known they were going we would have negotiated a far cheaper price.'

What hurts is that Braid has since learned that Bosman executives suggested to Messink and Bosman that Giant be offered a €1 million rebate to retain the business, but they refused to do so. 'Bosman knew there was a problem and never told us.' The fact that three other customers were leaving was reflected in the price, but Giant was not. Suddenly there were empty warehouses.

Additionally infuriating for Braid was the fact that Bosman had been reaping a 22 to 24 per cent net margin return from Giant, but lost the business to a 12 per cent net margin competitor. 'If he had come down to 15 or 18 per cent he might have held onto it, as the job he was doing for Giant was good enough. But for *half* the price? Well, of course they were going to move. If we had had Giant through that period, we would have made money, even at 15 per cent margin, and he would have had his €10 million payout.'

Mainfreight reacted, and at the time of writing had commenced court action seeking €11.2 million in damages.

Meanwhile, Braid is philosophical: 'It is pointless ranting and raving and getting emotional about it. Yes, the loss of Giant was a shock, it pissed us off, it has made life harder, but it's no good looking back over your shoulder. The reliance on too few customers in logistics is something we should have been more aware of, but it's what we do with what we have got that counts.

'What frustrates me the most is that there is so much more work out there. We have got to be focused on going out and gaining more business, bigger business, bigger customers. There is no point crying over spilt milk, it's happened. We must learn not to make the same mistakes again.'

Spilt milk indeed. Suddenly the big shed was half empty and logistics, the backbone of the company's profitability, was staring at red ink in what was a very competitive environment. While Braid is philosophical, he is also angry: 'Wim Bosman knew Giant was going and should have told us. Frankly, it leaves a sour taste.'

Through an aggressive price strategy new customers such as Beiersdorf, the global skincare company whose products include the Nivea range, and Unilever, the personal and home-care specialists, were gained. That returned 50 per cent of turnover, but with no similar impact on profit. This was business they obtained with sharp pricing — it was 2011, after all, and it helped to pay a part of the rental on the Bosman properties.

Meanwhile Newman tore down office walls, talked to the team as they worked on the warehouse floor, and travelled in trucks talking to drivers; talking, always talking. And the message got through. While Mainfreight might frown on such institutions as public relations departments, Bosman had one, and that team grasped the new way quicker than anyone. Soon, with no instruction from Newman, the Mainfreight 'pillars' were translated into Polish, Russian, Romanian, French and Dutch, and were on office walls the length of Europe.

Messink would point to the depth of his financial analysis and the breadth of his business performance indicators, which were so superior to anything Mainfreight produced. And, he would ask, 'How can you be successful?'

Newman would reply, 'Henk, at the end of the day you are probably better accountants than us, but that's why you were a small business and not likely to get any bigger. You have so much centralised control you ran out of capacity to keep your hand on every button. At Mainfreight we take every opportunity to decentralise the information, to decentralise the power and get people working together.'

At Bosman, if there was a tough issue on the table and the branch manager was not handling it, those higher up would just take over. Newman would explain patiently: 'Never, ever do it for them. Coach them through it. That way you get a more experienced manager who can cope better next time. Do it for them and all you get is someone who comes to you every time they have a problem.'

Messink agreed to a point. 'We spoiled our managers, did too much for them. When it came to finance, insurance and such things we told them not to bother as we took care of that. But Mainfreight has to learn it is different in Europe. They talk of aim, fire and see what happens. Forget it; it doesn't work in Europe, where people want to know why they are doing something, with a reason and an explanation. If you can't give one, they will not do it. In Europe, "Yes, yes" does not mean someone will do it.'

Newman responds with a smile. 'Watch and learn.'


MAINFREIGHT'S ACCOUNTANCY SYSTEM was simple for one very good reason: it was designed to be understood by branch managers and everyone in the team so they could grasp the financials and drive the business. The weekly figures were not presented to illuminate accountants, but so that everyone in the team understood precisely where the company was and what they might, as individuals, do to improve performance. There was no one in Mainfreight who did not understand what they were in business to do. They were there to make money.

Money was never far from Newman's mind. He had under his control one of the largest privately owned integrated transport and logistics providers in the Netherlands and Belgium, with fourteen branches across six European countries, with some 1500 team members. The services included consolidated transport of partial and full loads across Europe; road, sea and air transportation; warehousing, and other value-added services. It all made a strong strategic fit for Mainfreight. But there remained the small matter of all that disappearing business.

Then came some good news. Every year, John Deere selects a Supplier of the Year from all its worldwide suppliers. Wim Bosman was the 2010 winner, with John Deere declaring them an integral part of its success. Bosman was also recognised as a partner-level supplier for the second year in a row in the John Deere Achieving Excellence Program.

To understand the extraordinary relationship between John Deere and Bosman it's useful to meet Liane Philipsen, the 's-Heerenberg divisional manager of logistics. That she is elegantly tall became worthy of note the day she tripped at the head of one of the numerous steep flights of concrete stairs that are a peculiar design feature of Bosman warehouses. After tumbling from top to bottom she was rushed to hospital with a broken back. Days later she left her sick bed, in considerable pain, to make a presentation to John Deere executives.

Philipsen has but a single mission: 'To create added value.' And she delivers. Bosman had taken the buzzwords 'added-value logistics' and turned them into a reality by lowering the price for John Deere every year for the past ten years. And they improved margin at the same time.

Plested and Braid quickly realised that they had much to learn from the Bosman logistics people. Little wonder, then, that they sent one of them, René van Houtum, to run logistics in Australia. On the way he stopped to run the Everest marathon. Yes, he was Mainfreight material.

Philipsen manages a continuous improvement programme for all customers, no matter how long they have been with Bosman, sharing any monetary gain with them while ensuring increased margins with smart solutions. For John Deere they developed a photographic system that ensured the correct tyre was matched with the correct machine, a system that John Deere has since adapted for its own warehouses.

Philipsen's warehouses are quieter and more efficient than others, largely due to the number of women employed there. 'Not,' she is quick to point out, 'as a strategy of ours to put more women on the floor. We are merely a mirror of society, and that means a good balance of males and females.' It's a policy that is now being pursued in Mainfreight's New Zealand warehouses.

The Bosman relationship with John Deere goes back to 1998, beginning with handling garden mowers and progressing to the point where they would have a purpose-built workshop with specialist mechanics to deal with any issues across the entire range of machinery. There is now a worldwide relationship with John Deere.

WHILE THERE IS no doubt the loss of Giant Bikes was a major blow for the Bosman operation, there was now a growing relationship with Specialized Bikes, which offered a selection of quality mountain, road, downhill, BMX and children's bikes with an impressive global network. Thanks to Bosman, the relationship with Specialized Bikes now extends to Mainfreight in the US, Mexico and China.

But the future was seen as fast-moving food and consumer goods. Like Braid, Philipsen would remind the sales team, 'People can put off buying the new car but they will always want shampoo and food.'

The acquisition of the Wim Bosman Group provided Mainfreight with direct access to a robust wider European network, including exposure to the developing Eastern European logistics market. But while they had bought a land transport division as part of the Bosman package, Mainfreight's real target was the international business, labelled Sea and Air. It was quickly rebranded Mainfreight International, until it in turn would be rebranded around the world as Mainfreight Air & Ocean.

At this point Jon Gundy was transferred from New Zealand to bring his extensive experience in this field to bear. Gundy had come with the 2003 Owens purchase, as their national manager of international freight, and he had then merged and run the highly profitable Owens and Mainfreight International businesses. In Europe he inherited a business that had been losing money for six years — a full €2.2 million the year he arrived. It was a business Wim Bosman had been trying to sell for six years, almost succeeding twice, a business on the verge of being shut down when Mainfreight came on the scene. It employed 50 people, mostly in Rotterdam, with a measly €16 million turnover, and, in Gundy's words, 'looked good in the brochure but not so good on the books'.

But Gundy had not been sent to Europe to indulge in negative thoughts. Within six months he was talking of Bosman becoming the jewel in Mainfreight's crown within five to seven years, when he had a vision of it returning 50 per cent of group revenue. He was soon opening new branches and hiring men and women of equal vision, with China firmly in his sights as that country's liberated middle classes demanded goods 'made' in France and Italy. The irony was, of course, that these were often goods that had been manufactured in China before being exported to Italy for branding through an Italian buying house and then sent back to China. This is known as the U-turn trade.

China, as a domestic consumption market, was now the world's largest consumer economy, outstripping the US. Some estimates indicated that China had over 200 million people identified as middle class with disposable incomes. The growth of its own consumer market was a fundamental component of the Chinese economy. In terms of seafreight between Asia and Europe, Gundy was sitting on the world's biggest trade lane.

There was, as he put it, 'a tasty meal on the table'. But this view was tempered with a hefty dose of realism, as he recognised that the €16 million turnover was 'not even 0.001 per cent of the European trade'. Worse, Bosman was generally viewed in Europe as no more than a trucking company.

Gundy employed a simple tactic of targeting Bosman's 5000 customers, of whom a mere twenty were using the air and sea operations. They were not even being used for trade to the UK, and Gundy saw that as a damning indictment of the service or at least a lack of faith in it — on the part of both customers and team members. He put this down to a people issue, and began demanding positive energy, letting it be known that he was going to spend no more time or effort trying to get people over the line. They either came to work to make the boat go faster or they were left ashore.

He set about creating links with Bosman's own road and logistics people, 'persuading them to believe in us', determined that sales would grow from inside out. Bosman had had no mandate that one division should use another. Even the road division, which ran a fleet of Bosman-owned trucks, was no more than a preferred carrier that was required to compete for business with other outside carriers when the logistics division wanted freight moved. They were allowed to be slightly more expensive, as they carried Bosman advertising and ensured simpler invoicing that enabled the logistics division to retain greater margin.


THEY CERTAINLY DID things differently in Europe, and Braid conceded there was much to be learned. Rather than noisy, cumbersome forklifts, they used the far quieter and more manoeuvrable electric pallet jacks for handling freight. Braid made it his mission to convert New Zealand and Australia to this.

TOP — John Deere and Bosman have an extraordinary long-term relationship.
ABOVE — An aerial view of Mainfreight's transport and logistics facility in
Otahuhu, Auckland.

More interestingly, they loaded trucks from the rear rather than the side, as is the practice in New Zealand. In Europe land is expensive so they do not side-load as this requires longer docking facilities to park trucks alongside. Turning the truck round and loading from the rear requires much less land, effectively doubling the capable size of a business. Side-loading also involved using trucks and trailers with fabric curtain sides that could be rolled up. This notion is also frowned on in the US, where theft from such vehicles, even when they are stopped at traffic lights, is common. Indeed, it is considered sensible for trucks to drive through red lights in remote areas of the US at night, such is the risk of truck-jacking.

The 's-Heerenberg master warehouse, all 10 hectares of it, is testimony to the benefits of an all-concrete building: clean, quick to build, well-insulated and hygienic. Such warehouses were being built rapidly for Bosman in Romania, where a domestic distribution business had been opened in 2008 as the central Eastern European state developed from being more than a cheap labour production site into a consumer nation in its own right. Bosman was building warehouses close to the new motorway route from Istanbul to Budapest.

Russia was also viewed as a significant destination, with St Petersburg increasingly a port of major influence for Mainfreight. The Europe to Asia trade was even more exciting, with talk of a US$99 billion scheme to link Asia to North America via a 100-kilometre tunnel under the Bering Strait.

The Eastern European business certainly looked impressive. Apart from the notable Romania operation, there was Poland, where divisional manager Beata Krawczyk had the initial responsibility of recruiting and training drivers, at a third of the cost of a Dutch driver, for the international fleet. In Russia, Julia Shevkalenko had the initial role of gatekeeper, responsible for ensuring that the country's rampant corruption did not creep into the Bosman business.

Both women quickly tired of such administrative work and began expanding their respective businesses. Memorably, Bruce Plested and Don Braid went to visit Krawczyk's operation, expecting to find half a dozen Poles, to be greeted by a team of 32. She has now opened a second branch to cope with the amount of freight generated. Braid is convinced that Mainfreight has much to learn from the work attitude of the Eastern European team, who see opportunity and create business growth with the same work ethic

TOP — Rodd Morgan.
LEFT — René van Houtum.

that the Chinese team brought to the Mainfreight table. It all adds to an excellent base of profitability for those trade lanes between Europe, Asia and the US.

BRAID SEES GLOBAL growth in simple terms: 'It's not necessarily about expanding into the world to ensure that we control freight to New Zealand and Australia anymore. It is about becoming a truly international player in the international logistics market.'

The challenge was to convince multinational accounts that Mainfreight had all the competencies required. In this quest, having big names such as Unilever and John Deere certainly helped.

Lessons from Europe were making their way to Australia too. Bryan Curtis had moved back there from New Zealand in March 2011 to run the domestic operation. He made no secret of his desire to grow the business by 25 per cent per annum. Curtis had latched on to the need to sum up the business to a prospective customer in an elevator journey between two floors. He had it down to six words: 'Delivered 99 per cent on time.'

Times were tough in Australia, which had two economies — mining and the rest — with mining on a boom and the rest in severe pain. The mines were paying school-leavers, with no university education, twice what they would earn in the cities. Curtis was having to pay a storeman A$70,000 just to start. Growing the business was one thing; making money, let alone margin, was quite another.

The solution, as always, was quality. 'Price is important,' Curtis says, 'so get the quality right and you can ask for more.' The words '99 per cent on time' weren't just a slogan.

This was also the message René van Houtum brought with him from Ostend, Belgium, where he had worked for Bosman before the takeover. He would explain to incredulous Australians the John Deere story of reducing costs and increasing margin by the simple expedient of improving quality. The secret was to always seek ways to improve efficiency without spending any more money.

Australia was a long way behind Europe when it came to quality. Van Houtum discovered vast discrepancies when he did stock counts for big customers, meaning they were misdirecting or losing stock. His solution for improving quality was to make greater use of IT, with radio-frequency scanners. His counter to the argument that the scanners didn't work: 'So find out why, and make them work. It comes down to human error.'

The Australian expansion continued, Mainfreight opening branches in Newcastle and Townsville as it moved closer to customers in the regions to involve them in the fully integrated supply-chain process. Strangely, this intensification of the branch network was in contradiction to the activity of their competitors, who were retrenching. But not Mainfreight, which had a host of new services including the handling of seed and grain, perishables, cars, bulk wine, spirits and chemicals, while also emerging as specialists in handling mining projects.

René van Houtum also brought with him the Bosman belief that graduates should be challenged on a daily basis. Yes, they should work on the shop floor, but every day they should also be given time behind a desk with challenges to solve. If not, they take their experience and their brains somewhere else.

The impact of all this would be annual revenue growth for the Australian operation of close to 30 per cent as the company's thirty-fifth anniversary loomed in 2013.

Mainfreight Asia was equally buoyant, with revenue increasing by 30 per cent and profitability up by a stunning 66 per cent. The four newest branches — in Xiamen, Tianjin, Qingdao and Singapore — were now well established, making a total of twelve Asian cities with more planned, and CaroTrans mirroring this branch development. That said, Mainfreight remains frustrated at the rate of growth in such a large market.

The Asia/US/Asia trade routes had overtaken trade from Asia to Australia and New Zealand in terms of volume, and there was an expectation that air- and seafreight between Asia and Europe would surpass the US trade lane growth within five years. Such was the development potential from the Bosman acquisition.

THE CONTINUOUS EXPANSION within the US now meant there were 25 branches, with new offices in San Diego and Portland, and new line-haul routes to complement existing services to Toronto from Chicago daily, Newark weekly, and Philadelphia twice per week. There was also a weekly two-way road service between Los Angeles and Newark. And they were taking on more owner-drivers in Newark, Los Angeles, Atlanta, Chicago and Dallas. Customers' freight was increasingly being picked up and dropped off in Mainfreight-branded owner-driver trucks.

If they wanted proof of their acceptance it came when they won a Civil Reserve Air Fleet Licence (CRAF). This gave them the authority to handle any US government or military shipment to and from any point in the world by approved civil aircraft.

The emphasis across the global operations was on a performance rather than a volume business. Rodd Morgan in Australia sums it up: 'If your business is simply about making something the cheapest it can be then you are rooted, because that's very easy to imitate. You may have the greatest phone but how easy is it to take apart, copy and reproduce cheaper? Now, the complete logistics strategy, that's more difficult to copy.

'We help our customers make money because they have no need for warehouses, trucks, IT or an international network. We have a total package to make them more efficient, more profitable. Win-win.'

Well, that is the theory, but in Australia, the land of 'give us your cheapest price and now knock off 10 per cent', no matter how persuasively or glibly you put that argument, it is only really when a customer has been burned by poor service that they buy into the quality argument. Even then, as Morgan has learned, 'The more you give, the more they want.'

The emphasis, not just in Australia but around the world, was now on gaining the respect of the customer and giving them confidence that Mainfreight understood the driving forces of their particular business.

And they were looking further afield still, this time to India. Braid had taken part in a trade mission to the subcontinent with New Zealand's Prime Minister John Key. He returned convinced India could be a huge opportunity for Mainfreight. There was a burgeoning middle class with a desire for high-quality fresh food. He found supermarkets that just could not get enough strawberries, and he let it be known that if money was no problem, Mainfreight should immediately start a cool-store supply chain in India.

A staggering 40 per cent of India's harvested food spoils on its way to market because the infrastructure is so appalling. With no refrigeration service, apples picked in the lower Himalayas spend three days in open trucks before reaching the shops. To put scale to this market, Mainfreight was shipping 200,000 TEUs — 20-foot equivalent units — around the world. This from their entire global network. Braid met a supermarket operator in Mumbai who was shipping 100,000 such containers out of Hong Kong alone for his outlets in India.

When he reported back on all this to his board, they had a single question: 'How do we do it?'

THERE HAS ALWAYS been sensitivity in Europe about CaroTrans moving into a market where they had good relations with a mass of quality agents. No one will easily forget how much business fell into their laps when the likes of Shipco and NACA decided to establish in Europe, with a corresponding flight of agency business to CaroTrans. How much business might they too lose?

CaroTrans might have been distancing itself from the retail business, but the fact is 25 per cent of its business was directly with customers, not freight forwarding companies. Fonterra was Mainfreight's largest account on home territory, but in the US it was handled by CaroTrans, not Mainfreight USA. That came down to their vast experience in the agricultural business, handling seeds, irrigation equipment and, of course, dairy products. Similarly Ecolab, another leading New Zealand company, with a raft of personal and household hygiene products, had its imports handled by CaroTrans for close on a decade, rather than Mainfreight.

The salesman in Michael Forkenbrock makes no secret of his simple message: 'If you want retail we do retail, if you want wholesale we do wholesale.'

Bruce Plested counters this view with the point that CaroTrans offers a simple service that suits giant companies that are seeking the cheapest possible seafreight option yet are capable of making their own customs, warehousing and delivery arrangements. But Mainfreight Air & Ocean offered a far more sophisticated service to its clients. In short, CaroTrans is a volume business, without the host of services that Air & Ocean provides.

Don Braid's fear for Europe was that if they did not establish their own foothold they would see a continuation of the small-business approach of their agents. He would constantly remind everyone that Mainfreight had outgrown small businesses run by owners with lifestyle aspirations. 'We have moved on, it is inhibiting our growth, and the same can be said for the CaroTrans agencies.'

Braid saw CaroTrans being held back by the agent network, which was not growing more imports into the US. Finally, in 2012, they took the plunge and opened a CaroTrans office in Le Havre, the second busiest port in France. Braid described this move as 'one small step for CaroTrans in Europe'.

As for the fears from within the ranks that CaroTrans agents would take business elsewhere: 'If we worry about what someone is going to do we will never go anywhere. There were worries about us buying Target, and what harm it might do to CaroTrans, and today we are a bigger business. So, what does that say?

'They are unfounded fears. We have to be sensible about relationships, but you can't have a fear all the time about what your parent or agent is going to do. You have to believe that what the parent is doing is good for the company.'

Then, at his provocative best, Braid adds, 'If not, then maybe the child needs to be adopted out. We cannot afford for CaroTrans to hold us back from developing the Mainfreight brand.'


MAINFREIGHT'S FIRST 35 years have been years of extraordinary growth, driven by a combination of natural expansion and takeovers. At times the company has doubled in size by acquisition. Each such purchase has been endlessly analysed for lessons to be learned.

The Mogal, Daily Freightways and Owens purchases were all highly successful and while there are always lessons to be learned, the fact they were domiciled in New Zealand, operating in exactly the same space as Mainfreight, meant not too many mistakes were made. Indeed, they were all quickly brought into profit and challenged Mainfreight's dominance within the group.

The same, as we have seen, cannot be said for the CaroTrans and Target purchases in the US, K&S and Halford in Australia, or Bosman in Europe. Welcome to the Mainfreight global experience of normalised accounts, where the same mistakes were made again and again.

Bruce Plested and Don Braid are both highly sensitive to the censure that has come their way for what some critics perceive as weak due diligence. Plested in particular is adamant that Mainfreight makes strategic decisions to purchase, and all the due diligence in the world will not change that. However, he concedes that mistakes were repeated with acquisitions in Australia, the US and Europe.

As companies are prepared for sale the first thing they tend to stop spending on is IT. Operating and accounting systems are propped up for the short term — never for the future. Bosman was a classic case in point; money had not been spent on upgrading the system. Companies being readied for sale will do anything they can to improve the look of their books.

The purchase of K&S Express and CaroTrans both involved acquiring distressed small businesses from inside larger companies. Both businesses were operating accounting systems that were part of the larger company's computer system. They did not inherit a stand-alone computer system. Once the scale of the K&S debacle became clear there was the disastrous attempt to implement a new system from New Zealand, much to the anger of customers who saw their rates increase without explanation. It was similar with CaroTrans, as IT guru Kevin Drinkwater was dispatched to the US to create a 'start from scratch' operating and accounting system. The exercise took him out of play for nigh on three years. Today Mainfreight is wary of buying a small part of a bigger business that does not have its own operating and accounting package.

Owens was something of an exception, as it had a brand-new, world-class, NZ$13 million system that had been recommended by bright-eyed consultants. Within weeks Mainfreight knew it was inadequate, wrote it off in the books, and replaced it with the Mainfreight system for just NZ$25,000. Braid was astounded at what he saw as the 'naivety and arrogance' of the consultants, who had been sold a dumb system they didn't understand, and didn't want to take any responsibility for it. Braid remains furious. 'Consultants like that can stuff a business and then walk away wiping their hands, denying any culpability.'

Overrated computer systems aside, Owens was a listed company so Mainfreight knew exactly what it was buying from publicly available information. Braid knew what they were acquiring and what they would sell. They might not have been able to negotiate the price, but there was a high degree of certainty about what they would be getting. And remember, when the dust settled and unwanted managers and directors had all been dealt with, Mainfreight paid NZ$63.5 million and then reaped NZ$67 million by selling unwanted assets. Plus, they retained the core business, which went on to make handsome returns.

Don Braid looks beyond mere operating systems to the lessons

Don Braid, on the road in Europe for Mainfreight.

they learned from poor management and weak directors. Yes, they were quick to get rid of such impediments — Mainfreight cleaning out Mogal on day one, and firing the mass of Owens' management and directors on day two — but the lesson for him was, 'We never ever want to have a Mainfreight board or senior management team as weak as that or we will have big problems. The lesson is constant self-evaluation. We must keep looking at ourselves.'

The fact is, companies with top management teams and effective directors do not come up for sale all that often. 'If there is a lesson to be learned it is better to buy the corporation and flick off what we don't need, rather than take a piece of something,' Braid reflects.

The Bosman experience would also confirm the wisdom of retaining a proportion of the purchase price until the promised results come to fruition. This strategy had proved its worth with the Halford purchase, and with Bosman they insisted on that €10 million being withheld to achieve a €20 million EBITDA. Reduced revenue meant that money was retained by Mainfreight, and a further €5 million was placed in a lawyer's escrow account to cover any issues that arose post-sale. It was money that went on immediate hold when Mainfreight launched its court action for €11.2 million in damages.

TALK SOME MORE to Plested and Braid about lessons learned, though, and it is not long before the much-vaunted Mainfreight culture comes up. Ever since the painful experience of attempting to impose a Kiwi-style culture on Australia, Mainfreight has taken a determined approach to allowing the numerous nationalities within their global enterprise to adapt the company culture to suit their own approach to life and business.

As we've seen, the policy now is to bring managers to New Zealand for an injection of 'blue blood' so they can return home and spread the gospel. There was an initial theory that this should take two years, but experience has taught Don Braid that that may not be long enough and that people should stay 'for as long as it takes'.

For Mainfreight culture read 'the way we do things, the way we conduct ourselves'. The fact is, people from much larger countries do have difficulty with the notion that a company from a country of four million people can teach them *anything*, let alone how to manage a business. It takes time. Braid now accepts that, hence the 'for as long as it takes' caveat.

'Much of what we do, our approach, can be seen as small-company thinking, and the challenge we have is to keep that as we grow bigger. If we fail to instil that then it is our responsibility and we have to keep working at it.'

Don Braid is insistent that buying Bosman was the right thing to do. 'We have a business in Europe that gives us a different agenda.' Now they are positioned with a platform for further growth, and exposure to the growing economies of Russia, Poland, Turkey and beyond.

And, yes, K&S came with a big entry cost — NZ$10 million in one year alone — but the acquisition established Mainfreight Australia, where they now have a flourishing business. Otherwise they would have stagnated in New Zealand.

Braid is emphatic that while Mainfreight is not a prolific acquirer of businesses, when it does step into the ring it is for a strategic purpose. 'They have to fit the jigsaw. Bosman was a critical missing piece for us, essential to our global aspiration, as was K&S.'

Just as the Daily Freight acquisition taught them the advantages of multiple branding in a small market, where parochialism leads to greater brand loyalty, they also learned to be ever vigilant about margin. Mainfreight disciplines always improve margins. This is the art of ensuring that every branch is truly accountable, that any quote includes every cost all the way down the line before margin is allocated. No branch can buy business and then expect another branch to take the hit. By all means make a strategic decision to gain business with a competitive price, but you cannot ask anyone else in the business to drop their price for their share of the work.

And when buying, beware of normalised accounts. Braid admits to chuckling whenever he hears this word. 'Normalised means they are fudging. It's a classic. What they are saying is, "If we take out the problems . . . in a perfect world . . . this is what the figures would look like." We laugh when we hear the word normalised.'

Normalised accounts are something the Mainfreight accounting systems can iron out, but blockers are quite another matter. Blockers are those who don't buy into the Mainfreight culture, and typically think they know better. Plested and Braid concede that, as witnessed, time and time again they have inherited such people

Mainfreight founder Bruce Plested: 35 years at the helm.

through acquisition and failed to act quickly enough to remove them. Blockers and their followers never become what Mainfreight refers to as 'one of us'.

The lesson has to be to act decisively. But there is always the worry that such people may have relationships with customers, and even other people within the company, who will react badly to such a move. Braid is now insistent the lesson has been learned that if you act with momentum, 'you don't get attached to people'.

There have been other critical lessons on acquisition too. Take your time fixing them, and lift service levels before adjusting prices so customers stay with you. Be careful of changing the name of the business, especially if it has or has had a good reputation. This can cause destabilisation of customers and some team members. Beware the folly of equity-raising. Mainfreight raised funds for the Owens acquisition with an issue at NZ$1.30 a share, too little by far.

And remember, people don't sell well-managed, profitable companies. No matter what you are told, expect to find low prices, low service levels and long credit terms. Every time.

# WHERE

# NEXT?

On Thursday 26 July 2012, Mainfreight held its seventeenth annual general meeting since going public. Bruce Plested stood before the shareholders and talked about profits that had increased by 39 per cent; global sales up by 35 per cent, and how in the past five years net profit had increased by 62 per cent and sales by 99 per cent. Then he explained how they had done it.

'Our growth strategy has been to have strong businesses in other countries. These businesses then operate between themselves. This gives us real competitive advantage against opposition companies who are reliant on agents to follow up sales leads or perform services.'

Then, strangely for Plested, he went on the defensive. 'For this reason it is disappointing that some commentators regard it as a negative that we are in Europe or the US or wherever. The very fact that we are in those places assists in the activity and profits of all the other countries in which we operate. All are inextricably linked with each other, and contributing to each other's profit and success.'

Here was a man who had just celebrated his seventieth birthday on 14 March by personally gifting the equivalent of NZ$1000 to each of the more than 4500 team members who had been employed by the company for a year or more. There were people in Asia and Europe who thought it was NZ$1000 for the branch to have a few drinks and celebrate. That was exciting enough. When it dawned that they were to get NZ$1000 each, it was a jaw-dropping moment.

When it was Don Braid's turn to address the meeting, he talked of the numbers. Sales revenue exceeded NZ$1.8 billion, producing an EBITDA of NZ$138 million with a net profit of nearly NZ$66 million. Braid described the results as 'satisfactory', with the European contribution of €16.5 million 'disappointing' but offset by not triggering the agreed earn-out of €10 million to Mr Bosman. They were working on replacing the lost business, and here there was more than a hint that the loss of Giant Bikes

Jordan Tekoronga and Daniel Hobbs of Mainfreight Perishables Christchurch.

had been a blow. But the space left in their warehouses was quickly being filled.

Then the good news. Multinational customers were looking for global supply-chain competency, and Mainfreight was active in the three largest freight trading markets in the world: Asia, the US and Europe.

He had reason to be pleased about Europe, Braid told the meeting. They had opened further offices in Lyon, France; Hamina, Finland; Moscow, Russia; Cluj-Napoca, Romania; and Katowice, Poland. And they had established new Air & Ocean branches in Brussels, Paris and Amsterdam. And, of course, the CaroTrans office in Le Havre, France. He had high hopes for the newly separated domestic business in the US, while its international or Air & Ocean business, as they now called it, had a newfound focus on the Asian and European trade lanes.

Braid spoke of disappointment with the CaroTrans performance, which was below 'expectation', with lower export volumes, and the Asian operations had also 'disappointed', though there was an assurance that this under-performance would be countered by greater sales effectiveness.

Then, the twist. The global empire might have been struggling just a tad, but Australia and New Zealand were more than satisfactory, with a strong focus on the food, beverage and DIY-related sectors. This continued strong growth had required expansion across both countries. There was a new facility on Wellington's Aotea Quay, officially opened in March 2012 by Prime Minister John Key. The event was marked, in the Maori tradition, by the presentation of beautiful feather cloaks to two retiring directors, the men who had been there at the beginning and who had helped steer Mainfreight through troubled waters and on into triumph: Neil Graham and Don Rowlands.

There was a NZ$15 million state-of-the-art home for both Mainfreight Transport and Mainfreight Air & Ocean, a terminal built on KiwiRail land, allowing inbound and outbound rail services and including electric fork hoists and pallet jacks and more rear loading of road vehicles. This brought the total number of Mainfreight rail-served facilities to thirteen, with Palmerston North, Invercargill, Blenheim, Christchurch, Kaitaia and Hamilton high on the priority list for similar terminals.

Mainfreight's annual spend with KiwiRail exceeded NZ$35

million per annum, and Braid was emphatic that the nation was better served by a rail network under well-managed government control. All they needed was a government that also understood the port situation. New Zealand is in a bizarre situation for a country of four million people, having no fewer than thirteen ports competing against each other for business. Braid is of the view that fewer, more specialised container ports are the answer: two in the North Island at Auckland and Tauranga, and possibly one in the South Island. The balance would specialise in activities such as logs, gas and ferry services. If this does not happen, Braid foresees the day when the international shipping lines will operate via Brisbane, using a small ship to port-hop around New Zealand. This would add both transit time and costs for import and exports.

The investment in property is classic Mainfreight strategy. Braid sees this as building on a solid foundation rather than sand, with ownership of the key facilities that generate revenue all part of the 100-year philosophy.

This is the policy in both New Zealand and Australia, while in Europe Braid is quick to point out that they might have paid a multiple of six times EBITDA for a business that has struggled, but it came with €45 million of property. Asia and the US are different, in his book: 'We don't yet know what we will need and have no idea how big we will be. Until we get real traction and size, it will be a little while before we own property there.'

Braid was not making excuses. 'The world economic climate is what it is, and likely to be the operating environment for a while to come.' He knew there was more bad news to come out of the Europe operation, and while analysts were quick to point an accusing and critical finger, when it came to percentage of group revenue, the figures as at March 2012 made interesting reading.

|  | Revenue | Team | % Group Revenue |
| --- | --- | --- | --- |
| **Europe** | €245m | 1483 | 23.0% |
| **Asia** | US$29m | 196 | 2.0% |
| **USA** | US$332m | 544 | 22.7% |
| **Australia** | A$385m | 1236 | 27.5% |
| **New Zealand** | NZ$449m | 1779 | 24.8% |

ASIA, WHILE AT the bottom of the Mainfreight league table, had
opened its eighth branch operation in mainland China at Chengdu,
the capital city of Sichuan Province, one of the most important
economic, transportation and communication centres in western
China. With a population of over fourteen million people, this
historic city is the showcase for China's drive to develop the central
and western regions of the country. Mainfreight's operations
and coverage had more than doubled in the past two years, with
eleven operations in the region, covering Singapore, Hong Kong,
mainland China and Taiwan, with Thailand and Vietnam about
to open. Critically, they were positioned to take advantage of the
fast-growing domestic markets in China, a country that is home to
20 per cent of the world's population.

Braid makes no bones about what Mainfreight expects from the
team today. He hammers the need for constant improvement, just
as Bruce Plested did at the Flock House meeting seventeen years
earlier. But Don Braid is now speaking on a world stage, not in a
college hall in the backblocks of New Zealand.

'Yes we need constant improvement; that incremental gain from
continually striving to be better already delivers so much, particularly
in terms of quality. But we should not be coming to work "just to
do a bit better", we also need real step change especially in these
regions of huge potential — Asia, the US and Europe. Why don't
you come to work to make a real difference, to create a company
that is world class, that has real size about it? Because we have the
bones to do that.'

Braid told the meeting he would be frustrated at the US business
returning a weekly profit of US$80,000 when every Auckland
branch was returning NZ$100,000 a week. 'We should not be
happy until we are doing US$500,000 a week in the US. In a market
that big a million a week is certainly possible.

'Let's create a business that is bigger and better. Eighty thousand
a week is pissing into the pot.

'Those are the things that frustrate us. Sure, they look at me the
way they looked at Bruce, so I identify with how he was feeling at
Flock House. Mainfreight was going through the same thing then,
albeit in a smaller way, as what we have today.'

Braid looks to the future with a determination to do better.
'We need to be better, and not just a bit better. We require some
real step change. CaroTrans in the States has got to have strong

TEAMWORK
34 YEARS AGO IT WAS ABOUT A COUPLE OF KIWI BLOKES WHO HAD EACH OTHER'S BACKS. TODAY IT'S ABOUT ONE 5000-STRONG TEAM DELIVERING THE ULTIMATE MAINFREIGHT EXPERIENCE.

A page from Mainfreight's 2012 annual report.

import growth; Bosman has to grow its Air & Ocean and Logistics businesses to make up for the Giant loss; and China has to go gangbusters for in-country sales to create a business relative to the size of that market. The more people making decisions and leaps of faith the better off we will be as a business.'

There are analysts who wonder how this global expansion might impact on the company. Braid just shrugs this off: 'The New Zealand market has yet to understand we are a global business playing in a global marketplace.'

He expanded on these views and the state of New Zealand's performance when he was invited to write a 'think piece' for the *New Zealand Herald* that was published in early 2013. The *Herald* had asked him to ponder the question, Why isn't New Zealand working?

'Frankly, we think it *is* working,' Braid wrote. 'But at what level of its full potential, might be a better question. How can we improve what we have and, importantly, how do we find significant growth to satisfy future New Zealanders?

'As a nation we need long-term policies, with investment in infrastructure and business,' he wrote. 'Under the current mandate of three years, our politicians get about a year to implement anything worthwhile (in between taking on the mantle of government and getting research and plans in place for the first year, followed by battening down during the third year to avoid criticism that would impact on re-election). At an individual level New Zealanders also must take a stake in the game by exercising a measure of responsibility and voting for policies that are good for the country as a whole, rather than placing their individual wants and needs ahead of the community's.

'Of course, as a nation highly dependent on exports, we must continue to encourage more growth in this area. Where would we be if we had not had our dairy industry and Fonterra? Setting targets as the current Minister of Economic Development has done, of taking our export growth from 30 per cent of GDP to 40 per cent, is to be admired. In fact this government has begun setting more targets, and the more of this we can have the better. We all need targets to aim for, but it is not just about exports.

'For the team at Mainfreight it is the 100-year vision, the determination to take our business global that is earning valuable "export" dollars. Some might say in an unconventional manner, but one that is succeeding. There is a lack of understanding, both at government level and in general, of what our overseas earnings mean for New Zealand. Mainfreight may not be an exporter in the traditional sense of the word, but of the NZ$66 million profit earned in the last financial year, 56 per cent, or NZ$37 million, was from our businesses offshore. Those funds contributed to our strong growth, safeguarding the ongoing employment of our team members, providing the ability to invest in better facilities and allowing us to pay dividends to our New Zealand shareholders.

'We need to encourage more New Zealand businesses to internationalise or globalise themselves; call it what you will.

'As New Zealanders we are well thought of in most countries; our honesty, straight talking, "yes, it is possible" approach is appreciated and can be a key to our success. We are seen as a nation of achievers. We are able to see gaps in larger markets that the lazier, larger corporations have neglected. Our skills have been honed by the smaller, more competitive New Zealand environment. We just need to encourage more companies to get off their backsides and take on the risk and challenge of offshore development.

'Many will transform themselves for the better, ultimately delivering additional revenue and tax paid profits that come home. This will be the life blood of this country in the years to come. Furthermore, the enhanced skills and internationalisation of our business community will pay dividends for future generations.

'The current government has begun this process with the Prime Minister and his trade minister putting enormous hours into trade missions and developing trade agreements with a number of nations. Using these platforms to establish New Zealand businesses in other countries is an excellent initiative. Let us all in business take the opportunities presented for larger, more strategic growth rather than the whinging and moaning we are all sometimes guilty of in the face of challenges. Encouraging our media to cover these events and companies in a more positive manner will also be helpful. Celebrating New Zealand business success as we do our sporting success will go a long way to encouraging strong business development.

'To have New Zealand working at its full potential, we need to have more confidence and belief in our ability to compete on the world stage. Too many of our business leaders limit their horizons, thinking that New Zealand is the only market they can operate in. We need our business community to internationalise and grow our economy on the back of their success in larger, international markets. We *are* good enough!'

WHAT CANNOT BE denied is that Mainfreight has been the second best performing company on the New Zealand stock exchange for the past fifteen years. Business analyst and commentator Brian Gaynor makes the point that when Mainfreight started, the average company lasted 39 years, while today the lifespan is nearer to twelve years. They either go bust or they are absorbed by someone else. This shorter life-cycle is a reflection of a much tougher, more competitive environment. Most companies that began when Mainfreight did would have stopped twenty years ago with the owners taking a million or so each into retirement. Which makes it all the more extraordinary that the mantra of Mainfreight being a 100-year company has undergone a shift over time, subtle but illuminating; the 100-year vision is now not simply a finite point, but rather something that starts afresh each and every day — an evolving vision, the long-term view a way of life.

And in Gaynor's view, what makes Mainfreight different is their 'foot on the accelerator' approach.

Braid's problem now, as he sees it, is to keep the foot to the floor while ensuring all around him grasp that the global journey is only just beginning.

'The job we have in front of us is believing we can actually become New Zealand's biggest company by size and market capitalisation by our fiftieth anniversary. That's in 2028. That's not far away.'

Law Wai Hung: Mainfreight delivering in China.

QUITTER

NEVER V

WINNER

NEVER C

Appendices

# A selection of Mainfreight truck sayings

- A good friend is one who walks in when the rest of the world walks away
- A good laugh and a long sleep are the best cures
- A home without books is like a house without windows
- A turtle can't move forward unless he sticks his neck out
- All you need to have fun is one good friend
- Always keep your word
- Attention is to people what fertiliser is to flowers
- Attitudes are contagious
- Be a player, not a spectator
- Big trees catch wind
- Children are like wet cement, whatever falls on them makes an impression
- Children are our most valuable natural resource
- Choose the less travelled path
- Common sense is genius dressed in its work clothes
- Creative thinking is inspired by limited funds
- Diplomacy is thinking twice before saying nothing
- Discover the gifts of everyday life
- Don't sweat the small stuff; and it's all small stuff
- Doubt is the key to knowledge
- Education is the enemy of poverty
- Every day is a new opportunity
- Everyone is beautiful with a smile
- Give people more than they expect and do it cheerfully
- Good conversation should be exhausting
- He who never made a mistake, never made a discovery either
- I don't have to attend every argument I'm invited to
- Ideas are funny things; they only work if you do

- If you fail to plan, you are planning to fail
- If you think education is expensive — try ignorance
- Leave everything a little better than you found it
- Life is not a spectator sport, join the game!
- Minds are like parachutes, they only function when open
- Never test the depth of the water with both feet
- Peace of mind is always present; you just have to learn how to find it
- Quality is remembered long after the price is forgotten
- Question your prejudices
- Quitters never win, winners never quit
- Reach for the high apples first; you can get the low ones anytime
- Read every day
- Ready, fire, aim. The way to learn is to begin
- Some people walk in the rain, others just get wet
- Success is a journey not a destination
- Tell those that you love how you feel
- The best way to escape your problem is to solve it
- The best way to stay healthy is to eat properly and exercise
- The door to success is labelled 'push'
- The harder I work the luckier I get
- The man on top of the mountain didn't fall there
- The only place where success comes before work is in the dictionary
- The only thing worth stealing is a kiss from a sleeping child
- There is nothing in a caterpillar that tells you it's going to be a butterfly
- Throughout history, there will be only one of you
- Watch for big problems, they disguise big opportunities
- We do not inherit the land, we borrow it from our children
- With passion, anything is possible
- You ain't got music you ain't got life
- Your children need your presence more than your presents

# The Mainfreight share price
## 1996–2012

**NZX: MFT**

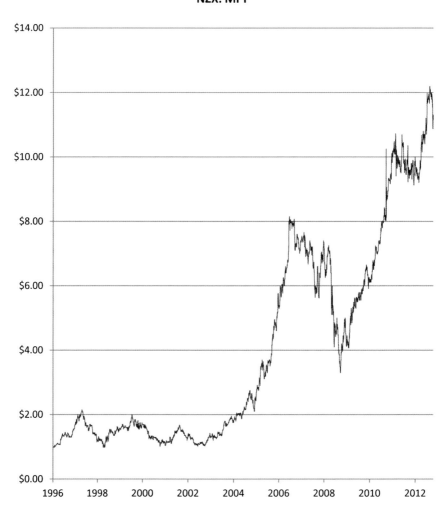

# Proud to work
# at Mainfreight

**NEW ZEALAND CaroTrans Auckland** Eyah Al-atafi, 10 Dec 2012; Lisa Bardon, 20 Sep 2010; Trudy Burt, 21 Feb 2005; Joshua Chellatamby, 21 Jan 2008; Cameron Couper, 11 Sep 2007; Lucio DiBello, 25 Jan 2010; Bruce Fruean, 3 Nov 2007; Steve Hendry, 28 Feb 2000; Katrina Nathan, 22 Jun 1998; Julien Schnorr, 28 Jun 2010; Nicky Smith, 2 Feb 2005; Erika Todi, 9 May 2011; Will Young, 14 Jul 2008. **CFS Auckland** Dale Abernethy, 10 Nov 2009; Tere Benedito, 11 May 1997; Mike Dunn, 26 Jul 1993; Norm Gasgoigne, 20 Dec 2010; Anthony Kirk, 26 Mar 2012; Mike Ladyman, 5 Mar 2007; Brent Marks, 1 Nov 2010; Ye Wang, 5 May 2008. **Chemcouriers Auckland** Sam Bollard, 12 Oct 2009; Wayne Buchanan, 3 Nov 2008; Christopher Byrne, 5 Jun 2003; Nikesh Chhana, 21 Feb 2008; Emily Cox, 26 Sep 1988; Ryan Cox, 28 May 2012; Leanne Drube, 6 Aug 2001; Yevgeniy Dryden, 4 Mar 2013; Villi Fatamaka, 11 May 2007; Max Finau, 20 Oct 2010; Kodie Hamilton, 12 Mar 2012; Kitty Henson, 24 Jan 2011; Luke Matthew Hiroa, 15 Jul 2010; Daniel Holder, 8 Nov 2004; Noel Hughes, 30 May 1994; Hans Huisman, 1 Apr 2003; Nicholas Kale, 1 Apr 2002; Isi Kaliopasi, 7 Feb 2011; Allan Keene, 1 Apr 2004; Michael Keith, 27 Mar 2001; Nagendra Kumar, 01 Mar 2008; Iulieta Leafa, 01 Apr 2013; Trevor Mitai, 16 Dec 2002; Nigel Mouat, 1 Apr 1993; Allan Murray, 2 Feb 1998; Gillian Murray, 6 Jan 2004; Ashley O'Connor, 5 Feb 2010; Mark Pakuru, 10 Oct 2007; Jayshree Patel, 10 Apr 2007; Kishor Patel, 29 Oct 1991; Henry Peti, 1 Apr 2005; Georgina Shelton-Agar, 23 Aug 2011; Andrew Smith, 20 Jan 2003; Gail Street, 2 Apr 1991; Greg Stringer, 11 Mar 2002; Milasa Tamapeau, 16 Dec 2002; Brenton TeRehu, 27 Jan 1998; Michael Thomas, 12 Jan 2004; Barry Thompson, 8 Feb 1999; Matt Tod, 1 Apr 2004; Noa Tohi, 23 Aug 2004; Kini Toloa, 30 Jun 2008; Sosaia Nomani Tupou, 4 Oct 2010; George Ulutaufonua, 10 May 2006; Wayne Walker, 1 Apr 1991; Sylvia Xie, 21 Apr 2010. **Chemcouriers Christchurch** Pitone Ah Kuoi, 24 Mar 2008; Isaac Davis, 15 Mar 2010; Chris Donaldson, 12 Sep 2002; Bridget Hansen, 25 Aug 2003; Alex Hubers, 6 Jun 2004; Graham Jackson, 1 Aug 2004; Grant Kilty, 1 Aug 2002; Charles Koudys, 12 Nov 2012; Karina Laughton, 5 Mar 2007; Charlie Powell, 1 Oct 1980. **Chemcouriers Mt Maunganui** Dennis Simpson, 1 Apr 1997. **Chemcouriers Wellington** Daryl Hutchinson, 1 May 2005; Brendon Jepson, 12 Feb 2007; Shane McDougal, 9 Jul 2001; Graeme Ngatai, 1 Aug 2008; Graham Ralston, 1 Aug 1996; Rodney Warsnop, 16 May 2007. **Daily Freight Auckland** Richard Aitken, 17 Jan 2011; Fazeel Ali, 13 Feb 2009; Arthur Atoaga, 9 Apr 2003; Allan Aufai, 16 Apr 1998; Tolua Aufai, 11 Sep 2007; Altaf Baba, 20 Oct 2008; Taimur Badhniwalla, 14 Sep 2007; Mark Balhorn, 1 Jun 1996; Russell Barry, 1 Aug 1992; Adrian Betterton, 30 Jul 2012; Beau Birtwhistle, 19 Nov 2012; Jacob Bower, 22 Feb 2011; Raymond Brown, 24 May 2010; Martin Cannon, 14 Mar 2011; Raghu Chinchalker, 4 Sep 2006; ZhenTao Chung, 15 Feb 2010; Anthony Covic, 2 Jul 2012; Edward Creedy, 28 Feb 2011; Jim Cullen, 24 May 1972; Tracey Curtis, 3 Jun 2003; Paul Derbyshire, 15 Jan 2004; Chetan Desai, 11 Dec 2006; Sidney Ene, 8 Oct 2007; Siera Fatu, 26 Jun 1989; Lydia Fohe, 5 Jan 2011; Soteria Folaumoeloa, 15 Feb 1995; Roger Hallen, 11 Aug 2003; Martin Hamilton, 5 Jun 2012; Candice Harrison, 24 Jan 2011; Vosa Henare-Vaihu, 21 Jul 2008; Joshua Hepple, 21 Mar 2011; Sam Hiko, 7 Jun 2011; Dorie Hindman, 7 Feb 2005; Gavin Holm, 14 Jun 2005; Malcolm Holm, 30 Jun 2003; Devon Holt, 7 Dec 2009; Nathan Humphreys, 23 Oct 1996; Max Kaleopa, 31 May 2010; Watson Kauvalu, 6 Aug 2007; Murray Kendall, 1 Sep 2005; Jordon Killen, 30 May 2011; Lionel Knox, 25 May 1981; Asnil Kumar, 22 Oct 2010; Yasbeen Kumar, 14 Jul 1998; Katalina Latana, 18 Oct 2010; Roger Leckner, 1 Oct 1997; Paul Leydon, 1 Feb 1990; Ray Linton-Brown, 27 Jan 1972; Loseli Manu, 21 Feb 2011; Hanna Matthews, 14 Nov 2011; Nick McConnochie, 21 Nov 2011; Shasta Mishra, 28 Feb 2007; Ben Monro, 11 Mar 2013; Sue Moses, 7 Mar 1988; Richard Mua, 29 May 2006; Benjamin Mulipola, 15 Feb 2011; Dave Murray, 01 Sep 1991; Solomon Na'a Koloke, 4 Apr 2011; Niraj Nand, 26 Nov 2012; Khalid Naved, 1 Dec 2011; John Newby, 18 Aug 1977; Christie Oliveti, 16 Jan 2012; Tim Ottenhof, 31 Jan 2012; Talau Paila, 6 Aug 2007; Saurabh Patel, 23 May 2011; Phillip Payne, 1 Feb 2001; John Poland, 18 Aug 2008; Tai Poleka, 22 Feb 2011; Kumar Rajan, 14 Jan 2008; Daniel Riddell, 1 Mar 1999; Lloyd Rivers-Smith, 15 Jul 1977; Terry Rogers, 16 Apr 2003; Tua Ropati, 29 Mar 2004; Roy Savage, 1 Sep 2005; Jatin Shah, 28 Jan 2013; Riki Short, 15 Jul 2003; Wesley Siakumi, 11 May 1977; Edward Simamao, 15 Oct 2007; Jai Singh, 13 Jun 2012; Lakhbir Singh, 4 Sep 2006; Parmjit Singh, 25 Aug 2010; Lesley Smith, 19 Apr 2004; Mike Smith, 1 May 1998; Terry Takairangi, 7 Feb 2006; Anneluisa Tanoai, 29 Oct 2007; Michael Tapper, 1 Feb 1968; Jennifer Tuhi, 3 Jul 2003; John Tui, 14 Jan 2008; Sheryl Waite, 30 Apr 1990; Grant Wallis, 1 May 1998; Vincent Wang, 5 Dec 2012; William Weekes, 21 Nov 1999; Brett Whitehead, 3 Jul 2006; Hayden Young, 22 Feb 2010. **Daily Freight Christchurch** Sheik Ali, 25 May 2009; Adam Banas, 26 Nov 2012; Jacob Bent, 30 May 2011; Isobel Bowman, 12 Oct 2011; Colin Brown, 1 Jan 1995; Beverley Canovan, 11 Oct 1999; Daryl Carter, 1 Feb 2007; Terrene Christmas, 24 Feb 2010; Bill Clark, 3 Oct 1988; Maurice Colville, 11 Mar 2005; Susan Davies, 25 Aug 2008; Megan Delaney, 5 Jan 1999; Carole Dixon, 14 Dec 2009; Craig Edwards, 23 Jul 2007; Martyn Ellis, 30 Mar 2005; Ken Ganseburg, 30 Jul 1973; Ross Hawken, 29 Oct 2002; Iain Henderson, 2 Nov 1992; Thomas Hira, 28 Jan 2008; Simon Jackson, 23 Aug 2010; Noel Jordon, 15 Jan 2003; Keith Kennedy, 21 Mar 2012; Vaugh Keefe, 1 Apr 2002; Abbey Kirk, 8 Mar 2012; Steve Lilley, 1 Jul 1998; Jacob Maikuku, 26 Jul 2010; Jared Maioha, 5 Mar 2013; Darryn McDonald, 01 Apr 2003; Lachlan McGhie, 28 Nov 2011; Doug McMillan, 1 Oct 1992; Shannon Merito, 13 Sep 2011; Harry Morris, 24 Jul 2006; Sam Morton, 31 Aug 2009; Steve Moule, 30 Mar 2004; Jayne Munslow, 17 Oct 2005; Deane Murray, 7 Dec 2009; Katie Newsome, 14 May 2007; Nikki Oliver, 5 Feb 1992; Luke Percasky, 9 May 2005; Tony Ringdahl, 5 Nov 2001; Mikala Smith, 13 May 2008; Craig Stewart, 11 Apr 1994; Carl Stringer, 26 Oct 2010; Ben Teale, 14 Jan 2008; Mark Tomlinson, 1 Oct 2002. **Daily Freight/Chemcouriers Hamilton** Jenny Cliffe, 13 Jan 1997; Barry Douch, 1 Apr 2003; Neil Douch, 9 Sep 2001; Edward Hemara, 2 Feb 2010; Tom Kumitau, 1 Apr 2002; Ernest Tauai, 19 May 2008; Lamar Ten Wolde, 7 Nov 2005; Jodi Vaughan, 18 Dec 1995. **Daily Freight Wellington** Ken Adams, 1 Jun 1989; Phil Amaru, 1 Aug 1972; Ross Braybrook, 6 Dec 2010; Martyn Bryant, 17 Nov 2003; Jason Caddis, 5 Mar 2007; John Campbell, 17 Oct 2001; Daniel Cornick, 21 Feb 2007; Sam Ede, 31 Mar 1997; Seila Fiso, 24 Aug 1984; Pat Henderson, 1 Feb 1997; Rukua Kavakura, 23 Aug 1999; Paul MacCormick, 1 May 2010; Michelle Mikara, 1 Dec 1993; David Priestley, 8 Feb 1973; John Salanoa, 26 Apr 2004; Ron Satherley, 22 Sep 2003; Lynette

Sinden, 23 Jun 1995; Alex Walters, 1 Oct 2004. **Mainfreight Ashburton** Nicky Butler, 1 Feb 2010; Ross Butler, 1 Nov 2010; Christopher Frost, 1 Feb 2010; Trevor Irving, 4 Feb 2013; Barry Linwood, 9 Jan 2012; Jared Orme, 25 Feb 2013. **Mainfreight Auckland** Hannah Abraham, 27 Sep 2006; Wiki Abraham, 9 May 2005; Jon Absolum, 19 Mar 2007; Maree Absolum, 23 Oct 2003; Ronald Ahmed, 2 Mar 2009; Kevin Aldridge, 1 Apr 1997; Shameen Basha, 2 Apr 2001; Prakash Bechan, 12 Apr 2005; Hayden Bell, 1 Nov 2000; Stu Bennett, 1 Apr 2000; Michael Bing, 27 Nov 2007; Don Braid, 9 Aug 1978; Kym Brett, 13 Aug 1994; David Brown, 10 Sep 2004; Hohepa Brown, 15 Apr 2002; Mark Brown, 14 Jul 2010; Mike Brown, 24 Apr 2012; Alex Campbell, 10 Nov 2009; Rex Campbell, 22 May 1995; Vania Chalmers, 3 Sep 2010; Shamal Charan, 18 Jul 2011; Bernard Chiondere, 10 Jul 2006; Yvonne Chissell, 7 Nov 1988; Milan (Jnr) Cihak, 9 May 2003; Milan (Snr) Cihak, 22 Sep 2008; Bryan Clark, 2 Nov 2011; Paul Cole, 1 Apr 2000; Scott Collings, 14 Sep 1992; Nikki Cooper, 18 Sep 2006; Simon Cotter, 1 Jan 2013; Larry Coulter, 13 Oct 1993; Andrew Coulton, 12 Jul 2010; Kerry Crocker, 10 Nov 1980; Robert Croft, 5 Jun 2012; Ioana Davis, 4 Jul 2005; Jonathan Davison, 8 Aug 2011; Lee De Cook, 3 Mar 2011; Robert De Haan, 31 Jan 2012; Martin Devereux, 29 May 2000; Edward Dickie, 4 Feb 2013; Kevin Drinkwater, 1 Apr 1986; Tom Dyson, 19 Nov 2012; Alan Edwards, 1 Jun 2002; Hayden Elwarth, 21 Jun 2010; Katarina Ene, 21 Jun 2006; Craig Evans, 6 Mar 1987; Tavita Fainu'u, 30 Aug 2004; Kevin Gee, 25 Sep 2006; Carl George, 31 Jan 1995; Nitaan Glentworth, 8 Nov 2010; Neil Graham, Life Member; Mitch Gregor, 19 Nov 2001; Aaron Hallett, 24 Feb 2013; Travis Hari, 7 Mar 2005; Levi Harris, 27 Sep 2010; Justin Hart, 22 Aug 2011; Mohammed Hassan, 1 Sep 2003; Joshua Haunga, 8 Aug 2011; Mona Hellens, 3 Dec 1987; Alfred Hetaraka, 13 Jul 2001; Emmet Hobbs, 25 Mar 2003; Charlotte Hoeft, 15 Sep 2009; Brett Horgan, 5 May 2008; Carl Howard-Smith, 6 Mar 1978; Bill Hoy, 25 Jul 1996; Quinnton Hubbard, 31 Mar 2008; Lesley Huia, 14 Jul 2003; Graeme Illing, 1 May 2000; Chris Isaia, 26 Oct 2010; Richard Jane, 1 Jul 2002; Tom Jane, 16 Nov 2010; Ella-Lee Jarvis, 15 Oct 2012; Fred Kalman, 12 May 1989; Emma Katavich, 21 Jul 2003; John Kaukas, 1 Oct 1999; Joe Kawau, 9 May 1988; Nic Kay, 3 Feb 1997; Alex Keen, 18 Apr 2006; Abdul Khan, 29 Sep 2006; Zarik Khan, 1 Oct 2007; Shalini Kumar, 11 Apr 2005; Lowrance Lal, 1 Apr 2007; Releesh Lal, 1 Aug 2007; Mark Lane, 10 Apr 1995; Julian Lawton, 30 Nov 2009; Wilson Li, 1 Sep 2003; Fiu Mapusua, 14 Jun 2010; Corina Mareela, 15 Apr 1997; Robert Mareela, 20 Apr 2005; Glenn Matthews, 13 Mar 1989; Vanessa Maxwell, 17 Feb 1995; Vaughan McDonald, 8 Mar 2010; Andrew McKenzie, 1 Mar 1997; Rachel McKenzie, 7 Feb 2007; Dean McLaughlin, 21 Jul 2008; Paul Miller, 1 Oct 2007; Bryan Mogridge, 25 Mar 2003; Zabid Mohammed, 25 Aug 2008; Dennis Morar, 5 Jan 1999; Sonya Mortensen, 28 Feb 2000; Michael Munns, 27 Jun 2005; Lui Naoupu, 9 Dec 1996; Michael Neale, 2 Nov 2010; Alan Neithe, 16 May 1988; Kevin Nepia, 1 Sep 2002; Jared Nuku, 31 Aug 2005; Zedekiah Nuku, 30 Aug 2005; Lucy Owen, 28 Jul 2011; Luke Paine, 5 Nov 2001; Maureen Paine, 20 Jun 1995; Israel Paul, 3 Oct 2011; Tom Paul, 3 Oct 2005; Maurie Phillips, 1 Oct 1999; Leon Pirake, 15 Feb 1995; Bruce Plested, 6 Mar 1978; Tipi Poa, 6 Oct 2008; Shayne Porter, 13 Dec 1999; Aviksh Prasad, 3 Apr 2008; Richard Prebble, 31 Mar 1996; Rowan Preston, 4 May 1998; Craig Radich, 1 Jun 1990; Cameron Reibel, 10 Jan 2011; Irene Richards, 21 Feb 2012; Keith Robb, 1 Oct 2001; Robert Robertson, 17 Feb 2005; Jason Rogers, 4 Apr 2005; Thomas Rolleston, 2 Feb 2010; Daniel Rowe, 18 Feb 2013; Don Rowlands, Life Member; Peter Sadler, 18 Jun 2012; Mohammed Saleem, 4 Aug 2008; Anil Sami, 23 Feb 2004; Tarlochan Sarai, 8 Aug 2009; Carol Selwyn, 14 Jul 1985; Geoff Sharman, 17 Nov 1997; Vavega Siliga, 16 May 2005; Carolyn Sim, 16 Nov 1998; Donna Sim, 25 Nov 1996; Harry Sima, 14 Mar 2005; Michelle Simmons, 25 Jan 1988; Manjit Singh, 11 May 2009; Vinod Singh, 7 Jul 2008; Navin Singh Sidhu, 13 Mar 2013; Dansey Smith, 22 Feb 2000; Pat Smith, 9 Dec 1996; Clinton Smith, 3 Feb 2003; Regan Somers, 29 May 2002; Stephen Speight, 6 Nov 2003; Jason Street, 1 Aug 1994; Glen Symons, 4 Apr 1994; William Tae, 22 Nov 2011; Jamane Tarau, 13 Sep 2005; Tuaine Tarau, 3 Mar 2003; Michael Taufa, 13 Sep 2004; Andy Taunga, 15 Feb 1995; Suzanne Taunton, 25 Sep 2006; Allan Taylor, 14 Dec 2007; Norm Teio, 1 Apr 2005; Holley Thoresen, 23 Jan 2012; Bruce Tierney, 14 Aug 2003; Rachael Timmo, 3 Mar 2003; David Tolson, 16 Mar 1971; Kevin Tram, 3 Apr 2012; Eddie Tuhakaraina, 10 May 2004; Ketan Undevia, 28 May 2007; Steve Ward, 20 Oct 2008; Abdul Wazeem, 1 Jun 2007; Bradley Wearing, 13 Jul 2010; Mellissa Wearing, 20 May 1996; Matt Wedding, 1 Apr 2002; Kyle Weir, 21 Jan 2008; Daniel Wells, 7 Jan 2008; Tina Whineray, 1 Sep 1988; Sheree Whitehead, 26 Apr 2004; Debbie Williams, 29 Nov 2002; Greg Williams, 6 Nov 2006; Rob Williams, 24 May 1993; Roy Williams, 23 Jan 2006; Tim Williams, 14 Mar 1984; Alicia Wilson, 28 Apr 2008; Caitlin Wilson, 7 Feb 2012; Clive Wilson, 10 Dec 2012; Hamish Wilson, 17 Jan 2011; Scott Wilson, 9 Sep 2002; Kelvin Winstanley, 6 Sep 2010; Greg Wong, 1 Apr 2006; Jareth Wong, 23 Jul 2007; Vern Wright, 1 Mar 2004; Lauren Yerex, 6 Apr 2010. **Mainfreight Blenheim** Ken Anderson, 8 Apr 2008; Ray Bradcock, 23 Oct 2007; John Cleary, 1 Feb 2004; John Falconer, 1 Apr 2006; Allan Harper, 15 Feb 2010; Steve Heffer, 24 Apr 2006; Peter Jones, 23 Jan 2006; Shane Kennedy, 7 Mar 2011; Janet Landon-Lane, 12 Apr 2005; Andrew Pillans, 30 Jun 2003; Rhonda Pillans, 23 Jul 2012; Amanda Sanft, 8 June 2009; Shane Smythe, 14 Nov 2011; Murray Snowden, 3 Dec 2007; Ratana Te Kanawa, 3 Sep 2012; Phillip Thompson, 23 Nov 2009; Murray Wallis, 11 Jul 2009. **Mainfreight Christchurch** Philip Black, 1 Jul 2008; Debbie Blackburn, 7 Dec 1993; Dean Buick, 4 Jul 2011; Chris Burrowes, 7 Feb 2000; Chad Chamberlain, 6 May 2004; Donald Chamberlain, 5 Nov 1998; Mathew Chamberlain, 16 Oct 2002; Rhys Chamberlain, 17 Jan 2011; Egon Chmiel, 1 Jun 2007; Dennis Christmas, 1 May 1999; Stu Clarke, 13 Aug 2001; Rhyl Cole, 21 Jan 2005; Sara Cole, 12 Mar 2012; Robin Cook, 17 Apr 1989; Sue Cook, 13 Apr 2006; Angus Cowlin, 12 Oct 2010; Mike Crawford, 31 Oct 2011; Ross Dalzell, 1 Jun 2006; Sally Dalzell, 12 Oct 1998; Robin Davids, 29 Nov 2005; David Dodge, 2 Dec 2003; Brian Dunlop, 1 Apr 2001; Alicia Frew, 24 Oct 2007; Rob Garriock, 29 Mar 2005; Sarah Garriock, 1 Apr 2010; Steven Grace, 8 Mar 2004; Mike Griffiths, 16 Mar 1992; Robert Halkett, 12 Mar 2012; Elijah Hapi, 21 Feb 2012; Michael Heremaia, 1 Feb 2012; Karl Hicks, 1 Jul 2007; Alan Howard, 1 Jul 2008; Nathan Hyde, 1 Sep 2008; Daniel Ireland, 6 Oct 2003; Russell Jackson, 7 Feb 1989; Desiree Jones-Jackson, 9 Oct 2006; Russell Kamo, 15 Jan 2009; Jason Lamb, 24 Jun 2012; Karen Lamb, 5 May 1998; Carolyn Lee, 6 Aug 1997; Lisa Martin, 7 Jan 2022; Jordan McGillivray, 15 Feb 2012; Patrick McGillivray, 17 Mar 2008; Robert McGillivray, 30 Jun 1997; Joseph McKay, 20 Aug 2008; Laurie McMahon, 21 Dec 1987; Neil McRobbie, 18 Dec 1987; Colin McTurk, 11 Feb 2004; Bob Murdock, 16 Jan 2012; Caryl Murdock, 10 Feb 2011; Shawn Murphy, 10 Apr 2010; Mark Nicol, 1 Aug 1998; Mark O'Keefe, 17 Sep 2008; Geoff Radford, 5 Oct 2004; Darryl Reid, 17 May 2006; Paul Robertson, 1 Jul 1999; Kieran Rowe, 1 Mar 2004; Ben Sharp, 1 Mar 2005; Wendy Smith, 22 May 2002; Stephen Tahere, 14 May 2012; Greg Tanner, 8 Jun 1999; Jacob Taurua, 17 Dec 2010; Noreen Taurua-Watson, 29 Mar 2004; Cynthia Thomas, 3 Oct 2011; Lindsay Thomas, 7 Aug 2007; Stuart Tyler, 5 Nov 2012; Steven Voyce, 1 Jul 2002; Russell Waters, 3 Aug 2006; Henry Whyte, 5 Dec 2011; Angela Williams, 10 Jun 2008; Jason Woods, 14 Mar 2005; John Wright, 27 Apr 1994. **Mainfreight Cromwell** Paul Arras, 5 Feb 2001; Megan Bradley, 24 Aug 2011; Josephine Cranston, 19 Jul 2004; Russell Decke, 1 Dec 2008; Marlene Graham, 12 Dec 2007; Joanna Heath, 14 Jul 2008; Arthur Higgan, 11 Sep 2012; Brent Jones, 5 Jan 2005; Kevin Madden, 5 Nov 2007; Sam O'Leary, 18 Feb 2013; Samantha Peterson, 27 Mar 2013; Julz Rickard, 2 Feb 2011; Tracey Rickard, 18 Mar 2010; Dean Shaw, 01 Oct 2010; Trevor Smith, 17 Aug 2011; Craig Steer, 1 Feb 2010; Shane Steer, 8 Mar 2010; Kaylene Thompson, 28 Jun 2004; Paddy Tuohy, 25 Oct 2007; Derek Wardell, 11 Aug 2017; Gary Woods, 12 Feb 2013; Deborah Wright, 13 Sep 1999; Paul Wright, 3 Nov 1983. **Mainfreight Dunedin** Jeff & Janine Blanc, 01 Dec 2007; Tim Brasier, 1 Apr 2001; Lenny Brisbane, 15 Jul 2008; Barry Clark, 21 Dec 2001; Graeme Clark, 3 Aug 2009; Greg Colston, 1 Sep 1998; Wayne Day, 2 Feb 2004; Rex Edwards, 1 Dec 1980; Pat Folimatama, 20 Feb 2012; Suzanne Fox, 20 Feb 2013; Carl Gardner, 1 Apr 2008; Fiona Guildford, 20 Feb 2006; Paul & Natalie Johnston, 9 Sep 1996; Kamm Kawau, 1 Apr 2005; Matt Keane, 1 Apr 2006; Peter Kerr, 7 Jan 2008; Yvonne King, 24 Jul 2000; Chris Marsden, 17 Oct 2005; Leah Maxwell, 1 Sep 1997; Shayne McAndrew, 25 Nov 2006; Doug McElhinney, 1 Jun 2005; Mark McElhinney, 1 Apr 2005; Kelly McKenzie, 28 Jul 2008; Shae McKenzie, 11 Apr 2011; Ryan

McLean, 29 Oct 2007; Doug Melrose, 5 Oct 1988; Lindsay Miller, 8 Aug 1997; Alana Mutch, 5 Jul 2004; Cameron Power, 15 Jan 2001; Vaughan Rohan, 1 Feb 2000; Tony Russell, 2 Dec 1996; Derek Saville, 1 Feb 2004; Mark Smith, 28 May 2012; Steve Smith, 1 Dec 2010; Robert Stout, 30 Aug 1999; Melissa Winklemann, 27 Feb 2012. **Mainfreight Gisborne** Riaz Ali, 26 Nov 2012; Kayne Arahanga, 29 Dec 2010; Blake Farrell, 8 Nov 2012; Margie Freeman, 14 Apr 2008; Ryan Griffin, 25 Jun 2012; Anton Hill, 23 Nov 2012; Wayne Lee, 20 Nov 2001; Chloe Mannix, 11 Oct 2012; James Mataira-Kaiwai, 4 Oct 2012; Brent McIntosh, 3 Nov 2008; David McKinnon, 3 Dec 2012; Dave McLauchlan, 1 Apr 1992; Elaine McLauchlan, 1 Oct 1997; Judith Miller, 19 Dec 2010; Margaret Muir, 15 Aug 2011; Sahad Rafiq, 16 Nov 2012; Alan Robinson, 8 Dec 2010; Willie Robinson, 17 Nov 2010; Mike Rutherford, 16 Apr 2008; Glen Sainsbury, 2 Apr 2008; Sally Taylor, 8 Sep 2011; Samuel Wanoa, 23 Aug 2012; Ben Williams, 15 Mar 2006. **Mainfreight Greymouth** Eddie Banks, 5 Jan 2009; Paul Cleland, 15 Nov 2010; Richard Dalzell, 19 Jul 2012; Wayne Dalzell, 17 Dec 2007; Troy Gerrard, 26 Nov 2011; Dwayne Hackett, 21 Dec 2002; Andrew Havill, 22 Nov 1987; Gavin Holmwood, 7 May 2012; Moana Johnsen, 21 Feb 2005; Keith Lavery, 22 Oct 2001; Scott Lemon, 7 Nov 2008; Jamie McGeady, 7 Feb 2007; Darryl Nichols, 6 Jul 2011; Jeff Older, 19 Jul 2012; Glen Redmond, 30 May 2011; Warren Rose, 17 Dec 2012; Quentin Scott, 16 Jan 2012. **Mainfreight Hamilton** James Baker, 30 Jan 2006; Gordon Baker, 1 Mar 1994; Luke Barlow, 28 Jan 2008; Patrick Barton, 17 Feb 2012; Ashleigh Blair, 23 Nov 2011; Robert Bryers, 27 Jul 2009; Charlie Camenzind, 24 May 1993; Charlotte Carpenter, 3 Nov 2011; Lee Clark Jnr, 1 Apr 2003; Barry Clifford, 19 May 2008; Louise Day, 10 Jan 2005; Randall Dennis, 14 Dec 2007; Dwayne Dickey, 15 Jun 2004; Ray Dixon, 4 May 1987; Daniel Dobbyn, 9 Jul 2012; Paul Douch, 2 Feb 2005; Robert Douch, 1 Dec 2007; Gavin Duncan, 28 Feb 2011; Keith Edwards, 7 Aug 2009; Bob Eva, 1 Jan 1985; Donna Everaarts, 25 Aug 2005; Nikolette Fahey, 24 Mar 2010; Ryan Gadsby, 26 Dec 2007; Wayne Goodwin, 1 Apr 1992; Jocelyn Gordon, 25 Mar 2008; Murray Gordon, 1 Apr 1991; Dameon Govind, 10 Nov 2010; Justin Gower, 28 Nov 2011; Melanie Greenbank, 6 May 2002; Andrew Hall, 26 Mar 2003; Kylie Hansen, 28 Mar 2011; Shane Hansen, 8 Nov 2011; Craig Hawira, 14 May 2012; Carlos Hicks, 22 Feb 2010; Wentworth Hicks, 4 Aug 2008; Dion Huisman, 1 Sep 2009; Hamish Jackson, 9 Mar 2009; Maurice Jarrett, 9 Jan 2006; Sam Johnson, 1 May 1992; Tracey Johnson, 15 Aug 2011; Gareth Jolly, 2 Jul 2007; Denise Kearns, 28 Apr 2003; Haami Kingi, 20 May 2003; Phillip Koopu, 30 Oct 2007; Murray Lasenby, 16 Jun 2008; Denis Laws, 1 Jun 1991; Keegan Lewis, 1 Aug 2012; Roxanne Logan, 25 Jun 2012; Stuart MacLennan, 12 Nov 2012; Julie Anne Madden, 5 Apr 2004; Peter Manutai-Esau, 2 Jul 2007; Francis Maxwell, 8 Sep 2008; Bridget Monrad, 4 Jan 2012; Richard Mountney, 1 Apr 2008; Robert Muru, 1 Jul 2005; Marie Oliver, 22 Feb 1999; Terry Phillips, 1 Aug 2011; Shane Pratt, 1 Apr 2007; Fabian Purcell, 8 Jun 2009; Bonty Ranapiri, 19 Apr 2004; Des Reynolds, 1 Jan 1985; Colin Richardson, 1 Jan 2009; Darren Richardson, 1 Apr 1994; Vaughn Sargent, 20 Aug 2008; John Scandlyn, 31 Oct 2002; Debbie Schollum, 6 Mar 2006; Vanessa Semmens, 5 Mar 2012; Tama Skipper, 5 Jun 2007; Shaun Smith, 13 Mar 2000; Mike Stockley, 10 Sep 2001; Able Tangitutu, 15 May 2006; Trudy Te Aho, 27 Feb 2006; Graig Te Awahuri, 1 Oct 2012; Frank Te Wani, 22 Dec 2010; Te Ate Walker, 21 Nov 2011; Wayne Warrender, 01 Jul 2009; Tyne Wats, 09 Jul 2012; Piko Wineera-Hemara, 7 Sep 2011. **Mainfreight Invercargill** Jason Bishop, 9 Jun 2011; Jackie Buckley Gray, 5 Jul 2010; Dean Cribb, 7 May 2012; Ian Garrick, 5 Jan 1988; Jason Gray, 25 Mar 2011; Murray Magon, 1 Sep 2007; Lisa McGilvray, 2 Dec 2002; Nathan McKay, 28 Sep 1999; Andrew McLean, 19 Aug 2002; Stephen Monaghan, 26 Oct 2010; Dean Reynolds, 2 Apr 2013; Harry Reynolds, 5 Jan 1988; Kate Sandri, 5 Sep 2011; David Searle, 9 Dec 2010; John Searle, 3 Jan 2001; Kelly Thorburn, 26 Apr 1999; Leonna Turner, 30 Jun 2008; Ross Wells, 16 Sep 1981; Jeanette Williams, 18 Feb 1985. **Mainfreight Kaitaia** James Poulson, 15 Sep 2008; Tunney Thrupp, 21 Jan 2013. **Mainfreight Masterton** Bob Dougherty, 1 Jun 1987; Charles Simpson, 24 Mar 1999; Dave Wilton, 31 Dec 2012. **Mainfreight Mt Maunganui** Alan Allport, 2 May 1988; Eric Ashe, 21 Apr 2007; Claire Atkins, 21 Feb 2000; Colin Belk, 24 Jan 1985; Carl Bergersen, 21 May 2012; Brent Brosnan, 14 Nov 2003; Rob Bull, 1 Mar 1993; Mark Cate, 1 Nov 2009; Anthony Chadwick, 27 Sep 2002; Darren Chadwick, 15 Dec 2003; Ashley Collett, 19 Jul 2011; Greg Conning, 7 Feb 2006; Richard Currie, 1 Jul 2004; Caitlin Darby, 12 Dec 2011; Dipak Dayal, 11 Jun 2002; Neville Emery, 21 Feb 2000; Hazel Fisher, 29 Oct 2009; Leroy Gavan-Smith, 9 Jan 2010; Mandy Goff, 7 May 2012; Dean Gordon, 1 Feb 2010; Paul Grimes, 20 May 2002; Jenna Haerewa, 23 Apr 2012; Yana Heath, 4 Aug 2003; Rhonda Hemming, 13 Feb 2012; Ray Hewlett, 1 Nov 2005; Kate Hilhorst, 4 Jul 2011; Craig Hine, 1 Apr 2000; Mark Johnson, 8 Jun 2009; Melissa Josephson, 2 Apr 2002; Chris Kendrick, 1 Aug 2002; Jordon Lilley, 16 Apr 2012; Andrew Lockyer, 1 Jan 2010; Sharon Lockyer, 1 Jul 2003; Murray McCarthy, 18 Aug 2004; Kyla McGregor, 16 Jun 2003; Fay Mikaere, 13 Nov 1989; Marcel Milner, 1 Jun 2000; Karson Muller, 10 Jan 2005; Rick Ngatai, 1 Nov 1993; Delcie Oliphant, 1 Aug 2006; Reuben Ranui, 9 Jan 2006; Mark Robinson, 29 Jan 2008; Lindsay Roper, 1 Nov 2005; Andy Sayle, 1 Jul 2008; Bevan Scott, 2 May 2012; Ranjit Singh, 1 Mar 2005; Leroy Smith, 27 Oct 2010; Courtney Stevenson, 13 Jun 2011; John Stewart, 21 Jun 2006; Lindon Tawhiti, 3 Mar 2003; Kelvin Teasdale, 6 May 2010; Lee Tuhura, 20 Mar 2006; Chris Webb, 1 Nov 2003; Maurice Webb, 1 Apr 2003; Schirelle Wildbore, 21 Aug 1989; Tracey Wright, 7 Nov 2005; Ryan Zimmerman, 26 Mar 2012. **Mainfreight Napier** Rachel Akuhata, 29 Oct 2009; Cameron Archibald, 18 Feb 2013; Kelly Barnett, 7 Jun 2004; Jeff Chapman, 29 Nov 2004; Kaylene Corin, 18 Sep 2007; Michael Delamere, 6 Nov 2006; James Farrell, 15 Feb 2010; Fraser Garnett, 18 Jan 2010; Tui Haami, 22 Sep 2010; Carey Jackson, 25 Jun 2012; Jason Kennedy, 19 Apr 2004; John Mackay, 21 Apr 1992; Tony Maddock, 16 Apr 2012; David Mason, 30 Aug 2007; Andrea Mill, 18 Apr 2005; Corbin Mills, 10 Dec 2012; John Montgomery, 10 May 2007; Henare Morton, 1 Jul 1995; Wayne Mullins, 1 Apr 1989; Kaye Ngapera, 16 Dec 2005; Kerryn O'Neill, 31 Mar 1993; Jenny Pedersen, 7 Apr 2008; Brent Redington, 29 Sep 2007; Scott Russell, 9 Aug 2011; Glen Scott, 30 Jul 2007; Darryn Scurr, 27 Jan 1994; Peter Simeon, 18 Mar 2013; Dylan Smith, 5 Sep 2011; Carl Spindler, 19 Sep 2011; Noel Stubbs, 2 Oct 2006; Nathan Tough, 2 Apr 2004; Craig Walker, 8 Jun 2010; Bill Whyte, 30 Jul 2012; Andrew Wickham, 3 Oct 2011. **Mainfreight Nelson** Paul Brown, 8 Sep 2008; Darren Chandler, 1 Apr 2002; Amy Climo, 6 Dec 2010; Corey Gower, 11 Nov 2002; Ray Gregory, 01 Apr 1996; Aimee Groome, 14 Mar 2007; Craig Groome, 23 Jun 2008; Saki Huch, 5 Mar 2013; Tracey Hughes, 11 Apr 2011; David May, 1 May 2012; Samantha May, 18 Mar 2013; Andrew Mctier, 26 Nov 2012; Leigh Rout, 9 Jun 2008; Bill Simmiss, 1 Feb 1995; Maree Toa, 4 Oct 2004; Graeme Towns, 28 Dec 2005; Bary Turner, 28 May 2012; Pam Waddington, 1 May 1991; Hohaia Walker, 3 Sep 2007; Neil Watson, 17 Oct 2005; Nick Watts, 01 Oct 2005; Brett Yates, 7 Jan 2002; Brad Young, 1 Mar 2001; Kelly Young, 23 Oct 2007. **Mainfreight New Plymouth** Jess Burkhart, 19 Jul 2010; Lane Bynon-Powell, 18 Mar 2002; John Davidson, 17 Feb 2003; Jonathan Davies, 14 Oct 2011; Cori Delves, 28 Feb 2011; Shannon Emmerson, 15 Aug 2006; Aaron Farley, 1 Nov 2001; Margaret Gay, 1 Feb 1999; Glenn Gordon, 29 Mar 2010; Shane Kauri-Mence, 14 May 2012; Benjamin Leaf, 18 Jul 2005; Steve Longstaff, 1 Apr 1994; Tony Martin, 16 Apr 2007; Cody Mason, 23 Oct 2012; Reuben Mason, 1 Apr 2001; John McKenna, 26 Jun 2007; Kayne Newman, 26 Mar 2012; Brendon O'Rourke, 17 Oct 2005; Rick Payne, 1 Apr 2005; Lane Powell, 18 Mar 2002; Gavin Roper, 11 Aug 2008; Steven Short, 17 Apr 2008; Tony Smith, 1 Jul 2004; Maree Stockwell, 15 Apr 2013; Cara Young, 6 Apr 2010. **Mainfreight Palmerston North** Craig Claire, 22 Jan 2013; Brett Cuttle, 2 Apr 1987; Peter Darroch, 1 Oct 1993; Brian Douglas, 10 Oct 1992; Shane Foot, 31 Oct 2004; John Fraser, 10 Jan 2003; Colin Gainey, 3 Mar 1995; Chris Graham, 21 Sep 2008; John Graham, 29 Jul 2002; Lilly Graham, 20 Aug 2007; Marsh Graham, 10 Jul 2008; Suzan Graham, 10 Feb 2003; Rana Heka, 31 Jan 2011; Robin Jago, 1 Mar 1988; Vanessa Johnson, 7 May 2012; Tuhi Kimura, 13 Oct 2008; John King, 13 Apr 2011; Rex Lambert, 2 Oct 2008; Craig Lowe, 13 Oct 2008; Stacey Luke, 1 Sep 2008; Tipu Luke, 8 Sep 2009; Zeke Mako, 12 Jul 2010; Mitch Maxwell, 3 Dec 2012; Rebecca McBride, 18 Mar 2008; Ross McDonald, 1 May 1994; Kevin McDougall, 1 Nov 2002; Scott McIntosh, 10 Apr 2008; John Mitchell, 1 Oct 1991; Lorraine Mitchell, 28 Jan 2013; Tracey Mitchell, 4 Aug 2008; Keri Monk, 3 May 2004; Keith Mudgway, 31 Jan 2002; Mike Murphy, 14 Jan 2013; Nick Page, 1 Dec

2008; Scott Payne, 7 Jan 2008; David Petersen, 7 Mar 2010; Ray Prideaux, 20 Jun 1994; Etu Rongotaua, 4 Aug 2008; Robert Rongotaua, 22 Nov 2010; Elvis Rowlands, 10 Feb 1997; Michael Smith, 14 Dec 2009; Wendy Stewart, 19 Oct 2009; Josh Stimpson, 1 Oct 2012; Keven Stuart, 11 Oct 2012; Bryan Taiaroa, 2 Dec 2009; Nathan Taiaroa, 14 Dec 2009; Peter Thorby, 21 Mar 2012; Albert Tovio, 14 Feb 2005; Michael Tunnicliffe, 5 Nov 2002; Jason Waho, 3 Dec 2012; Peter Waho, 11 Mar 2013; Wayne Wildbore, 6 Jun 2004; Jackie Williams, 1 Apr 2008; Uti Woodley, 12 Jul 2010. **Mainfreight Paraparaumu** Greg Howard, 15 Mar 1999. **Mainfreight Rotorua** Carl Gage, 1 Aug 2011; Greg Camenzind, 30 Oct 2007; Gary Dunseath, 1 Mar 2013; Wayne Ellis, 3 Apr 2006; Dave Farrell, 23 Mar 1987; Leonie Gardiner, 15 Apr 2004; Chris Hall, 18 Apr 2005; Barbara Harrison, 30 May 2011; Benjamin Jenkins, 28 Sep 2011; Raena Lacey, 12 Nov 2007; Rhys Leeke, 4 Jan 2010; Kerry Maxwell, 16 Nov 2009; Ray Maxwell, 1 Mar 2000; Robert McGowan, 2 Feb 2009; Randal McMahon, 15 Nov 2011; Taare Meredith, 20 Feb 2007; Bill Ngawhika, 8 Aug 2011; Graeme Ngawhika, 15 Sep 2004; Percy Powell, 10 Nov 2004; Damien Radesic, 24 Sep 2003; Ainsley Speak, 24 Sep 2007; Travel Taura, 1 Apr 2011; Matthew Thompson, 1 Mar 2005. **Mainfreight Taupo** Nev & Janna Haumaha, 4 April 2011; Willy Haumaha, 25 Jan 2009; Nick Hyde, 8 Feb 1993; Jenny Payne, 29 Dec 1997; Brendan Smith, 20 Feb 2008. **Mainfreight Thames** Phil Frost, 25 Oct 2010; David Henderson, 4 Aug 2008; Andrew McLeod, 1 Aug 2003; Dhenby Muller, 6 Dec 2010; Kiu Muller, 18 Feb 1985; Lance Paul, 4 Aug 2008; Wayne Powell, 4 Aug 2008; John Reynolds, 5 Jan 2011. **Mainfreight Timaru** Greg Anderson, 17 Jan 2008; Nigel Blackler, 2 Sep 2002; Hollie Borcovsky, 11 Jul 2012; Sandra Breen, 7 Feb 2006; Simone Brett, 7 Feb 2012; Jarrid Cooper, 6 Sep 2010; Dave Ennis, 31 Mar 2008; Andrew Fearn, 27 Aug 2012; Jamie Frewen, 6 Oct 2011; Pete Hollamby, 7 Feb 2012; Jordon Howey, 20 Dec 2012; Lisa Howey, 22 Jun 2009; Geoff Kerr, 4 Sep 2009; Murray & Juliet Kippenberger, 1 Apr 2000; Nathan Kippenberger, 8 Dec 2003; Renee LeLievre, 24 Jan 2013; John Lyon, 7 Jan 2013; Karen McKerrow, 26 Jul 2011; Katrina Mehrtens, 6 Dec 2012; Wayne Mills, 12 Mar 2013; Nicholas O'Keefe, 30 Apr 2012; Ryk Ormsby, 20 Nov 2006; Grant Paisley, 14 May 2012; Nerita Pearce, 21 Apr 2010; William Armstrong, 18 Jul 2011; Neil Schaab, 10 Nov 2011. **Mainfreight Wanganui** Innes Campbell, 4 Feb 2002; Daryl Edmonds, 13 Aug 2007; Darren Ellwood, 21 Mar 2011; Lyn Johnston, 4 Mar 2004; Ricky Katene, 11 Aug 2004; Jason Kibblewhite, 22 Sep 2003. **Mainfreight Wellington** Michael Akavi, 3 Nov 2011; George Albert, 15 Apr 1991; Peter Ansell, 21 Nov 2011; Craig Armstrong, 1 Mar 2004; Lynette Baker, 1 Mar 2003; Richard Bell, 6 Apr 2010; Sarah Bennison, 20 Feb 2012; Ian Black, 21 Dec 1987; Colin Bradshaw, 1 Jul 1995; Dempsey Broad, 1 Aug 2008; Lenard Bryant, 11 Jun 2012; Scott Carson, 5 Dec 2011; Regan Chase, 24 Apr 2003; Paul Connelly, 31 Dec 2007; Sam Dale, 13 Jun 2011; Matt Dalton, 8 Aug 2011; Harry Davey, 1 Feb 2005; Byron Dennis, 15 Mar 2010; Paul Fincham, 7 Oct 1996; Darron Fisher, 1 Oct 2003; Pouevalu Fiso, 1 Sep 2011; Selena Franklin, 1 Mar 2004; Luciano Giacon, 1 Jun 1980; Campbell Gray, 19 Mar 2012; Mereana Gray, 11 Aug 2008; Ben Harris, 25 Sep 2006; Ken Harris, 28 Jun 1995; Corey Hayden, 5 Jun 2012; Nathan Hilder, 11 Nov 2011; Scott Hilder, 1 Sep 2004; John Holton, 12 Nov 1997; John Hutchinson, 1 May 2006; Mayana Joseph, 12 Apr 2007; Daniel Jupp, 28 Jun 2004; Teddy Kameta, 3 Jan 2013; Brian Kelly, 15 Aug 1994; Maresa Kilepoa, 31 Mar 1989; Wayne Kilgour, 14 Feb 2000; Steve Marsh, 1 Oct 2005; Richard Maxwell, 10 Oct 2002; Mike McAlister, 19 Sep 2002; Andrea McCafferty, 11 Feb 2002; Nathan McEldowney, 7 Jan 2003; Robert McGrath, 1 Apr 1994; Steven McGregor, 12 Feb 2007; JD McMeekin, 26 Mar 2012; Herini Moeahu, 23 Nov 1987; Liz Moore, 28 Nov 2011; Caleb Morehu, 3 Oct 2011; Vincent Morehu, 6 Oct 2011; Bob Patterson, 1 Mar 1989; Dean Piper, 1 Mar 2004; Greg Piper, 1 Nov 1993; Jade Redfern, 23 Oct 2012; Adam Reeves, 24 Sep 2001; Tony Roberts, 28 Jun 1997; Michelle Romaine, 26 Jul 2005; Zach Rowe, 1 Aug 2012; Graeme Scahill, 1 Apr 1990; Tracey Scurrah, 1 Nov 2010; Pisa Seala, 7 Jun 2005; Johan Soetman, 1 Jul 1995; Jade Soliga, 7 Mar 2011; Megan Stallard, 5 Jun 2007; Mike Stevens, 12 Mar 2012; Timothy Stewart, 4 Jul 2011; Okalani Teuila, 1 Apr 2004; Stuart Thorn, 7 Apr 2003; Seamus Tyler-Baxter, 21 Nov 2011; Segaula Va, 31 Jan 2005; Damien Vaisagote, 19 Oct 2010; Barbara Vincent, 1 Feb 1988; Bob Vincent, 3 Aug 1985; Julie Ward, 17 May 2004; Ross Ward, 27 Aug 2007; Haedyn Wicks, 24 Jul 2002; Fiona Wilson, 4 Feb 2013; Gemma Wright, 10 Dec 2007; Teryle Yeates, 16 Apr 2012. **Mainfreight Westport** Lorraine Absalom, 13 Oct 2008; Gwen Lineham, 1 Jun 2008; Terry Lineham, 1 Jun 2008; Warren Lineham, 1 Jun 2008. **Mainfreight Whangarei** Manon Austin, 2 Oct 2007; Anthony Beazley, 29 Jan 2008; Anil Bhatia, 15 Aug 2011; Sarah Bleakley, 9 Oct 2006; Jim & Heather Bond, 29 Oct 2012; Rob Caie, 1 Jul 2010; Dean Critchley, 11 Jul 2011; Mary Edmonds, 28 Feb 2005; Jeremy Elliott, 1 Aug 2009; Owen Gilchrist, 31 May 2010; Brendon Harris, 16 Oct 2006; Pieter Lambrechts, 17 Oct 2008; Keiran Lynn, 13 May 2008; Shaun Mangal, 18 Jun 2012; Shiv Mangal, 18 Aug 2008; Matthew Maraki, 11 Jul 2011; Rod McTavish, 1 Feb 1980; Joe Reihana, 20 Aug 2012; Jose' Restrepo, 3 Sep 2012; Kevin Roberts, 1 Mar 1999; Douglas Tarau, 7 Feb 2013; Dave Tarawa, 5 Jun 2012; Dane Ten-Wolde, 3 Mar 2008; Desirae Watkins, 13 Sep 2004; Joseph Yearbury, 4 Apr 1994. **Mainfreight Air & Ocean Auckland** Behnaz Bahmani, 26 Oct 2010; Darren Barboza, 24 Feb 2010; Ross Benn, 2 May 1994; Matthew Beveridge, 18 Jan 2010; Sonya Buckle, 7 Apr 2008; Vicky Burgoyne, 12 Mar 2002; Jeremy Burnet, 25 Jan 2010; Tracey Burns, 13 Apr 2012; Penelope Burt, 11 Feb 2002; Don Campbell, 12 Jul 1982; Liz Castillo, 7 Jun 2005; Todd Chandler, 23 Jun 1994; Wilsyn Chang, 9 Jan 2012; Dianne Clemens, 12 May 1985; Tracy Cleven, 29 Sep 2004; Alice Colenbrander, 12 Sep 2011; Sam Cooper, 23 Apr 2012; Jennifer Daji, 27 Jun 2005; Sean Dillon, 2 Oct 1984; Shane Douglas, 21 Apr 1992; Christina Ewe, 21 Feb 2005; Ben Fitts, 15 Jan 2007; Ed Gafney, 4 Apr 2011; Daniel Glover, 28 May 2012; Mark Glover, 9 Aug 2006; Ian Graham, 21 Jan 2008; Abby Gundy, 12 Sep 2011; Canoe Halagigie, 9 Apr 1996; Manu Halagigie, 12 Sep 2006; David Hayne, 6 Dec 2005; Stefanie Henry, 1 Mar 2011; Emma Howard-Smith, 7 Dec 2009; Ben Inatoti, 2 Mar 2004; Jan Kesha, 2 Apr 1995; Kura Kiria, 21 Jul 2000; Tarun Kumar, 24 May 2007; Kara Lawson, 18 Mar 2008; Catherine Le Vert, 13 Jan 2003; Michelle Lemmens, 12 Jan 2004; Jabin Leung Choi, 3 Dec 2012; Paul Lowther, 20 Jan 1989; Daniel Mapp, 12 Dec 2011; Mark Mastilovic, 23 Jul 2007; Paul McNeill, 27 Jan 2004; Lisa Mitchell, 15 Mar 2004; Simona Nelisi, 27 Oct 1999; Phillip Nelson, 10 Nov 2008; Elle Nilsson, 1 Feb 2012; Sarah Olo, 2 Dec 2007; Jacob Pascoe, 21 Jun 2010; Joel Pereira, 16 Jun 2003; Amanda Pritchard, 7 Feb 2012; Rachael Richardson, 25 Feb 2002; Paul Riethmaier, 3 Apr 2006; Karen Roberts, 17 Aug 2000; James Sellers, 7 Jan 2013; Arina Serbanescu-Oasa, 21 Jan 2013; Sheila Singam, 9 Dec 1999; Rashni Singh, 11 Oct 2004; Charlie Sionetuato, 9 Feb 2004; Karen Smith, 1 Mar 2010; Giovana Tabarini, 6 Nov 2007; Andrew Thomson, 10 Jul 1995; Robert Tucker, 30 Jun 2008; Iki Vaka, 12 Oct 2007; Raju Vegesna, 26 Aug 2002; Raewyn Vela, 20 May 1996; Michael Wakefield, 1 Feb 2012; Cici Wang, 5 Jun 2007; Antoinette Ward, 5 Apr 2004; Annette Webb, 2 Nov 1998; Jessica Williamson, 21 Jan 2013; Joanne Wright, 8 Apr 2013; David Zhao, 22 Feb 2010. **Mainfreight Air & Ocean Christchurch** Gemma Allan, 27 Aug 2012; Jacinda Baynes, 16 Jan 2006; Alexandra Brook, 19 Nov 2012; Julie Bryce, 25 Oct 2007; Kevin Coman-Wright, 3 Apr 2012; Hayden Cook, 28 Feb 2000; Doreen Delahunty, 3 May 1994; Alana Evans, 2 May 2012; Anastasia Farrakhova, 5 Mar 2012; Tommy Fitzgerald, 15 Mar 2010; Daniel Hobbs, 15 May 2008; Jethro Lochhead, 23 Jul 2012; Megan Lockie, 20 Jun 2011; Jason McFadden, 27 May 2002; Jason Newton, 29 Mar 2010; Matthew Newton, 7 Jan 2008; Hamish Robertson, 1 Oct 2011; Rachel Robertson, 20 Sep 1999; Devan Smith, 28 Aug 2006; Kitt Taylor, 5 May 2008; Sonia Taylor, 29 Mar 2010; Chelsey Tiweka, 26 Sep 2011; Matthew Ward, 2 Apr 2013; Helen Watson, 17 Jul 1995; Elaine Wong, 17 Apr 2000. **Mainfreight Air & Ocean Dunedin** Nicky Jackson, 14 Jun 2010; Teresa O'Connell, 27 Jun 2011. **Mainfreight Air & Ocean Hamilton** Chris Carmichael, 29 Jan 2008; Greg Waylen, 16 Aug 2004; Amber Woodward, 15 Jan 2007. **Mainfreight Air & Ocean Napier** Levi Kroot, 22 Feb 2010; Monique Peary, 17 Feb 2003; Chris Rodgers, 12 May 2003; Melinda Thomson, 30 Apr 2007. **Mainfreight Air & Ocean Nelson** Stuart Bryson, 2 Dec 2008. **Mainfreight Air & Ocean New Plymouth** Shaun Buckley, 28 Jun 2004; Jo-Ann Heggie, 28 Nov 2011; Rebecca Le Prou, 29 Jan 2008. **Mainfreight Air & Ocean Palmerston North** Tim Bray, 14 Jun 2010. **Mainfreight Air & Ocean Tauranga** Abdul Abdul, 5 Oct 2009; Pauline Bettoniel, 5 Nov 2007; Margie Brunton, 21 Feb 2011; Duncan Byron,

14 Apr 2003; Bronwyn Gower, 20 Nov 2001; Nada Gvozdenovic, 31 May 1999; Cameron Hill, 22 Nov 1999; Robyn McCarthy, 10 Sep 1990; Linda Mitchell, 8 Nov 2010; Nicole Mitchell, 15 Jan 2007; Dennis Pearce, 5 Apr 2004; Julie Scott, 16 Feb 1995; Catherine Simmons, 1 Jun 1993; Shane Williamson, 12 Feb 2001; Grant Yeatman, 1 Feb 2011. **Mainfreight Air & Ocean Wellington** Erle Betty, 16 Oct 2000; Joseph Coffey, 8 Jan 2007; Natalie Curley, 10 Mar 2003; Chrissy Douglas, 24 Jul 1997; Paul Fredrickson, 28 Apr 2003; Natasha Jacobs, 30 Aug 2010; Briony Larsen, 21 Mar 2011; Jeff Larsen, 22 Mar 1999; Robert Little, 24 Jun 1992; Callum Quayle, 10 May 2010; Scott Rice, 9 Nov 2009; Trevor Rice, 4 Jan 1985; Julie Robert, 6 Apr 2006. **Mainfreight Air & Ocean Whangarei** Jason Morgan, 24 Aug 2009. **Mainfreight FTL North Island** Dean Chadwick, 23 May 2011; Lance Chadwick, 26 Oct 1976; Cory Duggan, 4 Nov 2007; Peter Flett, 21 Dec 2012; Dave Freeman, 23 May 2011; Prem Goundar, 10 Sep 2012; Mike Haycock, 26 Sep 2011; John Linton, 18 Jan 2012; Bruce Lowe, 15 May 2012; Paul Mahon, 30 Jul 2012; Warren McKee, 15 Jan 2007; Karen Powell, 26 Nov 2003; Laurence Purchase, 01 Jul 1998; Mike Swindells, 2 Feb 2004; Sandy Teddy, 27 Sep 1993; Jarden West, 7 May 2012; Martin Weismann, 28 Oct 2010; Michael Woodham, 28 Feb 2011. **Mainfreight FTL South Island** Nathan Anderson, 1 Apr 2003; Carey Barnes, 27 Mar 2012; Trevor Bray, 24 Jul 2011; Tony Bremner, 7 Aug 2012; John Buttolph, 1 Jul 2000; Matt Cave, 7 Jul 2011; Tom Feng, 29 Oct 2009; Terry Hucklebridge, 19 Aug 2011; Paul King, 2 Apr 2012; Lee McMillan, 4 Aug 2011; Tom Morgan, 2 Jul 2012; Rene Niovara'Dave, 1 Nov 1994; Tere Phillips, 1 Aug 2011; James Price, 15 Apr 2002; Rob Renwick, 24 Nov 2004; Jamie Sansom, 14 Aug 2011; Pat Smith, 1 May 1983; Heath Woollett, 31 Oct 2011. **Mainfreight IT New Zealand** Anthony Barrett, 2 Apr 2001; Donna Barrett, 10 Oct 2005; Nilesh Bhuthadia, 2 Feb 2000; Jennine Cosgrave, 3 Feb 1998; Richard Daldy, 2 Jul 2007; Paul Derbyshire, 3 Sep 1983; Mark Hales, 23 Jan 1996; David Hall, 7 Feb 2005; Gary Harrington, 6 May 1996; Alistair Hughes, 13 Oct 2008; Logan Lim, 15 Mar 2010; John McStay, 10 Nov 2003; Marissa Monteroso, 7 Apr 2003; Jason Moroney, 27 Oct 2005; Bhavesh Patel, 2 Nov 2009; Jamie Ross, 5 Aug 1996; Raagni Sahay, 28 Jul 2003; Dennis Shikhu, 14 Jun 2004; Pateriki Te Pou, 18 Jan 2010; Jamie Thomas, 01 Apr 2008; Glen Thompson, 1 Jun 2011; Roger van Dorsten, 21 Jun 1999; Peter Webster, 2 Feb 1970; Paul Woller, 5 Feb 2001. **Mainfreight Logistics Auckland, Mainfreight Lane** Joseph Bell, 24 Sep 2007; Sam Bisset, 23 Jul 2012; Gurinder Bryah, 10 Dec 2012; Jeremy Chin, 9 Aug 2010; Pio Filipo, 4 Feb 2013; Neil Harding, 29 Oct 1998; Will Harding, 7 Jan 2013; Nina Hutchinson, 14 Jan 2013; Thomas Jones, 30 Apr 2007; Cristina Lumby, 14 Sep 1992; Avao Mataafa, 26 Nov 2007; Albert Miratana, 1 Mar 2010; Vash Nathu, 14 Jan 2013; Chris Park, 15 Nov 2007; Dipesh Prasad, 24 Oct 2012; Satish Prasad, 7 Jul 2008; Dwayne Rowsell, 21 Feb 2012; Tony Sagaga, 12 May 2003; McCrae Sloper, 15 Feb 2011; Leslie Smith, 2 Mar 2011; Chris Teika, 28 Jun 2007; Dean Walters, 25 Oct 2011; Faisal Zafiri, 4 Feb 2013; Thomas Steel, 1 Feb 2006. **Mainfreight Logistics Auckland, Manu Street** Greg Abel, 7 Jan 2013; Marcus Brown, 25 Jul 2012; Richard Cowper, 29 Aug 2002; Shannon Hegan, 12 Feb 2007; Mo Khan, 25 Sep 2009; Allan Lowe, 17 Jan 2011; Lucille Matthews, 9 Jul 2012; Bruce McKay, 12 Jun 1995; Layne Neho, 11 Mar 2013; Gary Potatau, 25 Aug 2011; Jaswant Prasad, 9 Jul 2007; Ash Ryder, 14 Feb 2011; Daniel Sharma, 25 Jul 2012; Kim Sipeli, 10 Apr 2003; Cory Smith, 11 Apr 2011; Piesi Tama, 29 Mar 2004; Travis Thompson, 18 Jun 2012; Jamiee Tito, 25 Jul 2012; Andy Tongia, 11 Oct 2004; Kim Webber, 6 Aug 2012. **Mainfreight Logistics Auckland, Neales Road** Gordon Blakeborough, 5 Oct 2011; Chance Edwards, 4 Aug 2008; Poe Elama, 25 Jul 2012; Vinay Goundar, 9 Jan 2006; Thomas Hills, 11 Feb 2013; Teni Iofesa, 26 Apr 2004; Kerri Jones, 29 Sep 2008; Roni Lal, 12 May 2008; Jin How Lock, 25 Mar 2013; Johnathan MacDonald-Tainui, 4 Mar 2013; Stuart Mokalei, 4 Jun 2008; Jason Rogers, 8 Mar 2010; Dave Singh, 21 Jul 2009; Harmanpreet Singh, 26 Jun 2012; Cody Watts, 24 Jan 2000; Jeremy Williams, 3 Apr 2006. **Mainfreight Logistics Auckland, O'Rorke Road** Catherine Ashton, 1 Jul 2004; Edward Bird, 31 Jan 2012; Ken Bracey, 28 Jun 1995; Shayna Creighton, 4 Feb 2013; Shirley Cunneen, 12 Jan 1998; Kim Curtis, 28 Apr 1997; William Katu, 4 Feb 2008; Fotu Mau, 1 Oct 2006; Patrick Patalesio, 21 Jan 2009; Lyn Rogers, 22 Nov 1999; Amasaia Valu, 24 Mar 1998; Sione Valu, 12 Jun 1995. **Mainfreight Logistics Auckland, Westney Road** Kaushik Balan, 25 Jul 2011; Dave & Kay Batchelor, 1 Apr 2001; Yogesh Bhana, 9 Jul 2007; Stephen Bucheler, 20 Mar 2006; Joe Castle, 12 Jun 1995; Jill Cooper, 11 Aug 2001; Rory Edwards, 1 Feb 2013; Brian Gill, 1 June 1976; Damien Goddard, 1 Mar 2005; Rene Hill, 14 Jan 2013; Ross Hobson, 7 May 2012; Jan Hustler, 10 Jan 2005; Severe Iosia-Sipeli, 15 Jan 2008; Deborah Jackson, 30 Jul 1997; Syvon Katuke, 21 Nov 2011; Levi Kite, 19 Sep 2011; Rudy Kopara, 18 Apr 2012; Sonal Kumar, 14 May 2012; Esmond Lum, 13 Dec 2012; Morris Maaka, 12 Jan 2012; Brenda Nolan, 26 Jun 1998; Ken Odhiambo, 17 Mar 2008; Simone Panapa, 8 Feb 2012; Tangi Pekepo, 4 Apr 2005; Jai Prasad, 4 Jun 2002; Richard Ralm, 5 Dec 2011; Luke Rudolph, 26 Apr 2004; Rhys Stunell, 14 Nov 2011; Mulivai Televave, 30 Apr 2001; Patrice Temanu, 8 Oct 2007; Celia Tepania, 28 May 2002; BJ Upokomanu, 7 Apr 2009; Samantha Van Wyk, 19 Nov 2008; Mladan Yagmich, 2 Apr 1990. **Mainfreight Logistics Christchurch** Wayne Busson, 5 May 1997; Amelia Camp, 6 Aug 2012; Elliot Clayton, 2 Jul 2012; Israel Davey, 27 Feb 2012; Karn Evans, 23 Jun 2008; Robert Hayes, 5 Sep 2005; Bernard Jagers, 26 Apr 2005; Keyur Shah, 30 Nov 2009; Dave Knight, 30 Jan 2006; Geoff Lulham, 21 Oct 1991; Justin McCarthy, 6 Aug 2001; Simon Nicolson, 19 Nov 2012; Aslyn Pennington, 30 Apr 2012; Mark Ritchie, 23 Sep 1996; Sandra Ritchie, 12 Jul 1999; Garth Sutton, 13 Sep 1995; Kirk Simpson, 25 Jun 2012; Derek Thelning, 24 Jan 2011; Dean Williams, 12 Dec 2011; Jamie Young, 10 Jun 2001. **Mainfreight Logistics Dunedin** Geoff Baird, 21 May 1984; Martin Swann, 18 Aug 2008; Bruce Wilson, 26 Nov 2004. **Mainfreight Metro Auckland** Faizal Ali, 2 Oct 2005; Tiaz Ali, 10 Jul 2011; Joseph Anae, 29 Jun 2009; Zubin Bhathena, 5 Jul 2005; David Clarke, 29 Dec 2010; Bhavjot Dhillon, 16 Jul 2012; Sheldon Eden-Whaitiri, 15 Feb 2010; James Fuamatu, 3 Mar 2008; Kevin Geard, 1 Apr 1998; Nicole Harris, 23 Aug 2004; Theresa Herbert, 21 May 2002; Naushad Hussein, 4 Aug 2008; Ashwin Karan, 1 Apr 2006; Arfran Khan, 30 Jul 2012; Nazim Khan, 1 Nov 2000; Nishant Kumar, 9 Nov 2010; Aatish Lal, 13 Feb 2012; Kayne Levy, 20 Apr 2011; T.K. Lolo, 2 Jun 2009; Ken Mahon, 4 Mar 2013; George Mason, 14 May 2012; Tommy Miller, 17 May 2011; Sha Narayan, 1 Apr 2010; John Paul, 7 Sep 2010; Suresh Prasad, 8 Jun 2009; Amit Pratap, 10 Jul 2012; Shakeel Sahim, 5 Sep 2012; Simon Sahim, 23 Jun 2012; Mez Sethna, 8 Jan 2007; Shail Shiron, 23 Jul 2009; Mohammed Shahadat, 1 Jul 2012; Narinder Singh, 1 Oct 2011; John Siret, 5 Sep 2011; Michael Straessle, 20 Jun 2012; Sheena Symons, 2 Jun 2004; Lisa Tagoai, 17 Sep 2001; Thomas Tetai, 14 Sep 1998; John Teu, 28 Jul 2009; Ropisone Toma, 7 Mar 2005; Darren Turner, 1 May 2001; Phillip Wood, 29 Feb 2012; John Woollams, 7 Apr 2002. **Mainfreight Metro Christchurch** Trish Allan, 7 Sep 2006; Malcolm Baird, 13 Apr 2004; Kelly Brooks, 22 Sep 2008; John Cowlin, 24 Sep 2007; Hana Ferguson, 1 Jun 2010; Daniel Goldie, 5 Jan 2009; Heather Green, 7 Mar 2005; Russell Hayes, 1 Apr 2001; Tim Hitchings, 3 Jan 2013; Ian Johnson, 21 Oct 1999; Darryl Maxwell, 18 Jul 2011; Karl Murdoch, 10 Feb 2011; Wayne Robertson, 1 Sep 2008; Geoff Teehan, 25 Jul 2011; Doug Warren, 21 Jul 2011; Joe Weng, 17 Jul 2012. **Mainfreight Metro Wellington** Ala Aiono, 11 Apr 1988; Tecye Tevita, 1 Jul 2002; Sega Va, 1 Mar 2006; Rhys van Boheemen, 18 Mar 2013. **Mainfreight Mobile Auckland** Nicholas Gray, 2 Jul 2007; Ioasa Ioasa, 30 Mar 2009; Clayton Tito, 1 Oct 2001. **Mainfreight Port Operations Auckland** Mike Attwood, 4 Jun 2002; Rose Cross, 15 Jul 1996; Tony Cutelli, 1 Sep 2007; John Dash, 16 Mar 1989; Mark De Hoog, 21 Nov 2011; Rob Dickinson, 6 Nov 1995]; Gerald Goff, 10 Nov 2009; Muni Gounder, 1 Apr 2001; Jacqui Hogan, 20 Sep 2010; Bryan Hohepa, 3 Aug 2008; Brian Hurn, 1 Apr 1983; Salendra Kumar, 28 Feb 2012; Oriana Laumea, 19 Aug 2009; Graeme Lloyd-Smith, 1 Sep 1997; Andrea Morgan, 26 Apr 2004; Ronald Prakesh, 16 Feb 2008; Carl Price, 18 Jun 2012; Russell Shand, 1 Apr 2002; Tiffany Sio, 16 Jan 2012; Andrew Tautari, 1 Apr 2000; Dennis Tautari, 1 Sep 2002; Kevin Timmo, 13 Jun 2011; Trudy Timmo, 30 Aug 2004. **Mainfreight Port Operations Christchurch** Russell Carnegie, 1 Apr 1998; Dean Coates, 1 Apr 2003; Adrian Ferguson, 22 Jul 1999; Vaughan France, 19 May 2008; Tony Green, 10 May 1981; Tracy Hapi, 24 Sep 2001; Eddie Hiku, 1 Apr 1991; Christine Kennedy, 10 May 1999; Neil Miller, 1 Oct 2011; Barry Rodwell, 1 Apr 2002; Gary Sellars, 1 Jul 1999; John Williamson, 1 Apr 1996. **Mainfreight 2Home Auckland** Ray Brown, 1

Mar 2002; Leon Cassidy, 6 Sep 2004; Darren Cummins, 1 Mar 2003; Cindy Estreich, 16 Feb 2004; Tama Fasavalu, 27 Oct 2004; Ross Fisher, 3 Mar 2003; Edward Freeman, 29 Dec 2010; Emma Gilman, 4 Feb 2013; Shaun Hona, 3 Oct 2012; Chad Lawrence, 8 Mar 2012; Yvette MacLennan, 6 Aug 2007; Bronson Mareela, 26 Apr 2010; Damon Matthews, 22 Sep 2010; Sabbir Mohammed, 1 Mar 2003; Adrian Mokaraka, 1 Mar 2006; Max Muaulu, 16 Sep 2002; Rueben Munday, 1 Nov 2005; Geoff Pulford, 20 May 2003; Mohammed Shahim Khan, 20 Dec 2010; Navin Sharma, 1 Mar 2003; Andrea Sikuea, 1 Mar 2010; Grant Smith, 3 Nov 1981; Dion Solomona, 14 Feb 2007; Allan Tango, 1 Mar 2003; Lee Tuimauga, 19 May 2003; Arthur Tusa, 23 Feb 2007; Peter Wallis, 1 Mar 2003; John Wehi, 9 Feb 2011; Jeremy Wells, 5 Nov 2008. **Mainfreight 2Home Christchurch** Timothy Challis, 30 Jan 2006; Greg Cooper, 1 Nov 2008; Kelly Dean, 3 Oct 2011; Mansell Diamond, 1 Apr 2005; Jaysin Hurrell, 8 Sep 2003; Howard McGhie, 15 Jan 2001; Paul Mitchell, 1 Apr 2003; Samuel Mitchell, 1 Nov 2008; Wayne Pahl, 1 Sep 2011; Robert Poasa, 1 Apr 2003; Nicky Scott, 4 Jun 2007; Khamus Sisikefu, 8 Jun 2011; Ed Thomas, 1 Jul 2005; Kamen Withington, 23 May 2011. **Owens Auckland** Mohammed Ahmad, 16 Jun 2002; Frank Aholelei, 23 Oct 2007; Danny Ashik, 12 May 2007; Adam Awhitu, 1 Mar 2005; Kevin Babbington, 16 Apr 2004; Bob Bain, 22 Jun 2000; Graeme Bent, 22 Feb 2010; Pauline Bent, 22 Sep 2008; Yogesh Bilas, 22 Sep 2009; Debbie Brady, 30 Apr 1990; Michael Brown, 3 Apr 2012; Louise Byrne, 21 Jan 2013; Sami Chand, 31 Jan 2012; Lauren Chissell, 8 Jun 2010; Ricky Clark, 13 Sep 2012; Murray Craig, 3 Aug 1987; Alvin Datt, 9 Jan 2006; Arron Davis, 30 Apr 2001; Bobby Dean, 15 Mar 2001; Carl Dreaver, 1 Sep 1997; Daniel Edmonds, 8 Feb 2012; John Fahey, 14 Feb 2011; Aoese Fruean, 29 Oct 2007; Lisa Haycock, 21 Jan 2008; David Heka, 30 Jan 2001; Chase Inia, 21 Jan 2013; Telea Kasipale, 18 Mar 2003; Victor Kasipale, 14 Apr 2008; John Katu, 27 Dec 1989; Melanie Katu, 5 Dec 2003; Raymond Kendall, 25 Oct 2006; Dorrie Killen, 23 May 2007; Anshu Kissun, 5 Jun 2012; Kuldeep Kumar, 8 Nov 2010; Nitesh Kumar, 1 Dec 2010; Ravin Kumar, 1 Apr 2007; Nick Lenehan, 8 Mar 2010; Hayden Lilley, 26 Nov 2011; Rebekah Lopau, 29 Dec 1997; Pravin Maharaj, 23 Oct 2001; Joylene Malofie, 28 Jun 1999; Rhoda Malveda, 20 Mar 2002; Mary McCloughen, 22 Feb 1993; Scott McCormick, 14 Jan 2013; Glenn Mei, 3 Oct 2011; Jackie Mein, 10 Apr 2006; Thomas Merriman, 14 Nov 2011; Joseph Mohammed, 23 Oct 2011; Reza Motadeli, 1 Apr 2003; Joseph Nand, 1 Apr 2006; Tarryn Neal, 22 Jun 2010; John Palelei, 29 Dec 2010; Timo Palemene, 27 Jun 2012; Kim Peacock, 12 Nov 2002; Lisa Pearce, 7 Sep 2000; Ben Pillay, 23 Feb 2012; Adrianne Pongi, 13 Aug 2001; Hamish Quinn, 6 May 2007; Nileshni Rattan, 17 Oct 2007; Jason Reynolds, 18 Apr 2005; Joel Roberts, 6 Mar 2012; Gerrard Robinson, 14 May 2001; Sukhi Samra, 1 Oct 2010; Alex Scheirlinck, 12 Nov 2012; Aklesh Sharma, 1 Apr 2005; Salendra Sharma, 1 Apr 2005; Vinnie Sharma, 8 Mar 2004; Dinesh Singh, 11 Oct 2010; Niraj Singh, 6 May 2002; Raj Singh, 24 Mar 2004; Greg Smith, 12 Dec 1990; Ryan Smith, 5 Jul 2004; Warwick Smith, 1 Jul 1996; William Smith, 15 Nov 1999; Shayne Tall, 12 Dec 1994; Joseph Tatafu, 29 May 2006; Tuaileva Tatafu, 11 Mar 2012; Patrick Tau, 28 Jun 2004; Wallace Tauariki, 23 Aug 2010; Lance Taurere, 6 Sep 2012; Bernard Tautari, 1 Apr 2002; Danielle Te Tai, 3 Feb 2011; Tevita Temo, 1 May 2008; Paul Timmo, 14 Sep 2010; Paul Tolson, 8 Jun 1992; Louise Warren, 26 Jul 2006; Christopher Wearing, 15 Aug 2011; Rebecca Weber, 31 Jan 2013; Simon Wi, 1 Apr 2003; Candy Worden, 7 Oct 2002; Lauren Wright, 12 Nov 2012; Jim Wright, 2 Oct 2000. **Owens Christchurch** Cindy Aitchison, 26 Sep 2011; John Bradshaw, 1 Apr 1998; Dylan Burbery, 28 Apr 2008; James Carr, 1 Nov 2012; Alicia Coles, 7 Feb 2012; John Creedon, 25 Oct 2011; Wietske De Groot, 9 Mar 2010; Owen Donald, 6 Nov 1995; Alistair Harris, 14 Jul 1999; Cassandra Hunt, 26 Jul 2010; Deane Hunt, 15 Apr 1996; Kim Jung Hwan, 19 May 2008; Keith Kenyon, 6 Apr 1998; John Kerr, 1 Apr 1990; Robert King, 12 Sep 2007; Lindsay McKewen, 20 Mar 2012; Andrew Lysons-Smith, 16 Jul 2007; Graham McHarg, 1 Aug 2000; Rachael McKelvie, 16 Jul 2012; Alan Morgan, 11 Aug 1997; Shay Muir, 2 Apr 2012; Lawrence Narayan, 22 Mar 2010; McGee Nimmo, 1 Oct 2001; Ronnie Pawson, 9 Aug 2010; Ian Reid, 17 Aug 2008; Murray Roberts, 1 Apr 1996; Graham Ryan, 3 Apr 2006; Freya Schroeder, 10 Oct 2011; Jimmy Shearman, 25 Jun 2008; Jennifer Sheppard, 17 Apr 2001; Cecilia Shey-Castillo, 29 Jan 2013; Christopher Smith, 26 Mar 2013; Rowan Traue, 1 Apr 2006; Andrew Vercoe, 17 Apr 2012; James Whittle, 12 Sep 2011; John Wynyard, 7 Jul 2005. **Owens Hamilton** Wayne Bryant, 1 Jul 2007; Ron Hawkings, 1 Apr 1977; Lindsay Meredith, 1 Nov 1999. **Owens Wellington** Zealin Bishop, 1 Mar 2009; Albie Mahuika, 1 Jun 1993; Tess Mapiva, 12 Feb 2010; Cambridge Moore, 29 Aug 2005; Toi Morehu, 28 Apr 2008; Bob Patterson, 1 Mar 1989; Josh Satherley, 8 Jun 2010; Yohan Soeteman, 1 Feb 2005; Mark Sutherland, 6 Sep 2010; Jonathan Zwart, 26 Oct 2010. **Owens Logistics Auckland** Sam Anson, 14 Nov 2011; Jason Byun, 10 Apr 2012; Paul Claydon, 4 Feb 2013; Antonio Collings, 1 Dec 1997; Angela Diaz, 6 Oct 2008; Patislo Feo, 14 Sep 2009; Johnathan Gravatt, 25 Feb 2013; Ronnie Halagigie, 13 Jan 2007; Jenna Hudsen, 30 Jul 2012; Russel Langsdale, 17 Jan 2012; Konelio Leone, 10 Jun 2002; Alex McDonald, 23 Oct 2012; Colin McPherson, 27 Apr 1998; Caleb Mills, 16 May 2012; Noorali Pirani, 26 Aug 2006; Mateo Tino, 15 Mar 1999; Mark Upokomanu, 24 Jun 2004; Sam Vaisima, 1 Feb 2007. **Owens Logistics Christchurch** Renee Barnes, 1 Apr 2012; Grant Breach, 23 Jul 1990; Michael Brierley, 18 Jan 2010; Simon Cowper, 11 Jul 2005; Diane Franks, 23 Aug 1999; Chunguang Hu, 7 Apr 2008; Darren Jerard, 10 Jan 1996; Andrew Kay, 12 Nov 2001; Andrew Maxwell, 22 Jul 2002; Guy McMenamin, 10 Mar 2008; Prasenjit Paul, 19 Dec 2011; Brynley Riches, 26 Aug 1996; Cara Smith, 18 May 2011; Nikita Swarts, 25 Nov 2011; Jeff Walker, 5 Jan 2012; John Wolfrey, 19 Sep 1996; Robert Woods, 4 Apr 2005. **Owens Metro Auckland** Robert Ballard, 6 Oct 2008; Patrick Chong-Nee, 4 Sep 2006; Gary Gailas, 1 May 2008; Amanda Gavin, 30 Apr 2007; Azard Hussain, 1 Oct 2012; Tony Inia, 9 Mar 1995; Tevesi Inukihaangana, 1 Apr 2005; Tom Kasipale, 26 Mar 2002; Steve Kirk, 15 Oct 2009; Rahul Kumar, 16 Aug 2011; Shane Mohammed, 4 Feb 2013; Cheaten Patel, 7 Dec 2009; Bimal Prakash, 16 Nov 2011; Mahend Prasad, 16 Jul 2012; Anwaar Riza, 7 Jun 2011; Mark Sampson, 17 Oct 2011; Meherzan Sethna, 24 Sep 2012; Hardeep Singh, 12 Nov 2012; Jagjit Singh, 3 Sep 2012; Carlos Standen, 5 Feb 1998; Alex Tukuafu, 30 May 2008; Chang Wan Kim, 17 Aug 2007; Kevin Yao, 2 May 2011. **Owens Tankers** Maurice Clarke, 27 May 1997; Joe Curtis, 28 Sep 2005; Tom Davis, 17 Mar 1997; Jock Dixon, 7 Feb 2005; Stu Lennon, 16 Jan 2006; Guy Small, 1 Jun 1983; Marilyn Syms, 5 Jan 1998; Pule Taliaoa, 14 Mar 2011; Martin Ward, 11 Jan 2010. **Training New Zealand** Courtney Bould, 5 Dec 2011; Trace Donaghey, 9 Jun 1997; Gordon Jackson, 4 Mar 1984; Erica Jaffray, 20 Apr 1995; Rachel Oswald, 8 Jun 1998; Evan Pilcher, 24 Jan 2011; Ange Quedley, 22 Jul 1996; Alexia van der Zanden, 30 Nov 2009. **AUSTRALIA CaroTrans Adelaide** Mark Fricker, 28 Apr 2008; Vikki Julian, 1 Apr 2012. **CaroTrans Brisbane** Emma Atkin, 23 Jul 2001; Jade Fogwell, 28 Aug 2006; Melanie Hill, 13 Aug 2012; Melyssa Hobbs, 10 Nov 2005; Stamatiki Londy, 7 Jun 2010; Jacinta Marriott, 4 Sep 2008; Jordan Tofa, 18 Feb 2008. **CaroTrans Melbourne** Christopher Barnes, 8 Aug 2011; Sindy Bartlett, 20 Sep 2010; Paula DiBella, 16 Oct 2000; Michelle Groves, 20 May 2003; Christopher Gulizia, 21 Nov 2011; Andrew Jackson, 3 Jul 2006; Rebecca Macrae, 21 Sep 2009; Kate Marosy, 28 May 2007; Travis Thorogood, 22 Nov 2010; Hayley Vinci, 11 Jan 2010. **CaroTrans Perth** Joseph Covino, 10 May 2010; Paul Rees, 19 Oct 2009. **CaroTrans Sydney** Paul Bell, 31 Jan 2011; Michael Blackburn, 2 Feb 2004; Nick Dimovski, 24 Sep 2007; Joey Farhat, 31 Jul 2007; Diana Galeski, 21 Jun 2010; Marika Lenzo, 22 Nov 1994; Simon Lloyd, 15 Dec 2008; Kylie Miller, 25 Feb 2008; James Warren, 5 Feb 2007; Kate Winterburn, 22 Jun 2005. **Chemcouriers Brisbane** Joe Branagan, 17 Dec 2012; Michael Jarman, 1 Apr 2012; Colin Vearer, 18 Nov 1996. **Chemcouriers Melbourne** Brian Aspinall, 16 Aug 1993; David Carswell, 26 Mar 2012; Scott Jones, 7 Apr 2008; Jason Kennedy, 15 Jan 2007; Cameron MacLean, 30 May 2011; Vedrana Mrdic, 7 Nov 2011; Quinn Sherriff, 2 May 2011; Brendon Walker, 1 Feb 2013. **Chemcouriers Sydney** Liam Hastings, 14 Nov 2011; Matthew Howell, 21 Jan 2013; Oliseni Lolomanaia, 10 Dec 2012; Timothy Meredith, 1 Feb 2010; Bill Perese, 12 Jun 2012; Natasha Perese, 12 Jun 2012; James Pickett, 21 Nov 2011; Jody Savage, 26 Oct 2009; Kris Williams, 4 Feb 2008. **Mainfreight Adelaide** Peter Alexopoulos, 1 Jul 2011; Hayley Barnes, 15 Sep 2008; Georgina Brown, 20 Feb 2012; Fred Cammarano, 22 Apr 2003; Chris Cammarano, 17 Jan 2011; Pauline Cammarano, 4 Nov 2004; Trevor Clayson, 10 Oct 2006; Katrina de Koning, 14 Mar 2006; Kellie Dimech, 1 Mar 2010; David Ey, 15

Mar 2011; Luke Farrugia, 18 Apr 1994; Meagan Flynn, 21 Jun 2005; Frank Fontanelli, 15 Nov 2002; Terry Forst, 27 Feb 2012; Arthur Gentle, 21 Sep 2009; Patrice Hall, 29 Jan 2013; Richard Harper, 1 Jul 2011; Hamish Hill, 6 Jun 2011; Shaun Hurrell, 6 Mar 2013; Andrew Jones, 8 Feb 2010; Robert Jones, 27 Feb 2012; Jody Knight, 13 Sep 2010; James Lawless, 12 Apr 2006; Nilton Leao, 17 Jun 2010; Roger Manuel, 15 Dec 1986; Deborah Moore, 8 Oct 2009; Kim Pawsey, 27 Mar 2009; Lee-Anne Phillips, 20 Jun 2011; Stephen Phillips, 29 Jan 2007; Wayne Powell, 11 Jul 2008; Joanne Reimann, 2 Aug 2010; Lynne Rooney, 9 Feb 2010; Guiseppe Rugari, 10 Jun 2005; Byron Sampson, 14 Sep 2005; Garry Semmler, 11 Apr 1989; Davinder Singh, 3 Sep 2012; Justin Stoyanoff, 13 Sep 2011; Tom Stoyanoff, 18 Nov 2008; Andrew Tait, 14 Sep 2012; Steve Thorpe, 15 Nov 2002; Nick Tzevelekos, 13 Sep 2005; David Walker, 28 Sep 2009; Aaron Ward, 21 Mar 2012; Anthony Winstanley, 26 Mar 2012. **Mainfreight Albury** Nick Apostolovski, 14 Nov 2011; Jayden Beaumont, 16 Nov 2011; Matt Bonnfield, 1 Sep 2011; Carol Burton, 14 Jan 2013; Geoff Donovan, 13 Jul 2012; Kelby Elkner, 2 Apr 2012; Samuel Hargreave, 3 Dec 2012; Vince Harris, 19 Sep 2011; Andrew Holland, 11 Jan 2012; Tristan Kirkham, 13 Aug 2012; Bridgett Leddin, 28 Nov 2012; Andrew Mayne, 1 Sep 2011; John Ritchie, 25 Feb 2013; Jagpreet Singh, 13 Nov 2012; Robert Whitehurst, 28 Sep 2012; Kevin Wood, 1 Sep 2011; Stephen Wood, 28 Oct 2011. **Mainfreight Ballarat** Conor Dillon, 13 Nov 2012; Gabrielle Doolan, 19 Nov 2012; Matthew Friend, 14 Nov 2011; Jenine Harris, a Jan 2012; Cindy Lipplegoes, 13 Mar 2012; Brian Lloydd, 15 Mar 2001; Luke O'Shannassy, 16 Jul 2012; Barry Rix, 21 May 2012. **Mainfreight Brisbane** Steve Ace, 11 Oct 2005; Bernard Ashcroft, 1 Sep 2003; Camran Bahry, 16 Sep 2011; David Barrett, 30 May 2008; Steven Beaumont, 14 Mar 2011; Brent Bevin, 16 Apr 2010; Molly Boswell, 6 Mar 2012; Kenneth Brown, 2 May 1986; Mitch Bryan, 21 Jun 2010; Chris Burgess, 30 Apr 2012; Daniel Carlyle, 18 May 2011; Katrina Casey, 14 Feb 2013; Ritesh Chand, 12 Mar 2013; Rajnesh Chand, 31 Jan 2011; Rikeshni Chand, 31 Jan 2011; Bruno De Sousa, 9 Feb 2011; Kaitlin Dowel, 14 May 2012; Mas Eden, 24 May 2011; Tai Etuale, 5 Jul 2011; Roy Faifai, 5 Sep 2007; Troy Fale, 11 Mar 2013; Daniel Fenunuti, 17 Jan 2013; John Follent, 15 Oct 2012; Marty Fry, 1 Nov 1999; Stephanie Goldsack, 3 Aug 2012; Ross Griffin, 1 May 2003; Amanda Groves, 4 Mar 2010; Andrew Gruia, 31 Mar 2009; Louise Guilfoyle, 27 Sep 2011; Angelina Harper, 23 Jan 2012; Bruce Harper, 23 Jan 2012; Connor Harper, 20 Feb 2012; Morgan Hill, 23 Nov 2009; Stella Hobbs, 7 Nov 2011; John Holpen, 3 Feb 2000; Yvonne Ili, 7 Jan 2013; Ryan Ingall, 29 Jan 2013; Christian Ionut Istrate, 28 Mar 2011; Steve Jefferson, 19 Oct 2009; Chris Johnson, 8 Mar 2012; Amanda Johnston, 30 Jan 2007; Steve Jovanovic, 31 Jan 2012; Dallas Keevers, 1 May 2000; Jayson King, 7 Sep 2011; Linda King, 4 May 2012; Phillip King, 1 Feb 2010; John Kinsella, 16 Aug 2010; Peter Kinsella, 15 Dec 2009; Manu Korovulavula, 16 Apr 2012; Bradley Lahey, 19 Mar 1990; Kate Lindsay, 14 Feb 2011; Megan Livingstone, 15 Sep 2009; Garry Love, 2 Sep 2011; Natu Manao, 7 Mar 2005; Gautham Manchikalapudi, 20 Jul 2012; Brittany Martin, 21 Feb 2013; Shaun Martin, 1 Mar 2010; Tina Martin, 21 Nov 2011; Wayne Mcardell, 25 Nov 2011; Dave Miller, 31 Jan 2011; Michael Murray, 16 Aug 2011; Abendra Naidoo, 25 Sep 2008; Zoltan Neer, 29 Jun 2012; Mihaly Nemeth, 2 Dec 2011; Nikki Norman, 1 Aug 2007; Ross Palmer, 30 Dec 2002; Terry Petero, 1 Mar 2005; Nina Purvis, 7 Dec 2009; Emma Ryan, 13 Feb 2013; Nicholas Ryan, 19 Nov 2012; Tibor Sandor, 24 May 2011; Ashleigh Santoso, 30 Apr 2012; Samantha Schafer, 2 Aug 2010; Erika Simon, 8 Feb 2010; Liesel Stevens, 13 Apr 2012; Charles Sutcliffe, 14 Jul 2010; Zoltan Takacs, 28 Sep 2012; Ashley Taylor, 13 Feb 2008; Rebecca Taylor, 21 Sep 2011; Samantha Taylor, 21 Sep 2011; Sunil Thakkar, 1 Jun 2012; Jamie Thompson, 1 Jun 2012; Kerry Tilbrook, 27 Jun 2011; Pita Togia, 15 Oct 2012; Vesi Tuautu, 29 Jan 2007; Steve Turner, 15 Jan 2007; Zoltan Udvardi, 14 May 2008; Terence Utai, 20 Feb 2012; Uhila Vakameilalo, 16 Jan 2012; Michelle Van Den Ende, 11 Jun 2009; Maraea Wharemate, 15 Aug 2011; Kevin Whitty, 5 Apr 2012; Amanda Wiersma, 7 Jan 2013; John Wills, 14 Mar 2012; Byran Wong, 14 Apr 2005; Joshua Wood, 9 May 2011. **Mainfreight Canberra** David Britton, 13 Dec 2010; Kimberley Brown, 23 Feb 2010; Anthony Bruce, 13 Aug 2008; Adrian Crowther, 11 Feb 2013; Paul Hourigan, 14 Feb 2013; Leah Jones, 28 May 2007; Nathan Robson, 13 Mar 2009; Baljinder Singh, 12 Dec 2012; Jaxson Taylor, 5 Mar 2012; Chris Vlek, 7 Feb 2011; Ford Watene, 6 Mar 2006. **Mainfreight Gold Coast** Paris Knight, 4 Nov 2010; Chris Were, 5 May 2009; Judith Were, 22 Dec 2012. **Mainfreight Melbourne** Bachtiar Abdul Rahman, 11 Apr 2012; Max Adam, 18 Jan 2012; Vijay Ahluwalia, 12 Mar 2010; Brigitte Allen, 21 Nov 2011; Suranda Amukotuwa, 13 Mar 2012; Shane Anderson, 20 Aug 2007; Nelson Aravjo, 23 Mar 2007; Mali Barber, 1 Apr 2011; James Bennett, 1 Aug 2011; Craig Britto, 9 Sep 2008; Kath Brown, 14 Aug 1997; Liem Bui, 12 Mar 2010; Paige Cameron, 3 Apr 2012; Aaron Campbell, 8 Aug 2011; Vince Cecil-Daniel, 10 Apr 2012; Ervis Celo, 21 Feb 2011; Bin Jing Chen, 22 Aug 2007; Jean Claude, 1 Jan 1996; Steve Cooper, 1 Apr 2011; Dhillon Cornell, 22 Nov 2010; Steve Cornell, 19 Jan 2010; Bryan Curtis, 6 Sep 1980; Daniel Curtis, 10 Feb 2012; Peter Daly, 22 Jun 2005; Andrea D'Cruz, 25 Mar 1997; Thomas Deveny, 30 Jan 2012; Kim Devine, 26 Mar 2012; Kevin Dicker, 11 Feb 2013; George Dong, 23 Mar 2007; Luke Drosos, 5 Sep 2012; Sean Dunn, 21 Nov 2012; Jamie Eagan, 16 Nov 2012; Albert Edwards, 16 Aug 2000; Monique Fage, 19 Oct 2009; Catherine Flaherty, 17 Sep 2012; Arthur Floros, 13 Sep 2004; Ebony Fraser, 13 Dec 2010; Semi Godinet, 1 Sep 2005; Emma Gordon, 30 Mar 2012; Jason Govaars, 31 Jul 2009; Ross Grace, 17 Oct 2011; Peter Grindal, 7 Jun 2006; Chloe Guillemain, 12 Mar 2013; Douglas Hartwick, 4 Feb 2010; Faye Henderson, 4 Jul 2011; Kath Hill, 14 May 2007; Thuyet Ho, 10 Mar 2006; Nick Hodges, 25 Jun 2012; Scott Huntley, 14 May 2007; Saadat Hussain, 11 Feb 2013; Dung Huynh, 13 Oct 2011; Ivica Ilovaca, 4 Oct 2010; Jordan James, 19 Oct 2010; Jesse Jansz, 25 Sep 2003; John Kalogeropoulos, 6 Aug 2003; Jack Kanakaris, 25 Feb 2008; Benjamin Keane, 15 Oct 2012; Maureen Kemp, 1 May 2011; Denis Knight, 4 Feb 2013; Miki Kolek, 6 Sep 2004; Michael Kozman, 3 Apr 2012; Michael Kuzmanovski, 5 Nov 2004; Tenille La'Brooy, 28 Nov 2002; Joey Latorre, 13 Nov 2009; Brandon Lawler, 22 Mar 2010; Kevin Lloyd, 7 Sep 2009; Mike Mai, 14 Oct 2008; Brok Maihi-Taniora, 3 Oct 2011; Tiziana Martin, 29 Dec 2009; Andrew Mase, 17 Dec 2012; Nicholas Matthews, 15 Oct 2012; Leonard Mburu, 15 Dec 2010; Patrick Mburu, 6 Mar 2006; Lachlan McCaig, 24 Apr 2012; Matthew McLeod, 6 Feb 2004; Joshua Meads, 17 Sep 2011; Katrina Miller, 7 May 2012; Danita Minchington, 14 Sep 2012; Desiree Moenoa, 19 Sep 2011; Sumarni MohdShairy, 18 Sep 2000; Rodd Morgan, 1 Apr 2003; Raied Morogy, 26 May 2010; Benny Moser, 3 Jul 2006; Ferdi Muaremov, 27 Sep 2010; Edward Mulvenna, 1 Nov 2010; Muamer Muratovski, 3 May 2007; Shenol Muratovski, 15 Aug 2011; Shertim Muratovski, 19 Apr 2010; Surender Nagulapally, 7 Sep 2010; Krishna Naidu, 31 Oct 2007; Clifford Nash, 12 Aug 1999; Mark Ngaruhe, 3 Aug 2001; Nhiem Ngo, 14 Jun 2012; Vu Ngo, 11 Jul 2008; Ken Nguyen, 30 Mar 2005; Sang Nguyen, 22 Aug 2007; Tony Nguyen, 12 Aug 2008; Ving Nguyen, 17 Dec 2007; Huey Nguyen, 4 Feb 2013; Tien Nguyen, 6 Mar 2006; Devon Ng-Youne, 23 Jan 2008; Bill Nikopoulos, 4 Feb 2013; Jade Northcott, 7 Feb 2011; Osman Osman, 17 Feb 1997; Erina Palmer, 3 Oct 2011; Santbir Palsingh, 6 Mar 2013; Gheorghe Pasla, 3 May 2011; Jenny Paterakis, 2 Sep 1998; John Pegiou, 4 Nov 2009; Ray Pepper, 9 Nov 1998; Alexander Perelman, 28 Sep 2012; Hung Pham, 22 Aug 2007; Paul Pipilakis, 5 Dec 1995; Presley Purcell, 1 Oct 2011; Christopher Raditsis, 6 Dec 2012; Terry Rawiri, 20 Dec 2010; Glenn Reed, 22 Apr 2003; Sue Rexter, 26 Jul 2005; Malcolm Reynolds, 4 Feb 2003; Sian Rogers, 13 Dec 2012; James Ryan, 6 Sep 2010; Dina Sadinlija, 13 Mar 2007; Zoran Savic, 13 Jun 2003; Trevor Scharenguivel, 4 Nov 1996; David Scott, 26 Jun 2000; John Seaver, 30 May 2011; Antarpreet Sekhon, 15 Jun 2009; Suman Shaganti, 11 Feb 2013; Rupesh Sharma, 14 Jun 2011; Stuart Simpson, 4 Apr 2005; Darshdeep Singh, 12 Aug 2011; Ranbir Singh, 10 Jun 2011; Andrew Smith, 17 Jan 1990; Maryann Stellini, 3 May 2010; Janaya Symons, 17 Oct 2011; Hanh Hq Ta, 28 Sep 2012; Willie Tapuala-Unasa, 28 Nov 2012; Rawiri Thompson, 29 Sep 2009; Sridhar Thutkuri, 22 Sep 2008; Nicole Tierney, 3 Dec 2012; Riki Tipene, 17 Mar 2008; Rima Tipene, 8 Feb 2012; Tinika Tipene, 6 Feb 2012; Turoa Tipene, 24 Sep 2003; Thanh Tran, 15 Sep 2011; Cindy Trew, 13 Jun 2003; Lanh Truong, 29 Oct 2008; Van Be Truyen, 17 Dec 2007; Romney Tui, 10 Apr 2012; Chanel Utupo, 26 Oct 2011; Aline Van Buiten, 3 Apr 1995; Leon Vieyera, 3 Aug 2012; Estelita Vincent, 5 Apr 1993; Leigh Vlasblom, 13 Feb 2008; Richard Vlasblom, 3 Apr 2000; Tommy Vo, 15 Nov 2002; Srdan Vukovic, 30 Aug 2002; Massey Wade, 5 Mar 2012; Jennifer Wanigasekera, 20 Jul

2005; Kelly-Jo Wells, 3 Jan 2012; Stacey Wells, 6 Apr 2010; Andrew Weymouth, 1 Jan 2010; Willie Wharewera, 1 Jul 2010; Ashlee White, 2 Jun 2008; Brad Williams, 13 Jul 2010; Helen Williams, 18 Sep 2003. **Mainfreight Newcastle** Jessica Black, 10 Dec 2012; Rodney Byrne, 3 Sep 2012; Brett Cullinan, 2 Apr 2012; Lily Davis, 1 May 2012; Greg De Lautour, 15 Mar 1999; Ruth De Lautour, 11 Mar 2002; Geordie Farish, 31 May 2010; Emma Fitzgerald, 24 Sep 2012; Dylan Heins, 5 Mar 2012; Gregory Hillier, 1 Apr 2011; Katie Longfellow, 25 Aug 2010; Ian Macpherson, 3 Apr 2009; Tanya Milne, 20 Sep 2010; Alessandra Morgan, 25 Feb 2013; Michael Parkinson, 20 Dec 2011; Robert Piltz, 15 Jul 2002; Dale Sharp, 22 Mar 2012; Andrew Smith, 21 Jul 2003; Jason Willoughby, 26 May 2011; Shane Wiseman, 13 Feb 2009. **Mainfreight Perth** Ben Baugh, 14 Mar 2008; Karl Baxter, 24 May 2011; Shaun Birmingham, 8 Nov 2010; Nick Blundell, 14 Sep 1992; Chris Bowyer, 26 Nov 2012; Christopher Brookshaw, 28 Sep 2012; Stephen Bull, 19 Nov 2007; John Clancy, 1 Apr 2011; Hannah Conway, 29 Jan 2013; Rau Cooper, 22 Feb 1989; Lydia Davis, 25 Sep 2012; Michael DiMaggio, 4 Feb 2013; Raquel DiMaggio, 7 Nov 1996; Terence Duckworth, 28 Jun 2012; Brenton Eagle, 19 Nov 2012; Atila Emin, 21 Dec 2011; Damien Faass, 16 Dec 2011; Niall Fahy, 13 Dec 2012; Jeffrey Field, 13 Aug 2012; Aden Gelmi, 15 Nov 2012; Jesse Gray-Morgan, 28 Oct 1997; David Gurney, 15 Dec 2009; Daniel Harvey, 28 Oct 2010; Bob Hawksworth, 30 Jun 2008; Valerie Jeisman, 2 Oct 1996; David Kake, 21 Nov 2011; Julia Kirkby, 12 Oct 2010; David Leon, 12 Aug 2011; Robert Magee, 19 Nov 2012; Nikki Maru, 7 Mar 2006; Raymond Mccagh, 12 Jan 2012; Susanne Meechan, 23 Jul 2007; Kayn Notarangelo, 14 Jan 2013; James Packau, 23 Jan 2013; Brent Paekau, 7 Nov 2011; Tony Pain, 9 Sep 2009; Malcolm Papa, 14 Sep 2009; Alexander Penter, 2 Jan 2013; Douglas Rawiri, 26 Mar 2012; Neville Reeves, 9 Oct 2000; Lori Reid, 24 May 2010; Robert Rix, 3 May 2011; Paul Rucins, 17 Dec 2012; Benjamin Sharp, 1 Dec 2012; Scott Taumata, 10 Jan 2011; Graeme Tilley, 29 Oct 2012; Jim Trajanovski, 24 Mar 2008; Lauren Woodward, 8 Nov 2011. **Mainfreight Sydney** Ashraf Abdelhalim, 24 May 2011; Muchsin Alaydrus, 30 Aug 2010; Rebecca Alexander, 31 Jan 2012; Christian Aliste, 12 Jun 2003; Fadi Al-Mallou, 15 Feb 1992; Sharon Ama, 4 Oct 2005; Sonny Aneteru, 29 Oct 2012; Anthony Bigeni, 11 Aug 2008; Tony Bilir, 18 Jun 1905; Michael Blitvic, 24 May 2011; Krishna Boppana, 13 Sep 2011; Elle Boulos, 27 Jan 2010; Beau Briggs, 27 Feb 2012; Christopher Brkovec, 27 Jun 2011; Clinton Brock, 7 Sep 2011; Laisenia Burewe, 3 Nov 1994; Gavin Butler, 5 Jan 2010; Patrick Butler, 11 Apr 2011; Ashleigh Cameron, 6 Oct 2009; Kristen Cameron, 20 Aug 2007; Bevan Chambers, 16 Nov 2011; Avinesh Chand, 10 Nov 2005; Nilesh Chand, 10 Mar 2006; Navin Chandra, 23 Aug 2007; Salvin Chandra, 7 Jun 2006; Adrian Chanthavong, 4 Apr 2005; Raelene Codd, 10 Aug 2010; Stacey Collier, 24 Aug 2009; Amy Connelly, 28 Nov 2011; Michael Dairy, 10 Aug 2004; James Darby, 19 Jan 2009; Pamela Dilucchio, 18 Apr 2005; Alan Ebadi, 12 Aug 2011; Roland Eid, 31 Mar 2009; Danny Ellyard, 19 Sep 1990; George Epenian, 27 Aug 1997; Sinan Fazlilar, 27 Apr 2010; Emelito Feliciano, 1 Jun 2012; Amelia Fifita, 9 May 2012; Kristen Flood, 10 Aug 2009; Asipeli Fotofili, 5 Jul 2010; Tevita Fotofili, 22 Jun 1994; Joseph Franco, 9 Apr 2010; Debbie Geary, 24 Feb 2003; Tayfun Gezer, 3 Oct 2005; Nicholas Gleeson, 14 Oct 2002; Imran Goraya, 29 Aug 2011; Emma Gordon, 23 Mar 2012; Thomas Han, 13 Jan 2011; Ray Hanson, 20 Jun 1905; Geoffrey Heard, 23 Sep 1988; Jane Henry, 22 Aug 2011; Darren Hill, 3 Oct 1997; Ron Hill, 15 Apr 2001; Kingi Hoskin, 2 Apr 2001; Dean James, 21 Feb 2005; Natalie James, 13 Sep 2007; Salesh Jay, 1 Nov 2006; William Kahle, 10 Jun 2011; Roger Kaiser, 15 Oct 2007; Jim Karipis, 22 Jun 2012; Chrissy Kaufusi, 16 Apr 2012; Ben Keans, 31 Oct 2011; Robert Kelly, 6 Feb 2012; Sarah Kimmings, 21 Jul 2008; Sachindra Krishnan, 14 Mar 2013; Pramod Kumar, 7 Jun 2006; Umesh Kumar, 29 Oct 2008; Van Le, 9 Jan 2012; Tulipe Lolenese, 22 Aug 2011; Beverley McHugh, 16 Sep 2002; Robert Meredith, 4 May 2012; Darron Miles, 1 Jun 2012; Daneile Moana, 31 Jul 2000; Helena Moana, 12 Sep 2011; Susan Morrow, 24 Sep 2012; Magele Muaulu, 25 Oct 2010; Avinesh Naidu, 3 Jul 2012; Sam Narayan, 10 Mar 2004; Katherine Nemorin, 23 Nov 2004; Quoc Nguyen, 17 Jun 2008; Derek Ormsby, 7 Dec 2012; Suza Paceskoski, 7 Oct 2005; Cindy Page, 10 Jun 2003; Dylan Paniora, 19 Sep 2011; Eva-Lynn Patai, 11 Jul 2011; Mick Pepper, 22 Dec 2011; Siprachanch Phanoraj, 12 Feb 2007; Luke Phillips, 18 Oct 2012; Motiana Pisu, 1 Aug 2011; Wi Pohatu, 30 Sep 2004; Soane Potesio, 14 Sep 2009; Michelle Purvis, 3 Jul 2000; John Rapa, 21 Nov 2005; Mike Reid, 15 Nov 1980; Gary Ritchie, 1 Nov 2006; Blade Ross, 9 Aug 2012; Rotohiko Ross, 29 Feb 2012; Ray Rylewski, 8 Apr 2005; Eddy Saade, 5 Nov 2012; Taha Sabbagh, 7 Apr 2012; Daniel Salelesi, 13 Aug 2007; Saipele Salelesi, 7 Sep 2006; Robert Sandys, 2 Nov 2009; Strantz Schaumkel, 24 Oct 2011; Amy Schumann, 16 Apr 2007; Robert Seisun, 1 Jun 2005; Mirsad Serifovic, 28 Nov 2012; Chrissy Seve, 9 Nov 2011; Ozair Siddiqui, 10 Aug 2010; Randhir Singh, 27 Apr 2004; Jonathan Speedzenburg, 1 Jun 2005; Rangimarie Takiari, 8 May 2006; Jack Te-Atua, 19 May 2008; Liam Thompson, 28 Sep 2009; Zoran Trenkoski, 17 Sep 2004; Alex Vatau, 12 Mar 2012; Filipine Vave, 15 May 2000; Sione Vave, 4 Mar 1998; Mark Vincent, 12 Aug 1993; Frank Violi, 8 Feb 2005; Denise Vitellaro, 5 Dec 2002; Elinor Whitcher, 5 Jul 2011; Reg Woonton, 25 Sep 1991. **Mainfreight Townsville** Jay Bax, 17 Nov 2008; Marla Costabeber, 7 Mar 2011; Jessica Cuming, 22 Oct 2012; Karen Lloyd, 25 Mar 2013; Stephen Nolan, 14 Dec 2012; Joshua Nunan, 27 Oct 2012; Jordan Ryter, 4 Feb 2013; Shane Staunton, 13 Jul 2012. **Mainfreight Air & Ocean Adelaide** Samuel Bennett, 9 May 2012; Diana Christie, 3 Apr 2009; Jaimie Collyer, 21 May 2012; David Coughlin, 3 Dec 2012; Jodie Dirksen, 4 Jan 2011; Svetlana Kasyanov, 30 Aug 2010; Lisa Raimondo, 21 Aug 2000; Jessica Rankin, 2 Nov 2005; Skye Sargent, 1 Apr 2010; Mitchell Stint, 3 Jan 2012. **Mainfreight Air & Ocean Brisbane** Jennifer Ablett, 6 Oct 2008; Lee Amour, 2 Mar 1998; Patricia Anderson, 24 Oct 2011; Stephen Anderson, 1 Jul 2003; Christopher Bamford, 28 Mar 2007; Monicque Bamford, 2 Jan 2007; Drew Bowler, 17 Jan 2011; Georgia Buck, 13 Sep 2006; Julia Connolly, 22 Aug 2011; James Duncan, 20 May 2010; David Hall, 26 Oct 2009; Laureen Keller-Mills, 16 Aug 2010; Lyncoln Keresoma, 9 May 2011; Karen King, 21 Feb 2013; Lisa Laing, 12 Apr 2010; Deanne Lingard, 4 Feb 2008; Craig McNaughton, 10 Apr 2007; Christopher Meacham, 22 Oct 2012; Renee Mesinovic, 30 Jun 2003; Sara Payne, 16 Jan 2006; Danielle Prodger, 2 Jan 2013; Jessica Pursey, 7 Sep 2009; Darren Ramsden, 20 Jun 2011; Katelyn Ritson, 14 Jan 2013; Melanie Sheppard, 19 Jan 2010; Tony Skinner, 14 Jan 2013; Chantelle Stiege, 5 Nov 2001; Ian Thomas, 10 Oct 2011; Peter Tombling, 27 May 2008; Penelope Tumai, 28 Mar 2011; Emily Vardy, 7 Feb 2011; Ognjen Vuksanovic, 20 Jun 2005; Laureen White-Cain, 21 Nov 2011; Peng Zhou, 25 Mar 2013. **Mainfreight Air & Ocean Melbourne (Melrose)** Gary Atkins, 3 Dec 1979; Daisy Attard, 30 May 1994; Jade Barker, 3 Oct 2011; Melissa Bartlett, 25 Nov 1986; Jacky Brailsford, 5 Jan 2010; Christopher Brown, 28 Feb 2011; William Brown, 4 Jun 1985; Rebekah Burgoyne, 1 Sep 2012; Callum Burns, 10 Mar 2010; Laura Burns, 29 Mar 2005; Monica Cahill, 25 Sep 2006; Natalie Calvano, 1 Aug 2005; Tony Capuano, 16 Nov 2009; Jessica Clayton, 15 Jun 2010; Kenneth Clough, 18 Aug 2008; Lisa Colombo, 1 Mar 2007; Rebecca Conte, 5 Dec 2011; Megan Cooper, 22 Nov 2010; Rob Croft, 12 Apr 2010; Johanna Dahmen, 11 Oct 2004; Craig Daly, 31 May 1999; Vijaya Dasari, 10 Dec 2007; Kirsty Davis, 24 May 1999; Grant Draper, 21 Apr 1997; Josephine Fava, 1 Apr 2008; Damien Ferris, 29 Sep 2008; Alana Field, 5 Sep 2011; Dale Foote, 23 Sep 2003; Louise Gallardo, 31 Jul 2006; Greg Giarratana, 18 Aug 2003; Suzanne Gibson, 17 Dec 2007; Fiona Goodwin, 10 May 1999; Rachel Grover, 1 Nov 2011; Tyson Hanmer, 16 Feb 2012; Jordan Harding, 12 Mar 2013; Ryan Hatty, 22 Nov 2010; Edmila Hebel, 23 Jun 2003; Nicole Hegeman, 21 May 2001; Rachel Hilton, 25 Mar 2008; Sean Hutchinson, 26 May 2003; Janberk Ilhan, 15 Nov 2010; Aneta Jankovski, 13 Nov 2006; Lisa Jordan, 8 Mar 2004; Carolyn King, 30 Jun 1989; Troy Kirwan, 19 Oct 2005; Jasna Kovacevic, 12 Aug 2004; Franky Kranen, 25 Mar 2008; Rajini Kumari, 16 Feb 2004; Tracey Lane, 12 Mar 2003; Mandy Lazaridis, 14 Nov 2011; Christopher Lebon, 7 Jan 2008; Jenny Lee, 2 Jun 2003; Ping Ping Liang, 1 Feb 2013; Jing Liao, 12 Sep 2011; Xiu Lin, 18 Nov 2011; Christopher Lindroos, 4 Jun 2001; Lee Liu, 24 May 2010; Chi Luong, 3 Jan 2012; Rose Marra, 1 Aug 2002; Sarah Martin, 24 Apr 2008; Mercedesz Matskassy, 4 Oct 2004; Rachel McGregor, 6 Mar 2000; Roslyn Meli, 1 Sep 1992; Tatiana Mendel, 6 Apr 2010; Salvatore Milici, 15 Oct 2007; Shane Moroney, 15 Jul 2011; Silvina Moyano-Soccio, 14 Nov 2011; Brian Mueller, 20 Dec 1993; Janine Nemeth, 6 Mar 2006; David Patterson, 5 Jul 2004; Graham Patterson, 5 Oct 2009; Hai Pham, 29 Sep 2003; Kristian

Phillips, 29 May 2001; Grace Polgar, 5 May 1997; Catherine Rankin, 4 Jan 2010; Graham Robinson, 1 Jul 2007; Leasa Rowley, 18 Aug 2008; Dean Ruffell, 19 May 2003; Karli Ruhle, 21 Nov 2011; Brendan Ryan, 28 Jan 1992; Melanie Savona, 19 Jul 1999; Anthony Schembri, 7 May 2012; Luke Sekoa, 6 Sep 2010; Funda Sener, 12 Jan 2004; Shara Shanahan, 16 Jan 2006; Christopher Soriano, 28 Nov 2011; Jason Spiteri, 13 Aug 2007; Shobhana Sriram, 28 Jun 2010; Xiaoxia Sun, 27 Sep 2010; Paula Suwart, 3 Oct 2005; Brittany Thorogood, 21 Nov 2011; Stephen Thorogood, 27 Aug 1985; Richard Tomlinson, 28 Sep 2009; Julie Torrini, 5 Sep 2011; Paolina Tortora, 1 Apr 1992; Jarrad Tucker, 26 Feb 2008; Nicholas Veanes, 18 Sep 2012; Daniella Verlaque, 2 Jan 2006; Connie Vinci, 14 Mar 2000; Joyce Wain, 28 Nov 1994; Kendal Walsh, 1 Jul 1996; Joanne Warway, 18 Jun 2002; Paige Woodhouse, 1 Mar 2010; Samantha Worton, 30 Mar 2007; Stephanie Zenonos, 3 Jan 2012. **Mainfreight Air & Ocean Melbourne (Springbank)** Khled Abbas, 20 Mar 2010; Paul Berias, 17 Dec 2004; Debra Carr, 6 Dec 2010; Jonathan Caruso, 13 Dec 2010; Vincent Caruso, 19 Apr 2010; Kerry Cogan, 10 May 2001; Ryan Darmanin, 16 May 2005; Travis Dellar, 1 Jul 1999; Julia DiBella, 24 Mar 2003; Corey Dulson, 25 Mar 2008; Gaze El-Ali, 8 May 2011; Daniel Farrugia, 4 Feb 2008; Mario Farrugia, 1 Jul 1995; Angelina Fernandopulle, 4 Jul 2007; Michela Giarratana, 22 Feb 2010; Benjamin Green, 27 Oct 2009; David Grossman, 2 Jan 1993; David Mallia, 14 Jun 2005; Pam Moussiades, 5 Sep 2005; Matthew Mudge, 21 Jun 1995; Luise Ockardt, 4 Jan 2011; Suleyman Tahir, 4 Nov 2009; Riki Takerei, 12 Dec 2011; Tane Takerei, 20 Aug 2010; Peter Truda, 18 Mar 2010; George Tsiogas, 14 Feb 2011. **Mainfreight Air & Ocean Newcastle** Jason Storey, 29 Aug 2011. **Mainfreight Air & Ocean Perth** Amanda Aiken, 16 May 2011; Rebecca Colton, 5 Mar 2013; Jessica Hayes, 11 Aug 2008; Jocelyn McCagh, 18 Jul 2011; Colleen Ovens, 21 Mar 2011; Bronwyn Wassell, 28 Apr 1994; Ronnie Wong, 6 Sep 2010; Li Zhang, 2 Oct 2012. **Mainfreight Air & Ocean Sydney** Mohammed Ashifdar, 27 Feb 2007; Lucy Atai, 1 Feb 2011; Jennifer Bayad, 19 May 2011; Helen Baziotis, 28 May 1990; Theodore Billing, 9 Jan 2006; Darren Bird, 17 Mar 2008; Corey Braid, 1 Dec 1998; Mirjana Bridge, 27 Aug 2007; Samantha Burton, 18 Apr 2012; Luke Chance, 30 Jul 2012; Renjia Chen, 17 Nov 2011; Dermot Clark, 5 Sep 2011; David Coe, 15 Apr 1985; Rowan Cooke, 19 Feb 2007; Kerrie Coombes, 8 May 2012; Julie Costopoulos, 20 Jun 2007; Matthew Crealy, 18 Feb 2008; Julie Deang, 26 Nov 2012; Paul Dixon, 14 Mar 2011; Slav Donevski, 8 Mar 2010; Craig Dunphy, 3 Mar 2008; Paul Enriquez, 9 May 2011; Alla Ermoliev, 1 Jul 2010; Conor Farrell, 14 Jun 2006; John Finocchiaro, 28 Feb 2011; Salvatore Forzisi, 4 Jan 2005; Natalee Fox, 4 Oct 2005; Jian Gao, 6 Dec 2006; Paula Gomez, 24 Nov 2008; Tyne Green, 30 May 2005; Natalie Grilo, 16 Apr 2012; James Hartigan, 19 May 2000; Melissa James, 29 Jan 2008; Garry Jamieson, 20 Dec 1999; Dongzi Jia, 15 Aug 2011; Morgan Jones, 15 May 2012; Peter Joyce, 25 Feb 2008; Vanessa Kidd, 5 Nov 2007; Chanel Lazarevska, 19 Apr 2010; Felipe Leyton, 20 Jun 2011; Vanessa Lowe, 20 Oct 1997; Janina Manalese, 24 Jun 2002; Damien Mascord, 17 Mar 2008; Stuart McCartney, 8 Nov 2004; Damien McNamara, 12 Feb 2007; Robert Miller, 3 Dec 2012; Pamela Millhouse, 28 Jul 1997; Jessica Molyneux, 25 Feb 2008; Mariam Najjar, 4 Oct 2011; Joumana Nasr, 12 Sep 2005; Tony Naumoff, 25 Feb 2002; Natalie Nikolovski, 30 Aug 2010; Steven Pavitt, 27 Feb 2013; Brianna Piasini, 26 Mar 2012; Mark Posa, 11 Dec 2000; Zeallian Prasad, 25 Nov 2011; Kate Pryor, 3 Jul 2007; Margaret Reynolds, 22 Apr 2003; Sofia Rida, 31 Oct 2005; James Robertson, 3 Oct 2005; Rosa Samaha, 12 Apr 2010; Bruce Scott, 6 May 2011; Hayley Smith, 29 Nov 2012; Claire Smithies, 23 Jan 2013; Melissa Stanley, 2 Jan 2008; Raymond Starkie, 7 Mar 2012; Lee Symons, 23 Apr 2007; Elizabeth Tadic, 16 Jan 2013; Brendon Timihou, 28 Jun 2011; Riwa Wiki, 13 Oct 2004; Philip Wilson, 15 Jul 2002; Kit Ying Woo, 8 Sep 2008; Hua Yu, 19 Dec 2011; Lirong Zhou, 23 May 2011. **Mainfreight Air & Ocean Perishables Sydney** Aaron Angeles, 10 Apr 2012; Lisa Harrison, 5 Dec 2011; Debra May, 27 Oct 1997; Melinda Pickard, 1 Feb 1990; Markus Raab, 19 Mar 2007; Imran Shaikh, 3 Dec 2011; Karam Zebib, 15 Apr 2008. **Mainfreight Air & Ocean Townsville** Shane Bird, 21 Nov 2005. **Mainfreight FTL Adelaide** Brian Cook, 22 Nov 2004. **Mainfreight FTL Brisbane** Paul Bellamy, 30 Aug 2004; Angela Topp, 12 Mar 2012. **Mainfreight IT Melbourne** Darrel Byrnes, 26 Aug 2008; Rob Cotter, 30 Jun 1988; Jonathan Holmes, 24 Mar 2003; Michael Hood, 9 Jan 2006; Mario Lonigro, 27 Apr 2011; Ian Mavric, 22 Mar 2004; Andrew McLeod, 1 Jul 2010; Darryn Petricevich, 1 Feb 1992; Pagona Petricevich, 21 Dec 2009; Benjamin Renehan, 15 Oct 2004; Kate Ryan, 12 Jun 2000; Marija Vukovic, 19 Apr 2004. **Mainfreight IT Sydney** Belinda Bright, 14 Jun 2005; David Coen, 16 Apr 2012; Rachael Moore, 4 Feb 2002; Debbie Rawiri, 1 Mar 2012. **Mainfreight Logistics Adelaide** Kendall Anderson, 8 May 2007; Scott Knight, 10 Oct 2011. **Mainfreight Logistics Brisbane** Timothy Craig, 30 May 2011; Paul Fraser, 9 Feb 2004; Tyrone Hall, 26 Nov 2012; Gordon Hay, 2 Apr 2001; Wesley Iosia-Sipeli, 10 Apr 2012; Stephen Jones, 7 Dec 2009; Barry Keleher, 12 Oct 2011; Matthew Little, 20 Mar 2013; Christine Meekings, 25 Jun 2007; Daniel Mullins, 29 Aug 2011; Eric Taylor, 14 May 1993; Fiona Trebilcock, 16 Dec 2002; Riley Tryhorn, 2 Apr 2012; Simon Wishart, 12 Mar 2012; Tracey Young, 10 Mar 2008. **Mainfreight Logistics Melbourne (Noble Park)** Hamish Bradley, 30 Nov 2009; Olivia Bradley, 22 Oct 2010; Mensur Burnic, 9 Mar 2010; Thomas Clarke, 5 May 2010; Dale Cranston, 26 Oct 2011; Mafutaga Galuvao, 25 Sep 2012; Wayne Harris, 1 Feb 2000; Patrick Kerr, 16 Feb 2004; Daniel Martin, 1 Jun 2006; Stuart McKell, 16 Jan 2012; Audrey Puni, 3 Sep 2007; Theresa Tahi, 10 Oct 2011. **Mainfreight Logistics Melbourne (Somerton)** Aladin Basic, 8 Jan 2007; Kevin Bradley, 21 Jan 1969; Jeremy Collins, 16 Jul 2007; Nathan Day, 1 May 2012; Joshua Devine, 18 Aug 2008; Bradley Greer, 7 Aug 2000; Tony Henderson, 6 Oct 2009; Patrick Iese, 27 Jun 2011; Dianne La Velle, 20 Jun 1995; Esekia Manuele-Malagaoma, 4 Apr 2007; Rhonda Marroun, 20 Aug 2007; Andrew Marshall, 14 May 2010; Andrew McNally, 27 Aug 2012; Peter McNally, 24 Feb 1992; John-Paul Melody, 15 Sep 2011; Lieselotte Michels, 1 Mar 2012; Michal Oczek, 14 Jun 2011; Donald Quartermain, 14 Nov 2011; Gabriel Simonetti, 17 Dec 2007; Michael Sulzberger, 15 Nov 2012; René Van Houtum, 21 Feb 1994; Jake Van Meel, 13 Feb 2012; Luke Van Meel, 4 Jul 2011; Ger Vang, 1 Sep 2010; Dietmar Venkort, 19 Feb 2007; Hamish Woods, 17 Jul 2006. **Mainfreight Logistics Melbourne (Sydney Road)** Paul Boud, 13 Nov 2012; Sam Bradley, 11 Dec 2012; Nicholas Dinneen, 22 Aug 2008; Toso Fretton, 12 Apr 2004; David Honer, 29 Nov 2011; Mile Jovanovski, 13 Sep 2010; Colm Scully, 15 Jun 2010; Valentin Teles, 27 Dec 2012. **Mainfreight Logistics Perth** Helen Brookshaw, 6 Aug 2007; Philip Connell, 24 May 2004; Craig Ellis, 4 Feb 2013; Katie Gray-Morgan, 18 Jan 2011; Tracey Ironui, 11 Oct 2010; Toni Letch, 26 Apr 2006; Pauline Poi, 13 Nov 2009; Paul Read, 5 Feb 2007; Wade Stagg, 6 Feb 2012; Todd Vallerine, 8 Oct 2012; Dean Williams, 14 Aug 1997. **Mainfreight Logistics Sydney (Moorebank)** Michael Bell, 2 Apr 2012; Troy Bennett, 8 Jan 2001; Krystal Blackadder, 24 Jan 2011; Ray Camillire, 10 Dec 2002; Rayfort Collins, 17 Oct 2011; Pramendra Datt, 9 Aug 2010; Martin Geers, 2 Apr 2012; Matthew Gowman, 26 Apr 2010; Joe Harris, 28 Oct 2010; Larissa Harris, 21 Dec 2011; Vivienne Harris, 18 Dec 2000; Aris Izmirlian, 4 Jan 2011; Leanne Jones, 2 Apr 2012; Denny Mankin, 4 Oct 2010; Donna Martin, 24 Jan 2011; Thi Nguyen, 1 Jul 2011; Doris Pace, 17 Oct 2011; Melanie Pace, 12 Mar 2013; Gordon Pairama, 19 Jul 2007; Fernando Puglia, 4 Oct 2010; Lee Purvis, 2 Jul 2012; Alex Rivera, 2 Apr 2012; Channa Rodrigo, 28 Nov 2011; Karl Rutherford, 25 Jan 2008; Olotele Salanoa, 1 Aug 2011; Alistair Soares, 2 Oct 2012; Tracey Tihema, 2 Aug 2010. **Mainfreight Logistics Sydney (Prestons)** Dylan Burgess, 7 Nov 2011; Ray Burgess, 4 Oct 1996; Charlie Camilleri, 24 Oct 2007; Frankie Camilleri, 1 Nov 2010; Vedran Crnovodja, 15 Oct 2012; Matthew Dickson, 26 Nov 2012; Alvina D'Souza, 24 Oct 2011; Scott Green, 16 Jan 2012; Simon Hart, 2 Feb 2006; Kris Maddaford, 29 Nov 2010; Kerin Mamo, 2 Feb 2011; Glenn McDonald, 14 Feb 2011; Pohorambage Nilantha, 9 May 2007; Nicole Oncescu, 4 Jan 2010; Shaun O'Reilly, 15 Oct 2012; Vitda Pangnanouvong, 28 May 2012; Catherine Pasnin, 15 Aug 2011; Keith Penman, 1 Sep 2005; Janice Phillips, 12 Oct 2005; Wiari Sekene, 24 Jan 2011; Karena Shell, 31 Jan 2011; Jason Sloan, 25 Oct 2010; Chris Soares, 11 Jan 2010; Aaron Vallely, 18 Aug 2010; Maria van der Nagel, 12 Jun 2008; Mary Wall, 25 Mar 2008; Shane Zielonka, 27 Oct 2008. **Mainfreight Metro Brisbane** Jayson Baxter, 15 Jun 2007; Arnold Corpuz, 15 Jul 2011; Kieran Dawkins, 30 Nov 2010; Scott Dawson, 18 Nov 2011; Gavin Douglas, 30 May 2006; Christopher Gordon, 12 Mar 2010; Martin James, 15 Jul 2011; Gary Knuckey, 8 Feb 2013; Davide Mancini, 17 Jul 2008; Andre Mcconnell,

26 Mar 2012; Peter Mclean, 30 Sep 2011; Darius Molsovan, 18 Sep 2008; Adrian Opris, 16 Jan 2012; John Platt, 7 Aug 2008; Manoj Punj, 1 Jul 2011; Michael Sheen, 14 Feb 2013; Gordon Simpkins, 13 Nov 2001; Harvinder Singh, 10 Jan 2012; Jasbir Singh, 15 Jul 2011; Vinod Sreeramoju, 22 Dec 2010; Jason Steele, 8 Feb 2013; Kareena Sullivan, 10 Apr 2007; Damien Taylor, 18 Feb 2013; Tara-Leigh Walker, 1 Nov 2011. **Mainfreight Metro Melbourne** Yilma Asherbire, 4 Aug 2010; Allan Ballantyne, 13 Mar 2009; Timothy Brown, 17 Nov 2011; Melissa Dick, 25 Mar 2013; Natasa Dimakis, 6 Oct 2008; Bill Fraser, 14 Jul 2010; Gianni Gallardo, 21 Apr 2008; Rifet Gorovic, 13 May 2002; Bob Inoue, 7 Jan 2004; Jaspal Janda, 16 Oct 2012; Jovan Jovanovski, 25 Sep 2006; Milorad Kirkovski, 2 Oct 2009; Stevo Krstevski, 6 Jan 2012; Antony Papalia, 19 Jan 2010; Zandro Racasa, 16 Oct 2012; Jasvir Sing, 21 Sep 2012; Vikramjit Singh, 17 Oct 2012; Robert Tanevski, 24 Jul 2012; Zoran Tomic, 20 Feb 2012; Benny Vodiloski, 14 Jul 2010. **Mainfreight Metro Sydney** Arthur Alexiou, 31 Jan 2010; Haider Al-Haider, 14 Oct 2008; Erwyn Bolina, 28 Nov 2011; Deni Bozinovski, 30 Apr 2010; Fadi Brais, 20 Aug 2012; Ahmet Celik, 8 Nov 2011; Tah Eldarwich, 22 Jun 2012; Hilal Fawaz, 28 Dec 2012; Francesco Ferreira, 9 Nov 2007; Andrew Gailani, 14 Mar 2013; Hadi Ghafary, 11 Nov 2010; Rgheed Ghdhaib, 14 Mar 2013; Arthur Hatzianestis, 29 Feb 2008; Jamal Jaber, 2 Apr 2012; Paul Jones, 18 Feb 2013; Kire Josevski, 29 Jun 2007; James Kanard, 30 Apr 2010; Nick Karapalevski, 20 Apr 2011; Muy Heng Khao, 24 Sep 2012; Anup Kumar, 14 Mar 2013; Said Lahroudi, 27 Sep 2012; Thanh Le, 30 May 2008; Grant Lee, 17 Mar 2009; Yong Li, 21 May 2012; Brooke Moretti, 28 Feb 2011; Thai Nguyen, 9 Apr 2010; Glenn O'Riley, 30 Aug 2005; Dean Parker, 4 May 2010; Gaya Prasad, 13 Jan 2006; Lindsay Puckeridge, 31 Jan 2008; Ali Rahal, 14 Mar 2013; Devender Singh, 29 Oct 2012; Craig Smith, 2 Oct 2001; Steven Spano, 22 Oct 2012; Saso Sutarov, 20 Dec 2012; Riad Taha, 21 May 2012; Nikolce Tasevski, 10 Jun 2011; Goran Trajkoski, 8 Sep 2009; Jason Truong, 28 Sep 2012; Craig Whitaker, 15 Aug 2011; Peter Wilson, 27 Jun 2005; Ghulam Zohori, 24 Aug 2012. **Owens Brisbane** Shareen Ali, 1 Mar 2010; George Athos, 14 May 2012; Ben Avery, 20 Jul 2011; Ian Bavister, 8 Feb 2013; Desmond Bertram, 9 Feb 2000; Danny Capner, 19 Nov 2010; David Carvolth, 15 May 2012; Jose Conjera, 20 Nov 2006; Darren Copland, 9 Feb 2006; Maurice Cowen, 14 Jan 1994; Marc Cranmer, 28 Jul 2011; Jamie Davis, 17 Dec 2007; Anthony Hazcat, 14 May 2012; Shayne Hobson, 29 Oct 2009; Clive Kennedy, 5 Apr 2010; Brian Key, 3 Feb 2006; Rob Liston, 2 Apr 2008; Niki Londy, 13 May 2002; Dominic Lupo, 16 Jan 2006; Lisa Mahy, 18 Apr 2005; Paul May, 6 Apr 2010; Murray McMahon, 23 May 2000; Glen Mcrae, 15 Sep 2010; Alan Milliner, 22 Nov 2010; Geoff Milne, 4 May 2012; Robin Moore, 12 Mar 2012; Jason Moore, 13 May 2012; Bill Morton, 8 Feb 2013; Robert Ngamoki, 23 Mar 2010; Michael Phillips, 21 Nov 2011; Randall Provost, 8 Feb 2013; Neil Randall, 3 Dec 2006; Mark Redman, 12 Nov 2009; Trevor Roberts, 21 Feb 2006; Graham Sailes, 31 Oct 2004; Rod Sheriff, 21 Sep 2012; Trevor Smith, 4 Sep 1996; Timothy Stewart, 5 Mar 2012; Matthew Termin, 23 Aug 2010; Ricky Thomas, 11 Oct 2010; Martin Vandeweem, 30 Mar 2006; Paul Williams, 22 Jul 2005; Thomas Wilson, 20 Nov 2009; Dyer Wroe, 26 Sep 2011; Les Wroe, 21 Dec 2012. **Owens Melbourne** Zlate Apostolovski, 22 Oct 2012; Lincoln Butter, 10 Jan 2013; Ian Callen, 15 Feb 2011; Mathew Coles, 27 Feb 2013; Greg Cook, 11 Jun 2007; Daniel Cozzolino, 30 Oct 2012; Brett Dintinosante, 6 Feb 2012; Susi Dombrzalski, 18 Mar 2013; Matthew Dunne, 14 Jan 2013; Kolio Falealii, 1 Dec 2011; Lindsay Gray, 5 Jun 2006; Wayne Hoare, 3 Sep 2007; Alex Josifovski, 5 Nov 2012; Vasko Josifovski, 24 Sep 2012; Roy McCarthy, 15 Dec 2012; Rodney Patterson, 25 Jun 2012; Jaiden Pickering, 4 Feb 2013; Michael Rana, 1 Nov 2010; Nigel Rouse, 16 Aug 2012; Martin Sammut, 16 Jan 2012; Joseph Tejada, 10 Dec 2012; Peter Valdemarin, 20 Dec 2011; Marcus Van Loon, 19 Apr 2011; Jeff Woods, 20 Jun 2011. **Owens Perth** Sandra Ali, 19 Jun 2006; Aryan Bhardwaj, 5 Mar 2012; Swarn Brar, 1 Oct 2012; Philip Cabassi, 1 Mar 2013; Samantha Cox, 10 Oct 2011; Praneil Deeplaul, 1 Feb 2012; Nicole Hurley, 12 May 2008; Jaskarn Khangura, 24 Sep 2012; Stephen McDonald, 22 May 2012; Jeffery McGough, 1 Feb 2013; Gethash Ramlukun, 8 Aug 2012; Steven Schmidt, 1 Apr 2012; David Shine, 1 Feb 2012; Tejwant Singh, 24 Sep 2012; Shane Willcox, 29 Aug 2012. **Owens Sydney** Scott Beauchamp, 1 Feb 2010; Mark Boyd, 28 Sep 2009; Christian Brohoquis, 16 Apr 2012; Stephen Butler, 6 Jun 2011; Hirdesh Chand, 23 Oct 2006; Cameron Clode, 28 May 2001; Craig Connors, 4 Oct 2011; Rubinco Corboski, 17 Feb 2000; Scott Davies, 7 Jan 2013; Brian Doyle, 1 Jul 1999; Justin Howlett, 16 Apr 2012; Josepine Kimberley, 1 Jun 2011; Benjamin MacDonald, 7 Feb 2011; Paul McCracken, 1 Aug 1993; Vale McKenzie, 1 Jul 2006; Nathan Preval, 22 Jul 2002; John Rawling, 23 May 1994; Pasqua Riservato, 14 Sep 1998; Karyn Seed, 9 Mar 2011; Steven Slezak, 14 Jan 2013; Harry Belongiannis, 1992; Alec Cakovski, 1991; Roberto Catalano, 27 Aug 2012; Sam Catena, 2002; Bill Debrincat, 1 Jul 2008; Peter Disibio, 1988; George Evangelou, 2000; Glen Finlay, 1 May 1998; Vangel Gramosli, 25 Jul 2011; Colin Hanson, 1991; Brian Hogarty, 2000; Ivo Hudec, 1998; Keith Jones, 1991; Paul Jordon, 1 Jul 2008; Paul Konstantinidis, 12 Jun 2012; Jamie Kukeski, 2004; Steve Lipovac, 16 Jun 1905; Ali Madrajat, 19 May 2012; George Mantzakos, 2000; Dean Marks, 1 Jul 2008; Glenn Marshall, 13 Jun 1905; Robert Michael, 1 Jul 2008; Cuong Nguyen, 2004; Colin Ogrady, 27 Jun 1905; Danny Petrevski, 2007; Goran Petrevski, 28 Jun 1905; Van Pham, 1992; Reino Repo, 1 Apr 1999; James Russell, 1991; Jan Sloma, 2000; Nick Soldatos, 1 Jul 2008; Keith Stone, 1 Jun 1998; Ronald Stone, 15 Jun 1905; Graeme Syphers, 1993; Anastasios Validakis, 2008; Eddy Wosik, 1992; Henryk Wroblewski, 1992; George Xenos, 1 Jul 2008; Sotirios Xenos, 1 Jul 2008. **Training Australia** Sarah Averill, 23 Dec 2010; Aaron Bond, 1 May 2000; Gabrielle Fage, 27 Sep 2010; Natalina Fisher, 22 Sep 2008; Rachel Gallo, 7 Jan 2013; Stephen Kay, 15 Aug 2011; Colleen Moore, 23 Apr 2001; Shona Taylor, 10 Jun 2003; Samantha Ward, 2 Feb 2004. **ASIA CaroTrans Guangzhou** Alex Yang, 11 Jun 2012. **CaroTrans Hong Kong** Jerry Chan, 18 Apr 2006; Ray Chan, 18 Apr 2011; Coey Cheuk, 8 Apr 2013; Sharon Lee, 15 Jul 2010; Judy Leung, 21 Jun 2010; Maggie Leung, 4 Jan 2008; Eric Ng, 9 May 2012; Elton Poon, 16 Oct 2001; Yoko Suen, 25 Oct 2010; Pearl Szeto, 29 Aug 2008; Kristy Tai, 11 Jan 2008; Janly Wai, 19 Aug 2008; Daffy Wong, 1 Jun 2007. **CaroTrans Ningbo** Cindy Chen, 16 Dec 2010; Rain Shan, 1 Aug 2007; Michelle Wu, 19 Mar 2012; Carl Xu, 28 May 2012. **CaroTrans Shanghai** Doris Bao, 1 Mar 2011; Joan Ji, 1 Jul 2002; Elaine Lu, 2 Jul 2012; Tom Qu, 5 Nov 2012; Helen Sun, 1 Aug 2001; Benny Tang, 30 Jun 2010; Evoone Tang, 2 Jul 2010; Sanny Zheng, 4 Jul 2011. **CaroTrans Shenzhen** Ken Guo, 17 May 2011; Lavender Wang, 26 Jul 2006; Cecliy Xiong, 16 Feb 2013. **Mainfreight Chengdu** Share Du, 2 Jul 2012; Daniel Rae, 19 Dec 2011; Enid Shi, 26 Jun 2012; Shelly Xiao, 25 Mar 2010. **Mainfreight Guangzhou** Jarvis Cai, 16 Aug 2010; Dick Deng, 31 May 2009; Lance Feng, 15 Mar 2010; Andy He, 1 Feb 2012; Frankie Li, 6 Sep 2010; Kidd Li, 19 Sep 2010; Lina Lin, 1 Feb 2008; Jane Liu, 5 Nov 2009; Judy Liu, 27 May 2008; Natalie Liu, 5 Nov 2009; Wendy Niu, 1 Nov 2007; Angela Wang, 23 Sep 2008; Castie Wu, 7 Jul 2010; Wing Wu, 4 Jan 2013; Raymond Zhuang, 1 Feb 2012. **Mainfreight Hong Kong** Chris Chan, 17 Nov 2011; Cynthia Chan, 16 Apr 2012; Edmond Cheng, 21 Feb 2007; Aubery Cheung, 30 Nov 1998; Derek Cheung, 24 Jan 2008; Connie Cho, 7 May 2012; Aldous Chu, 18 Jun 2012; Cary Chung, 1 Jun 2011; Sam Fung, 5 Jul 2010; Karen Ho, 12 Dec 2011; Joe Hsieh, 1 Feb 2012; Kurt Kwan, 4 Oct 2004; Patrick Kwok, 10 Mar 2010; Shing Lam, 7 Oct 2010; Wing Lam, 26 Sep 2011; Gary Lau, 7 Apr 2003; Joyce Lau, 30 Aug 2012; Hung Law, 3 Nov 2011; Andy Lee, 25 Feb 2013; Jouann Lee, 16 Aug 2004; Matthew Lee, 3 Jul 2007; Bonnie Leung, 14 Feb 2013; Jason Leung, 10 Sep 2012; Michael Lofaro, 1 Oct 1989; Wah Low, 3 Dec 2012; Franky Lui, 16 Sep 2008; Rai Ng, 30 Oct 2012; Burt So, 1 Apr 2010; Ricky Tong, 22 Jul 2010; Michelle Wong, 27 Dec 2012; Rose Wong, 14 Jan 2013; Kennis Yau, 21 Feb 2013; Sherman Yuen, 9 Apr 2008; Daniel Yun, 3 Sep 2008; Nichi Zhui, 25 Jun 2007. **Mainfreight Ningbo** Vicky Chen, 27 Jun 2011; Catherine Ge, 18 Oct 2010; Charlie He, 1 Mar 2012; Eric He, 23 Aug 2010; Yolanda Hong, 12 Jan 2009; Lisa Li, 18 Mar 2013; Sunny Sun, 5 Mar 2012; Daisy Wang, 1 Sep 2008; Wesker Wang, 26 Jun 2012; Emily Wu, 6 Jun 2012; Sara Xie, 16 Nov 2009; Joice Xu, 9 Jul 2008; Hannah Yang, 5 Sep 2005; Paul Ye, 3 Nov 2008; Klark Yu, 16 Sep 2010. **Mainfreight Qingdao** Jim Guo, 7 Mar 2013; Gary Hu, 5 Sep 2011; Sabrina Huang, 16 Sep 2011; Eva Jiang, 15 Jun 2011; Michael Lin, 14 May 2011; Amanda liu, 15 Jun 2011; Fred Wang, 29 Mar 2012; Jessica Wang, 4 Jan 2012; Vicky Zhao, 15 Jun 2011. **Mainfreight Shanghai** Milo Cai, 7 Jan 2013; Squall Cai, 21 Jun 2010; Joy Cai, 6 Jul 2012; Lucy Chen,

1 Dec 2007; Selina Chen, 6 Jul 2009; Queen Cheng, 1 Apr 2009; Joanna Fan, 30 Jul 2010; Frank Fei, 1 Jul 2006; Somnus Gu, 2 Jul 2012; Patrick He, 27 Jul 2009; Wendy Hu, 18 Mar 2013; Linda Huang, 1 Jun 2000; Elaine Hui, 1 Jul 2007; Lan Ji, 1 Aug 2012; Andy Liu, 1 Jun 2011; Anny Liu, 1 Mar 2003; Cici Liu, 6 Apr 2010; Andy Lling, 1 Aug 2009; Liarena Lu, 28 Jan 2013; Rody Luo, 1 Jul 2000; Echo Mao, 18 Mar 2013; Frances Mei, 17 Feb 2013; Momo Miao, 24 Oct 2011; Cindy Qi, 1 May 2003; Miko Ren, 5 Aug 2010; Seven Shi, 5 Jul 2012; Jenny Shui, 1 Aug 2002; Lillian Sun, 12 Aug 2009; Cherry Wang, 30 Mar 2011; Daniel Wang, 24 Jan 2013; Sophie Wang, 22 Jul 2008; Wing Wang, 9 Feb 2011; Aren Wu, 9 Jul 2012; Fanatic Xu, 9 Oct 2010; Matt Xu, 1 Nov 2012; Una Xu, 11 Mar 2011; Jerry Yang, 9 Oct 2010; Lily Yang, 20 May 2009; Kelly Ye, 18 Mar 2013; Doris Yuan, 8 Oct 2011; Sarah Yuan, 18 Mar 2013; Billy Zhang, 1 Aug 2001; Suki Zhang, 6 Nov 2005; Vivien Zhang, 1 Nov 2010; Jessica Zheng, 2 Jul 2012; Martin Zhong, 11 Feb 2011; Ricky Zhou, 16 Feb 2013; Suzy Zhou, 1 Jul 2000. **Mainfreight Shenzhen** Lily Huang, 15 Nov 2010; Steafan Lei, 5 Mar 2012; Sasa Liang, 3 Dec 2012; Sunny Lin, 9 Oct 2005; Sophie Liu, 7 Jun 2010; Raymond Lo, 1 Aug 2003; Hellen Peng, 21 Jun 2010; Samantha Sun, 4 Mar 2013; Crystal Wang, 2 Apr 2007; Evonne Wu, 25 Mar 2013; Soy Wu, 15 Oct 2010; Yuki Wu, 13 Oct 2009; Lucy Xiong, 21 Apr 2011; Sindy Yang, 5 Nov 2012; Paul Yuan, 1 Nov 2010; Aily Zhang, 1 Apr 2008; Cindy Zhang, 19 Jun 2007; Evan Zhang, 14 Aug 2006; Seven Zhang, 20 Mar 2013; Jenny Zhong, 23 Apr 2012; Canni Zou, 26 Oct 2006. **Mainfreight Tianjin** Carol Chen, 12 Jul 2010; Suzy Chen, 3 Sep 2012; Grace Mu, 12 Jun 2010; Cindy Ran, 2 May 2012; Ada Wu, 15 Nov 2011; Catherine Xie, 8 Oct 2010. **Mainfreight Xiamen** Renny Chen, 1 Jul 2010; Sally Chen, 8 Mar 2010; Tina Chen, 1 Jul 1994; Colin Cheng, 1 Jul 2011; Jessica Chou, 4 May 2010; David Wang, 1 Jan 1995; Anna Zhuo, 16 Apr 2012. **Mainfreight Taiwan** Carol Chang, 18 Mar 2013; Jenny Chen, 1 Aug 2012; Anna Chen, 1 Aug 2008; Emily Chen, 2 Apr 2007; Mei Chen, 11 Dec 2006; Mia Cheng, 10 Aug 2009; Joan Chiu, 14 Jan 2013; Rita Hsiao, 25 Jun 2012; Una Huang, 8 Aug 2000; Andy Jou, 11 Sep 1985; Debbie Ku, 25 Jul 2011; Nicole Kuo, 25 May 2006; Candy Lee, 1 May 2005; Kelly Lin, 11 Aug 2009; Yvonne Peng, 1 Jul 2012; Lily Shen, 19 Jul 2011; Stanley Su, 1 May 2012; Trista Tang, 28 Jun 2007; Sam Tu, 18 Jan 2010; Chloe Wu, 3 Nov 2009. **Mainline Singapore** Huang Yong Goh, 10 Jan 2011; Stephanie Goh, 2 Apr 2012; Shawn Lim, 3 Jan 2012; Simon Song, 17 April 2013, Peggy Yeo, 1 Nov 2012; Jillian Zheng, 14 Feb 2013. **CANADA Mainfreight Toronto** Shayne Cannon, 28 Feb 2013; Andrew Hall, 7 Jan 2013; Tricia Ougrah, 17 Sep 2012; Paul Taylor, 1 Jun 2012. **CHILE CaroTrans Santiago** Marcelo Hermosilla, 6 Jun 2011; Carolina Ibarra, 11 Mar 2013; Raul Katz, 1 Jun 2010; Yasna Moreno, 18 Apr 2011; Beatriz Osorio, 2 Jan 2012; Jaqueline Salviat, 16 Apr 2012; Crisly Santis, 18 Apr 2011; Wilfredo Soto, 14 May 2012. **MEXICO Mainfreight Mexico City** Fernando Ruiz, 16 Jul 2012; Jesus Calzada, 1 Oct 2012; Ana Cristina Cornejo, 1 Apr 2013; Eréndira Dueñas, 1 Apr 2013. **USA CaroTrans Atlanta** Emily Bonilla, 18 Jul 2011; Lindsay Brazier, 9 Jul 2012; Stephen Faulkner, 25 Jun 2012; Ginger Holland, 21 Aug 2006; Kacylle Mohammed, 24 Apr 2012; Ismael Perez, 24 Dec 2012; Wayne Pierre, 9 Apr 2008; Veronica Schock, 18 Dec 2000. **CaroTrans Baltimore** Steve Greenfield, 17 Jul 2008; Christopher Hamilton, 13 Jun 2011; Susan Kahl, 23 Nov 1981; Meredith Mc Kay, 28 Oct 2009; LisaL Tryon, 21 May 2001; Michelle Underwood, 10 Oct 2005. **CaroTrans Boston** Kerrianne Doneghey, 5 Jan 2009; Lauren Gannon, 23 Mar 2011; Brian Moorhead, 2 Apr 2012; Ede Salvadore, 24 Sep 2007; Sarah Stone, 13 Feb 2012; Thomas Swain, 26 Aug 2006; Virginia Valentine, 13 Nov 2006. **CaroTrans Charleston** Patricia Anderson, 10 Sep 1993; Renee Basnett, 11 May 1998; Kerr Ann Carter, 3 Jul 2006; Wicks Dickson, 3 Apr 2012; Kellyanne Dix, 3 May 2004; Jenny Harper, 12 Jul 2004; Clay Jones, 15 Jun 2006; Nicholas Leugers, 9 Jan 2012; Lucinda McCorkle, 9 Sep 1997; Sarah Michael, 3 Dec 2012; Mark Stowell, 8 Jul 2002. **CaroTrans Charlotte** Shelly Bisanar, 23 Jun 2003; Linda Denning, 24 Sep 2007; Jamie Gunnells, 17 Oct 2005; Michael Haywood, 4 Oct 2010; April Pride, 4 Oct 2010. **CaroTrans Chicago** Nicole Bobor, 3 Jul 2006; Susan Brockway, 22 Jun 2005; Janice Brunning, 28 Nov 2005; Olga Cazares, 14 Nov 2005; Lorenzo Cometa, 13 Jun 2005; Elisabeth Conboy, 15 Sep 1997; Kristine Connolly, 29 Apr 2002; Cezary Czech, 12 Jan 2009; Barbara Hunt, 3 Mar 2005; Joan Janacek, 20 Apr 1998; Lisa Johnson, 5 Dec 2005; Debbie Klodzinski, 28 Aug 2006; Peter Kowalski, 28 Mar 2011; Sarah Lucas, 18 Sep 2012; Daniel Lynch, 11 Jan 2010; Carol Malak, 13 Apr 1998; Annalisa Marchiafava, 14 Apr 2008; Pamela Mata, 16 Sep 2002; Timothy Merchut, 7 May 2012; Mark Milan, 24 Sep 2007; Patricia Moran, 26 May 1998; Nicole Muschong, 15 Sep 2008; Lynn Ocasio, 13 Aug 2012; Kelly Pate, 14 Apr 2008; Catherine Petersen, 7 Nov 2005; Valerie Pierucci, 7 Jul 2008; Grace Sarsfield, 3 Jun 2008; Christopher Stearns, 1 Oct 2012; James Stutzman, 6 Feb 2007; David Valadez, 6 Jul 2004; Ana Maria Vietoris, 29 Oct 2007; Anna Villafane, 9 Jul 2007; Andrew Weisse, 22 Jul 2002; Joseph Zeno, 7 May 2001; Dana Zeno, 24 Dec 2012. **CaroTrans Cleveland** Diana Beaman, 9 Apr 2007; Krystle Bouchahine, 27 May 2008; Ryan Cantwell, 25 Aug 2008; Annamaria George, 21 Feb 2011; Vicky Haddad, 7 Jun 2010; Abigail Malson, 28 Nov 2011; Magdalena Piktel, 2 May 2005; Lori Radca, 13 Jul 2006; Christopher Sever, 24 Jan 2011; Christopher Wilson, 12 Jul 2004; Elaine Yeager, 4 Oct 2004. **CaroTrans Dallas** Michael Bara, 1 Aug 2011; Jerry Boyle, 28 Nov 2011; Keith Morris, 14 Feb 2011; Philip Rubalcaba, 13 Feb 2012. **CaroTrans Houston** Matthew Britton, 12 Jan 2009; Marcos Cazares, 27 Sep 2010; Sharon Jay, 1 Apr 1996; Norman Johnson, 10 Oct 2006; Alissa Prestridge, 7 Apr 2010; Stephen Rivas, 19 May 2010; Mylinda Winton, 9 May 2011. **CaroTrans Los Angeles** Maria Aldana, 3 Sep 1998; Oliver Aldana, 1 Oct 2004; Mercedes Bitong-Noche, 20 Aug 2001; Jean Bouldin, 23 Jan 2006; Jessica Chargualaf, 16 Aug 2000; Kari Christopher, 22 Oct 2007; Andrew Dickie, 14 Jun 1996; David Duyao, 25 Jul 2007; Elsa Gomez, 20 Nov 2006; Siamack Heshmati, 4 Feb 2008; Theresa Iamaleava, 25 Aug 2003; Katrina Jones, 28 Apr 2008; Claudette Kwiat, 13 Feb 2006; Theresa Langell, 5 Sep 2007; Thuc Ly, 3 Dec 2012; Patricia Maahs, 8 Jan 2001; Alice Macgregor, 4 Feb 2002; Nelson Mendoza, 4 Feb 2008; Grant Morrison, 6 Nov 2000; Giovanni Napoles, 11 Jun 2012; Rodnina Pese, 7 Nov 2000; Carol Rebullar, 6 Nov 2006; Nancy Silva, 1 Jul 1998; Janice Tabios, 9 May 2011; Mark Taitingfong, 18 Apr 2005; Rowina Tauanuu, 25 Sep 2000. **CaroTrans Miami** Michael Amundson, 8 Nov 2010; Milton Carballo, 6 Feb 2012; Maria Henriquez, 31 Aug 2009; Maria Huete, 6 Sep 2011; Gregory Meier, 9 Jul 2008; Susana Melara, 25 Aug 2008; Juan Melendez, 29 Nov 2010; Roberto Montoya, 21 Aug 2006; Jorge Montoya, 15 Aug 2005; Hugo Sequeira, 8 Oct 2007; Lester Sevilla, 23 Dec 2007; Christian Supplice, 10 Jul 2012; Maria Veiga, 3 Jan 2006; Beatriz Zaldivar, 21 Jan 2008. **CaroTrans New Jersey** Blanca Aguirre, 24 Feb 2003; Francisco Almonte, 8 Jan 2013; Maria Amorim, 1 Jun 2005; Jonathan Arico, 28 Jun 2011; Yisel Barrett, 5 Jan 2004; Erik Berger, 16 Oct 2000; Ana Bermeo, 22 Jun 2005; Lueder Bitter, 1 Jun 1998; Kai Campbell, 4 Oct 1999; Michelle Chan, 4 Apr 2011; Jose Chariez, 2 Feb 2009; Kerry Conn, 21 Nov 2005; Kelly Creson, 23 Oct 1997; Gary Dreuer, 10 May 2004; Beth Embry, 5 Jul 2005; Natalie Espino, 29 Apr 2002; Michael Forkenbrock, 7 May 2001; Marina Gilyadov, 3 Mar 2008; Jessica Hernandez, 7 Nov 2011; Norihiro Hisanaga, 1 Dec 2001; Kenneth Hogan, 23 Jun 2008; Gregory Howard, 18 Jun 1984; Antanina Imbriaco, 15 Oct 2001; Christopher Johnson, 14 Jun 2010; Riyaz Jordan, 29 May 2000; Derek King, 22 Nov 2010; Takehito Kashiwabara, 27 Mar 2006; Latonia Kornegay, 16 Jul 2001; Alexander Kosachev, 18 Mar 2013; Janet Lanni, 8 Sep 2009; Laura Litchholt, 12 Feb 2001; Ishani Lokuliyana, 18 Mar 2013; Ioannis Lourmas, 27 May 2003; Christine Mackey, 25 Jan 2010; Oluseun Makinde, 19 Nov 2007; Samuel Martinez-Arias, 21 Feb 2011; Theresa Maxie, 22 Sep 2008; Debra Mccarty, 3 Mar 2003; Abdul Mirza, 8 Jan 2001; Jessica Murphy, 5 Jan 1998; Shraddha Nayak, 22 Mar 2010; Victoria Naboa, 20 Feb 2012; Tyler Nichols, 11 Feb 2013; Camise Normil, 6 Feb 2006; Yuzuru Onishi, 24 Mar 2008; Diane Pirozzi, 25 Jan 1999; Kelly Preziosa, 12 May 2008; Kelly Rodriguez, 2 Jun 2003; Nancy Silva, 15 Oct 2001; Yenny Villafuerte, 20 Nov 2012; Mary White, 2 Jan 1990; Heidi Zhao, 2 Apr 2007; Rita O Reilly, 27 Aug 2001; Barbara Parker, 16 May 2005; Joseph Pimentel, 17 Jul 2006; Cindy Rafart, 6 Nov 2006; Giuilherme Ribeiro, 10 Oct 2012; Julianne Santiago, 20 Jul 2010; Matthew Spartz, 20 Sep 2000; Cynthia Suggs, 8 Sep 1983; Jeryck Villahermosa, 18 Jan 2006. **CaroTrans San Francisco** Jessica Angell, 7 Nov 2008; Winnie Cien, 9 Jul 2007; Heather Jeffries-Million, 15 Mar 2010; Eddie Miranda, 1 Jun 2006; Mark Tanelli, 13 Mar 2006. **CaroTrans Seattle** Brian Allcorn, 8 Feb 2012; Andrea Cherry, 26 Sep

2000; Adam Whelpley, 15 May 2008. **Mainfreight Albany** Mike Byrnes, 9 Apr 2012; Eileen Ceccucci, 16 Nov 1991; Lisa Gaetano, 11 Aug 2008; Heather Hackney, 4 Feb 2013; Sean Hennessey, 20 Aug 2012; Bryce Hicks, 5 Aug 2004; Karen Ikokwu, 15 Jun 2003; Agnes Maciorowski, 15 Jun 2004; Tom Magier, 11 Jul 2011; Angela Meyer, 1 Aug 2011; Rebecca Monette, 16 Jan 2012; Nicole Moon, 2 Sep 2008; Mike Morrissey, 24 Feb 1997; Robert Narcavage, 10 Jan 2011; Elinor Seeley, 8 Aug 2011; Tracy Zayac, 10 Apr 2006. **Mainfreight Atlanta** Bill Agnos, 18 Feb 1997; Rebecca Alterman, 19 Mar 2012; Denise Davis, 12 Sep 2011; Brent Fetcher, 6 Feb 2012; John Freeman, 8 Nov 2007; Ron Hein, 18 Feb 2013; Debbie Johnson, 5 Feb 2003; Brian Martin, 21 May 2012; Janine Mayo, 1 Aug 2011; Matt Mayville, 24 Mar 2003; Jeff Meese, 10 Sep 2012; Ted Mitchell, 22 Nov 2010; Don Rainey, 8 Mar 2010; John Roberts, 18 Feb 2013; Steven Rydzewski, 11 Mar 2013. **Mainfreight Charlotte** Johnny Collins, 22 Apr 2002; Clarence Jr Davis, 26 Nov 2012; Greg Deshields, 12 Apr 2012; Scott Hopkins, 1 Sep 2010; Tyrone Neville, 20 Sep 2010; Naomi Parfait, 19 Apr 2012; Julie Power, 22 Apr 2002; Nathan Proctor, 2 Jul 2007; Melinda Rhames, 5 May 2010; Beth Rosenbrock, 28 Nov 2005; Mike Rosenbrock, 11 Apr 2011; Conrad West, 14 Oct 2002. **Mainfreight Chicago** Michael Baldus, 19 Mar 2010; Suzanne Berner, 18 Oct 1999; Adrian Gallardo, 1 Feb 2011; Tina Geuder, 25 Oct 2011; Tracey Goering, 6 Jul 2004; Nathan Goodman, 11 Oct 2010; Theresa Griffin, 28 May 2010; Lori Hageline, 8 Feb 1999; Nadine Hatfield, 13 Apr 1998; Mark Hines, 29 May 2007; James Hughes, 30 Jul 2012; Matt Janik, 3 Dec 2012; Tom Kurtzer, 14 Sep 2009; Nicole Militello, 27 Oct 2008; Aaron Nash, 13 Sep 2010; Jennifer Nudi, 31 Jan 2005; Dan Osterhout, 27 Jun 2011; Mike Redden, 10 May 2010; Tim Reich, 2 Jul 2012; David Rogalski, 16 Apr 2002; Troy Rybandt, 7 Dec 2010; Desiree Santos, 6 Sep 2006; Jon Shaw, 25 Oct 2010; Bradley Siciliano, 19 Dec 2011; Rich Sobchinsky, 31 Aug 1998; Brian Speer, 30 Apr 2012; Stephen Zopp, 28 Jun 2011. **Mainfreight Columbus** John Griffin, 1 Jul 1989; Chris Khan, 1 Jan 1990; Jason Meyer, 14 Jun 2004; Steve Rea, 2 Jan 2012; Malik Smith, 25 Mar 2004; Tonia Uhrlg, 30 Jul 2000. **Mainfreight Dallas** Lane Adamson, 25 May 1992; Karen Aguilar, 24 Oct 2011; Misae Amemiya, 16 Apr 2012; Elizabeth Branson, 25 Mar 2008; Ashley Burns, 31 Oct 2011; Jessica Campbell, 1 Mar 2008; Tracey Clark, 20 Aug 2003; Brandon Confer, 30 Jul 2007; Diane Cox, 9 Nov 2006; Marty Cryer, 11 Mar 2002; Richard Dean, 14 Oct 1998; John Dunn, 22 Oct 2002; Glenn Eranger, 15 Apr 1993; Scott Eranger, 30 Jun 1990; Ricardo Espino-Barros, 9 Jan 2012; Debbie Hendrix, 15 May 1993; Shelby Hill, 20 Aug 2007; John Hitz, 12 Jan 2009; Lori Hull Garcia, 6 Oct 2005; Joshua Johnson, 7 Mar 2007; Diane Johnson, 28 Jun 2010; Tim Karlen, 30 Aug 2010; Heather Kosowski, 19 Mar 2012; James Lawless, 30 Apr 2012; Mary Leake, 1 Mar 2000; Paul Lidberg, 6 Jun 2011; Todd Luney, 29 May 2012; Andy Morales, 20 Jun 2011; Alan Nadeau, 4 Aug 2003; Jamie Patterson, 7 May 2012; Keith Price, 14 Jun 2010; John Ramirez, 2 Jan 2013; Steve Scott, 7 Aug 1989; Zack Shepherd, 13 Dec 2010; Amy Strong, 6 Jun 2011; Dacia Tribble, 1 May 2012; Jimmy Wallace, 4 Mar 2013; Falanna Warren, 31 Aug 2010; Michelle Worden, 4 Oct 2011; Tom Zalesky, 16 Apr 1987. **Mainfreight Detroit** Sandra Alviani, 21 Apr 2008; Edward Richardson, 26 Jun 2006. **Mainfreight Houston** Carol Beilman, 9 Apr 2012; Linda Callahan, 4 Oct 2010; Brian Culver, 24 May 2004; Stefanie Davis, 24 Sep 2012; Keith Devillier, 2 Aug 2010; Freddie Gonzales, 9 Feb 1999; Blanca Holliday, 27 Jun 1991; Tim Huth, 16 Apr 2012; John Ladd, 28 Feb 2011; Mark Mccrory, 6 Feb 2006; Michael Pilgrim, 14 Aug 2007; Corey Powers, 11 Mar 2013; Scott Rood, 4 Apr 2007; Rachael Whitehead, 26 Jul 2010. **Mainfreight Los Angeles** Alfredo Actual, 29 Aug 2011; Alonzo Alviso, 7 Feb 2011; Bob Andrews, 29 Jan 2001; Javier Angulo, 7 Jun 2002; Manny Arceo, 13 Dec 1999; Dave Barker, 8 Sep 2008; Brendon Belesky, 5 Nov 2004; Linda Bettencourt, 24 Jun 1997; Leslie Bivens, 28 Sep 1998; Ed Blancarte, 27 Dec 1999; Jay Bradberry, 8 Oct 2012; Jason Braid, 1 Sep 1998; Darnelle Briant, 2 Jan 2001; Eugenio Bungalon, 4 Jan 2010; Peter Burke, 24 Jun 1997; Rodney Buskeness, 14 Apr 2000; Matt Cable, 1 Nov 2011; Raquel Canas-Thompson, 3 Dec 2007; Monique Castillo, 26 Mar 2012; Cynthia Castro, 14 Jan 2013; Nathan Chaney, 4 Oct 2011; Nelson Cheung, 28 Aug 2000; Janet Clark, 13 Sep 2010; Kenny Cobos, 18 Feb 2013; Frank Crossan, 1 Dec 2008; Helba Cudny, 1 Feb 2012; Steve Curle, 1 Aug 2008; Maryjane Dauis, 9 Nov 2011; Jaime Delgado Rios, 1 Jul 2011; Analisa Dennis, 7 Feb 2000; Harsh Dharamshi, 19 Apr 2010; Denis Dillon, 21 Sep 1998; Tom Donahue, 6 Oct 2006; Alicia Dorris, 3 Dec 2012; Barry Ehrreich, 5 Jul 2006; Jessica Emonin, 29 Aug 2011; Taschana Epps, 16 May 2012; John Eshuis, 1 Oct 2001; Jackie Estrada, 24 Mar 2008; Ron Frady, 14 Aug 2000; Byron Franks, 15 Feb 2010; Vicki Friedland, 18 Jan 2000; Jackie Ganther, 18 Nov 2002; Luv Ganzon, 22 Aug 1999; Jose Garcia, 22 Mar 2010; Jose Garcia, 6 Jul 2011; Rae Glamuzina, 31 May 1999; Jeremiah Gregersen, 26 Nov 2007; Fernando Guzman, 30 Apr 2012; Alta Heacock, 3 Jan 2011; Brian Heidrich, 29 Jan 2007; John Hepworth, 19 Jun 1989; Lisa Herrera, 4 Jan 2010; Karen Hill, 5 Jul 2000; Melissa Holmes, 11 Aug 2008; Judy Hua, 29 Nov 1999; Bong Deuk Hwang, 14 Nov 2011; Gabriel Ibarra, 14 Nov 2011; Christie Ireland, 20 Sep 2010; Nico Ireland, 18 Jul 2011; Steve Jefferson, 9 Sep 2002; Roxana Jimenez, 17 Apr 2000; Patti Jimenez, 9 Dec 1999; Jeff Johnson, 6 Jan 2000; Seife Kidane, 22 May 2000; Jonathan Kirwan, 3 Jan 2012; Talia Lamiano, 7 Oct 1997; Alex Laseen, 14 Mar 2011; Espy Leanos, 1 Jun 2010; Jason Lee, 20 Feb 2012; Kara Lewczyk, 18 May 1998; Cesar Limas, 14 Nov 2011; Carlos Linares, 14 Nov 2011; Jarrod Lovell, 4 Apr 2011; Tony Lucio, 19 Aug 2011; Daniel Lund, 26 Feb 2007; Ely Lupian, 26 Jul 1999; Alberto Macias, 28 Nov 2011; Christian Magana, 7 Mar 2012; Devita Magdalena-Ralston, 26 Oct 2009; Annabel Mahnke, 12 Jul 2010; Desiree Martinez, 24 Jan 2000; Alex Mcgarry, 9 Aug 2010; Bob McGhee, 17 May 2006; Barry McLemore, 28 May 2008; Craig McRitchie, 29 May 1995; Craig Meador, 24 Jun 1997; Andrew Meeson, 19 Jul 2010; Edwin Melgar, 14 Nov 2011; Adrienne Minoia, 27 Jun 2011; Rigo Mora, 30 Aug 2004; Marie Morales, 19 Dec 2000; Eric Moreno, 28 Nov 2011; Mike Moval, 11 Jul 2011; Silvia Mueller-Thompson, 8 Feb 2010; Cora Mullen, 20 Jun 2011; Jeff Nallick, 12 Feb 2007; Mark Neumann, 23 Apr 2007; Erik Ohler, 23 Jun 2008; Maria Ortiz, 7 Oct 1996; Sean Osborn, 23 Jul 2012; Joe Parada, 22 Nov 2010; Jonathan Perez, 11 Feb 2013; Sandra Phillips, 24 Jan 2000; Abel Pineda, 29 May 2012; Alvaro Ramirez, 14 Nov 2011; Craig Robb, 7 Feb 2011; Olivia Rodriguez, 12 Mar 2001; Sam Safotu, 16 Jan 2013; Juan Sagrero, 17 Oct 2012; Lee Sailiata, 13 Jun 2011; Abel Salazar, 29 Oct 2012; Myrna Salazar, 8 Sep 1997; Henrique Sanchez, 7 Jul 2011; Efrain Sanchez, 7 May 2012; Erika Sandler, 4 Sep 2012; Jose Serrano, 5 Feb 2007; Paul Sharpe, 26 Nov 2012; Brent Sipl, 14 May 2007; Lindsey Sivesind, 7 Feb 2011; Anita Smith, 26 Feb 2001; Ron Solano, 14 Jun 2000; Maggie Soul, 17 Mar 2003; Yung Sun, 31 Mar 2003; Sal Swift, 11 Jun 2012; Nathan Thomas, 4 Jan 2001; Suzy Tziboy, 18 Apr 2011; Tom Valentine, 1 Jan 1986; Carl Vangorden, 26 Jan 2009; Isela Vazquez, 5 Sep 2006; Lilia Villanera, 1 Oct 1990; Eduardo Villasenor, 7 Feb 2011; Sam Washington, 18 Feb 2013; Susan Weiher, 20 Sep 1999; Dallas Wymes, 9 Nov 2009. **Mainfreight Memphis** Steve Chadwick, 19 Jul 2010; Grant Garcia, 28 Jan 2013; Tony Garza, 17 Jun 2002; Owen Hodson, 8 Aug 2011; Nick Reynolds, 30 Nov 2011; Jeff Solbrack, 3 Sep 2001; Jon Solbrack, 26 Apr 2012; Duryea Williams, 21 Dec 2009. **Mainfreight Miami** Batilda Alvarado, 15 Jan 2001; Juan Arteaga, 25 Feb 2013; Mary Daniels, 21 May 2008; Danay Del Valle, 27 May 2008; Steve Long Iv, 29 Nov 2010; David Martinez, 29 Oct 2012; Adalgicia Porras, 16 Jun 2010; Eduardo Rivera, 8 Nov 2010; Ervin Vasquez, 13 Jun 2005. **Mainfreight Minneapolis** Michael Benjamin, 19 Aug 2008; Scott Brunclik, 31 Jan 2013; Heather Zoccoli, 21 Jan 2013. **Mainfreight Newark** Raul Ambriz, 17 Oct 2011; Emilio Andino, 27 Jun 2011; Yoysett Baker-Gonzalez, 7 Jun 2010; Carmen Barbato, 1 Jan 2013; Marcelle Barboza, 5 Aug 2010; Carol Bausch, 30 Apr 1989; David Bubb, 29 Apr 2005; Rosaura Candelario, 8 Mar 2010; Christine Correia, 30 Aug 1989; Jim D'Amico, 20 May 1989; Roseann Forminio, 10 Dec 2012; Michelle King, 4 Dec 2003; Mary Ann Kish, 6 Jun 2011; Louie Lara, 20 Aug 2010; Feng Yan Li, 10 Nov 2008; Terry Lindell, 19 Mar 2012; Tony Mazza, 14 May 2012; Shane Michalick, 30 Sep 1985; Jade Michalick, 26 Nov 2012; Ellen Mullery, 1 Feb 1970; Lauren Queli, 24 Aug 2009; Oscar Rossini, 21 Mar 1989; Charles Ruddell, 30 Nov 2009; Irma Ruiz, 7 May 2012; Debbie Rumore, 20 May 1990; Nicole Salcedo-Twaddle, 5 Sep 2006; Renata Sampaio Outler, 2 Oct 2006; Umang Shah, 11 Feb 2013; Kenny Silveria, 3 Aug 2011; Danny Skipper, 7 Jan 2013; Rich Smith, 24 Apr 2006; Ron Stickle, 24 Jun 1997; Nick Stickle, 12 Mar 2001; Abdul Taylor, 6 Mar 2013; Johanna Toro, 24 Mar 2008; Danielle Torsiello, 11 Feb 2013.

**Mainfreight Norfolk** Sean Dunleavy, 28 Oct 2008; Steve Harklerode, 9 Jun 2008; Carol Koch, 7 Dec 2009; Matt Mays, 7 Sep 2010; Adam Renner, 8 Aug 2011; Kelly Roberts, 7 Sep 2010; Nancy Sanchez, 13 Nov 2006; Sara Santos, 13 Feb 2012. **Mainfreight Pasadena** Blanca Avalos, 13 Aug 2012; Matt Friedman, 14 Dec 2009; Jim Lynn, 2 Jan 2013; Marco Martinez, 13 Aug 2012; Nick O'Brian, 3 Dec 2012; Aaron Pina, 27 Aug 2012. **Mainfreight Philadelphia** Scott Doggett, 30 Jul 2012; Matt Gummel, 3 Sep 2012; Pat Lesser, 3 Sep 2012; Bill McClay, 3 Sep 2012. **Mainfreight Portland** Jacqueline D'Angelico, 27 Dec 2010; Megan Longoria, 22 Oct 2012; Daniel Mulligan, 13 Jun 2011; Sara Sauter, 8 Nov 2010. **Mainfreight San Diego** Karen Amador, 20 Sep 2010; Melissa Green-Ysais, 15 Sep 2010; Brenda Rensfield, 27 Sep 2012. **Mainfreight USA Support Center Phoenix** Joseph Brouillard, 28 Sep 2009; Sandy Downing, 10 Apr 2012; Danie Frady, 12 Nov 2009; Michelle Grabek, 25 Feb 2013; Daniel Hutcheson, 18 Feb 2013; Pat Kirwan, 29 Mar 1993; Jason Kirwan, 5 Apr 2010; Bill Minard, 24 Jan 2011; Greg Sutton, 11 Feb 2002; Jeremy Thomas, 28 Sep 2009; Ivette Valenzuela, 27 Aug 2012. **BELGIUM Mainfreight Antwerp** Cindy Baeselen, 13 Mar 2000; Nadja Bougria, 4 Sep 2000; Ilhan Cakici, 2 Jul 1990; Maria De Saeger, 14 Jul 2003; Peter Decock, 23 Mar 1999; Kevin Dieltjens, 17 Oct 2011; Herman Elst, 15 Jan 1997; Patrick Frederickx, 1 Oct 2000; Philippe Hellebuyck, 12 Aug 2002; Francois Janssens, 23 Mar 1998; Tom Lathouwers, 22 Oct 2007; Karen Meeus, 12 Jul 1999; Viviane Megens, 6 Mar 2000; Robert Mergan, 17 Sep 2006; Gitta Pottiez, 15 May 1995; Luc Takx, 3 Sep 2007; Wesley Teck, 16 Jul 2000; Daniel Van Beylen, 1 Mar 2008; Hilde Van Den Boom, 1 Aug 2001; Marcel Van Elshocht, 1 Nov 1969; Glenn Van Hoof, 22 Feb 2010; Kathy Van Meerbergen, 1 Jun 2010; David Van Sandt, 1 Jan 2011; Arno Wackerghom, 14 Feb 2007; Parcifal Wackerghom, 1 Aug 1996; Ines Waegemans, 11 May 1998. **Mainfreight Brussels** Katrien Baes, 1 Sep 2011; Sven Duchene, 16 Jan 2012; Christine Tisson, 8 Oct 2012; Christine Van Geesberghen, 27 Jun 2011; Laura Zenebergh, 6 Feb 2012. **Wim Bosman Genk** Steven Bleys, 1 Jul 2006; Rosolino Castronovo, 1 Jan 2011; Daniel Di Pardo, 1 Dec 1998; Kevin Fourrier, 1 Jun 2007; Frederik Gielis, 1 Mar 2012; Ivo Leurs, 20 Sep 1999; Ann Loos, 1 Sep 2000; Daniel Mathot, 1 Jan 2005; Patrick Medats, 1 Jun 2011; Debby Missfeldt, 14 Jun 2004; Peter Olaerts, 16 Jun 2009; Karolien Orlandini, 1 Aug 2008; Sander Smeekes, 1 Jan 2011; Eddy Stals, 1 Mar 1996; Antoine Thuys, 3 May 2010; Antonetta Trobbiani, 1 Sep 2006; Ronny Van Cauter, 18 Oct 2004; Ann Vanhaeren, 15 May 2006; Tom Verlinden, 1 Jan 2005; Joseph Willems, 1 Jul 2006. **Wim Bosman Oostende** Tonnie Abbenhuis, 1 Mar 2012; Hamid Abbou, 1 Sep 2012; Jos Allemeersch, 2 Jul 2007; Tom Ampe, 1 Oct 2008; Dries Anthonissen, 1 May 2012; Ignace Arnou, 11 Aug 2008; Nic Astaes, 15 Dec 2008; Jozef Baeyens, 13 Aug 2007; Kurt Bakker, 19 Sep 2011; Barbara Bartorelli, 1 Jul 1997; Adel Belal, 16 Jul 2012; Wim Benony, 16 Jan 2006; Guy Bentein, 8 Mar 1996; Quentin Bentein, 2 May 2005; Anzor Beshiev, 29 Jan 2007; Lesly Billiet, 25 Aug 2008; Roger Blanckaert, 9 May 1979; Natalie Blomme, 10 Jul 2006; Nancy Bober, 12 May 2003; Alain Bockhodt, 4 May 2009; Marc Bogaerts, 4 Jun 2008; Kevin Boghmans, 13 Aug 2012; Riad Boumaza, 12 Sep 2011; Carine Bovy, 1 Jun 1996; Daniel Brats, 6 Aug 2007; Annick Brokken, 16 Jan 2012; Jurgen Buffel, 1 Aug 2009; Neil Calingaert, 21 Sep 2009; Patrick Callant, 1 Sep 2006; Walter Callewaert, 1 Jan 2012; Daniel Capriotti, 22 Sep 2008; Liliane Carels, 1 Sep 2009; Mario Carette, 1 Aug 1997; Annemie Casier, 21 Sep 1998; Ivan Casier, 4 Feb 2002; Cedric Cattrysse, 18 Jul 2011; Alex Cazzato, 11 Feb 2013; Haik Chatchatryan, 28 Jan 2013; Naida Claes, 2 Jan 2002; Griet Cloet, 3 Jan 2005; Bruno Clybouw, 14 Dec 2009; Kristof Cool, 16 Aug 2010; Jimmy Cooleman, 26 Jan 2009; Dennis Cools, 1 Jul 2011; Alex Corbisier, 26 Aug 2002; Koen Costenoble, 1 Nov 2011; Filip Cremer, 1 Jan 1998; Carl Criem, 13 Aug 2007; Maggy Crombez, 13 Aug 2007; Eddy Cuylle, 1 Feb 2011; Stijn David, 26 Mar 2007; Philippe David, 17 Oct 1997; Christophe De Backer , 16 Apr 2012; Bruno De Bruyn, 16 Jan 1995; Kris De Buck, 7 Sep 2009; Bruno De Busscher, 15 Nov 2010; Alain De Corte, 13 May 2008; John De Cuyper, 17 Sep 2012; Jordy De Gheselle, 11 Feb 2013; Thomas De Gols, 10 Sep 2012; Christine De Grande, 1 Dec 2010; Tessa De Groote, 21 Mar 2011; Rita De Jaeger, 16 Jan 2006; Christian De Loof, 10 Dec 2007; Tom De Love, 6 Feb 2006; Dirk De Maeseneer, 29 Jan 2007; Hannelore De Muynck, 5 Nov 2012; Kevin De Preter, 16 Jan 2006; Ingrid De Rechter, 22 Jan 2010; Peter De Smet, 1 Sep 1997; Romina De Smul, 19 Jul 2010; Tatjana De Vogelaere, 1 Jan 2012; Didier De Wannemacker, 29 Jun 2009; Koen De Wever, 12 Apr 2010; Steve Deboysere, 15 Sep 2008; Pascal Debrabandere, 2 Oct 2007; Rudi Debras, 18 Apr 2011; Johan Debruyne, 13 Aug 2007; Annelien Deceuninck, 13 Sep 2010; Jean-Pierre Declercq, 17 Oct 2011; Herve Decloedt, 21 Mar 2011; Peter Deconijnck, 26 May 2008; Martin Defour, 8 Apr 1991; Bjorn Degraeuwe, 1 Feb 2011; Anita Dekens, 1 Oct 2012; Franky Delanghe, 1 Mar 1991; Thierry Delbaere, 28 Aug 1989; Robert Deman, 29 Jan 2001; Mario Demey, 18 Jul 2011; Raymond Denblijden, 1 Dec 1998; Roderick Denblyden, 1 Jan 2012; Nicolas Deputter, 19 Jan 2009; Caroline Depuydt, 17 Sep 2007; Steven Depuydt, 1 Jun 2006; William Dereeper, 19 Aug 1991; Aude Derycke, 4 Sep 1995; Alain Deschacht, 17 Sep 2012; Kim Desmet, 1 Oct 2001; Celine Devloo, 1 Sep 2011; Lili Devriendt, 23 Nov 1988; Fanny Dewanin, 21 Mar 2011; Jean-Francois Dewever, 2 Oct 2000; Matthias D'Hont, 18 Feb 2008; Christine D'Hont, 12 Oct 2009; Andy D'Hoore, 20 Jun 2011; Erwin Dieusaert, 4 Feb 1985; Jordy Doornaert, 1 Jan 2012; Niels Duchateau, 1 Aug 2012; Steve Dumalin, 12 Jul 2004; Jean Dumon, 1 Oct 2007; Jimmy Duriez, 12 Sep 2011; Frederik Eeckloo, 18 Jan 2007; Nizar El Ali, 6 Oct 2008; Toufik El Khiari, 1 Sep 2012; Udo Engels, 20 May 1991; Piotr Ernest, 24 Sep 2012; Chris Everaert, 14 Feb 1990; Cengiz Fani, 30 Oct 2006; Henk Feys, 30 Nov 2009; Karol Flak, 14 Jun 2010; Krzysztof Flak, 14 Jun 2010; Griet Fleerackers, 18 May 2009; Miguel Focke, 12 Oct 1998; Wim Foulon, 17 Aug 2011; Kenny Francois, 9 Jul 2007; Kevin Gailliaert, 17 Oct 2011; Sadri Gani, 11 Jun 2001; Krzysztof Gasch, 21 Mar 2011; Ivan Gavrilovic, 29 Jan 2007; Mathieu Geelen, 10 Jan 2005; Noel Geers, 2 Dec 1996; Iris Geselle, 1 Jan 2007; Francois Gesquiere, 16 Aug 1990; Redgy Goethals, 2 May 2005; Christophe Goossens, 19 Sep 2005; Glenn Grunewald, 22 Jan 2007; Hannes Gunst, 15 Dec 2008; Sabrina Haeghebaert, 1 Jan 2013; Gilbert Haelewyck, 16 Feb 1987; David Haerinck, 16 Jul 2007; Davy Haers, 5 Oct 2010; Jeffrey Haevermaet, 20 Aug 2007; Dieter Hamers, 1 Mar 2010; Jessy Hardy, 3 Sep 2001; Marvin Haspeel, 14 Nov 2011; Abdelsattar Hassan, 11 Feb 2013; Kevin Hellemans, 1 Oct 2008; Daniel Helsen, 22 Mar 2010; Francis Hennebert, 1 Aug 1994; Dominique Hillebrandt, 26 Mar 2007; Mario Holemans, 31 Aug 2009; Miguel Hollevoet, 1 Aug 2005; Gaetan Hoslet, 1 Jan 2001; Claudine Houkx, 3 Apr 2006; Catherine Houtteman, 1 Apr 2010; Jan Houwen, 1 Feb 1993; Rebecca Hovaere, 1 Aug 2012; Wilfried Hullebus, 15 Feb 1999; Sylvie Hullebus, 17 May 2005; Dave Huwel, 21 Dec 1998; Glenn Huwel, 6 Aug 2001; Aleksander Ignatenko, 22 Oct 2007; Roland Janssen, 21 Feb 1977; Pascal Janssens, 19 Apr 2010; Yves Janssens, 12 May 2003; Eddy Jonckheere, 11 Aug 2003; Gregor Jouret, 9 Jul 2007; Fabrice Junion, 9 Oct 2006; Gari Justianz, 6 Aug 2007; Samuel Kamden, 29 Jan 2007; Burim Kastrati, 1 Jan 2011; Bert Kegels, 12 Mar 2007; Homayoun Khezri, 25 Oct 2004; Liedewij Kieboom, 6 Aug 2012; Michel Klutsch, 20 Oct 2003; Yves Knockaert, 6 Dec 1999; Sini Konig, 20 Sep 2010; Konstantin Kovaliov, 17 Sep 2012; Werner Kraft, 9 Feb 1987; Khanpacha Krymsoultanov, 16 Jul 2007; Sylwia Kuczynska, 11 May 2009; Jozef Kujawa, 11 Jun 2010; Abdelaziz Labane, 2 Aug 2010; Robert Lambrecht, 14 Apr 1998; Geert Lapon, 1 Jan 2003; Peter Laseure, 11 Feb 2013; Jurgen Lecluyse, 16 May 2011; Joke Lepeire, 1 Jul 2006; Marie Christine Lesage, 16 May 2006; Oleg Logounovitch, 2 Aug 2010; Veronique Lootens, 2 Jan 2006; Massivi Lubaki, 13 Nov 2006; Eddy Maeckelberghe, 12 Jun 2006; Kim Maenhout, 16 Jun 2003; Marc Maerten, 1 May 1989; Stefan Maertens, 16 Mar 2005; Joseph Maertens, 24 Mar 2003; Romain Maes, 2 Jun 1997; Marc Marey, 9 Jul 1990; Didier Martinat, 7 May 2012; Scott Menten, 1 May 2011; Bram Merlevede, 17 Dec 2007; Eddy Mestdagh, 2 Jun 1997; Benny Mestdagh, 19 Aug 1991; Luc Meulemeester, 1 Sep 1997; Leo Meuris, 3 Jul 1989; Miroslaw Mleczak Pawel, 12 Nov 2012; Dennis Moelans, 1 Mar 2013; Monaam Moknassi, 8 Oct 2001; Stefan Monteny, 4 Feb 2011; Aurelie Moreau, 17 Sep 2012; Roger Mortier, 7 Jun 1993; Filip Muylle, 6 Apr 1999; Shana Mylle, 14 Mar 2011; Karen Naesen, 12 Feb 2007; Steven Naessens, 1 Feb 2011; Robby Nagy, 16 Apr 2012; Ireneusz Niedzwiedz, 14 Mar 2011; Krystian Niedzwiedz, 20 Sep 2010; Fidele Nzuzi Kindanda, 17 Sep 2007; Pete Onyekwere Chukwunyere, 16 Jul 2012; Chris Osstyn, 15 Jan 1990; Ives Parmentier, 18 May 1987; Walter Parmentier, 17 Mar 1986; Anthony Pauchet, 17 Feb 1997; Sergio Perre, 12

Sep 2011; Zsolt Petrak, 21 Mar 2011; Nick Petyt, 1 Feb 2011; Jean-Pierre Pierloot, 7 Apr 2008; Damian Plata, 9 Jun 2008; Pascal Polfliet, 4 Nov 2002; Andrew Popelier, 1 Dec 2011; Bart Porreye, 30 Nov 2009; Katrien Portier, 18 Sep 2000; Gregory Prevot, 10 Mar 2003; Wim Pyra, 6 Dec 1999; Glenn Quintijn, 1 Feb 2011; Dirk Ragaert, 1 May 2002; Freddy Ragaert, 15 May 2006; Veerle Ramon, 1 Mar 2012; Isabelle Renard, 11 Feb 2013; Liesbeth Reyskens, 1 Mar 2012; Jamshid Rezaie, 1 Jan 2012; Jacky Robaert, 14 Mar 2011; Jan Rodrigus, 16 Aug 2010; Adam Rogatzky, 5 May 2008; Glenn Rogiers, 17 Sep 2007; Didier Rosseel, 17 Sep 2012; Khalid Roudane, 21 Mar 2011; Nick Rouzere, 1 Jan 2012; Kurt Ryheul, 1 Jul 2011; Pol Sabbe, 26 Jul 2010; Peter Sabbe, 1 Jan 2012; Khalifa Salek, 1 Mar 2012; Marc Samaey, 25 Sep 2000; Nancy Schelstraete, 18 Oct 2010; Yves Scherpereel, 2 Mar 1998; Bram Schoutteten, 8 Aug 2011; Paul Schroyens, 6 Sep 2004; Sinclare Scott, 1 Mar 2013; Bram Segers, 21 May 2008; Andrzej Seibert, 1 Apr 2011; Marlies Sevenhant, 4 May 2011; Mohammed Issa Sherzad, 11 Feb 2013; Redgy Simons, 8 Jan 1996; Manga Singh, 1 Sep 2011; Didier Sinnaeve, 9 Aug 2004; Gregory Smetz, 1 Feb 2011; Julie Snauwaert, 2 Nov 2010; Bernard Soenen, 2 Aug 2010; Nicolas Jose Soto, 16 Aug 2010; Maximiliaan Spee, 14 Nov 2005; Marc Speliers, 14 Nov 2005; Guido Staels, 13 Apr 1992; Marc Stroobants, 29 Jan 2007; Jimmy Stubbe, 12 Jan 2009; Krzysztof Sulikowski, 28 Jan 2008; Darline Tanghe, 21 Mar 2011; Hugo Tanghe, 1 Dec 1981; Katchatuz Terterian, 14 Mar 2011; Mohamad Theibich, 11 Mar 2013; Robert Thirry, 11 Jan 1993; Sebastien T'Jonck, 17 Sep 2012; Julie Tolpe, 1 May 2011; Brian Tondeur, 26 Mar 2007; Dimitri Torreele, 28 Feb 2005; Niels Tratsaert, 7 Jun 2010; Marleen Tratsaert, 17 Sep 2001; Lukasz Tymkiewicz, 21 Mar 2011; Astrid Van Acker, 5 Nov 2012; Stefaan Van Aken, 1 Jan 1998; Kevin Van De Voorde, 1 Jan 2012; Bart Van Den Eynde, 1 Jan 2012; Franck Van Der Heyde, 5 Jul 1993; Eddy Van Hauwaert, 1 Jun 2010; Antoon Van Herck, 5 Sep 2011; Cedric Van Huffel, 31 Jul 2000; Martine Van Hyfte, 1 Jun 1995; Frederick Van Rapenbusch, 14 Mar 2011; Yves Van Vooren, 28 Oct 1996; Philip Vanacker, 11 Feb 2008; Pascal Vancoetsem, 17 Jun 2002, Sylvie Vancoppenolle, 15 Sep 2008; Erwin Vandamme, 3 Jul 2000; Kateleen Vandecasteele, 24 Apr 2006; Katrien Vanden Eeckhoute, 1 Apr 2010; Christiaan Vandenberghe, 10 Apr 2006; Isabelle Vandenberghe, 2 Apr 1990; Jean-Pierre Vandenberghe, 23 Oct 1989; Frederik Vandenbrande, 13 Aug 2007; Bart Vandenbussche, 3 Feb 1992; Kenneth Vandeputte, 1 Jan 2012; Patrick Vandeputte, 17 Sep 2012; Iselinde Vandergunst, 2 Oct 2006; Katrien Vandewalle, 8 Jan 2007; Rudy Vandewalle, 8 Apr 1987; Kristof Vandeweyer, 16 Apr 2012; Vincent Vandorpe, 6 Jun 2011; Sofie Vanhee, 12 Apr 1999; Ariane Vanhooren, 2 Jun 2008; Andre Vanhoorne, 4 Oct 1999; Jay Vanhou, 12 Oct 2009; Koen Vanhuysse, 17 Sep 1990; Rudi Vankerckhove, 14 Mar 2011; Frederic Vanmeenen, 2 Aug 2010; Jos Vanmullem, 1 Sep 2012; Rik Vanneste, 1 Jan 2012; Pascal Vanroose, 2 Jan 1990; Geert Vantyghem, 11 Oct 2010; Ronny Vanwelsenaers, 17 Sep 2012; Akash Varma, 1 Mar 2010; Oleg Vassiliev, 22 Oct 2007; Andy Verbrugghe, 2 Nov 1998; Stefaan Vercruysse, 6 Jan 1992; Elisama Verheecke, 1 Mar 2010; Fabienne Verhelst, 1 Jan 2012; Bart Verhulst, 6 Dec 2010; Carl Verhulst, 8 Sep 2008; Carol Verkempynck, 18 Jul 2011; Jacky Verlee, 23 Jul 2007; Dieter Verlinde, 13 Jun 2011; Serge Vermander, 16 Mar 2010; Marc Vermeire, 16 Jan 2006; Wim Verpoort, 1 Jun 1993; Bart Verschelde, 7 May 2012; Ingeborg Verschorre, 2 Dec 1996; Kevin Verstraeten, 1 Sep 2012; Lies Viaene, 1 Dec 2011; Dimitri Vierstraete, 17 Mar 2008; Patrick Volbrecht, 1 Aug 2012; Manu Volckaert, 7 Jan 2008; Jan Vroman, 15 Sep 2008; Linda Vyvey, 13 Aug 2012; Hugo Vyvey, 5 Nov 1987; Raymond Warnier, 4 Jan 2000; Geert Watteel, 23 Jul 2012; Jenny Weemaels, 11 Feb 2008; Arnold Weidler, 11 Feb 2008; Luc Willems, 14 Nov 2005; Ines Wouters, 20 Oct 2003; Nick Wyns, 21 Jun 2010; Sander Xhajaj, 18 Jun 2007; Marc Zaman, 4 Nov 1996; Amir Zand Karimi, 1 Jan 2011; Yury Zhauniarevich, 21 Mar 2011; Daniel Zonnekein, 17 Mar 2008. **FINLAND Wim Bosman Hamina** Petra Parviainen-Tohmo, 2 Apr 2012; Mia Paunonen, 19 Apr 2012; Satu Suortti, 16 Apr 2012.  **FRANCE Mainfreight Le Havre** Ophelie Decure, 1 Jun 2012; Marie Fohet, 1 Jun 2012; Chris Wilson, 8 Jul 2004.  **Mainfreight Paris** Eric Defonte, 2 Apr 2013; Alain Navarron, 2 Apr 2013; Cécile Rodier, 2 Apr 2013; Véronique Sabatier, 2 Apr 2013.  **Wim Bosman Lyon** Fabienne Bouchut, 25 Mar 2013; Lea Dedourge, 5 Sep 2011; Jean Louis Grosheitsch, 12 Mar 2012; Léonard Rizzo, 30 Aug 2012.  **Wim Bosman Paris** Fatiha Ait Kheddache, 14 Jan 2013; Abdel Majid Atoui, 7 Jan 2013; Teresa Aubert, 1 Apr 1997; Nicolas Bertrand, 2 Jan 2012; Marie Bissey, 17 Sep 2012; Martine Blandin, 7 Feb 1992; Stephane Bobu, 2 Jul 2007; Ludovic Bobu, 8 Sep 2008; Christophe Bobu, 2 Jun 2009; Jérome Chevreux, 9 Nov 2010; Fabienne Cochereau, 1 Jul 2005; Caroline Cordier, 3 Sep 2012; Sylvia Costa Neves, 17 Jun 2002; Orienty Danial, 17 Sep 2012; Daniel de l'Espinay, 4 Oct 2010; Jihad Demdoum, 21 Jan 2013; Isabelle Denon, 17 Sep 1998; Jeremy Despote, 2 Jan 2013; Thibault Detrouselle, 6 Mar 2013; Shama Devi, 9 Dec 2011; Cédric Diarra, 12 Feb 2013; Nadir Dramsy, 1 Feb 2010; Laura Dubois, 18 Jul 2011; Flavien Durpoix, 12 Nov 2008; Naima El Haddad, 10 May 2011; Fabien Esmoingt, 9 Dec 2011; Faten Essid, 1 Feb 2012; Joel Fagotin, 14 Apr 2008; Michael Farges, 28 Nov 2006; Philippe Fortin, 2 Aug 2004; Claude Grele, 7 Feb 2011; Jonathan Henault, 17 May 2010; Brigitte Herbomez, 2 Apr 1991; Laurent Janniaud, 2 Nov 2004; Lydie Jarrin, 2 May 2008; Samuel Justine, 1 Feb 2013; Zakaria Kada, 14 Jan 2013; Thierry Lacoudray, 9 Feb 2011; Emmanuel Landron, 3 Sep 2012; Raphael Lemoigne, 24 Sep 2012; Hervé Lenglet, 23 Mar 2011; Muriel Loube, 29 May 2012; Charles-Henry Maingard, 7 Apr 2008; Forconi Mattéo, 4 Apr 2013; José Maximilien, 2 May 1991; Vanessa Miet, 7 Oct 2002; Thierry Moisan, 28 Jun 1994; Jacques Niati, 1 Aug 2000; Riad Ouarga, 5 Feb 2013; Franck Pardo, 17 Dec 2012; Emmanuel Peccatte, 19 Apr 1999; Soda Ponn, 21 Jan 2013; Rachid Rahmani, 6 Oct 2006; Delphine Roucan, 9 Jul 2001; Chalcou Samuel, 2 Apr 2013; Remy Soares, 12 Feb 2013; Isberte Stanislas, 18 Jun 1992; Julien Vieville, 16 Oct 2003; André Voignard, 3 Oct 2011; Alice Voignard, 10 Apr 2012; Patrick Voinson, 5 Nov 2001; Théodore Yamanoglu, 1 Oct 2012.  **NETHERLANDS Mainfreight Rotterdam** Alex Brokx, 1 Apr 2013; Paul de Haan, 1 Sep 2008; Patrice de Ruiter, 15 Nov 2010; Ronald den Held, 30 May 2012; Alex Doornheim, 11 Apr 2012; Harrold Dost, 1 Feb 2009; Björn Febus, 1 Jun 2007; Rodney Fister, 10 Apr 2012; Cora Greven, 1 Oct 2005; Tiantian Gu, 13 Aug 2012; Jon Gundy, 2 Jun 1998; Bert Hoepel, 27 Feb 2012; Myckel Hoogendijk, 19 Feb 2010; Monique Kleijburg-Streefland, 1 May 2006; Danny Kok, 1 Jul 2010; Rhea Post, 1 Dec 2008; Niels Stadthouders, 19 Nov 2012; Kristian Stilting, 19 Feb 2007; Peter Stilting, 1 Oct 2002; Bart Termeer, 1 Aug 2012; Arthur van Amen, 1 Aug 2004; Bryan van Bezeij, 1 Mar 2012; Astrid van Dam, 1 Jul 2006; Yvonne van den Berg-van der Hout, 29 Jan 2007; Veronique van den Berge-van den Peerboom, 15 Aug 2008; Cor van den Heuvel, 1 Oct 2000; Sera van der Graaf, 1 Sep 2011; Patrick van der Hoek, 9 Jun 2008; Pascal van der Meer, 1 Oct 2012; Angelique Van der Spuij-van der Visser, 26 Sep 2007; Mariska van Schaik, 1 Feb 2005; Theo Verhagen, 1 Sep 1998; Jacco Wijker, 15 Nov 2010.  **Mainfreight Schiphol** Rob Duijnmayer, 24 Feb 1987; Esmee Heuvink, 1 Mar 2012; Angelique Keters, 4 Feb 2013; Mike Ligthart, 15 Jul 2011; Gideon Lioe-A-Tjam, 1 Feb 2012; Mels van Egmond, 1 Dec 1995; Arie van Saarloos, 16 Dec 1996.  **Wim Bosman C.E.E. 's-Heerenberg** Roel Beumer, 21 May 2007; Randy Bruns, 8 Jan 2007; Clemens Farwick, 1 Oct 2008; Nataliya Hakken-Vasylueva, 1 May 2007; Lyuba Hofstad-Li, 30 Jan 2012; Patrick Schonewille, 26 Apr 2011; Ronnie Sessink, 1 Aug 2005; Guus van der Stelt, 1 Dec 2000.  **Wim Bosman Clearance 's-Heerenberg** Angelo Daamen, 1 May 1997; Gerrie Heering, 1 Jan 1992; Fred Martens, 23 Apr 1990; Rieky te Grootenhuis-Hebbink, 1 May 1997; Gijs te Kaat, 1 Feb 2005.  **Wim Bosman Crossdock 's-Heerenberg** Bodo Apmann, 1 Nov 2007; Chantal Arts, 1 Jul 2007; Gert Beernink, 1 May 2005; Remco Berndsen, 28 Feb 2001; Willem Bijma, 1 Dec 2009; René Bisselink, 18 Sep 2006; Joost Boersma, 27 Aug 2012; Harold Bosch, 11 Mar 1988; Eef Bottcher, 21 Apr 2000; Jeroen Bouwman, 16 Aug 2004; Daniël Bouwman, 16 Feb 2012; Hans Bruggink, 28 Dec 1999; Tonny Buijl, 26 May 1986; Thorsten Claassen, 1 Feb 2002; Bahri Coroz, 17 Jul 2000; Ramon de Bakker, 8 May 1989; Leroy Elderman, 1 Oct 2000; Theo Engelen, 5 Oct 1993; Gert Essink, 18 Feb 1985; Derk Geersing, 13 Jul 1987; Robert Giezen, 4 Mar 1991; Hans Hageman, 1 Jan 2000; Patrick Helmink, 12 Sep 2005; Wilco Hendriks, 1 Oct 2003; Gerben Heymen, 1 Dec 1997; Bennie Jansen, 1 Jul 2000; Poldien Keurntjes, 1 Nov 2007; Erol Kilicdere, 23 Aug 2001; William Kniest, 1 Apr 1985; Harald Kuhfuss, 1 Dec 2000; Levent Kumurcu, 17 Sep 2007; Ellen Küppers-Kolkman, 1 Aug 2007; Mehmet Kurum, 11 Aug 2003; Jeroen Lakwijk, 26 Apr 1993; Uwe Lamm, 1 Nov 2007; Henk

Lammers, 25 May 1993; Peter Langenheim, 24 Apr 1991; Erika Laros-Bussing, 13 Aug 2001; Erik Leijgrave, 9 Aug 2004; Ronald Luikink, 1 Apr 1997; Björn Meunders, 1 Nov 2007; Luis Miguel, 20 Nov 2006; Peter Nagel, 14 May 2007; Michael Neils, 26 Jan 2011; Mohamed Osman, 1 Dec 2008; Ricardo Peters, 10 Oct 2005; Eric Raaijman, 1 Nov 2007; Theo Rengelink, 1 Apr 2000; Meriam Rengelink-Bongers, 18 Jun 2007; Guido Roes, 27 Jun 1988; Richard Ruthers, 4 Nov 1991; Dorie Rutjes-Janssen, 14 May 2001; Geert Steltjes, 1 Nov 1993; Gerry Stevens, 14 Jan 1991; Cor Straub, 1 Apr 1997; Karl Heinz Tabatt, 1 Dec 2007; Richie Tatoglu, 29 Apr 2004; Hein te Winkel, 14 Aug 2000; Dewi Tebeest, 16 Aug 2004; Raymond ten Haaf, 12 Sep 2005; Ralf Timmer, 1 Jul 2002; Jan Ursinus, 1 Sep 1979; Sebastiaan van Aken, 1 Feb 2009; Jeroen van Broeckhuijsen, 1 Aug 2004; Ruud van Buuren, 8 May 1989; Peter van de Kamp, 1 Apr 1997; Nico van den Heuvel, 2 Jun 1986; Gunther van Ophuizen, 1 Jul 2006; Francis van Zelst, 1 Nov 1989; Remo Verschueren, 30 Oct 2000; Willem Visser, 1 Jan 1991; Annette Wagener, 1 Nov 2000; Jurgen Wagener, 1 Nov 2000; Jeroen Weijers, 18 Jan 2001; Pascal Wevers, 1 Feb 2001; Marc Wijnsema, 1 Jan 2000; Henny Willemsen, 3 Mar 1986; Henri Winters, 1 Nov 1993; Jurgen Wolke, 1 Nov 2000; Thorsten Wolsing, 3 May 2004; Haci Yildirim, 1 Feb 2005. **Wim Bosman Forwarding 's-Heerenberg** Francisca Aaldering, 6 Apr 2000; Rob Aalders, 17 Jun 2002; Masis Agob, 1 Apr 2010; Erwin Arendsen, 1 May 2008; Pargol Azarbad, 14 Nov 2011; Salih Bal, 1 Jan 2008; Stefan Banning, 14 Jan 1985; Ina Beekhuizen-Roes, 3 Aug 1987; Pieternel Beekvelt, 1 Nov 2007; Tom Benning, 1 Feb 2005; Patrick Bergevoet, 20 Nov 2000; Marco Berndsen, 25 Sep 2000; Harriëtte Berndsen-te Dorsthorst, 30 Nov 1999; Hedy Berntsen-Hendriks, 1 May 1988; Edith Bijenhof-Wevers, 25 Mar 2008; Rianne Bisseling, 1 Jul 2007; Yvonne Bleekman, 1 Nov 1995; Stephan Bloemberg, 1 Jan 2007; Robin Boeijink, 1 Jun 1994; Tanja Bondarchuk, 1 Nov 2007; Erik Bongaerts, 14 Feb 2011; Hans Bruggeman, 30 Oct 2000; Jeroen Bruil, 1 Feb 2005; Robert-Jan Bruil, 2 Mar 1990; Gerda Buffinga-Feddes, 1 Oct 2006; Ilke Bultink, 3 Jan 2011; Dora Ciza, 26 Jun 2012; Arthur Dammers, 5 Jan 2009; Jeroen de Lange, 1 Apr 2001; Hannah de Maat, 12 Nov 2012; Bart Decnop, 1 Jun 2011; Jordy Dellemann, 1 Feb 2006; Irina Dobos, 3 Dec 2012; Tania Donis Psarou, 1 Jan 2001; Mirjan Donkers-Liebrand, 4 Sep 1989; Teun Doornenbal, 1 Sep 1999; Ivo du Plessis, 11 Feb 2008; Muhammed Durucan, 16 Jun 2008; Marcel Duvigneau, 18 Apr 1988; Corrie Ederveen, 1 Feb 1991; Ron Enzerink, 1 Mar 1995; Uwe Ferfers, 1 Dec 2004; Mark Feukkink, 14 Jun 1999; Anton Frauenfelder, 1 Feb 1993; Cristina Fülöp, 1 Feb 2001; Leander Geelen, 25 Jan 2007; Michael Gersjes, 1 Jan 2006; John Giezenaar, 3 Sep 1979; Thijs Graat, 1 Dec 2010; Hans Groothuis, 16 Mar 1984; Tamara Hakfoort, 1 Mar 1999; Ylaine Hansen-Böhmer, 1 Jan 2008; Dennis Heersink, 7 Jul 2003; Wessel Heezen, 1 Feb 2002; Patricia Heijnst, 1 Nov 2000; Marieke Heinen, 16 Oct 2006; Eddy Heister, 18 Dec 1989; Gerry Helmink, 14 Aug 2006; Jacqueline Hendriks-Ras, 19 Aug 1996; Anouck Hesseling, 1 Aug 2000; Wilco Hogenkamp, 1 Jun 1999; Sonja Holstein-Reumer, 7 Aug 2006; Ramon Hueskes, 1 Jan 2008; René Inkenhaag, 1 Sep 2002; Cindy Jansen, 8 Nov 1993; Bianca Jansen-Arntz, 6 Aug 2007; Femke Janssen, 16 Apr 2007; Koen Janssen, 4 Jan 1988; Douwe Kaastra, 15 Oct 2007; Senay Kaya-Özay, 5 Sep 2011; Liedewij Kieboom, 6 Apr 2010; Hans Kloosterboer, 1 Sep 1993; Jan Kniest, 13 Sep 1999; Miranda Kock-Augustijn, 26 Aug 1995; Marleen Kolkman, 27 Sep 2010; Wim Konings, 1 Feb 2007; Linda Korteweg, 1 Sep 2008; Rut Koster, 1 Feb 1997; Marcel Kramp, 1 May 2004; Martijn Kusters, 9 Jul 2012; Susan Kusters-Keurentjes, 1 Mar 2003; Kees Kuyvenhoven, 1 Sep 1990; Ivan Larsen, 1 May 2003; Mirjam Lieven, 1 Aug 2001; Chanine Loef, 1 Oct 2010; Paul Looman, 1 Apr 2000; Cilia Lorx, 1 Jan 1995; Tanja Loskamp-Verstegen, 26 Apr 2010; Angelique Lovink, 10 Oct 2006; Berni Luimes, 1 Nov 2001; Jurgen Lukassen, 1 Feb 1991; Jos Marissink, 11 Jun 1979; Monica Marissink-Jansen, 28 Jul 2003; Henk Martens, 22 Jan 2007; Hasima Mekic-Jasarevic, 1 Jan 2008; Gerd Meunders, 1 Aug 2000; Henny Meurs-Goorman, 1 May 1992; Lex Miechels, 1 Nov 2011; Antonie Moonen, 1 Sep 2005; Rosie Neervoort, 1 Apr 2000; Nathaniël Nguyen, 1 May 2012; Chris Nijland, 14 Oct 1998; Frank Overgoor, 15 Sep 1988; Cilia Peters-Boerboom, 18 Jan 1999; Patty Pijpers, 16 May 2011; Kees Plantinga, 18 Sep 2000; Esther Pol-Bolwerk, 1 Dec 2000; Levy Pomper, 21 Aug 2000; Marijn Pothoff, 1 Oct 2005; Ronald Putman, 9 Feb 1987; Peggy Reinders-van Koot, 1 Aug 1999; Erik Roelevink, 15 Sep 1997; Margo Rottger-Goorman, 1 Jan 1980; Sara Schildkamp, 22 Nov 2010; Jack Schweckhorst, 27 Mar 1992; Anita Seegers, 19 Jul 1993; Michael Siebenheller, 3 Jan 2011; Silvia Siemes-Aalders, 1 Jan 1995; Rob Silvius, 1 May 2007; Anneke Slotboom-Meulenbelt, 1 Jul 2006; Martin Sluyter, 1 Sep 1998; Mike Sommers, 22 Jun 1998; Yvonne Sommers-Böhmer, 15 Feb 1999; Angelique Stefas-Vinkenvleugel, 21 Jun 1993; Andrea Steinmeier, 1 Sep 2008; Diana Telenta, 21 Mar 2010; Karin Timmerman, 1 Feb 1986; Myrke Tinga, 12 Dec 2005; Ruud Tousain, 6 Jan 1986; Nick Trentelman, 1 Oct 2012; Bram Tromp, 4 Jun 2007; Andreea Urzica, 1 Sep 2011; Marga van Brandenburg, 6 Nov 2000; Rob van Bueren, 9 Jul 2007; Suzanne van Dam, 1 Sep 2005; Sjoerd van den Bos, 13 Apr 2009; Richard van den Brink, 27 Oct 2008; Joost van Gaalen, 1 Nov 2001; Henriette van Haaren-te Dorsthorst, 16 Feb 2004; Helga van Manen, 15 Aug 2011; Danny van Oostveen, 1 Aug 2000; Harald van Schooten, 18 Apr 2005; Nikky van Veluwen, 3 Jun 2011; Winfried van Vessem, 3 Jun 2009; Joost Verdouw, 1 Jul 2007; Fred Verholen, 4 Aug 1986; Roy Verploegen, 11 Sep 2006; Nick Verweij, 1 Apr 1996; Irene Visser, 12 Jan 2004; Sander Vreeburg, 14 Jun 2007; Lammert Wanders, 4 Jul 2005; Erwin Wanders, 9 Oct 2007; Martine Wegenhousen, 1 Jan 2011; Natalie Weijenbarg-Bos, 18 Dec 1995; Dave Welling, 3 Feb 2003; Annemieke Westerhof-Aalders, 7 Apr 1993; Mark Wevers, 1 May 2004; Kay Wijkamp, 1 Nov 2006; Cissy Wingelaar, 1 Nov 2008; Elles Winkel, 1 Jan 2004; Sander Wolsink, 1 Apr 1999; Oktay Yalcin, 1 Jul 1998; Frans Zuidgeest, 24 Feb 1997. **Wim Bosman Holding 's-Heerenberg** Arjan Albers, 1 Mar 2006; Danielle Arendsen, 14 Mar 2005; Lydia Baars-Kuster, 1 Jan 2001; Bastiaan Besselink, 1 Aug 1999; Annelies Bijsterbosch-van Leeuwen, 6 Feb 1978; Henk Bisselink, 14 Dec 1998; Leon Bleumink, 1 Jul 2006; Silvia Boerakker-Jansen, 15 Nov 1994; Sina Bosch, 1 Aug 2002; Marianne Boschker-Boom, 1 Apr 2008; Ilona Brugmann, 1 Dec 2008; Anke Caspers-van den Oord, 16 Jul 2001; Saskia Daams-Arts, 26 Sep 2000; Maarten de Graauw, 1 Jan 2009; Rudi Debras, 18 Apr 2011; Peter Derksen, 8 Oct 2008; Dinie Dijkman-Reessink, 1 May 1989; Nicole Driever-Ruess, 1 Jul 2002; Marjo Egging, 1 Jan 1990; Sander Elfring, 3 Jan 2005; Michel Engel, 1 Feb 1980; Niek Essink, 25 Aug 2008; Jeanette Frauenfelder-Frazer, 1 Apr 2001; Mike Freriks, 19 Apr 1989; Rosite Frielink-Gerrits, 19 Aug 2002; Joost Froeling, 1 Sep 2001; Joyce Hermsen, 1 Apr 2001; Chiel Hesseling, 24 Feb 2003; Marian Heuvel-Wissink, 4 Sep 2000; Sebastiaan Holleman, 1 Sep 2011; Monique Holleman-Oudhuis, 1 Feb 2005; Robin Hoogenraad, 9 Dec 2002; Arthur Hoogsteder, 7 Sep 1987; Ilse Jansen, 15 Jun 2009; Robert Jochoms, 7 May 1990; Doris Jolink-Wosnitza, 1 Oct 2008; Ross Kambel, 1 Aug 2011; Nicolé Karthe-Schweckhorst, 22 Jan 2001; Gera Kersjes-Brouwer, 1 Dec 2007; Marion Kloos, 21 Apr 2008; Wilma Kloosterboer-Bisselink, 14 Jan 1993; Wilfrank Knuiman, 16 Jun 2008; Evie Koolenbrander-Tinnevelt, 8 Dec 1986; Stina Kristiansson, 5 Feb 2001; Devlin Krul, 17 Oct 2011; Willy Kuiper, 17 Sep 1990; Jorne Lamers, 20 Mar 2013; Mike Lelivelt, 18 May 1998; Helmy Leuverink-Ebbing, 2 Jul 2012; Emile Lieferink, 18 Jul 2011; Mulugeta Mandefiro, 1 Oct 2011; Jan Willem Navis, 6 Jan 1977; Mark Newman, 30 Aug 1995; Silvan Obelink, 4 Sep 2006; Lucy Partridge, 1 Mar 2010; Chantal Peters-van de Zand, 17 Nov 1997; Shari Pieneman, 1 Oct 2011; Jonathan Ras, 1 Feb 2012; Angelique Remijnse, 4 Oct 1993; Rudi Rietman, 1 Mar 1989; Tammo Rietsema, 2 Oct 2012; Anita Roelofsen-Besselink, 1 Apr 2010; Nardie Rosendaal-Verweg, 14 Jul 2008; Sandra Ruikes, 13 Sep 1989; Mario Schoofs, 1 Jul 2007; Jürgen Schuimer, 20 Apr 2009; Annelies Spaan, 4 Sep 2000; André Sprenkeler, 1 Jan 2009; Carola te Grotenhuis, 1 Mar 2005; Giel ter Beek, 8 Jan 2007; Pim Teunissen, 5 Jul 2010; Monique Tuenter-ten Holder, 23 Apr 1997; Jelmer van Bergenhegouwen, 1 Jan 2008; Jules van de Pavert, 26 Jul 1976; Leonie van Driel-Evers, 1 Jan 2000; Nena van Londen, 19 Nov 2012; Aart van Silfhout, 8 Apr 2002; Marco Veenstra, 1 Feb 2009; Astrid Verbeeten, 9 Dec 1985; Gerdo Wenting, 3 Dec 2001; Wilma Wesselink-Hertgers, 26 Jan 2000; Marloes Wiendels, 1 Dec 2008; Erwin Willemsen, 17 Jul 1989; Sylvana Winters, 1 Apr 2013. **Wim Bosman Logistics Services Geleen** Wichart Achten, 11 Nov 1985; Patrick Baaten, 1 Jan 2011; Sven Bronkhorst, 1 Jan 2003; Jan Coenen, 28 Jan 1974; Richard Cords, 1 Jul 2011; Jos Cox, 1 Mar 1982; Ton Cuijpers, 1 Aug 1977; Mariëtte Debets, 1 Jun 2004; Marcel Destreel, 1 Sep 1988; Ger

Dormans, 16 Dec 1974; Anita Everaerts, 16 Feb 1981; Jeroen Evers, 30 Dec 2011; Ron Frijters, 9 Oct 2012; Peter Grammé, 1 Jan 2008; Jos Habets, 1 Jan 2009; Eddy Hermans, 1 May 1989; Joselien Hoen-Adams, 1 Aug 1986; Wim Jakobs, 1 Dec 1969; Mischa Jansen, 23 Jan 2006; Fred Kosack, 1 Feb 1977; Arno Kuijpers, 1 Apr 1986; Frans Larue, 1 Apr 1973; Jimmy Metekohy, 13 Mar 2013; Carola Mohren, 1 Sep 2010; Ton Moors, 2 Sep 1985; Leo op de Beke, 1 Mar 2012; Michel Pierik, 1 Oct 2004; Frank Ramakers, 17 Apr 1989; Anke Reijnders-Smits, 3 Oct 2011; Norman Ridderbeekx, 1 Mar 2004; Chris Roering, 1 Jan 1981; Bas Romein, 4 Mar 2013; Karl Schubert, 1 Oct 2006; Frank Senden, 22 Aug 1977; Marlies Soetelmans-Gerits, 9 Aug 1982; Louis Wijnen, 18 Jun 1980; Henk Wolner, 1 Feb 2012; Rob Zonneveld, 1 Feb 2008. **Wim Bosman Logistics Services 's-Heerenberg** Stef Aalbers, 1 Oct 2007; Gonzalo Ahumada, 1 Jul 2000; Wilbert Bach, 1 Mar 2011; Harry Bakker, 1 Mar 2005; Marcel Bax, 1 May 2007; Marianne Becker-Niersmann, 1 Feb 2013; Ingo Bergmans, 1 Feb 2013; Toon Berntsen, 9 Oct 1978; Christiaan Besselink, 1 Oct 2005; Dick Betlem, 1 Mar 1995; Andre Biermann, 15 Jul 2007; Thomas Bijl, 1 Mar 2005; Hans-Peter Bisseling, 1 Jul 2008; Jason Bloemendaal, 1 Jun 2006; Eric Boerboom, 1 Aug 1994; Wim Buijzert, 1 Oct 2000; David Buyl, 8 Oct 2007; Chow-Ling Chong, 16 Oct 2006; Richard Clappers, 1 Jan 1995; Martin Coenen, 5 Apr 1990; Geert Colenbrander, 20 Mar 2000; René Derksen, 10 Feb 1992; Nicole Donders, 1 Feb 2001; Toon Elting, 1 Sep 1999; Patricia Epskamp, 1 Apr 2000; Pato Espinoza Vasque, 6 Dec 1989; Jean-Gérard Fifis, 24 Aug 1992; Danielle Fifis-Oudbier, 1 Feb 2005; Edwin Geurts, 9 May 1994; Leo Geurts, 20 Nov 2000; Patrick Goossen, 1 May 2006; Detlef Hawranke, 1 Aug 1989; John Hegeman, 1 Jan 2000; Edwin Heijnen, 1 Mar 2005; Juliane Hein, 16 Feb 2006; Leon Heister, 10 Aug 2009; Jeanette Hendriks, 1 Jun 2008; Anouk Hendriksen-Evers, 1 May 1999; Jorg Heuer, 1 Jun 2001; Arjen Heyboer, 1 Mar 2000; Richard Huisman, 27 Mar 2000; Jeroen Jansen, 15 Aug 2000; Milo Janssen, 23 Oct 2000; Gerrie Jeene, 19 Feb 1990; Hubert Kamphuis, 1 Feb 1996; Oksana Keller, 21 Apr 2008; Anna Kersten, 1 Aug 2001; Jan Kieft, 1 Jun 2006; Theo Klein Tank, 6 Nov 1995; Nico Klein Wolterink, 1 Feb 2005; Berry Kluitmans, 1 Jan 1995; Judith Kniest, 19 Mar 2007; Niels Kok, 1 Dec 2006; Dennis Konstapel, 1 Jan 1999; Christian Koskamp, 1 Mar 1999; José Koster, 1 Mar 2012; Mels Koster, 17 Oct 2005; Sandra Krijgsman-Schneider, 1 Apr 2000; Jan Langeler, 1 Jan 1999; Astrid Lankreijer, 1 Jul 2007; Michel Lenderink, 1 Sep 2006; Corinne Lepine, 1 Nov 2006; Christian Leurs, 26 May 2008; Evelyn Liske-Roes, 5 Jun 2000; Dariusz Longer, 1 Feb 2013; Richard Louwe, 1 Feb 2005; Arjan Maas, 18 Nov 1991; Linda Maquine, 1 Mar 1999; Aafke Mateman, 1 Feb 2013; Johnny Maurick, 1 Sep 2006; Arjen Meijering, 8 Nov 1993; Sander Memelink, 14 Mar 2013; Maarten Mol, 8 Nov 2010; Nadine Muller, 21 Apr 2008; Mike Neidhöfer, 1 Jul 2008; Jarno Nuijen, 22 Mar 1999; Thomas Obermeit, 1 Jan 2010; Henk Peters, 4 Dec 1995; Erik Peters, 1 Sep 1998; Danny Peters, 1 May 2007; Liane Philipsen, 1 May 1997; Geurt Poel, 19 Mar 2007; Floris Proost, 1 Apr 2009; Michael Putman, 11 Jul 2005; Leoni Putman, 1 Jun 2008; Joop Reitsma, 18 Sep 2006; Bertie Reumer, 19 Mar 2007; Maarten Reumer, 1 Mar 2007; Franck Roodbeen, 1 Sep 1998; Joyce Ruesink, 1 Jul 2006; Servet Sahin, 1 Oct 2000; Vincent Schilp, 1 Dec 2005; Andre Schmidt, 1 Sep 2008; Donny Schonenberg, 1 May 1997; Geert Schoonderbeek, 1 Feb 2013; Jürgen Schöttler, 22 Oct 2007; Krzysztof Sedlak, 18 Jan 2008; Tonny Smeenk, 1 Sep 1999; Harry Smit, 1 Sep 2008; Erwin Smitjes, 1 Dec 1997; René Spaan, 11 May 1992; Tonny Stoffels, 1 Aug 1999; Sjoerd Teerink, 14 Sep 1992; Iris Timmermans, 1 Nov 2012; Rob van Aken, 1 Dec 1998; Herman van Amerongen, 28 Dec 2010; Eric van der Pol, 1 Apr 1997; Wilfried van Dulmen, 1 Dec 1986; Stefan van Gemmern, 1 Jul 2000; Roy van Gendt, 1 Sep 2006; Ceryl van Hasselt, 14 Feb 2011; Steven Vaughan, 15 Sep 2008; Daniela Veuger-Ardelean, 17 Jul 2006; Roger voor de Poorte, 1 Nov 2005; Boudewijn Vrolijks, 6 Jul 2000; Rémon Weerwag, 1 Mar 1994; Daniela Werdelmann-Nöthe, 1 Sep 2008; Gerbrand Wesselink, 1 Oct 2007; Martin Wierzbicki, 4 May 2012; Tim Wittenhorst, 1 Jun 2000; Bart Wolkenfelt, 15 Mar 2004. **Wim Bosman Transport 's-Heerenberg** Koos Aaldering, 8 Feb 2010; Diana Abbenhuis-Siroen, 13 May 1987; Theo Alofs, 13 Jul 1998; Johnny Amting, 1 May 2007; Freddie Anneveld, 15 Mar 1999; Sven Baars, 8 Apr 2013; Wilco Bannink, 1 Sep 2002; Torsten Becker, 1 Sep 2010; Aart Bendeler, 5 Nov 2008; Emrah Bilici, 3 Sep 2012; Toon Bod, 1 Feb 1997; Ivo Bod, 1 Mar 2006; Gerald Braam, 1 Dec 2008; Joan Brink, 9 Jan 1989; Ton Broekhuizen, 18 Apr 1984; Arno Broekhuizen, 15 Aug 1997; Gert Bruil, 18 Jan 2010; Gerjan Bulten, 1 Jul 2000; Herman Bussink, 2 Apr 2003; Lutz Carolin, 2 Jun 1992; Gerrit Cornelissen, 9 Feb 1970; Rinus de Jong, 1 Jul 2009; Hemmy de Reus, 14 May 1984; Rudi de Vries, 3 Oct 2005; Frits de Wind, 17 Aug 2001; Theo Deijnen, 10 Aug 1998; Bennie Dekkers, 9 Apr 1985; Bert den Brok, 1 Sep 1981; Thijs Derksen, 8 Dec 2010; Antoine Derksen, 29 May 1998; Paul Dieker, 13 Jun 1978; Jeroen Dieker, 18 Jan 2010; Herben Dimmedal, 1 Jan 2006; Wim Driessen, 4 Feb 1991; Jo Duis, 4 Feb 1985; Olaf Eenstroom, 1 Nov 2000; Marc Elting, 15 Sep 1997; Hans Engelen, 1 Sep 2000; Ramon Engelen, 16 Aug 1996; William Esman, 1 Jan 1997; Martin Essink, 7 Dec 1987; Corine Evers, 1 Jul 2002; Tommy Firing, 10 Jun 1996; Jürgen Fleuren, 25 Jun 1990; Jeroen Giezen, 1 Sep 2005; Cemil Gönc, 22 Aug 2008; Arjan Greven, 1 Mar 2007; Niek Hansen, 1 Sep 2010; Thomas Heezen, 11 Feb 2011; Stefan Heitink, 1 Sep 2011; Frank Hermanns, 9 Sep 1991; Erik Jan Heykoop, 8 Jan 1990; Henk Hijink, 13 Feb 1978; Ronny Hoefman, 1 May 2010; Erik Hoftijzer, 7 Mar 2011; Henk Holtland, 6 Nov 2000; Hans Holtslag, 13 Dec 1976; Jacques Huiskes, 4 Oct 2010; Rolf Hunting, 10 Nov 1987; Jurgen Huying, 1 Sep 2010; Frank Jansen, 18 Aug 1986; Frans Jansen, 1 Feb 2010; Dennis Jansen, 20 Jun 2000; Wouter Janssen, 3 Aug 1992; Herman Jolink, 1 Jun 2000; Gepko Jonker, 1 May 2010; Henk Kamphuis, 1 Oct 2006; Hudai Karakurt, 1 Jul 2010; Hennie Karsten, 1 Jun 1989; Danny Karsten, 1 Aug 2009; Dejan Kastein, 17 Jun 2007; Sami Kaya, 22 Sep 2002; Fons Keijser, 8 May 1978; Frank Ketelaar, 20 Sep 1991; Raymond Kock, 1 Apr 2007; Aaron Kock, 1 Feb 2009; Alan Kort, 7 May 1990; Mischa Koster, 5 Sep 2011; Kazim Kozan, 12 Jul 2010; Mehmet Kozan, 1 Jun 2008; Leo Kuiper, 19 Jan 2004; Gerard Kupper, 25 Jul 1977; Davy Küppers, 3 Sep 2012; Erik Lammers, 5 Jun 1979; Johan Lanters, 8 Aug 2003; Wygle Liebrand, 1 Apr 2004; Devlin Liebrand, 22 Oct 1990; Simeon Liebrand, 8 Mar 2010; Kevin Loef, 1 Oct 2011; Harrie Lucassen, 19 Mar 1984; René Luijmes, 2 Jul 1984; Casper Lukassen, 25 Jun 1998; Hishem Maksoud, 1 Feb 2006; Wim Marissink, 4 Jun 1984; Ferdinand Massop, 1 Feb 2001; Frank Medze, 14 Feb 1977; Arjan Meijer, 1 Sep 2000; Henk Meijer, 17 Oct 2011; Robert Meijer, 4 Sep 2002; Piet Melleé, 1 Sep 1999; Lars Mennink, 1 Aug 2011; Udo Middelkoop, 3 Sep 2012; Ronald Mijnen, 1 May 2010; Gerard Morren, 1 Oct 2003; Jeroen Morren, 5 Jul 2004; Christian Naujok, 1 Feb 2004; Hakija Nekic, 15 Nov 2010; Edwin Nienhuis, 7 Mar 1988; Harm Nijland, 5 Apr 2011; Barry Notten, 25 May 2010; Henry Oosterdijk, 1 Oct 2010; Thijs Papenborg, 25 Apr 2005; Mike Peelen, 20 Sep 2010; Marcel Peppelman, 1 Jul 1995; Willem Pietersen, 25 Nov 1987; Rob Polman, 13 Aug 1984; Thomas Prinsen, 16 Mar 2010; Dirk Pruiksma, 1 Jan 1975; Henk Reindsen, 18 Oct 1999; Ferry Rikhof, 1 Nov 2007; Léon Robbe, 29 Jun 1998; Bryan Roelofsen, 3 Sep 2010; Frank Roelofzen, 1 Nov 1997; Sandy Rossel, 1 Jun 2008; Erik Ruesink, 1 Oct 1995; Mark Ruesink, 1 Apr 2006; Maurice Ruesink, 1 Jul 1994; Roland Ruesink, 1 Jul 1992; Torsten Rüsch, 23 Sep 2001; Rob Rutten, 1 Mar 1984; Arno Rutten, 17 Jun 1996; Pascal Sas, 1 Mar 2001; Koen Schreur, 24 Feb 1987; Luc Schreur, 5 May 2003; Bennie Schut, 27 Sep 1982; Bertus Schuurman, 28 May 2001; Theo Schuurman, 20 Jun 2005; Nico Sewalt, 5 Jan 1998; Jimmy Sewalt, 1 Nov 2006; Willem Smits, 2 Jun 1997; Piet Speet, 25 May 1987; Ramon Starink, 1 Jul 1995; Harry Stevens, 1 Dec 2012; Johan te Lindert, 1 Feb 2006; Sietse te Mebel, 1 Sep 2010; Fred te Wiel, 6 Apr 1992; Frank Tempels, 19 Jun 1985; Roel ten Hagen, 11 Jul 1994; Ivar ten Tuijnte, 25 Mar 2013; Henri Tenten, 1 Aug 2001; Jeroen ter Beest, 19 Nov 1994; Leo ter Heerdt, 1 Mar 2006; Marcel ter Heerdt, 1 Oct 1997; Bertil ter Maat, 1 Nov 2008; Mart Terhaerdt, 21 Jul 2008; Bjorn Theijssen, 1 Jul 2001; Piet Thuis, 1 Jan 1992; Bob Timmermans, 11 Oct 2010; Hans Tomassen, 1 Oct 2001; Dirk van Boggelen, 11 Jun 2003; Frank van de Kamp, 13 Aug 2007; Robert van de Kamp, 1 Oct 1997; Marcel van de Wetering, 20 Sep 1990; Theo van den Berg, 31 Jul 2000; Timo van den Bos, 29 Oct 1990; René van den Broek, 21 Jun 1999; Ewald van den Heuvel, 19 Jun 2006; Henk van den Heuvel, 5 Jun 1979; Jos van der Zwet, 1 Feb 1988; Jurgen van Eerden, 1 Apr 2006; Kees van Grootveld, 12 Apr 1999; Kevin van Halteren, 24 Mar 2010; Wouter van Hartskamp, 1 Jun 2000; Gerard van Heeswijk, 23 Feb 1988; Luc van Marwijk, 1 Sep 2010; Hans van Niekerk, 29 Sep

2003; Maurice van Ree, 12 Jan 2004; Marco van Remmen, 1 Mar 2004; Sander van Schie, 10 Sep 1990; Rutger van Toor, 1 Mar 1999; Niko van Uhm, 1 Nov 1998; Jacques van Uum, 2 Feb 1988; Mark van Wessel, 9 Jul 2007; Bart Venes, 16 Dec 2005; Björn Visser, 1 Feb 1998; Theo Volkers, 16 Jun 2000; Edwin Vrogten, 7 Apr 1997; Jan Wassink, 7 Sep 1977; Joop Wassink, 15 Dec 2000; Rutger Wassink, 20 Jun 2005; Rien Wassink, 17 Jan 1995; Henk Wenting, 18 Oct 2010; Richard Wienen, 1 Jul 2005; Jeroen Wierbos, 1 Mar 1996; Patrick Willemsen, 30 May 2011; Ron Winters, 17 Feb 1988; Rene Wissing, 11 Apr 1977; Dave Wissink, 1 Jul 2008; Wilfried Wolbring, 1 Jul 1985; Patrick Wolswijk, 3 Sep 2012; Seydi Yanardag, 3 Sep 2012; Sakir Yilmaz, 15 Jul 2002; Ruben Zegers, 22 Aug 2005. **POLAND Wim Bosman Forwarding Katowice** Łukasz Ciszewski, 3 Sep 2012; Monika Golmento-Froń, 6 Jul 2012; Magdalena Sobota, 13 Aug 2012; Dariusz Szczerbiński, 18 May 2012. **Wim Bosman Forwarding Pruszków** Tomasz Barańczuk, 12 Jul 2012; Wojciech Bartoszewski, 11 Mar 2013; Stanisław Chrustny, 16 Sep 2010; Zdzisław Chrustny, 3 Nov 2010; Tomasz Chudzik, 30 May 2012; Radosław Citak, 6 Jul 2011; Anait Czarkowska, 10 Oct 2012; Stanisław Czarkowski, 26 Jun 2012; Jacek Czwojdrak, 9 Aug 2009; Krzysztof Dąbrowski, 1 Jun 2011; Grzegorz Dąbrowski, 4 Apr 2012; Michał Dworak, 7 Jul 2012; Krzysztof Dzieniszewski, 29 Feb 2012; Piotr Fijałkowski, 11 Mar 2013; Roman Gabryl, 29 Sep 2005; Marcin Gaze, 26 Jul 2007; Tomasz Gołąbek, 30 Mar 2008; Paweł Gozdalski, 3 Aug 2011; Radosław Grabelski, 6 May 2012; Zygmunt Hoffmann, 8 Aug 2012; Mirosław Jóźwiak, 4 Feb 2007; Katarzyna Juszkiewicz, 20 Jul 2009; Sławomir Kaczmarek, 29 Sep 2012; Bożena Kałuska, 1 Nov 2010; Robert Kaszewski, 27 Jul 2010; Artur Kłosiński, 23 May 2012; Rafał Knafel, 6 Mar 2013; Tadeusz Kompanowski, 4 Jul 2006; Robert Konieczny, 16 Jul 2009; Łukasz Koralewicz, 1 Nov 2007; Renata Korytkowska, 1 Jan 2009; Piotr Kościański, 2 Nov 2006; Anton Kozak, 25 Jul 2011; Mirosław Kozikowski, 23 Mar 2011; Janusz Krakowiak, 13 May 2007; Beata Krawczyk, 1 Apr 2005; Krzysztof Krawczyk, 12 Jul 2009; Sławomir Kudelski, 30 Sep 2012; Dawid Kuliński, 29 Sep 2012; Dariusz Kusztal, 2 Jan 2008; Jakub Łaś, 4 Nov 2012; Dariusz Lepczak, 19 Mar 2007; Ireneusz Lepczak, 5 Aug 2006; Sławomir Lepczak, 8 Jul 2007; Zygmunt Lepczak, 22 Oct 2006; Michał Lesiecki, 23 Jul 2010; Piotr Lesiecki, 23 Jun 2010; Piotr Łopaciński, 26 May 2009; Sławomir Maciejewski, 11 Jan 2012; Mariusz Majer, 22 Jun 2008; Marek Majewski, 23 Feb 2011; Arkadiusz Makówka, 2 Mar 2011; Andrzej Mandziński, 6 Oct 2005; Radosław Maranowski, 14 Sep 2010; Karol Miller, 1 Dec 2007; Katarzyna Mirgos, 20 Feb 2012; Tomasz Murawski, 28 Apr 2011; Bolesław Muszyński, 6 Jul 2011; Marek Olek, 7 Feb 2008; Katarzyna Olszewska, 26 Jul 2010; Piotr Orzechowski, 9 Nov 2011; Agnieszka Osmólska, 1 Jun 2012; Marek Perlic, 13 Jun 2012; Franciszek Pichnar, 12 May 2010; Zdzisław Pietrzyk, 2 Mar 2011; Daniel Piotrowski, 15 Jun 2011; Tomasz Podlewski, 14 Apr 2005; Kamil Polowczyk, 8 Oct 2012; Andrzej Poszelężny, 11 Sep 2006; Krzysztof Przybylski, 9 May 2010; Ryszard Puchalski, 1 Apr 2012; Bogdan Rakowski, 21 Sep 2005; Agnieszka Raunmiagi, 1 Mar 2006; Tomasz Rudzki, 18 Jul 2012; Andrzej Rzymowski, 6 Oct 2010; Lesław Sadza, 5 Oct 2010; Zbigniew Sejda, 22 Jan 2007; Tomasz Skoczek, 28 Feb 2010; Jacek Skorża, 18 Jan 2007; Marek Słupczyński, 29 Sep 2012; Karol Smugowski, 18 Dec 2012; Artur Sobótka, 11 Jul 2010; Mariusz Stachowiak, 13 Jul 2011; Dariusz Synowiec, 1 Nov 2005; Sylwester Szlendak vel Rybak, 13 Mar 2007; Grzegorz Szotowicz, 10 Apr 2012; Paweł Szraga, 23 May 2012; Mariusz Szrejber, 24 Apr 2012; Piotr Sztąberski, 13 Aug 2013; Joanna Szumlewicz, 23 Nov 2011; Krzysztof Szumlewicz, 26 Oct 2011; Sylwester Tarnowski, 28 Oct 2007; Tadeusz Tarnowski, 20 Nov 2010; Jacek Teresiński, 2 Jan 2012; Artur Tiupa, 2 Mar 2011; Mirosław Tomaszewski, 10 Nov 2010; Wiesław Toporek, 19 Jan 2011; Piotr Trawiński, 13 Sep 2009; Mariusz Uciński, 6 Oct 2010; Jarosław Ulewicz, 11 Jul 2012; Mirosław Walkowiak, 8 Jan 2007; Piotr Walkowiak, 15 Jan 2008; Henryk Weber, 20 Jul 2011; Andrzej Wegner, 20 Apr 2006; Hubert Wiśniewski, 16 Sep 2007; Bogdan Witanowski, 8 Jun 2011; Miłosz Witkowski, 2 Feb 2011; Tycjan Włodarczyk, 15 Jun 2011; Łukasz Wojciechowski, 1 Sep 2010; Piotr Wolański, 15 Sep 2010; Ryszard Wolański, 2 Jun 2010; Marcin Zamojski, 18 Jan 2007; Stefan Zieliński, 14 Sep 2011. **ROMANIA Wim Bosman Forwarding Cluj-Napoca** Attila Bandi, 8 Feb 2013; Ioana Blaj, 27 Jul 2012; Mihai Rus, 25 Oct 2012; Robert Vajas, 30 Aug 2012. **Wim Bosman Forwarding Ploiesti** Gheorghe Albina, 27 May 2008; Rony Andreescu, 9 Apr 2008; Teodor Anghel, 2 Sep 2008; Gheorghe Anton, 27 Aug 2001; Cristinel Apostol, 4 Nov 2011; Florin Apostol, 21 Apr 2008; Alina Avram, 30 May 2011; Maria Avram, 28 Nov 2007; Stelian Avram, 8 Jul 2009; Florin Baciu, 4 Oct 2000; Constantin Badaran, 14 Oct 2004; Mugurel Badea, 23 Aug 2005; Adrian Balalia, 20 Jun 2010; Catalin Balalia, 1 Mar 2011; Nicolae Barbu, 20 Sep 2011; Cristian Boaca, 6 Feb 2012; Ilie Bolanu, 10 Jul 1996; Iulian Bolanu, 19 Sep 2007; Ionel Bratu, 1 Nov 2007; Razvan Brumarescu, 10 Aug 2012; Gheorghe Calin, 23 May 2007; Mihaela Chircu, 24 Mar 2003; Gabriela Chirita, 21 Jun 2006; Marian Cioc, 16 Aug 2001; Marius Ciurea, 19 Jun 1999; Tiberiu Cojocaru, 21 Oct 2010; Mihai Constantin, 13 Aug 2012; Gheorghe Constantinescu, 14 Dec 2006; Alexandru Craciunica, 10 Jul 2009; Liviu Culea, 7 Dec 2004; Dragos Dinu, 19 May 2001; Neculai Dogea, 7 Oct 2010; Gheorghe Dumitru, 28 Sep 2011; Nicoleta Duta, 6 Dec 2004; Teodor Florea, 10 Apr 2012; Tudor Florea, 10 Apr 2012; Iulian Florescu, 3 May 2007; Cristina Florian, 26 Jul 1995; Romeo Gheorghe, 24 Oct 2012; Aurora Gherman, 18 Apr 2012; Cristina Ghinea, 8 Oct 2012; Alexandru Grigore, 5 Sep 2012; Claudiu Ilie, 14 Jul 2008; Emil Ion, 4 Nov 1992; Costel Ionita, 5 Dec 2007; Daniela Ionita, 8 Mar 2010; Dragos Jaravete, 1 Feb 2011; Lorena Jianu, 28 Oct 2002; Daniel Joita, 8 Oct 2012; Mariana Joitoiu, 18 Oct 2011; Gabriel Lepadatu, 1 Aug 2012; Daniel Lungu, 21 Jun 2010; Gheorghe Lupea, 12 Aug 2011; Nicolae Lupu, 11 May 2011; Cristian Maria, 1 Aug 2012; Adrian Marin, 1 Aug 2012; Alexandra Marinescu, 14 Mar 2013; Ioan Matei, 3 Jan 2008; Lucian Mazare, 13 Oct 2008; Sorin Mihai, 31 Jan 2012; Virginia Minea, 26 Nov 2010; Cristinel Mocanu, 22 Jul 2011; Bogdan Moisescu, 28 Nov 2011; Constantin Neagu, 9 Jun 2010; Petre Neagu, 19 Jul 2011; Ion Nefliu, 14 Apr 2008; Ion Negre, 23 Sep 1999; Ecaterina Negulescu, 19 Mar 2003; Tiberiu Niculescu, 16 Sep 2011; Marius Pana, 16 Jun 2010; Alexandru Panait, 11 Jan 2010; Marius Patrascu, 3 Oct 2008; Daniela Paun, 23 Nov 2009; Dumitru Pertea, 1 Sep 2005; Nicolae Petcu, 29 Jul 2011; Marian Petre, 16 Jun 2010; Cosmin Pirvan, 10 Jan 2012; Andreea Popa, 14 Mar 2013; Iulian Popa, 8 Jul 2011; Giani Popa, 5 Oct 2011; Mihai Popescu, 6 Feb 2012; Constantin Radu, 21 Jun 2010; Romeo Rosu, 3 Oct 2008; Iulian Rotaru, 15 Sep 1997; Ionela Sandu, 14 Apr 2008; Nicusor Scarlat, 17 Jul 2006; Marian Serban, 11 Jun 2007; Petre Solovastru, 7 Jun 2011; Cristina Stan, 23 Apr 2008; Gabriel Stan, 2 Jul 2007; Gabriel Stanciu, 1 Oct 2010; Ionut Stanciu, 20 Sep 2011; Vasile Stanciu, 27 Mar 2008; Romulus Stanescu, 30 Sep 2008; Adrian Stanescu, 23 Nov 2009; Adrian Stanila, 19 Jul 2001; Justina Stanila, 5 Jun 2000; Sebastian Stanimir, 21 Sep 2012; Ion Valentin Stefan, 2 Feb 2011; Valentin Stemate, 2 Apr 2012; Gabriel Stoian, 30 Sep 2011; Adrian Stoian, 27 Mar 2008; Ionut Strambeanu, 3 Oct 2008; Daniel Tanase, 18 Feb 2011; Dorin Tanase, 1 Aug 2012; Roxan Teodoru, 28 Aug 2006; Nicolae Toma, 9 Aug 2012; Luoana Truta, 26 Sep 2012; Marius Tudose, 4 Aug 2006; Simona Unger, 26 Nov 2010; Marius Zet, 3 Oct 2011. **RUSSIA Wim Bosman Forwarding Moscow** Maria Andreeva, 14 Sep 2009. **Wim Bosman Forwarding St. Petersburg** Maria Ageenko, 19 Sep 2012; Ksenia Chudak, 1 Oct 2010; Olga Chudak, 16 Jan 2012; Igor Frolin, 25 Oct 2010; Konstantin Gichin, 8 Nov 2012; Olisya Gribanova, 11 Nov 2009; Julia Klepikova, 8 Sep 2008; Roman Kondrashev, 27 Aug 2012; Boris Kryukov, 20 Apr 2011; Ekaterina Polkovnikova, 25 Oct 2012; Denis Scherbakov, 1 Aug 2011; Julia Shevkalenko, 5 Oct 2007; Vladimir Sladkov, 2 Jul 2012; Evgenia Stasina, 18 Jun 2007; Rodion Sukhorukov, 21 Jun 2010. **UKRAINE Wim Bosman Forwarding Kiev** Ivan Balakhonov, 12 Feb 2013; Marina Ivanets, 24 Sep 2012; Maxim Moshkivsky, 1 Oct 2012; Irina Murashko, 27 Aug 2012.

# Index

# Acknowledgements

I FIRST ENCOUNTERED the remarkable world of Mainfreight a decade ago when I recounted their formative years for an earlier book. They were then experiencing growing pains as they emerged from a trucking-company chrysalis and began the transformation into a global logistics company. Mainfreight was taking tentative steps in Australia, Asia and the US, with Europe a dream few dared mention. Ten years on and they have taken a culture that began as a way of life and developed it into a strategic tool that gives them enormous competitive advantage. To understand Mainfreight it is necessary to delve deep into its culture, and in this regard I am indebted to the following, in no particular order, for their unwavering assistance:

Nikki Cooper, for her particularly valuable help, Aline van Buiten, Andrea d'Cruz, Anthony Barrett, Bill Brown, Bryan Curtis, Bruce Plested, Bryan Mogridge, Brynley Riches, Carl George, Carl Howard-Smith, Carmel Fisher, Chris Dunphy, Chris Knuth, Brett Horgan, Christine Meyer, Martin Zhong, Craig Evans, Dave Scott, Don Braid, Emmet Hobbs, David McLean, Bryan Gaynor, Geoff Sharman, Glen Reed, Grant Draper, Greg Giarratana, Greg Howard, Neil Graham, John Hepworth, John Wright, Jon Gundy, Julia Dibella, Kathy Brown, Kerry Crocker, Kevin Drinkwater, Aubery Cheung, Mark Newman, Andy Ling, Mark Ritchie, Linda Vagana, Simon Cotter, Michael Lorimer, Martin Devereux, Michael Forkenbrock, Michael Lofaro, Ossie Osman, Nikki Cooper, Murray Calder, Gary Lau, Richard Prebble, Rodd Morgan, Carol Selwyn, Billy Zhang, Melissa Holmes, Rose La Vella, Don Rowlands, Jouann Lee, Steve Thorogood, Tim Preston, Annabel Mahnke, Gavin Macdonald, Cary Chung, Tim Williams, Cherry Wang, René van Houtum, Bertil ter Maat, Bryan Rene, Dick Betlem, Erik Berger, Peter Derksen, Dianne Clemens, Riyaz Jordan, Frans Zuidgeest, Guss van der Stelt, Henk Messink, Christianne Kuenen, Jason Braid, Joan Ji, Liane Philipsen, Elton Poon, Richard Vlasblom, Linda Huang, Mario Schoofs, Paul Looman, Shane Michalick, Tom Donahue, Wim Bosman and Suzy Zhou.